THE FUTURE OF SOCIALISM

THE FUTURE
of
SOCIALISM

by
C. A. R. CROSLAND

SCHOCKEN BOOKS · NEW YORK

The Future of Socialism was first published in the United
States in 1957. For this edition the original work has
been abridged and revised by the author.

First SCHOCKEN PAPERBACK edition 1963

Second Printing, 1967

Library of Congress Catalog Card No. 63-18395
Manufactured in the United States of America

CONTENTS

35438

PART FIVE

ECONOMIC GROWTH AND EFFICIENCY

PREFACE TO NEW EDITION

IT seemed better, when preparing this new edition of *The Future of Socialism*, not to revise the substance of the argument, but to concentrate on shortening the book to a more manageable size (for it was inordinately long!). In this way, new readers may judge for themselves how far the original analysis has stood the test of time.

In fact, were I completely revising the book, I should substantially alter only one major argument, that relating to economic growth. Here I was too optimistic—not about the *capabilities* of the full-employment mixed economy (for such economies have grown rapidly in Western Europe and Scandinavia), but about the Anglo-Saxon economies in particular. These have put up a lamentable performance in recent years; and the decline in their growth-rates, and the re-emergence of unused resources, would compel me now to modify (though only in an Anglo-American context) some of my remarks about economic planning, investment-attitudes, the danger of inflation, the disappearance of poverty, and the shift of power to the unions. But for the rest, the basic diagnosis and prognosis of the book seem to have been fully borne out by subsequent events.

This, however, readers may decide for themselves, since all the major arguments (though sometimes shortened) remain essentially intact and unrevised. The abridgement has necessitated some minor consequential re-writing; but the sense of the argument is, I think, scarcely ever changed.

In abridging, I have left out mainly the following: out-of-date statistics (e.g. on comparative growth-rates, or the cost of the social services), short-term economic analysis of the kind that quickly dates, a chapter on the 1945-1951 British Labour Government, and some discussion of issues in which interest has subsequently waned (such as the Rignano plan, or a large-scale capital levy). Cuts have also been made simply in the interests of brevity. But all the essential argument remains.

I would have liked not only to cut, but also to add; for there are, of course, other issues which have grown in importance and topicality since I wrote—the mass media, urban planning, the threat of Soviet growth, and so on. But again I preferred not to alter the book basically by incorporating new discussions into it. I have therefore dealt with these topics separately in a more recent book, *The Conservative Enemy*.

The layout of the book is as follows: Part One describes the new starting-point; that is, it analyses the significance of the changes that have occurred since the pre-war socialist programs were constructed. Part Two asks what meaning is to be attached to the concept of socialism in the light of these changes, and proceeds to define it in terms not of nationalisation or State planning, but of social welfare and social equality. Part Three discusses the welfare objective. Part Four deals with three allied questions: how social equality is now to be interpreted, how greater equality is to be justified when further redistribution will not obviously increase economic welfare, and how it is to be attained. Part Five discusses some of the economic implications of socialist policy. The concluding chapter peers rather further into a future in which collective social and economic issues may become less significant than the problems of leisure and private life.

C. A. R. CROSLAND.

House of Commons,
London.
August 1963.

THE FUTURE OF SOCIALISM

PART ONE

THE TRANSFORMATION OF CAPITALISM

I

———◆———

THE TRANSFER OF ECONOMIC POWER

1 *The Pre-war Socialist Assumptions*

SOCIALISTS in the 1930s, whatever their disagreements on long-term questions, were united on the immediate objec-/tives of a majority Labour Government. These were first the abolition of poverty and the creation of a social service state; secondly, a greater equalisation of wealth; and thirdly, economic planning for full employment and stability.

But many socialists, while assenting to these aims in principle, did so in a distinctly pessimistic frame of mind, thinking them probably unattainable within the existing economic framework. They believed, on the basis of a predominantly Marxist analysis, that capitalism itself must first be forcibly overthrown. Otherwise, reform would be rendered impossible either by the fact that the whole system was in process of decline, or, even while it still survived, by the entrenched power and reactionary attitudes of the 'capitalist ruling-class'.

The pervasive influence of this Marxist analysis in the 1930s was a reflection of an intellectual ferment without parallel in the history of the British Labour Movement, so traditionally and so doggedly anti-doctrinal. Under the impact of the 1931 slump and the growth of Fascism, more and more people came to mistrust a merely *ad hoc* reformist approach, and to feel that some more thorough-going analysis was needed to explain the catastrophe which appeared to be engulfing world capitalism.

The official Labour Movement remained somewhat unmoved by all this excitement, though faint echoes of it could be heard even from the direction of the National Executive.[1] But the younger generation of intellectuals absorbed itself furiously in the pursuit of theoretical truth. And for the most part it took to Marxism, which thus had to wait almost a century before achieving a major influence on the British Left.[2] The Fabian tradition offered no effective counter-attraction – indeed, its best-known leaders deserted, and became amongst the foremost exponents of the Marxist gospel.[3] The Hobsonian tradition, still strong in the I.L.P., was sufficiently close to Marxism not to constitute a rival doctrine – after all, had not Hobson been canonised by Lenin himself? A very few socialist thinkers stood outside the Marxist stream,[4] and a number of non-analytical works of a practical reformist nature were still being written.[5] But Marxism was the dominant intellectual influence; and it made a profound impact on my generation of socialists in their formative years before the war.

For this reason, and also because many who might have disclaimed the label Marxist shared the pessimistic attitude described above, I start by discussing the theory of capitalist collapse, and the metamorphosis of the 'capitalist ruling-class'; and so hope to arrive at a clearer view of the locus of economic power in the present 'mixed economy'. The next chapter discusses the performance of the Labour Government in respect of the three immediate objectives mentioned at the beginning of this chapter.

But first one preliminary word must be said. It will become clear in this and later chapters that in my view Marx has little or nothing to offer the contemporary socialist, either in respect of practical policy, or of the correct analysis of our society, or

---

[1] Cf. Mr. Attlee's *The Labour Party in Perspective* (Gollancz, 1937).

[2] The characteristic figure of the decade was Mr. Strachey, whose two books, *The Nature of Capitalist Crisis* and *The Coming Struggle for Power*, were as influential as they were typical of the period. In the political field Professor Laski was the outstanding influence (cf. *The State in Theory and Practice*).

[3] The most notable conversion, of course, was that of the Webbs themselves, who began by eschewing Marxism altogether and ended by embracing it whole. The outstanding younger Fabian figure, G. D. H. Cole, was also a leading (though never uncritical) exponent of Marxism (cf. especially *What Marx Really Meant*, Gollancz, 1934).

[4] Notably E. F. M. Durbin, *The Politics of Democratic Socialism* (Routledge, 1940).

[5] E.g. Mr. Dalton's *Practical Socialism for Britain* (Routledge, 1935), and Mr. Douglas Jay's *The Socialist Case* (Faber, 1937). These and similar books dealt essentially with short-term problems, and contained no long-run analysis of the future of capitalism.

even of the right conceptual tools or framework. His prophecies have been almost without exception falsified, and his conceptual tools are now quite inappropriate.

But this is no reason for adopting the current fashion, and sneering either at the man or his achievement. Intellectually he remains a towering giant amongst socialist thinkers, a man of the stature, in other fields, of Freud and Keynes, and very few others over the last hundred years. His analytical insight into the essential, dynamic nature of nineteenth-century capitalism, the range and sweep of his interests, his grasp of the crude reality underlying the surface parliamentary struggles, his passionate conviction, the wit and compelling power of his language – all these, even now, have an electric effect on the reader, and make the work of his contemporaries amongst the classical economists seem by comparison flat, pedestrian, and narrowly circumscribed. And his astonishing output was the work of a man in constant pain, who was often underfed, always poor, living usually in conditions of squalor and privation, with the dun and the bailiff never far away.

This was a feat of self-sacrificing devotion and dedication not often paralleled in the history of letters. No doubt Marx had many unpleasant traits of character; and his teaching, if only because it relates to conditions that have long since passed away, holds little relevance to-day. But the man was a dedicated genius; and only moral dwarfs, or people devoid of imagination, sneer at men like that.

II   *The Theory of Capitalist Collapse*

The belief that the 'inner contradictions' of capitalism would lead first to a gradual pauperisation of the masses, and ultimately to the collapse of the whole system, has by now been rather obviously disproved. Both total output and working-class standards of life have steadily risen. The British net national income, in real terms, was $3\frac{1}{2}$ times as high in 1938 as in 1870, and income per head $2\frac{1}{2}$ times as high;[1] and real wages moved roughly in line with income per head.

[1] A. R. Prest, 'National Income of the United Kingdom, 1870-1946', *Economic Journal*, March 1948.

Faced with this evidence of growth, Marxist scholars made various attempts to salvage something of the master's theory. For example, some maintained that the increasing misery was never expected to manifest itself until the latter days of capitalist decline, and that in fact 'the first foreshadowings of increasing misery appeared in the first decade of the twentieth century',[1] and still more plainly in the inter-war period. But even this modified version finds no support from the facts. The real national income rose by 55% from 1900 to 1938, and by 31% during the inter-war period.[2] Again the working class shared fully in the rise, with wages maintaining their proportion of the total. It is true that the rate of growth was lower in the inter-war period than during the second half of the nineteenth century, and that the 1931 depression was, by historical standards, exceptionally severe; but the growth nevertheless continued.

There was thus no evidence, even in 1939, of growing pauperisation, nor that capitalism as an economic system, painful and unsatisfactory in many ways though its performance was, was at all near the point of collapse. And now, for a decade since the end of the war, the British economy, whether or not we still choose to call it capitalist,[3] has singularly improved its performance. Full employment has replaced depression; the instability is vastly less; and the rate of growth appreciably more rapid. And my own view, which I discuss in detail in the economic chapters, is that the growth will continue, and that the future is more likely to be characterised by inflation than by unemployment.

This change in the economic climate, and hence in the starting-point for any analysis of the future, would alone suffice to outmode the greater part of the pre-war literature. It is easy to forget to-day, not merely how unanimous socialist writers were in anticipating the collapse of capitalism,[4] but how completely their analytical systems, their prophecies, and their recommendations, all hinged on this central belief. Faced with this awful, yet

---

[1] Cole, op. cit., pp. 112 seq.   [2] Prest, loc. cit.   [3] v. Chapter II.

[4] In a review of the economic literature of the 1930-1945 period, Professor D. McC. Wright notes that 'the majority of socialists and all communists assume that if any important time-span is to be considered, capitalism has no prospects, therefore the left tends to concern itself at most with the problems of transition'. ('The Prospects for Capitalism', in *A Survey of Contemporary Economics*, ed. Howard S. Ellis, Blakiston, 1948, p. 449.)

hopeful, prospect, they viewed the future with natural alarm, it is true, yet with the exhilaration which comes when the moment of decision is finally at hand, and all problems of choice are left behind. Since then, alas, the mischievous enemy has retreated, and gone into disguise as well; and the simple orders for a backs-to-the-wall defence must be countermanded, and replaced by a more elaborate but less exciting plan.

III *The Pre-war Power of the Business Class*

The second Marxist assumption, on which also much pre-war socialist analysis was based, was that society was effectively controlled by a capitalist ruling-class which held all or most of the important levers of power. Now Marxist theory does not, as later chapters show, provide a satisfactory basis for the analysis of either the class system or the distribution of power; its scope is too restricted, and the categories too narrow.

Nevertheless, if we confine ourselves to one particular aspect of *economic* power, and accept that we are not discussing the whole subject of power in modern society, we may say that the pre-war 'capitalist' class possessed this power to a marked degree, and wielded it with a good deal of ruthlessness.[1] This is the power to make, or at least predominantly influence, both the major production-decisions (whether, how much, how, what, and where to produce) and distribution-decisions (about the division of the national income between different social groups), the first being of course much easier to determine than the second. Such power requires effective control both at the perimeter (that is, in the firm or industrial unit) and at the centre (that is, at the seat of government).

The pre-war capitalist class broadly possessed this control. In some respects, it is true, its economic power had contracted over the years with the steady accretion of influence to both the

---

[1] The adjective 'capitalist' is not, it is true, entirely exact, since it has to embrace salaried business executives as well as industrialists drawing their power from the traditional capitalist source of industrial property-ownership. Nevertheless it is a not wholly misleading shorthand for the pre-war class of business leaders, many of whom still retained a considerable ownership stake in industry; while even those who did not continued to adopt a predominantly capitalist standpoint in the sense that they held the interests of property to be paramount.

political and industrial Left, and the general growth of democratic sentiment and social conscience. Yet in other ways it had
grown as a result of technical and economic changes. The trend
towards large scale in industry, and the inter-war trend towards
monopoly, meant that the decisions of a single firm or cartel had
an increasing impact on society; a smaller number of individuals
took decisions that affected a larger number of their fellow-
citizens. At the same time, the growth of monopoly weakened
the element of consumer influence which competition to some
extent preserves.

The economic power of the business class both at the perimeter
and the centre can best be gauged by recalling what was in
some ways the most symbolic, as in others it was the most traumatic, incident of the 1930s – the story of Jarrow.[1] Jarrow was
condemned, physically to a decade without jobs, psychologically
to a decade without hope, as a result of two decisions: first, to
close down the shipyard on which almost the whole town depended for its livelihood; secondly, to prevent, by the refusal of
a guaranteed share in a fully-controlled home market, the construction of a modern, integrated steel plant.

Now the immediate issue is not whether these decisions were
right or wrong from a strictly economic point of view, but what
they implied for the distribution of economic power. Both were
taken by private monopoly bodies (National Shipbuilders Security Ltd. and the Iron and Steel Federation). Both were taken
over the passionate protests of the workers and the local community, and in the face of a public opinion strongly aroused by
such dramatic incidents as the famous Jarrow hunger-march, as
well as by the flood of stories of local suffering and distress. Both
were taken solely in the light of short-term profit considerations,
and were influenced neither by the social and humanitarian arguments on the other side, nor by the long-term public interest in
the capacity and location of two such strategically important
industries. And both were taken with the sanction of the Government, despite the storm of protests and appeals.

The refusal of the Government to intervene afforded striking
evidence of the continued subservience of the political authority,
despite the revulsion caused by the Great Depression, to the

[1] For an account of this episode, v. Ellen Wilkinson, *The Town that was Murdered*
(Gollancz, 1939).

interests of business. Right-wing governments, largely composed of businessmen and wedded to an ideology of *laisser-faire*, were firmly opposed to interfering in the 'legitimate preserve' of private industry. When they did intervene, it was not to limit the economic power of private enterprise, but on the contrary to give additional sanction or support to its policies. Tariffs, industrial subsidies, Marketing Boards – all these interventions were at the behest of the producers concerned, and designed to strengthen their monopoly position. The weight attached by the Government to the (supposed) interests of the business class was most conspicuously (and painfully) demonstrated by its refusal to adopt any effective employment policy, whether the sort of expansionist anti-depression policy being widely tried out in other countries, or even a more limited policy of locating new factories in the Distressed Areas.

IV *The Loss of Power by the Business Class to the State*

To-day the capitalist business class has lost this commanding position. The change in the balance of economic power is reflected in, and may be inferred from, three developments. First, certain decisive sources and levers of economic power have been transferred from private business to other hands; and new levers have emerged, again concentrated in other hands than theirs. Secondly, the outcome of clashes of group or class economic interests is markedly less favourable to private employers than it used to be. Thirdly, the social attitudes and behaviour of the business class have undergone a significant change, which appears to reflect a pronounced loss of strength and self-confidence.

The most direct and obvious loss of economic power has been to the political authority, which now exerts control over a much higher proportion of economic decisions than before the war. The public authorities[1] to-day not only employ 25% of the total employed population, and are responsible for over 50% of total investment, but they wield a substantially greater power over business decisions even when these remain nominally in private hands.

This is largely a consequence of the explicit acceptance by

[1] Including the nationalised industries, which are discussed separately below.

governments of responsibility for full employment, the rate of growth, the balance of payments, and the distribution of incomes. The main instrument for exercising this responsibility is fiscal policy. Acting mainly through the Budget, though with the aid of other instruments, the government can exert any influence it likes on income-distribution, and can also determine within broad limits the division of total output between consumption, investment, exports, and social expenditure.

But it also exerts a powerful influence on production-decisions in individual industries – not only through a wider range of positive and negative indirect taxes (especially purchase-tax), which alter the pattern of demand and hence the relative attraction to producers of different lines of conduct; but, more important, through monetary, legislative, physical, and hire-purchase controls. It often fails to use these controls as effectively as the critics would like.[1] Nevertheless, it uses them to an extent which severely limits, as compared with the position under pre-war capitalism, the autonomy of business decisions.

Naturally the greater influence of the government would signify little if it were simply used to buttress the power, and underwrite the actions, of private business – if the state, in the Marxist phrase, were still the 'executive committee' of the capitalist class. But of course it is no such thing. The policies and attitudes of government are by no means the same as they were in the 1930s. The change is due mainly to a Leftward shift in the balance of electoral opinion, reflected not merely in six years of post-war Labour rule, but also in the significantly reduced majorities, by pre-war standards, of the succeeding Conservative Governments. Conscious of the slender electoral margin now separating the parties, and sensitive also to a fundamental change in public attitudes towards full employment and social welfare, these administrations have largely preserved the changes introduced by the Labour Government; and this has required the exercise of economic power on a scale, and in a direction, which would never have been countenanced by pre-war Conservative Governments.[2]

[1] *v.* Chapter XX.

[2] The possibility that the Conservatives may behave differently in future is discussed in Chapter II,, Section II. But to take one current example, no pre-war Conservative Government would have introduced the anti-monopoly legislation which has come from the present administration.

The reality of the change is attested by the different outcome of clashes of group economic interests. These most obviously take the form of disputes over the distribution of income. Since 1939, a considerable redistribution of personal incomes has occurred; and the gains have accrued largely to the workers, while the losses are at the expense of property-incomes – the share of net dividends, in particular, is much reduced. In addition, and indeed partly responsible for the smaller share of dividends, the taxation of profits is now much heavier than before the war despite an unceasing chorus of protests from business leaders. When private industry cannot even win its taxation battles against the government, something quite important must have changed.

Equally significant is the distribution of economic sacrifices in a crisis, for this reflects perhaps more accurately than anything else the ultimate location of power. Before the war, it was always the working class which bore the brunt. Since the war, the outcome has been quite different. It was a shrewd, though not over-friendly, American observer who remarked of the 1947 crisis that 'for the first time in British history the brunt of an economic crisis is not being borne by the workers'.[1] The best evidence of the change, at least during the period of Labour Government, was to be found in the intense antagonism of the better-off classes. 'Herein lay the whole secret of the middle classes' attitude to the Government, which ranged from white fury to hurt bewilderment. In 1921 they had suffered severely, but the working class had suffered too. . . . It was the same in 1931. . . . But now the Labour Government was talking about "equality of sacrifice", and the working class was not sacrificing anything; there weren't even any unemployed.'[2] Certainly the middle classes have come off distinctly better under the Tories. Yet a repetition of 1921 or 1931 is unthinkable even now; the national shift to the Left, with all its implications for the balance of power, may be accepted as permanent.

The other test lies in social and political attitudes. Here the contrast with both the facts and the expectations of the 1930s

[1] Herbert L. Matthews in the *New York Times*, 25 November 1947.

[2] Roy Lewis and Angus Maude, *The English Middle Classes* (Phoenix House, 1949), p. 95.

was complete, most obviously during the period of Labour rule. Pre-war socialists often anticipated violent, if not unconstitutional, opposition from private business; and a whole theory of 'capitalist sabotage', ranging from a flight of capital abroad to a 'strike of capital' at home, was constructed on this premiss. The event was very different. Investment proceeded briskly, and indeed had to be restrained; the opposition to nationalisation, although vocal, was never violent; firms and Trade Associations co-operated amicably with Labour Ministers; there was no hint of sabotage; and generally the atmosphere was one of amiable amenability, not untinged with nervousness.

All this was partly, of course, a reflection simply of the extreme unplausibility of pre-war Marxist analysis. But it also reflected a consciousness on the part of industry that the balance of power had altered. This consciousness (and also the diminished capitalist influence within industry itself) was most conspicuously demonstrated by the acceptance of voluntary dividend restraint during the Crippsian era. Despite the outcry in the City press, the degree of co-operation was remarkable, and a striking sign of weakened capitalist self-confidence. Certainly company chairmen continued to fulminate in their annual speeches; but their actions were the reverse of aggressive.

The fact that governments now exercise this pervasive economic power, and that they do so from motives other than a desire to prop up private business, would be sufficient by itself to outmode most pre-war, semi-Marxist analyses of class power. 'Whatever the forms of state', wrote Laski in 1937, 'political power will, in fact, belong to the owners of economic power.'[1] This was hardly a very helpful or plausible statement even in 1937, in the light of the history of Nazism and Fascism. But if we are to make misleadingly simple statements of this kind, it would be more accurate to turn Laski's statement on its head: whatever the modes of economic production, economic power will, in fact, belong to the owners of political power. And these to-day are certainly not the pristine class of capitalists.

---

[1] *Liberty in the Modern State* (Pelican Edition, 1937), p. 52.

v   *The Effects of Nationalisation on the Distribution of Power*

A second transfer of economic power has followed from the nationalisation of the basic industries. This has clearly diminished the power of the capitalist class. But more than this one cannot easily assert, for while everyone agrees on who has lost the power, not everyone agrees on who has gained it. The political authority now has, it is true, the power of Ministerial directive, of Parliamentary debate, and of investigation by Select Committee. On the other hand, many of the nationalised Boards consistently act in a very independent manner, which provokes constant complaints alike from workers, politicians, and economists. Indeed, some people think that the Boards are actually less 'accountable', and amenable to governmental control, than many private managements.

For practical purposes, therefore, economic decisions in the basic sector have passed out of the hands of the capitalist class into the hands of a new and largely autonomous class of public industrial managers. But since the political authority has at the same time acquired an explicit legal power over these new managers, even though it often chooses not to use it, the change does represent, in the last resort, an increase in the economic power of the state – though of course this leaves open the question of whether nationalisation is always the only, or the best, method of achieving this result.[1]

vi   *The Transfer of Power from Management to Labour*

Thirdly, there has been a decisive movement of power within industry itself from management to labour. This is mainly a consequence of the seller's market for labour created by full employment.

The relative strength of workers and employers does not, of course, depend solely on conditions in the labour market. It depends also on the political balance, the social climate, the degree of organisation of the two sides, and current views about

[1] *v.* Chapter XVIII, Section II, for a full discussion of this point.

the relation between wages on the one hand, and profits, employment, or the foreign balance on the other.[1] These factors had all changed in a manner favourable to labour even before 1939. Yet the strength of the Unions was still severely limited by large-scale unemployment; and they were obviously, and knew it, the weaker of the two contenders.

The change from a buyer's to a seller's market for labour, however, by transposing at once the interests, and therefore the attitudes, of the two sides, has dramatically altered the balance of power at every level of labour relations.

At the level of the individual worker, the decisive change relates to the question of dismissal. The employee, for whom dismissal before the war was often a sentence of long-term unemployment, can now quickly find a job elsewhere; and he has lost, in consequence, his fear of the sack, and with it his docility. The employer, on the other hand, who before the war could replace a dismissed worker from a long waiting-list of applicants for jobs, may now have difficulty in finding any replacement at all; and he has acquired, in consequence, a reluctance to dismiss, and himself has become more docile. Thus the balance of advantage is reversed, and the result is a transformation of relationships at the shop-floor level.

At the level of the plant or firm, the main change lies in the altered attitude of the two sides towards their ultimate weapons of coercion – the strike and the lockout. With unemployment, the employer can often well afford to endure a strike or initiate a lockout; the odds in the contest are on his side, while the cost of a stoppage, with stocks often high and market conditions unprofitable, may be relatively minor. But with full employment, the odds are quite different, since the workers can now hold out much longer; while the cost of a stoppage in terms of profits foregone is likely, with stocks perhaps low and a lucrative market demand, to be much greater. The employers' incentive to avoid strikes has thus increased in the same measure as the workers' prospects of winning them; the implications for the balance of power are obvious.

[1] Thus there was much less pressure for wage-reductions in 1931 than in 1921, partly because there was no general fall in prices as in 1921, but partly because employers now realised that competitive price-reductions would do them little good in the face of a rather inelastic consumers' demand, and with the certainty that their rivals would follow suit.

These implications extend to relations at the level of the industry, and hence to the question of wage-settlements. In addition, the high profits associated with full employmen' naturally incline employers more readily towards wage concessions, which can be more easily passed on to the consumer, or absorbed by rising productivity, than under conditions of depression. Indeed, so eager is the demand for labour to satisfy the prosperous full-employment market that employers are often themselves responsible for (sometimes *sub rosa*) wage increases.

The different outcome of labour-management disputes, as compared with before the war, testifies clearly to the shift of power. Wage-demands, now made annually in most important industries, are regularly conceded by employers to an extent which arouses constant alarm amongst economic commentators. Again and again a large wage-claim is submitted, which the entire financial press condemns as dangerous and unrealistic; a few weeks later it is quietly but generously settled by the employers concerned. To take two industries at opposite ends of the scale of prosperity, neither the engineering nor the railway unions to-day would feel much doubt about where the balance of industrial power lay. Indeed, people are now more nervous lest the Unions may *abuse* the new bargaining strength conferred on them by full employment.[1]

The outcome of strikes and lockouts is similarly a reversal of the customary pre-war pattern. In fact the employers have virtually abandoned the use of the lockout; while a much higher proportion of strikes culminate in a climb-down on the part of management. Indeed, employers have partially ceded their most fundamental power of all – to decide who, and how many, to employ; both these decisions are sometimes reversed under the threat of a redundancy strike, or a stoppage over the dismissal of a particular individual. This is a far cry from 'wage-slavery'.

But perhaps the change is most conspicuous, in terms both of actual policy and social attitudes, in the relations between the Unions and Conservative Governments. Here one can speak, without exaggeration, of a peaceful revolution. One cannot imagine to-day a deliberate offensive alliance between Government and employers against the Unions on the 1921 or 1925-6

---

[1] I am not concerned here with whether or not they do abuse it but simply with the fact that it exists.

or 1927 model, with all the brutal paraphernalia of wage-cuts, national lockouts, and anti-Union legislation; or, say, a serious attempt to enforce, as so often happened in the 1920s, a coal policy to which the miners bitterly objected.

Instead, the atmosphere in Whitehall is almost deferential, the desire not to give offence positively ostentatious. We see cordial and intimate meetings at No. 10. One Conservative Minister publicly rebukes a firm for declaring redundancy without prior consultation with the Unions. Another, forced to choose between the National Union of Mineworkers and a pressure-group of his own back-benchers, unhesitatingly chooses the former. The Cabinet firmly resists all efforts to bring Trade Union restrictive practices within the orbit of the Monopolies Commission. Industrial legislation is planned only after the most anxious consultation with the Unions. And in 1955, twenty-eight years after the Trade Disputes Act, the Conservative Government, in the face of considerable public clamour, unites in adamant opposition to proposals for 'outlawing' even unofficial strikes.

VII *The Psychological Revolution Within Industry and the Altered Role of Profit*

So far we have considered the loss of economic power by the business class as a whole to forces external to itself. But internal changes have also occurred within industry which significantly reduce the power of the capitalist class relative to other managerial classes. These changes were already perceptible before the war; but they have accelerated in the last decade.

The first, a consequence of the growing scale, complexity and technical intricacy of modern industry, is the increasingly specialised nature of business decisions. The gifted amateur is more and more at a discount; and even the professional top executive sometimes finds his decisions almost pre-determined (especially in regard to investment) by technological or research considerations. As a result, although the ultimate power of course remains in the hands of the top 'lay' management, more and more influence passes to the technical experts and specialists – the new 'organisation men' with the 'long-haired know-how', to use the current American slang: the plant engineer, the research chemist, the market research experts, the corporation lawyers, and the like. This partial change in the character of the decision-making function naturally calls for men with a different outlook and equipment, and therefore different interests and motives, from those of the traditional capitalist. One sign of the change is the growing number of scientists and specialised technicians appointed to boards of directors.

But much more significant, though many socialists are reluctant to admit it, is the change in the psychology and motivation of the top management class itself. This is partly, though by no means solely, a consequence of the now well-documented change in the composition of the business-executive class. The divorce between ownership and management, and the relative growth of the joint-stock corporation with fragmented shareholding, were of course already evident before the war. But the process has been further accelerated since by the continued growth in the scale and hence the financial requirements of industry, by a level of taxation which bears relatively more heavily on the small private business than on the public company, and by the effect of higher death duties in compelling the conversion of private into public companies. Business leaders are now, in the main, paid by salary and not by profit, and owe their power to their position in the managerial structure, and not to ownership. Meanwhile, the nominal owners have largely lost even the residue of control which they retained before the war.

And top management to-day is independent not only of the firm's own shareholders, but increasingly of the capitalist or property-owning class as a whole, including the financial institutions. As compared with the inter-war period, a higher proportion of profits is ploughed back into the business, and a higher proportion of capital expenditure is financed internally and not by recourse to outside capital. It is true that the Marxist prophecy of the transition to 'finance-capitalism', as industry fell more and more into the clutches of the City and the banks, was never at any time wholly fulfilled in Britain. But the financial difficulties created by the depression caused at least a trend in that direction before the war; and there were certain important industries in which management was, in consequence, extremely susceptible to outside financial pressure.

To-day, however, a decade of prosperity and high gross profits,

combined with a lower ratio of dividend distribution, has greatly
fortified the financial strength and independence of most public
companies. Despite the increased weight of taxation, undistributed profits are normally sufficient (taking industry as a whole)
to finance the whole of industrial capital formation – with a good
deal, indeed, to spare. Naturally some firms still need to borrow
or make new issues of share-capital; but internal company savings, relative to investment, are now higher than before the war.[1]
The economic power of the capital market and the finance
houses, and hence *capitalist* financial control over industry (in the
strict sense of the word), are thus much weaker. This change
alone makes it rather absurd to speak now of a capitalist ruling-
class.

The decline of capitalist control does not of course mean that
the profit-motive has disappeared, or that profits are less important. It is a mistake to think that profit, in the sense of a
surplus over cost, has any special or unique connection with
capitalism. On the contrary, it must be the rationale of business
activity in any society, whether capitalist or socialist, which is
growing and dynamic.[2] But with the divorce between ownership
and management, the role of profit has undergone a subtle
change, which leads to a consequential change both in the distribution of profit, and in the intensity with which maximum
profits are pursued.

The contemporary business leader does not want high profits
primarily as a source of high personal income or consumption;
since he does not own the business, he cannot, as his capitalist
predecessor often used to do, withdraw large sums from it for
his own enjoyment. Nor does he seek high profits primarily in
order the maximise the reward of shareholders. He seeks them –
partly, of course, because in the long run his own remuneration
depends on the success of the company: but mainly because his
social status, power, and prestige depend directly on the level of
profits. This is both the conventional test of business performance, and the source of business power. It determines both the
strength and prestige of the firm, and the power and social status
of its executives. Thus profit remains an essential personal and
corporate incentive – but largely as a source of strength and

---

[1] *v.* Chapter XVII.
[2] *v.* Chapter XVII, Section I.

influence, and not as an avenue to a privileged consumption-position for the capitalist. The implications for the distribution of income, as the shareholders' champions well realise and the figures of dividend payments demonstrate, are of course profound.

A further result of this change is a less aggressive pursuit of maximum profit at all costs. Profits are seen partly as a source of social prestige. But in the climate of the welfare state, they are far from being the only such source. The business leader can also acquire prestige by gaining a reputation as a progressive employer, who introduces co-partnership or profit-sharing schemes: or by being known to possess a high standing in Whitehall, and to have the ear of Ministers, an obvious candidate, perhaps, for Royal Commissions and National Advisory Councils; or by enjoying an outstanding local and civic reputation, as a benefactor, a helpful friend to the City Council, a member of the Court of the civic University; or by displaying obvious patriotism, and devoting a lot of time to the British Productivity Council; or simply by being an intellectual, who broadcasts and writes in Bank Reviews, or makes speeches at the British Institute of Management or Nuffield Conferences at Oxford. Such activities are increasingly common and well-regarded.

All this represents, I believe, a profound change in the social climate, which communicates itself even to the sphere of business decisions. Thus private industry to-day tends to be very sensitive to public opinion, and to its own notion of the public interest, even though no specific threat or sanction may have to be feared either from the government or from labour. This is evident even in respect of price policy. Price-determination is not now simply a matter of crude profit-maximisation, or invariably directed to the greatest possible exploitation of the consumer. It is at least influenced by notions of what constitutes a conventionally fair and reasonable price, which will be acceptable as broadly in the public interest, and immune from accusations of over-charging. For a long time after the war, for example, there were many goods, such as motor-cars, for which a huge pent-up demand existed, and which would have commanded an enormous price in a free market. Yet manufacturers, almost without exception, held prices down to what they considered a 'fair' and 'reasonable' level, well below the market or profit-maximising price. No doubt considerations of long-run goodwill played a part in this deliberate moderation; but the prevailing social climate also played a part.[1]

The traditional capitalist ruthlessness has largely disappeared from other spheres as well: from that of investment policy – few firms to-day, quite apart from the certainty of government intervention, would even try to repeat the Jarrow story; or policy towards competitors, dealers or suppliers, who are seldom driven into bankruptcy with quite the vigorous *élan* of thirty years ago; and most obviously, in the many ways described above, from labour policy.

The talk, and part of it at least is genuine, is now of the social responsibilities of industry – to workers, consumers, the locality, retiring employees, disabled workers, and in America, where business benefactions are on a gigantic scale, to universities, research foundations, and even symphony orchestras. Aggressive individualism is giving way to a suave and sophisticated sociability: the defiant cry of 'the public be damned' to the well-staffed public relations department: the self-made autocratic tycoon to the arts graduate and the scientist: the invisible hand, in Mr. Riesman's phrase, to the glad hand. Private industry is at last becoming humanised.

I do not mean that all businessmen now behave as though they were *manqué* philanthropists or social reformers – many manifestly do not.[2] But I do believe that the trend is in the direction I describe: that most businessmen are at least tinged by these more social attitudes and motives: and that those who most obviously express the change are coming to set the tone for industry as a whole. At any rate, we have here a definite contrast with a generation ago.

This psychological change of course fuses with, and reinforces, the change in attitudes to the state and the Trade Unions described above, and due simply to the loss of economic power. In practice one cannot disentangle the two influences, or say precisely which is cause and which effect. Nor indeed does it very much matter. Even supposing the motives behind the more diplomatic and humane behaviour to be of the narrowest and

[1] Resale price maintenance, contrary to what business spokesmen sometimes say, of course played no part at all so far as the manufacturers were concerned.

[2] And the exceptions are often outstanding for drive, efficiency, and innovation. The decline in ruthlessness may conceivably exact a price in terms of economic growth.

most self-interested kind, deriving solely from a consciousness of weakness, it would make no difference to our analysis – indeed it would be the more convincing proof of the altered configuration of power. And no doubt a large part of the change is to be so explained. Yet I doubt if this is the whole explanation – especially as the decline in the ideology of aggressive individualism even has its reflection within the business itself, where decision-making is more and more passing from the individual to the team.

This is not due solely to such technical influences as the greater number of variables and their increasingly specialised character, which virtually compel a group approach to decision-making. It is also due to a change in ethos, from the cult of the individual to the cult of teamwork. This explains the almost obsessive contemporary emphasis on co-operation, participation, communication, 'democratic leadership', 'permissive management', and all the rest of the slogans of 'progressive' management. The old-style capitalist was by instinct a tyrant and an autocrat, and cared for no one's approval. The new-style executive prides himself on being a good committee-man; and subconsciously he longs for the approval of the sociologist. He dreads any suggestion of high-handedness, or hint that he has failed to consult his colleagues. Above all the staff must work as a team; and where once the apt analogies for business behaviour were taken from war, now they are taken from sport. As one of the shrewdest observers of American industry has written: 'If our society comes to an end it will not be with a bang or a whimper. The sound track will be the soft tinkle of rimless glasses on a conference table.'[1]

VIII *The Political Power of Private Industry*

But whatever may or may not be happening in the realm of managerial psychology, it is indisputable that the economic power of the capitalist (i.e. industrial property-owning) class is enormously less than a generation ago; while even that of the managerial business class is significantly restricted by the new

[1] William H. Whyte, *Is Anybody Listening?* (New York, 1952), p. 223.

economic activism of governments, and the greater strength of organised labour.[1]

Nor am I personally much alarmed by the alleged political power of private industry. Socialists sometimes become very disturbed by the activities of such bodies as Aims of Industry, or the publicity campaigns launched by firms threatened with nationalisation, such as Tate and Lyle in 1950 or I.C.I. in 1955. But what is surprising over the last decade is not how much, but how little, aggressive 'free enterprise' propaganda there has been: and not how effective, but how ineffective, most of it has proved. The exceptional cases, where it has been both determined and effective, as in the two nationalisation instances just quoted, are largely to be explained by the failure of the Labour Party to put forward effective counter-propaganda, or to make clear to the country (and even to the workers in the firms concerned) just why it wanted to nationalise sugar in 1950 (but not in 1951 or 1955), and chemicals in 1955. And one can hardly blame an industry threatened with nationalisation for defending itself by any constitutional means; one only hopes that the Trade Unions (which in fact have more political power under a Conservative, than private industry has under a Labour Government) or the Co-operative Movement, if they were threatened by some Conservative electoral proposal, would be at least as vigorous and vocal in their own defence.[2]

Even the resistance of the steel industry in 1950-51, which met with such shocked surprise in some Labour quarters, does not appear to disprove this view.[3] It never went, in terms of political action, beyond what the Trade Union movement is well accustomed to undertaking. It was not economically effective, since steel output continued to rise under nationalisation despite the refusal of the industry's leaders to serve on the nationalised Board.

[1] It may also be said to be restricted, in another direction, by the probability – the evidence is not yet conclusive – that the degree of monopoly and concentration in the economy as a whole, after growing steadily for 40 years, decreased between 1939 and 1950 (though it appears to have increased again slightly since 1951).

[2] The fact that firms threatened with nationalisation often hurry to introduce profit-sharing schemes and the like may be taken as positively confirming the general argument of this chapter.

[3] And of course the acceptance by the steel industry, under the threat of nationalisation, of a Government Control Board with a power of veto over prices, and some powers of supervision even over investment decisions, is itself evidence of the altered balance of political power.

And it enforced the delay and awkwardness which it did only because the Labour Government had a Parliamentary majority of seven, a very brief expectation of life, and a widely suspected division in its own ranks over whether to nationalise or not. In the light of these weaknesses (and the fact that the industry appeared to be performing reasonably well), the ability to force through the nationalisation of the 'strongest bastion of capitalist power' suggests that we distinctly over-rate, not under-rate, the power of private industry.[1] I believe, for reasons to be explained in Chapter XVIII, that the argument for re-nationalising steel is irresistible. But it is not to-day, as it might have been in the 1930s, that a privately-owned steel industry wields a vast power of life-and-death, beyond the control of any government to limit, over either our political or economic destinies.

Of course the arguments presented in this chapter relate only to one manifestation of power in modern society, and that, in my view, of diminishing importance. Economic power, in the sense described in this chapter, and which rather naturally obsessed pre-war socialists when they were analysing capitalism, now poses fewer problems than other forms of power which have nothing to do with ownership or private industry as such, and indeed cut across the capitalist-socialist controversy.[2] These are first the power of the enlarged and bureaucratic state: secondly, the power of a small hierarchy of Court, Church, and influential newspapers, either to block reform or to impose its own social and moral standards on groups and individuals: and thirdly, the power of those who control the bureaucratic mass organisation, whether public or private – the B.B.C., the Coal Board, and the Trade Unions quite as much as I.C.I. or Unilever.

Some of these are discussed in later chapters.[3] I do not share all the current alarmism about the extreme menace which they present – what one might call respectively 'Crichel Down', 'Establishment', and 'managerial revolution' fears. Nevertheless I do believe that these aspects of power are of greater significance than the economic power to control production and

---

[1] For an opposite view, *v. The Labour Government and British Industry 1945-51* (A. A. Rogow and P. Shore, Blackwell, 1955).

[2] It is curious that the socialist, as opposed to the radical, tradition has comparatively little to say about any aspects of power other than the economic and political power of privately-owned industry.

[3] *v.* especially Chapters VI and IX.

distribution decisions, now that this is so much less concentrated and irresponsible than it was before the war.[1]

Again, statements about the decline in the economic power of the capitalist class are not to be taken as statements about *social* class. They do not imply that social class is necessarily any less pervasive or significant in Britain than it was, or even that no 'upper-class', in some sense of social status and prestige, can now be said to exist. Economic power is only one aspect of social class; and other aspects may remain just as relevant even though this one has diminished in importance. It is quite consistent to say both that Britain remains to an exceptional degree a 'class society', and that no ruling class exists in the narrow Marxist or economic sense.

The argument of this chapter is simply that the intellectual framework within which most pre-war socialist discussion was conducted has been rendered obsolete, first by the fact that the economy is growing at a rapid pace, and secondly by the fact that we now have a quite different configuration of economic power.[2]

These two fundamental changes call for a complete reappraisal of the socialist position – the more so since Labour's immediate policy objectives, which were listed at the beginning of this chapter, were also substantially achieved during the post-war years.[3] The amount of poverty was drastically reduced (though too much still remains). The social services were greatly expanded. The marked wartime levelling of incomes was carried over into peacetime. And full employment was maintained throughout the period.

[1] And now that the higher level and greater equality of purchasing power in any case make a divergence between 'production for use' and 'production for profit' much less likely (v. Chapters III and XX).

[2] In the light of certain events which have occurred since the text of this chapter was written, I must emphasise that the argument is about underlying trends, to which of course exceptions will continue to occur. I do not mean to imply that production will go up every year, or that recessions will never occur, or that no firms will ever act in a high-handed manner. But the trends here described are, I believe, irreversible.

[3] The unabridged edition contains a separate chapter describing this achievement in detail.

II

———◇———

IS THIS STILL CAPITALISM?

1 *The Extent of the Change*

THE changes already described in the previous chapter, and others not analysed here, amount to a considerable transformation of British society; and I suppose no liberal-minded person would deny that things were a great deal better in consequence. Affairs are conducted in a manner at once more just and more humane; and the angry clamour of past struggles is now heavily muffled. Recent years have witnessed nothing comparable to the violence of the post-1918 period, with its alternating succession of national strikes and lockouts; nor to the bitterness, a natural reaction to dole-queues, soup-kitchens and hunger-marches, which consumed the older industrial areas in the 1930s. The marked decline in political extremism is clear evidence of diminished social tensions.

It would, of course, be absurd to attribute the entire credit for the improvement to the post-war Labour Governments. Capitalism had been undergoing a slow, though painfully slow, metamorphosis since the turn of the century. Largely this was involuntary, in the sense that it was enforced by the rebellion of the non-capitalist classes against the unpleasant consequences of industrial *laisser-faire*, and by the growing power of the political and industrial Left. This was a prime reason why Marxist prophecies about the development of capitalism were never fulfilled in Britain, or indeed in any democratic country; as I wrote elsewhere, 'one of the errors the Marxists always made, on the basis of a faulty analysis of the nature of political conflict, was absurdly to under-rate the socio-economic consequences of political democracy.'[1]

But it was not only the anti-capitalist classes which called for change. The business classes, which, contrary to a curious pre-war socialist notion, do not indefinitely prefer to endure low profits and economic depressions rather than accept some measure of reform, were simultaneously losing their pristine capitalist faith and loyalty. And the economic reaction was reinforced by other and more subtle changes: the gradual evaporation within the bourgeoisie of the old unquestioning self-confidence, the simple conviction that unregulated capitalism must be the best of all possible systems: the steady growth of a genuine moral conscience about the miserable social and physical results of capitalism:[2] the political penetration of the middle classes in the 1930s, culminating in the astonishing phenomenon of the Left Book Club: and of course the psychological change, discussed in Chapter I, associated with the gradual supersession of capitalist by managerial personnel in industry. As a result, the anti-capitalist forces were attacking a citadel whose garrison was already weakened by dissension and defeatism.

Nevertheless, whatever the future potentialities of these underlying changes, the actual results were still rather small; and Britain in 1939 remained, basically, an unreconstructed capitalist society.

The war, on the other hand, was a most powerful agent of social change. A predominantly Conservative Government was compelled by military exigency to introduce many of the reforms for which the Labour Party had vainly pleaded during year after year of peace: government planning, full employment, redistributive taxation, new social services. The moral, that these measures were perfectly practicable and not merely the Utopian dreams of Left-wing visionaries, was not lost upon the electorate, which in 1945 firmly ejected the Conservatives for having neglected to do in peace what they so readily did in war.

Yet it is wrong to ascribe all that has happened simply to the

---

[1] *New Fabian Essays* (Turnstile Press, 1952), p. 35.

[2] Due partly to the influence of a minority of churchmen; the effect produced, for example, by the speeches and writings of Archbishop Temple should not be under-rated.

effects of the war. Past history shows that democratic peoples and governments always move to the Left during a war. The important question is whether they stay there afterwards. In Britain after World War I, and in many other countries after World War II, they did not, but retreated rapidly towards the pre-war norm. Wars are only permanently revolutionary if followed by Left-wing Governments which dig in, consolidate the changes, and use them as a basis for further advance.

This was the historic task of Mr. Attlee's Government. Just how successfully it was accomplished, people perhaps scarcely realise to-day. Memories are feeble; the changes are quickly taken for granted and accepted as part of the *status quo*; and it becomes impossible to recapture former moods and hopes.

It is therefore instructive to compare the achievement with pre-war expectations. The most relevant comparison is with the Labour Party's 'Short-Term Programme' of 1937. This was the most detailed and concrete programme of action to which the Party had ever committed itself. It was described as a list of urgent measures 'of Socialism and Social Amelioration, which a Labour Government would carry out during a full term of office when returned to power by the electors'.

Its salient features were as follows: (1) Finance: nationalisation of the Bank of England; control over new investment; redistribution of wealth by taxation. (2) Industry and Agriculture: powers of compulsory acquisition of land by public authorities; nationalisation of railways and other unspecified 'transport services'; nationalisation of coal, gas, and electricity. (3) Social Benefits: holidays with pay; school-leaving age to be raised to 16: improved pensions, workmen's compensation, and health services. (4) Distressed Areas: control over the location of industry.

It must not be thought that this programme, emanating as it did from the much-abused headquarters at Transport House, was an excessively timid creation of cautious politicians, and unrepresentative of general opinion on the Left. On the contrary, it was closely in tune with the thought of well-known socialists outside Parliament, to whatever wing of the Party they belonged. Professor Cole, Mr. Douglas Jay, and E. F. M. Durbin, in their works on socialism, all adumbrated very similar programmes as the most that could be expected of a Labour Government during its first term of office.[1] Indeed Mr. Strachey, at that time considered rather far to the Left, produced a 'Popular Front' programme for the Left Book Club which was incomparably more modest.[2] This was based, it is true, on the assumption that the Labour Party, in order to win a majority, would need to ally itself with non-socialists. Nevertheless, it was described as a set of measures which 'would modify the nature of capitalism to a serious extent', and 'must lead to Socialism' in the end. It consisted of six main items: (1) the promotion of public or mixed investment, (2) the lowering of the rate of interest to encourage private investment, (3) redistributive taxation, (4) higher social services, (5) a public banking system, (6) government control over the balance of payments.

It is evident from these programmes that the performance signally exceeded expectations. In each of the spheres mentioned, action went a good deal beyond what had been envisaged. Nationalisation, for example, embraced civil aviation, steel, road transport, and Cable and Wireless in addition to the industries listed in the official programme. Social service policy extended to family allowances, a comprehensive National Health Service, and a complete new structure, instead of minor improvements, of National Insurance. And in the fields of redistributive taxation, the level of employment, the Distressed Areas problem, the working-class standard of living, and government control over the economy, much more was achieved than most pre-war writers ever anticipated.[3]

None of this means that everything went right, or that more might not have been done, or that a great deal does not remain to be done. And of course the war helped to smooth the path of reform. It simply means, what is often forgotten to-day, that greater social changes had occurred by the end of the first majority Labour Government than the most sanguine amongst pre-war Leftists had expected.

[1] Douglas Jay, *The Socialist Case*; G. D. H. Cole, *A Plan for Democratic Britain* (Labour Book Service, 1939); E. F. M. Durbin, *The Politics of Democratic Socialism*.

[2] *Programme for Progress* (Gollancz, 1940). But it was not as modest as Sir Richard Acland's programme for a Popular Front Government, which was to consist of only four domestic promises: (1) to nationalise coal and the Bank of England, (2) to abolish the household means test, (3) to put an end to the 'site-value racket', and (4) to make milk cheap. (*Only One Battle*, Gollancz, 1937, p. 155.)

[3] Durbin, indeed, thought that hardly any social service improvements would be possible during the first period of office, and courageously called for a standstill on the standard-of-living while control over the economy was being consolidated.

II *The Danger of Conservative Reaction*

But are these changes very precarious? Is the whole new struc-ture vulnerable simply to a few years of Conservative reaction? There would be no point in getting very excited if everything was now to be undone, with Labour watching helplessly from the opposition benches.

Many such fears were expressed in 1951. I confess I never shared them. Of course it was always obvious that the Con-servatives would do reactionary things, and peel off several layers of what had been achieved: that they would alter the priorities, withdraw the frontiers of social control and ownership, and above all redistribute real income from poor to rich – by changes in taxation, reductions in subsidies, and the removal of controls. All these things have in fact been done; and more will be done in future. But it was never likely that the Conservatives would destroy the hard core of the achievement; and even if we suffer several more years of Conservative rule, I should still expect 75% of the reforms to remain intact.

This is partly because some of the changes cannot be undone by any practicable means whatever, being due not to Acts of Parliament, but to fundamental changes in the social framework. Thus the transfer of power described in Chapter I could not be substantially reversed by any Government, for its causes lie much less in legislation, than in changes in social psychology, the moral consensus of opinion, technology, and the internal structure of industry.

Even if this were not the case, a wholesale counter-revolution would still be rather unlikely. It is not, for one thing, in the nature of the British Conservative Party, which for all its clamorous fringe of backwoodsmen usually entrusts its leadership to cautious, realistic Peelites.[1] Indeed, it lacks the essential attribute of a counter-revolutionary party – a faith, a dogma, even a theory. A passionate desire to restore the past must rest on a deep attach-ment – moral, ideological, or theoretical – to the virtues of that past. And this the British Conservative, typically pragmatic and empirical, seldom has. His attachment is to the *status quo*, what

[1] For an excellent discussion of this whole question, *v.* Roy Jenkins, *Pursuit of Progress* (Heinemann, 1953).

ever the *status quo* may be; and his function is less to reinstate the past than to preserve the present.

This is particularly true to-day, since the immediate past was an era characterised by chronic depression, violent instability, and a singularly unheroic foreign policy. Nostalgically as Conservatives may think back to particular features of that era, such as the low taxation, they could hardly, by any feat of self-deception, beget a deep doctrinal or emotional devotion to pre-war society as a whole, or convince themselves that the 1930s were a glorious age, any defection from which is immoral as well as unwise.

The mood of the electorate provides, in any event, a sufficient guarantee against a sweeping counter-revolution. The voters, now convinced that full employment, generous welfare services and social stability can quite well be preserved, will certainly not relinquish them. Any Government which tampered seriously with the basic structure of the full-employment Welfare State would meet with a sharp reverse at the polls; and this knowledge acts as rather a strong inducement to politicians not to tamper. It is this which explains the otherwise curious phenomenon that the Conservatives now fight elections largely on policies which twenty years ago were associated with the Left, and repudiated by the Right: on increases in the social services, the over-riding claims of full employment, the prosperity of the wage-earners, and even, occasionally, the success of the nationalised industries! The fact that the political battle to-day is waged mainly on ground chosen by the Left is remarkable evidence of the change in national ideology.

It is significant, in particular, that the feature of post-war society which, for electoral reasons, is the least vulnerable to political reaction, namely full employment, is also one of the most decisive for the underlying balance of power. As an earlier chapter showed, it constitutes a basic cause of the shift of economic power away from the business class; and so long as it is maintained, then whoever governs at Westminster, the organised workers will remain the effective power in industry.

The Conservatives, then, besides acting as a barrier to further advance, will continue to make dents in the new social and economic structure; in particular, they will favour the better-off classes as much as they dare. But they will certainly not destroy the essential fabric.

III *Is Britain a Capitalist Society?*

Is there any sense in which the new structure can still be described as capitalist? This, obviously enough, is a matter of definition. But it is not the less important for that. Words such as capitalism, socialism, democracy, and communism have a strong emotional and propaganda content. It is therefore a matter of some importance whether a society (or a person!) is or is not labelled communist, or capitalist, or socialist, or democratic, since the label itself will influence people's attitudes towards the society (or person) in question. Verbal precision is therefore not a merely trivial or pedantic matter.

The word capitalism might reasonably be taken to mean one of two things. First, it might be used in a historical sense to describe the society which developed in nineteenth-century Britain after the Industrial Revolution, and which in its main outlines, although of course with modifications, persisted into the 1930s. This was in fact the sense in which the word first came into common use, having been chosen because the most conspicuous difference between industrial society, and medieval or feudal society, was the large-scale creation of industrial capital. Hence the word came to be applied to the whole of the society which grew up round, or on the basis of, this technological revolution.

On this historical definition, it is manifestly inaccurate to call contemporary Britain a capitalist society.[1] What, after all, were the salient features of that society, which fundamentally determined its social character?

(1) The autonomy of economic life, the decentralisation of economic decisions down to the individual unit of production, and the subordination of these decisions to (mainly) market forces; that is, what is crudely called *laisser-faire*. To-day, by contrast, as was shown in Chapter I, the state and the political authority have removed a wide, and strategically decisive, segment

---

[1] That is, unless we adhere to a literal interpretation in terms of large aggregations of industrial capital, in which case of course Britain is still a capitalist country – but so is Soviet Russia.

of economic decisions out of the sphere of purely market influences, and made them subject to deliberate political control. Through fiscal policy, and a variety of physical, legislative, and financial controls, the state now consciously regulates (or seeks to regulate) the level of employment, the distribution of income, the rate of accumulation, and the balance of payments; and its actions heavily influence the size of industries, the pattern of output, and the direction of investment-decisions. The passive state has given way to the active, or at least the ultimately responsible, state; the political authority has emerged as the final arbiter of economic life; the brief, and historically exceptional, era of unfettered market relations is over.

(2) At the level of the unit of production, decisions were effectively controlled by a class of private owner-managers, or capitalists, who (given the background of *laisser-faire*) largely monopolised economic power in the sense defined in Chapter I. This situation no longer exists even in the unit of production. In the basic industries, nationalisation has wholly deprived the capitalist class of its power of decision. But it has been similarly deprived in much of the private sector. The growth of the managerial joint-stock corporation has transferred the function of decision-making to a largely non-owning class of salaried executives, who suffer singularly little interference from the nominal owners. Even this new business class finds its freedom of action limited to an extent which its capitalist predecessors never did—partly by the growth in the role of government, but mainly by the growth in the power of labour, stemming generally from the rise in Trade Union strength and specifically from the altered conditions in the labour market. Thus the classical capitalist class of entrepreneurs has largely disappeared, at least from large-scale industry; while its successor, the business executive class, can certainly not be said to monopolise economic power even in the individual firm.

(3) Industrial capital was privately owned, as of course is implied in the previous point. This is still true of the greater part of industry. But its significance for social and economic relations has wholly altered for the two reasons just given, and with the results described below.

(4) The distribution of wealth was characteristically unequal for two reasons. First, the concentration of economic power in

the hands of one class meant that this class steered the distribution of income, so far as it could, in its own favour. Secondly, since this class was a capitalist one, at once the main source of new capital and the main agent of production decisions, strict economic considerations, quite apart from the balance of class power, necessitated an exceptionally large return to industrial capital-ownership relative to other sources of income.

To-day, as I pointed out above, the distribution of personal income has become significantly more equal; and the change has been almost entirely at the expense of property-incomes. Even more significant, the income accruing to the owners of industrial capital has dwindled to a negligible share of the total. Dividends net of tax are now only some 3% of all personal incomes after tax;[1] and even making a generous allowance for realised capital gains, this is a total reward to the 'capitalist' class which makes it startlingly clear that the economy is no longer basically capitalist-motivated, and that private share-capital is no longer, as it was under capitalism, the foundation and mainspring of the whole system. The demise of capitalism could almost be inferred from this one figure alone.

(5) Capitalism was historically associated with an explicit, assertive, and, in the perspective of history, unusual ideology. Its essential features were, first, the veneration of individualism and competition: secondly, an insistence on the absolute and unconditional rights of private property: thirdly, an intellectual belief that the unfettered exercise of private rights must, by 'the invisible hand' of economic competition, maximise the welfare of the community.

None of these beliefs could be said to form part of the ruling ideology in Britain to-day. The non-capitalist classes have always opposed an ideal of co-operation, social action, and collective responsibility to that of individualism; and as their power grew, so this ideal increasingly prevailed. No one would argue that in the contemporary Welfare State the dominant ideology was one of self-help or aggressive individualism.[2] And even within the business class itself, as Chapter I has shown, the worship of

[1] Gross dividends on ordinary shares in 1954 were £600 million, total personal incomes before tax over £14,000 million. Dividends, owing to the unequal distribution of shareholding, of course pay a much higher-than-average rate of tax.

[2] v. Chapter IV, Section IV, for a fuller discussion of the decline of the competitive ideal.

individualism has given way to a positive cult of team-work and group action.

Nor does anyone now much believe in the over-riding rights of private property.[1] Even Conservatives to-day seldom dress their claims in these terms; instead, they borrow moral standards and criteria that used to belong to the Left. It is significant that the opposition to nationalisation was usually based less on grounds of private property-rights, than on arguments about efficiency. And in so far as any ideology of property-rights persists, it is not within the new class of business managers, who find their sanction rather in performance and economic growth.

As for the dogma of the 'invisible hand', and the belief that private gain must always lead to the public good, these failed entirely to survive the Great Depression; and even Conservatives and businessmen now subscribe to the doctrine of collective government responsibility for the state of the economy.

(6) Lastly,[2] capitalism was characterised, largely as a consequence of these other features, by an intense class antagonism. Indeed this was inevitable in a society dominated by an aggressive economic ruling-class, whose power was yet increasingly challenged by an emerging class – the industrial workers. From the Peterloo massacre, through Chartism and the violence of pre-1914 syndicalism, to the bitter coal strikes of the '20s and '30s, the atmosphere was one of constant industrial tension, often verging on class war.

To-day this heavy, lowering atmosphere has largely lifted. Of course we still have strikes, hostilities, and periodic outbursts of emotion – perhaps even to a surprising extent.[3] But they no longer take the same prolonged, dogged, and embittered form. The disputes are conducted within more moderate limits; compromises

---

[1] v. Chapter XV, Section I.

[2] I am not sure what view should be taken of another feature of capitalism, at least according to Marx and Engels. 'Our bourgeois, not content with having the wives and daughters of the proletarians at their disposal, not to speak of common prostitutes, take the greatest pleasure in seducing each other's wives. Bourgeois marriage is in reality a system of wives in common. . . . It is self-evident that the abolition of the present system of production must bring with it the abolition of the community of women springing from that system, i.e. of prostitution both public and private.' (*The Communist Manifesto*, 1848.) This seems rather a harsh judgment on mid-Victorian morality. But I am not sure what it suggests for the argument of this chapter.

[3] v. Chapter VII.

are more quickly reached; and the militant language of class-war, the terminology of revolt and counter-revolt, is itself passing out of usage.

The more pacific character of the pursuit of power is reflected in the altered social and political attitudes of the different classes. Generally, the temper of political controversy is now much calmer. One could never to-day use descriptive language which seemed quite apt even twenty years ago. 'The forces of capitalism', wrote Laski, 'are highly integrated, [and] have the self-confidence which comes from the absence, so far, of any serious challenge to their authority. . . . All the main instruments of power and property are in their hands. . . . If democracy stands in the way, so much the worse for democracy. . . . If democracy will not stand much longer the poverty and unemployment . . . then they are prepared for the destruction of democracy.'[1] To-day this sounds like an echo from another world.

The attitude of the workers, both leaders and rank-and-file, has similarly lost its violent character. Some militants still occasionally speak in the accents of the class-war; but their social attitudes often belie their words. It is characteristic of a genuine class-war period, when the masses are rebelling against real oppression and exploitation, that the leaders identify themselves with their followers, not only intellectually and emotionally, but in their private and social lives.[2] They embrace a severe austerity, decline to mix socially with the governing class, and dedicate their entire lives, their hours of leisure as well as of work, to the prosecution of the struggle. The more amiable and sociable attitude of contemporary leaders, even on the 'militant' wing of the Left, is a significant sign of the change of mood – and, of course, a well-justified symbol of greater strength and self-confidence. And so far as the rank-and-file are concerned, their attitude is described in a prophetic remark of Engels: 'the masses have got damned lethargic after such long prosperity.'[3] But unlike him, not everybody would consider this a bad thing.

Thus almost all the basic, characteristic features of traditional

[1] *Liberty in the Modern State*, pp. 25 seq.

[2] That is, the genuine and trusted leaders, as opposed to the future deserters, like MacDonald, who are gradually seduced by the 'aristocratic embrace'.

[3] *The Correspondence of Marx and Engels* (Lawrence and Wishart, 1934), p. 86.

pre-1914 capitalism have been either greatly modified, or completely transformed. Does it then make sense to go on speaking as though contemporary Britain were still similar in kind to the society historically designated by the word capitalism? Surely not. And it is significant that our society is now different in kind from classical capitalism, not only in the socio-economic respects considered in this chapter, but in almost every other respect that one can think of – family relationships, population trends, sexual morality, personal religion, the position of women, literary and artistic standards, and so on. It would be curious if these profound changes in every part of what Marx called the 'superstructure' reflected no fundamental change in the underlying social and economic forces.

It therefore seems misleading to continue talking about 'capitalism' in Britain, as though the lines of battle were essentially the same as a generation ago. But the difficulty is that people feel happier if things are labelled; and they will not discard an old label unless a satisfactory new one wins acceptance. And no new terminology has come into universal vogue. The colourless 'Mixed Economy' and the rhetorical 'Welfare State' have gained most currency; but neither is a satisfactory descriptive label for contemporary British society.

I once rashly joined in the search for a suitable name, and in *New Fabian Essays* called the new society 'statism'. But it was, on reflection, a bad choice. It has come to be widely used, especially in the U.S.A., but as a synonym for 'collectivism', which was not the connotation intended. Having had no better idea since then, I have no intention of trying again. Nevertheless, I believe that our present society is sufficiently defined, and distinct from classical capitalism, to require a different name. It is, of course, always a matter of extreme doubt, indeed simply of personal judgment, when one can properly say of any evolving society, which avoids a complete upheaval, that a quantitative change has become a qualitative one, a change in degree a change in kind. Thus most historians would agree that it took six centuries of continuous evolution for full-blooded feudalism to develop into full-blooded capitalism; but they would disagree about the date at which the feudal features ceased to be, and the capitalist features became, the predominant ones which gave the society its characteristic tone.

Similarly people would disagree to-day (although the pace of change has been a great deal faster); and it can only be a personal judgment that capitalist features and attitudes no longer predominate, and that a change in degree has become a change in kind. But there is at least some powerful evidence to support the view.

IV The Growing Irrelevance of the Ownership of the Means of Production

But it might be objected that the word capitalism has often been used not in the meaning so far assumed, namely as a definition or description of a whole society: but simply to describe one feature of that society which was thought, rightly or wrongly, to be the basic determinant of all other features, namely, the private ownership of large-scale instruments of production. On this definition, any industrial society in which private ownership predominated, whatever its other features, would have to be described as capitalist; and contemporary Britain would be described simply as 75% capitalist and 25% socialist (assuming for the moment that socialism is defined equally narrowly in the converse sense).

Now it is a matter for argument which is the 'proper' definition of capitalism: that is, whether the word has normally been used in this narrow sense, or in the wider sense suggested above. But if the narrower definition is insisted on, we cannot of course prove that it is 'wrong'; we can only ask whether it retains any significance or interest if the assumption behind it turns out to be false; that is, if it appears that ownership is not the fundamental conditioning factor which determines the character of the society.

It seems clear that this assumption is not now correct, whether or not it was in the mid-nineteenth century. Let us return to Marx, from whom many socialists still derive their image of capitalism, and who was mainly responsible for this definition of the whole in terms of one of its parts.

The relations and modes of production which formed the basis of the Marxist analysis were twofold. First, the *technological* fact of large accumulations of industrial capital, leading inevitably to the factory system: 'the hand-mill creates feudal, the steam-mill capitalist, society.'

Secondly, the *social* fact that this capital, that is, the instruments of production, was 'alienated' from the workers who actually produced, and controlled by a separate class of owners. Thus the owners of labour-power and the owners of capital confront each other as two distinct and opposite economic classes, one of which must employ the other before production can begin. 'The separation of labour from its product was therefore the real foundation in fact, and the starting point, of capitalist production.' And again: 'Capitalist production therefore of itself reproduces the separation between labour power and the means of labour.'[1]

This separation, the fact that capitalist and labourer confront each other in the market as buyer and seller, leads inescapably to the basic features (in Marx's view) of capitalism: the economic fact of the 'exploitation' of the worker (that is, the appropriation by the employer of surplus value), and the social fact of the relation between capitalist and wage-labourer. From these two facts in turn spring all the other typical features of capitalism – the political domination of the owners, the class-struggles, the pauperisation of the masses, inequality, and the rest.

Now the whole argument hinges on the separation of the worker from the means of production, the alienation of control, and the confrontation of buyers and sellers of labour. And indeed Marx was correct, as sociologists to-day well realise, to isolate these factors as the determining influence on many social and economic relations. But the relevant question is: has this separation anything whatever to do with the actual *ownership* of the means of production, or does it arise inevitably from the underlying technological fact of complex and large-scale factory organisation? Surely the latter.

The only society in which it does not occur, and in which the worker alone, not being confronted by an employer, determines both the conditions on which his labour-power is used and the use to which the means of production are put, is a peasant or craft society, or at least a society of small-scale units. But as soon as society becomes 'capitalist' in the literal sense of being characterised by large agglomerations of capital, the separation is

[1] *Capital*, Vol. II, pp. 583, 591.

inevitable, whoever owns this capital. There must, merely on account of the huge numbers employed and the intricate sub-division of labour, be some central hiring organisation which decides who, and how many, and on what terms, to employ, and what use is to be made of their labour-power. Similarly there must, again owing to sheer size and complexity, be some central nucleus of managerial control, and chain of command, which takes the production and distribution decisions in a more or less centralised manner and by methods other than periodic mass-meetings of workers.

Thus irrespective of who 'owns' the means of production in the legal sense, both 'confrontation' and 'alienation' are inevitable; and someone other than the mass of workers must ultimately take the production decisions. The basic factor is not ownership, but large scale; and a collectivist economy, with no private owners, is no less characterised by the alienation of control than a capitalist economy. Indeed, even in the latter, ownership has less and less relevance to the question of control. The same trend towards large scale and complexity which alienates the workers from the means of production also alienates the owners. Capital requirements are so great that sole ownership gives way to frag-mented shareholding; and many large companies to-day have more shareholders than workers. Naturally the mass of share-holders is even less able than the mass of workers to control and co-ordinate the highly technical, managerial organisation which alone can take the decisions. Thus ownership becomes of less and less importance for two separate reasons, both deriving funda-mentally from the growth of scale: first, because the alienation of the workers is an inevitable fact whether ownership is 'capit-alist' or collectivist, and secondly because even 'capitalist' ownership is increasingly divorced from effective control.

Of course the pattern of ownership may still have some influence on what economic decisions are taken – though not necessarily in any particular direction, as is made clear below. But it is wholly irrelevant to the underlying fact of the alienation of the workers from the means of production. In Soviet Russia, just as much as in the United States, the employer and the labourer 'confront each other as buyer and seller'; the control centre is separated from the workers; and the possibility of exploitation, and of all the other features of 'capitalism', is present.

Since private ownership has little to do with the loss of control by the workers, and indeed is not itself the main source of control even where it still survives, it seems unlikely that the pattern of ownership will uniquely determine anything. Let us test this view against each of those basic characteristics of a society which have, historically, been of most concern to socialists.

First, political freedom and parliamentary democracy. Recent history demonstrates that these may (though of course they need not) exist in a largely privately-owned economy, and not in a collectivist one. Presumably no one would deny that they were present in Britain, and absent in Soviet Russia.

Secondly, class stratification, whether in the 'economic power' sense discussed in Chapter I or the wider sense discussed in Chapter VI, may be either more or less marked in a collectivist than in a privately-owned economy. The once-popular equation of state ownership and the classless society rested either on a tautological proof (that is, class was defined in terms solely of the presence or absence of private ownership, from which it followed that if there were no private ownership, there could be no classes), or on the assumption that when the state expropriated industry, no one class would control the state. But there was no logical reason why this should be true. Most people would judge that in Russia it is not, and that a distinct ruling-class exists, its power resting on control of the state machine. And so far as non-collectivist societies are concerned, the view that the distribution of class power depends on the pattern of ownership is disproved by the arguments set out in Chapter I. Indeed, if we compare the two extremes (in terms of ownership) of Russia and the U.S.A., it becomes obvious that both the distribution of economic power and the degree of social stratification depend on innumerable influences besides the ownership of the means of production; and a comparison between Britain in 1956 and in 1856 would of course show the same result.[1]

Thirdly, the degree of 'exploitation' – that is, the extent to which the workers, instead of being paid and consuming the whole value of what they produce, surrender some part in the form of 'surplus value' – again does not depend uniquely on ownership. It is determined primarily by the fiscal policy of the government, and by managerial decisions about the disposal

[1] v. Chapter VI for a fuller discussion of the question of class.

of profits.[1] A collectivist economy can extract as much surplus value as it chooses by means of heavy taxation and the ploughing-back of profits by state enterprises; while of course the need for surplus value, as a condition of capital accumulation and economic growth, is just as great in a collectivist as in a privately-owned economy. Indeed, if Soviet apologists are to be believed, and the rate of capital investment in Russia is what they say, then the world's first collectivist economy has extracted surplus value from its population on a scale never exceeded by any capitalist country in history.

Fourthly, the distribution of personal income is not uniquely determined by the pattern of ownership. It depends on the share of wages in the national income, the taxation policy of the government, and the behaviour of relative prices; and these in turn depend on many different factors such as the level of employment, the degree of competition, the strength of the Trade Unions, and above all the political complexion of the government. It is quite possible for income-distribution to undergo large changes without a major change in ownership, as it has done in Great Britain over the last fifty or a hundred years: for incomes to be more unequally distributed in a collectivist than in a privately-owned economy, as they are in Soviet Russia than in Britain or Scandinavia: and for personal incomes from property to be squeezed, even in a 'capitalist' country, to an almost negligible proportion of the total.

The same is true of the distribution of capital. This is determined by the structure of inheritance taxes, and the possibilities of accumulation during lifetime. The former is of course under the control of the political authority. But it is sometimes said that large accumulations during lifetime are inevitable in a privately-owned economy, since a sufficient supply of capital depends on high dividends and rapidly rising capital values. But this, I believe, is greatly to exaggerate the importance of the shareholder as a source of capital in the modern large-corporation economy. The matter is argued in detail in later chapters;[2] but the experience on the one hand of Germany, where the shareholder is of singularly little importance and the capital market quite different from our own, and on the other hand of Sweden, where

---

[1] This point is discussed in more detail in Chapter XVII, Section I.

[2] *v.* Chapters XV and XVII.

an exceptionally high level of investment is accompanied by only a modest rise in capital values, suggests that large private accumulations can be prevented even under a system of private ownership.

Fifthly, the degree of government planning does not depend exclusively on ownership. Post-war experience has shown that private industry can be subjected to a close degree of government control, while nationalised industries may behave in a rather independent fashion, and prove not altogether easy to plan.[1] Generally, there is no practical or theoretical reason why a collectivist economy should not operate solely under the influence of the price-mechanism, without interference by the government, nor why a privately-owned economy should not be subject, as the Nazi economy was, to state control of all major economic decisions.

Lastly, the status of the worker may be either better or worse in a collectivist than in a privately-owned economy. So far as real income is concerned, this depends partly on the share of wages in the national income, but in the long run mainly on the rate of growth of the economy; and there is no definite evidence that this must be higher in a collectivist society. So far as status at work is concerned, the Marxist criticism of 'proletarianisation', in the direct sense that most employees work for wages in mass factory units, is of course as easily levelled at Soviet Russia as at the United States.[2] But what really matters is the degree to which management is autocratic or democratic, the extent of joint consultation and participation, and the freedom of the worker to strike or leave his job. In all these respects the Soviet worker is more proletarianised than the British worker. He has no free Trade Unions to protect him, no right to strike, no freedom to change his job, no elaborate system of arbitration, and no political party to represent his interests in a democratic parliament. Deprived of individual rights and subject to autocratic management, he may well envy the British worker his free Trade Unions and looser discipline; the victim of periodic compulsory speed-ups, he may similarly envy the American worker his shorter hours and greater freedom. In this, as in the

[1] v. Chapter XVIII, Section II, for details.

[2] This point has been made by M. de Jouvenel in the course of a comparison of the Soviet and non-Soviet economies. (Paper presented to the Milan Conference of the Congress of Cultural Freedom, 1955.)

other spheres already mentioned, the ownership of the means of production decides much less than the character of the political system.

If we turn from society as a whole to the individual unit of production, we still find that the question of ownership is of less importance than other factors. The experience of nationalisation has shown that the public and private corporation face very similar problems, which indeed are common to all large-scale industrial organisations. Thus not only the Coal Board and I.C.I., but a Soviet State Trust, General Motors, and Volkswagen, all have much in common in respect of the economic and technical decisions which they have to take – how to determine wages, settle disputes, achieve a sense of participation, decentralise decisions, accumulate a sufficient surplus, and satisfy a critical public.

Nor do they *necessarily* differ (in the sense that their decisions are uniquely 'given' by their different patterns of ownership) in the approach which they bring to these problems. All are managerially controlled, none exist primarily to enrich the owners. And not only their economic motives, but also their 'social character' is often similar. This is because they are all controlled by men enjoying similar relations at work. Whether in a public or private corporation, the executives are paid by salary. They enjoy security of tenure, steady incremental increases in income, a more or less regularised system of promotion, and pension rights. They are appointed, and neither elected nor self-chosen; they work within a hierarchically-organised structure, and according to a systematic set of rules.[1] It is hardly surprising that they show a temperamental affinity – more, indeed, than either would have with the classical capitalist entrepreneur. This may be a good or bad thing. But it is a fact, and indeed one of the reasons why large-scale nationalisation has produced fewer changes than many socialists expected.

Is it then not clear that the ownership of the means of production has ceased to be the key factor which imparts to a society its essential character? Either collectivism or private ownership is consistent with widely varying degrees of liberty, democracy, equality, exploitation, class-feeling, planning, workers' control, and economic prosperity. And it is surely the degree to which

[1] *v.* Robert K. Merton, *Social Theory and Social Structure* (Glencoe, 1949), Ch. V.

these attributes are present or absent which makes people differentiate between societies.

This does not of course mean that ownership can have no influence whatever on the character of a society, or on what decisions are taken in these various spheres. It might be that private ownership was either a help or a hindrance to the attainment of certain goals, such as income-equality, or the diffusion of power, or a higher status for the worker. This question is left for discussion in later chapters. What it does mean is that the pattern of ownership, although it may influence, is unlikely to *determine* the extent to which such goals are attained. And even as an influence it is now less important than other factors, such as the managerial structure of industry, the level of employment, the strength of the Trade Unions, the general social climate, and above all the character of the political authority.

It therefore seems rather pointless now to define and distinguish societies according to this one criterion. The resulting classification would be a very misleading guide to the true character of the societies; nor indeed would it show any correlation with what a socialist would consider 'good' or 'bad'. If we persist in defining capitalism in terms of private ownership, and socialism in terms of collectivism, then as socialists we must say that we should prefer, or that the mass of workers would prefer, or that we should regard it as more just and moral, to live in Soviet Russia than in Britain, Sweden, or even the United States. Which only shows how completely these definitions have cut adrift from what people had in mind when they originally used the words.

I conclude that the definition of capitalism in terms of ownership, whether or not it was helpful 100 years ago, has wholly lost its significance and interest now that ownership is no longer the clue to the total picture of social relationships: and that it would be more significant to define societies in terms of equality, or class relationships, or their political systems. In any event, I personally think, as I argued earlier, that the proper definition of the word capitalism is a society with the essential social, economic, and ideological characteristics of Great Britain from the 1830s to the 1930s; and this, assuredly, the Britain of 1956 is not. And so, to the question 'Is this still Capitalism?', I would answer 'No'.

PART TWO

THE AIMS OF SOCIALISM

III

———◇———

THE TRADITIONS OF BRITISH SOCIALISM

1 *The Appeal to the Past*

I F this is not still capitalism, then what is socialism now about?
The Labour Party has not yet given a clear answer to this
question; indeed no one who has observed the Party since
1951, furiously searching for its lost soul, can have failed to sense
a mood of deep bewilderment. This mood is in no way discredit-
able. In the light of the legislative accomplishment, there is no
help to be got from searching the files of Transport House; while
in view of the change in the balance of economic power, most
pre-war analyses have lost their relevance, and the much-thumbed
guidebooks of the past must now be thrown away. It is small
wonder, in these circumstances, that the approach to a new policy
should be fumbling and hesitant, and that there should be a
note of irritation both about the demands for 'new thinking',
and then about the responses to it once it comes.

In this situation the simplest refuge, and the most common
cry, is to urge that we 'go back to socialist first principles'. This
sounds both easy and attractive. But unfortunately the phrase
'first principles' is ambiguous. Does it refer to basic ethical or
emotional aspirations? But these may have been the product of
a situation which has passed away. Or to particular policy objectives? But these may have been achieved, and so have become
irrelevant. Or to the ideological or theoretical justification for
these objectives? But this may have been outmoded by changes
in economic or sociological thought. Or to the means by which
these objectives were to be fulfilled? But there is no reason why

means that are suitable in one generation should be equally suitable in the next.

That one can easily browse amongst 'socialist first principles' without any new policies, or fresh contemporary justification for old ones, emerging at the end, was clearly shown in the most widely-read socialist book of this period.[1] This negative result is bound to follow unless it is made clear to what category of statement the phrase 'first principles' is held to apply. To take a particular case, which of the following is to be held sacred as a first principle: nationalisation of the means of production (the means to a particular objective), the appropriation by the state of property incomes (the objective), the labour theory of value (by which the objective was often justified), or the underlying aspiration towards equality? Very different answers for future policy would emerge according to which of these historically interrelated elements was picked out as the essential truth to be preserved.

There is the further difficulty that no single constant and consistent body of socialist doctrine exists. R. H. Tawney has written that 'like other summary designations of complex political forces, Socialism is a word the connotation of which varies, not only from generation to generation, but from decade to decade'. And not only has the doctrine varied through time, but different versions of it, as will be seen, are mutually inconsistent.

In the case of the British Labour Party, matters are additionally complicated by the fact that it was not founded on any body of doctrine at all, and has always preserved a marked anti-doctrinal and anti-theoretical bias. The foremost historian of the Party, writing of its formative years, speaks of 'a Socialism almost without doctrines . . . so undefined in its doctrinal basis as to make recruits readily among persons of quite different types'.[2] This may or may not have been a good thing;[3] but it was a fact, and

---

[1] Aneurin Bevan, *In Place of Fear* (Heinemann, 1952).

[2] G. D. H. Cole, *A Short History of the British Working-Class Movement, 1789-1937* (Allen and Unwin, 1937), Vol. III, pp. 22, 26.

[3] The British workers had already been rapped sharply over the knuckles by Engels for their inattention to doctrine. Writing in the 1870s, he congratulated the German workers on the fact that they 'belong to the most theoretical nation in the world, and have retained that theoretical sense which has been almost completely lost by the so-called educated classes in Germany'. He contrasts this happy state with 'the indifference to theory which is one of the chief reasons of the slow progress of the English working-class movement'. But in the end the intuitions of Keir Hardie proved a more reliable foundation than the theories of Lassalle and Kautsky.

one which makes it particularly hard to decide what are the correct dogmas to which we are now supposed to go back for inspiration.

But since the appeal to tradition is so appealing a catch-phrase, and lest, for all these difficulties, it should throw up the right answers, a brief résumé of traditional socialist doctrine is given in this chapter. I say nothing of the long pre-capitalist tradition of 'communism', stretching all the way from the early Christians to the Levellers, since modern socialism is concerned with an industrial society, and the doctrinal formulations of purely agrarian societies can have little relevance. But the following doctrines, listed broadly in chronological order, have been the most influential over the last 150 years.[1]

II A Summary of Socialist Doctrines

(1) *The philosophy of natural law.* This had its immediate inspiration in Locke, though of course it can be traced much earlier in philosophical history. But it was Locke (suitably interpreted) whose ideas provided a theoretical basis both for the English radicals who rejoiced at the French Revolution, and the early anti-capitalist writers of the Industrial Revolution. He was called in aid to prove that land was originally held in common, and that labour was the only true title to property. These two principles were used to support the revolutionary thesis that common possession, because natural, was therefore also just, and that private property must be abolished: and that all deductions from the produce of labour in the shape of rent, interest or profit were indefensible, and should be reclaimed by the community.

(2) *Owenism.* Robert Owen, believing that character and states of mind depended on economic environment, maintained that so long as the economic system was competitive, it would breed neither good character nor general contentment. Competition must therefore be replaced by a co-operative organisation of industry, with property held in common, and all labour treated

[1] For histories of this subject, *v.* M. Beer, *A History of British Socialism* (Allen and Unwin, 1940), Alexander Gray, *The Socialist Tradition* (Longmans, 1946), G. D. H. Cole, op. cit., and (an anthology of socialist writing) Henry Pelling, *The Challenge of Socialism* (Black, 1954).

as of equal status. This transition does not require class-war, industrial strikes, or even political action. It requires only that the upper classes should be converted, as they must be as soon as they perceive the reality of the situation, to the need for a new social order, which can then be built by a cumulative series of local co-operative experiments, with all classes gladly participating.

(3) *The Labour Theory of Value.* Derived from Ricardo, this was forged into a weapon of socialist propaganda by the English pre-Marxist socialists (Hodgskin, Bray, etc.), and became the predominant intellectual inspiration of the working-class anti-capitalist movement, and in particular of Chartism. Labour is the source of all exchange-value, yet receives only subsistence-wages. It therefore derives no benefit from the continuous rise in production, wages being held down by what Lassalle later called 'the iron law of wages', and the whole increase in wealth accruing to the capitalist and landlord in profit or rent. There is consequently an irreconcilable conflict between capital and labour over the distribution of the product; and this can only ultimately be resolved by labour's securing the whole value of what it produces. The struggle must be waged by a working class organised on militant class lines, and prepared to use either industrial or political action as circumstances dictate. (This is in marked contrast to Owen's reformist, Utopian belief in class co-operation.)

(4) *Christian Socialism.* The aims of the Christian Socialists bore a close resemblance to those of Owenism, though of course the inspiration was different – in the one case a Benthamite belief in universal happiness, in the other a concern with Christian ethics. But for both the essential evil was the competitive pursuit of private gain, and the objective a co-operative society of communal ownership, in which mutual love and brotherhood would replace the selfish antagonisms inevitably bred by competitive capitalism.

(5) *Marxism.* Like some earlier socialist doctrines, Marxist economics were based on a Ricardian labour theory of value, and a somewhat more refined theory of surplus value and exploitation. The worker, who could support himself by working only x hours a day, is in fact compelled to work x plus y hours; and the entire fruits of y accrue to the capitalist as surplus product.

There is therefore a basic conflict between workers and bourgeoisie, which must be fought out with all the weapons of class-
war. The root of capitalist power lies in the ownership of the
instruments of production; and the vital condition of success for
the working class is therefore the expropriation of these instruments. The struggle over their ownership will grow continuously
more bitter, for capitalism suffers from certain insoluble inner
contradictions which must lead to growing pauperisation, and
eventually to collapse and revolution.

The most novel and, as it has proved, most influential element
in this doctrine was the central role ascribed to the capitalist
monopoly of the means of production, and the insistence that
this must be replaced by state ownership as soon as the workers
have created a proletarian state. Marx was in truth the founder
of the State or collectivist tradition in socialism, as opposed to
earlier notions of communal or co-operative ownership.

(6) *The theory of rent as unearned increment.* This was developed
from the Ricardian theory of rent by John Stuart Mill, and was
later popularised, with for a time enormous success, by Henry
George. It was a doctrine directed primarily against landlords.
Economic progress causes a constant increase in land-values. This
goes to enrich the owners, although they have in no sense 'earned'
the increment, which would accrue to them though they were
totally passive and idle. It is the product solely of the fact that
land is in limited supply, and effectively monopolised by its
existing owners. Since it is clearly inequitable that the additional
wealth created by society should be sequestered by the landlords,
and since this deprives labour of its just reward, the land should
be nationalised, or at least land-values heavily taxed, so that
the increment may in future be enjoyed by the whole community.

(7) *William Morris and anti-commercialism.* Competitive commerce degrades the worker as producer. It drains the craft and
satisfaction out of labour; it destroys art and good design; and
it creates a vulgarised upper class, and an intolerable gap between
rich and poor. There is no help to be looked for from the state,
nor from Parliament, nor from the collectivist socialists, who are
likely merely to fasten a new bureaucracy and tyranny on the
worker. Competition must be replaced by small co-operative
units, and economic activity decentralised down to local communes. The need for a central state will then disappear, and

even the nation will lose its function. Once the twin evils of central state authority and commercialism have been eliminated, all wealth will be held in common, competitive antagonisms will fade away, and labour, performed for pleasure and not for profit, will again assume the dignity of a craft occupation.

(8) *Fabianism.* The early Fabians owed little to previous socialist thinkers, and in particular nothing to either Owen or Marx.[1] Their intellectual derivation was wholly non-socialist – from Ricardo, Mill, Jevons, and Henry George.

Specifically, they extended the Mill-George theory of rent as an unearned increment to other factors of production besides land. The owners of any factor which possessed a differential advantage would, with increasing prosperity, become possessed of large economic rents, measuring the natural superiority of the more favoured over the marginal establishments. But since these special advantages are normally inherent qualities of the factors of production concerned, the differential rents are a pure unearned increment: not the product of any efforts on the part of the capitalists themselves, but the automatic consequence of social labour and development. Land and industrial capital must therefore be emancipated from individual or class ownership, and vested in the community by nationalisation. Rent and interest will then accrue to the state, and can be equitably shared amongst the whole population (though not necessarily equally – if labour were to be granted its 'whole product', efficiency might suffer).

The Fabians stressed the virtues of collective (state or municipal) action not only in respect of ownership, but in every sphere. Any extension of collective at the expense of individual activity constitutes an advance towards socialism, including the registration by the state of playing-card makers, hawkers, dogs, cabs, places of worship and dancing-rooms.[2] This implies, of course, a view of the state diametrically opposed to that of Marx, who thought that nothing good could come out of the capitalist state, which must be overthrown and replaced by a workers' state *before* collectivism could be established. The Fabians, instinctive gradualists and permeators, believed on the contrary that reform could come through the existing capitalist media.

[1] Their contempt for Marx was reciprocated on his behalf by Lenin, who called them 'filthy froth on the surface of the world labour movement'. (Quoted by Gray, op. cit., p. 485n.)

[2] Sidney Webb, *Fabian Essays* (1931 edition), pp. 44-7.

(9) *The I.L.P. tradition.* This has been extremely influential, but is not easy to define. It was the early Independent Labour Party that Professor Cole had in mind when he wrote of 'a Socialism almost without doctrines . . . a broad movement on behalf of the bottom dog';[1] and what there was of doctrine was a simple amalgam of previous doctrines. Yet there is still something distinctive about the I.L.P. tradition. This unique element is neither doctrinal nor intellectual, but rather a particularly strong insistence, largely Nonconformist in origin, on the brotherhood of man, on fellowship, service, and altruism. This is stressed not only in a domestic context, but equally in relation to other countries. The internationalist tradition of the Labour Party stems far more from the 'international brotherhood of man' appeal of the I.L.P., than from the 'workers of the world, unite!' slogan of the Marxists. It is this generous, idealistic, deeply religious emphasis on brotherhood and altruism which justifies us in identifying the I.L.P. as a separate influence – and one very different in spirit from the Fabian, as may be seen from the contrasted reactions of the two bodies to the Boer War.

(10) *The Welfare State or paternalist tradition:* the rejection of the *laisser-faire* doctrine that the state has no obligation to its citizens (save for the protection of property), and indeed a positive obligation to remain inactive: and the affirmation of the opposite view that the state must accept responsibility for preventing poverty and distress, and for providing at least a subsistence minimum of aid to such citizens as need it.

This has not always been a distinctively socialist doctrine – indeed, it was only in the era of classical competitive capitalism that the 'night-watchman' view of the state (to use Lassalle's phrase) was prevalent. The opposite view was normal up to the time of the Industrial Revolution, and of course is now once more widely accepted outside the socialist parties. But the *laisser-faire* view prevailed for the whole of the nineteenth century; and since during that period the socialist movements were the only serious anti-capitalist force, the paternalist view of the state came to be associated with them. It runs through many of the doctrines mentioned above, and others not mentioned here. It can perhaps be traced back first, amongst socialist thinkers, to Louis Blanc, but more reliably to Lassalle and the German Social-Democratic

[1] op. cit., p. 22.

Party. In Britain, it may be said to be implicit in much of the Chartist propaganda for universal suffrage, and traces of it can be found in S.D.F. and early I.L.P. writings. But it was the Fabians who first gave it strong overt expression. Since then it has become, in the shape of demands for social security and a guaranteed national minimum, perhaps the most deeply-felt item in Labour policy.

(11) *Syndicalism and Guild Socialism.* On the continent, Syndicalism constituted a separate tradition in its own right (especially in the Latin countries), with deep roots in anarchism, a long literature, and many famous exponents. But in Britain continental syndicalism held only a brief sway in the immediate pre-1914 years, and British Guild Socialism owed as much to Ruskin and Morris as to the C.G.T. or the I.W.W.

Guild Socialism was a violent reaction against collectivist state socialism. The state socialists mistook the problem by failing to see that the central evil of the capitalist system was not private property-income, but the wage system, or 'wagery'. This evil would not be eliminated by collectivisation, which would merely throw up a new industrial bureaucracy, as unpleasant as the old. It could be eliminated only by establishing workers' control in industry by means of syndicalist industrial guilds. This alone would guarantee justice to the worker as producer. It is of no use to look to Parliament or the state to create this transformation; it requires revolutionary strike action by the Trade Unions. The whole emphasis is on the worker as producer, not as consumer: on workers' control, not the division of income: and on the Trade Unions, and not the state, as the spearhead of advance.

(12) *The doctrine of planning.* This was a late development in socialist thought, and attracted scarcely any attention before 1914.[1] It was largely a response to the increasingly severe incidence of unemployment in the inter-war period, combined with the apparent success of the Soviet Five-Year Plans; and it later became caught up in the Keynesian Revolution (though Hobson still deserves credit as an early prophet). By the late 1930s a

---

[1]Shaw's preface to the 1931 edition of *Fabian Essays*, for example, is wholly concerned with unemployment and the need for socialist planning (plus an end to the Parliamentary Party system) to cure it. But his original essay, and his preface to the 1908 edition, were exclusively concerned with unearned surplus value, and made no mention of planning.

variety of arguments were being used to support the case for planning – academic theories of 'imperfect competition', Pigovian welfare economics, the maldistribution of incomes, the distinction between 'production for use' and 'production for profit', and so on. But the essential argument was based on unemployment; and from 1931 onwards planning for full employment became the first objective of Labour policy.

III *The Predominant Themes*

What emerges from this brief catalogue? Above all the variety and heterogeneity. It is this which makes it impossible to isolate any one orthodoxy to be consulted now for guidance about the future.

It is obvious enough that socialist thought varies through time, and that different doctrines prevail at different periods. This is as it should be. It is not even surprising that different doctrines should be supported at the same time – Owenism and Chartism, Marxism and Christian Socialism, Fabianism and Guild Socialism; there must always be divergent views on the right emphasis and order of priorities, and these will prevent a uniformity of thought. The trouble is that some of the divergences are not a matter simply of emphasis or the right priorities. They are fundamental, and the doctrines mutually inconsistent.

Thus Fabian collectivism and Welfare Statism require a view of the State diametrically opposed to the Marxist view. The syndicalist tradition is anti-collectivist. The Marxist tradition is anti-reformist. Owenism differs fundamentally from Marxism and syndicalism on the class-war. Morrisite communes and Socialist Guilds are incompatible with nationalisation: and so on.[1]

How then to decide which is the correct scripture? It is, of course, impossible. All we can do is to pick out certain recurrent

---

[1] And if anyone doubts the mutual hostility of these various schools of thought, he has only to read any passage in Marx on any other socialist thinker (save naturally for Engels); or he can refer, to take a later English example, to the early literature of the Guild Socialists – 'Collectivists may take their choice:' wrote Mr. Cole, 'they are knaves, who hate freedom, or they are fools, who do not know what freedom means, or they are a bit of both.' (*Self-Government in Industry*, p. 231.) After this outburst, references to 'the dotards of the *New Statesman*', or 'the Sir and Lady Oracle of the Labour Movement', seem positively courteous.

themes (whether mutually consistent or not) which have exercised a predominant influence, and which are common to more
than one school of thought: and ask whether they are applicable
in Britain to-day. In so doing, we need to distinguish in each
case between the objective, the means and policies chosen to
carry out the objective, and the ideologies or theories by which
the objectives and the choice of means are justified.

Five predominant themes can be distinguished (though they
often overlap): the appropriation of property incomes, co-
operation, workers' control, social welfare, and full employment.

(1) The objective of the appropriation by society of the rewards
of capital (rent, interest, profits) by means of the abolition of
private property, and the substitution for it either of communal
co-operative ownership (the land reformers, Owen, Morris) or
collectivist state ownership (Marx, the Fabians, the modern
Labour Party), the collectivist view naturally gaining ground
with the growth of large-scale units.

The theoretical justification has varied through time, but the
constant element has been the theory of a surplus product, due
to the effort of labour, but impounded by the owners of property.
This theme, of the exploitation of the worker, runs through all
the natural law doctrines, the deductions from Ricardo's theory
of value, the Marxist theory of surplus value, the Mill-George
theory of rent, and the generalised Fabian theory of unearned
increment.

Few of these justifications have stood the test of time. Not
many people to-day accept the doctrine of *ius naturale*, or the
Ricardo-Marx labour theory of value,[1] or the theories of Henry
George.[2] This, however, is of no great importance, since a
desire to diminish extravagant property incomes can be quite
soundly based on a normative judgment about equality, such
as Robert Owen made when he argued that inequality created
social discontent, or on a moral objection to large unearned
incomes.

---

[1] Even Mrs. Robinson, in her gallant endeavour to rehabilitate Marx as an
economist, is forced in this connection to quote Voltaire's *mot* that you can kill a flock
of sheep by witchcraft if you give them plenty of arsenic at the same time, and to
admit that the labour theory of value serves mainly to provide the incantations.
(*An Essay on Marxian Economics*, p. 27.)

[2] I am assuming in particular that no socialist now thinks the worker should be
paid the whole value of his product – some surplus value must be extracted for capital
accumulation (*v.* Chapter XVII). The objection is to large property *incomes*.

But, more serious, the means chosen to carry out the objective are not, in contemporary Britain, necessarily the most appropriate ones. The Labour Party having decided, rightly, to pay full compensation, the transfer of industries to state ownership does not have any large or immediate effect on the distribution of income.[1] Over the long run there is, of course, a connection; but even in the long run other methods of redistribution are now seen to be simpler and more effective. As a determinant of relative shares in total income, the ownership of industrial property is less important than the level of employment, the behaviour of prices, government controls (e.g. over rent or dividends), and above all taxation policy; and a determined government can restrict property incomes more easily than by the collectivisation of industry with full compensation. In addition, nationalisation has thrown up certain stubborn and largely unexpected problems which, so long as they remain unsolved, in any case make it impracticable to rely on public ownership as the main method of raising wages at the expense of property incomes.

In fact the other methods have already gone some way to fulfilling the desired objective. There has been an important transfer from property-incomes to wages since 1939; and the distribution of wealth is now much more egalitarian. Certainly much remains to be done; but fiscal policies offer a simpler and quicker way of doing it than wholesale collectivisation.[2]

This does not mean that nationalisation may not be justified on other grounds, nor that over the long period it has no influence of any kind on income-distribution, nor that the egalitarian objective to which it was directed has lost its relevance. It simply means that the ownership of the means of production, as the last chapter has already shown, is no longer the *essential* determinant of the distribution of incomes; private ownership is compatible with a high degree of equality, while state ownership, as the Russian experience has demonstrated, may be used to support a high degree of inequality.

(2) The objective of substituting for unrestricted competition and the motive of personal profit some more social organisation and set of motives, by means either of co-operative undertakings

---

[1] For a detailed discussion of this point, *v.* Chapter XIX, Section I.

[2] *v.* Chapters XII and XIII for a discussion of further egalitarian fiscal policies.

or state ownership. (R. H. Tawney, a magisterial authority in these matters, considers this objective to be the basic element in socialism.)[1] It has two sources of inspiration.

(a) The first is ethical, and springs from a desire to replace competitive social relations by fellowship and social solidarity, and the motive of personal profit by a more altruistic and other-regarding motive. The combination of competition and the profit motive was equally offensive to Robert Owen (because it militated against human happiness), the Christian Socialists (because it ran counter to Christian ethics), Ruskin and Morris (because it bred ugliness and commercialism, and debased the quality of labour), and the pioneers of the I.L.P. (because it denied the brotherhood of man).

Few will quarrel with this ethical aspiration towards a more fraternal and co-operative society – indeed, it is remarkable how it anticipates the writings of many contemporary sociologists. The difficulty is to find the framework within which it can be fulfilled. So far as social organisation is concerned, it will clearly not be fulfilled simply by eliminating industrial competition, since this constitutes only a small (and diminishing) part of the sum total of competition in modern society. We are now more vividly aware of the wide extent, in any country having pretensions to equal opportunity, of feelings of emulation, rivalry, and competitive envy; indeed, the more successful the Left is in equalising opportunities, the more all-pervasive must competition (for jobs, promotion, social prestige) become – whether or not the organisation of industry is formally competitive.

Industry itself, moreover, has become a great deal less competitive since these doctrines were in their prime, so much so that it is now an applauded object of government policy to make the private sector rather *more* competitive. There is little risk, in view of the mild and refined character of the British business-man's competitive instinct, that this will set citizens too violently at one another's throats; and this reinforces the point that there are now more pressing causes of antagonism to be attended to than competition between capitalists.

In addition, most people would now feel doubts about Robert Owen's view of the relation between social organisation and individual character. On the one hand, we know enough to perceive

[1] In his Introduction to Beer, op. cit., p. vii.

that the simple act of replacing individual by group or collective relationships does not necessarily make people more contented, or fraternal, or amiable; while on the other hand, we know too little to dogmatise about how groups can or should be organised in such a way as to achieve these desired results.[1] And the traditional means are either wholly inappropriate, or not sufficient in themselves: small-scale co-operative units are not practicable under modern conditions, while state ownership, as at present conceived in terms of nationalised public boards, does not self-evidently induce a co-operative spirit or sense of social solidarity – at the very least the point remains unproven.

When we turn to the question of personal motives, we find again that developments over the last century have served to complicate the issue. Those socialists who think it immoral and degrading that men should work for money, and not for loving-kindness or social duty, cannot now fasten on profit as the only object of their obloquy; for profits are no different in kind as an incentive from piecework earnings, bonus systems, or even the incentive of a rise in salary. And the steady spread of incentive payments has extended the system of differential rewards for differential effort over so large a part of the population that merely to abolish industrial competition or private ownership would do little to alter matters – the money incentive is just as pervasive under monopoly or public ownership. Even assuming, moreover, that people would work better and be happier, or that the moral tone of society would be improved, if they no longer worked for personal gain, it is increasingly hard, in view of the growth of large-scale production, to see the institutional framework within which a change in motives could be effected.[2] Again the traditional means do not provide a sufficient answer; guilds and communes are ruled out on technical grounds, and state ownership has not produced the hoped-for change. Although, therefore, the aspiration has clearly not been fulfilled, the method of attaining a more co-operative society must be re-appraised in the light of technical changes and greater knowledge.

(*b*) The second objection to private profit and competition was economic, and related to the actual material results of classical capitalism. Poverty, slums, malnutrition – these were ascribed

---

[1] These points are discussed in more detail in the next chapter (Section IV).
[2] *v.* next chapter, Section IV.

to the fact that production was carried on for profit and not for use, and was directed to satisfying the demands of the rich before the needs of the poor. Only public ownership would ensure a more equitable and socially desirable allocation of resources.

Now it is quite true that production for profit, conducted within a framework of very unequal incomes, must give a distribution of resources highly distasteful to socialists, because it takes no account of needs, however urgent, but only of monetary demand. It is further true that the means chosen (state ownership) could in principle fulfil the objective of a different and more equitable distribution of resources.[1]

But the objective can also be achieved by other means, and has been largely so achieved to-day. The statement that production for profit gives a bad distribution of resources (caviar for the rich before milk for the poor) is only a shorthand. What is meant is that production is undertaken for profit: that the distribution of purchasing power determines what is profitable: and that if this is very unequal, then the wants of the rich will be met before the needs of the poor. But if purchasing power is distributed more equally, it becomes more profitable to produce necessities, and less profitable to produce luxuries. The objection is thus fundamentally not to the role of profit, which is merely to reflect and communicate the distribution of demand, but to the distribution of demand itself – to the fact that the rich had so much money to spend on caviar, and the poor so little to spend on milk.

But to-day the redistribution of incomes, and the rise in working-class purchasing power, have banished the worst effects of production for profit by calling forth a quite different pattern of output. It is now highly profitable to produce articles, whether necessities or luxuries, for mass working-class consumption; indeed, by far the greater part of production for the home market takes this form. Moreover, a further weapon is at hand – fiscal and physical controls – which can also be used, and was widely used by the Labour Government, to enforce a pattern of output even on privately-owned industry different from that which the price-system, left to itself, would call forth. These influences now

[1] I say 'in principle', because in practice the nationalised industries have not always proved either amenable to government planning, or themselves capable of contributing to a more intelligent allocation of resources (v. Chapter XVIII, Section II).

give an allocation of resources much nearer to what most people would consider desirable; that is, far more resources than previously are devoted to satisfying the wants of 90% of the population, and far fewer to satisfying those of the richest 10%. And if a further move towards an 'ideal' distribution is desired, this can be easily accomplished without an extension of state ownership.[1]

Thus the historic anti-competitive theme, in both its aspects, provides a second case where so much has changed that the traditional doctrine now seems over-simplified, and new ways of fulfilling the aspiration either have been, or can be, or must be found.

(3) The objective of workers' control. Syndicalists, Morrisites and Guild Socialists, all starting from the belief that the central feature of capitalism was the exploitation of the worker, had as their common objective the control of industry by the actual producers. The means chosen were various – control by the Trade Unions, or Socialist Guilds, or Morrisite communes. But the ideological justification was always a syndicalist version of Marxism, based essentially on the twin notions of 'wagery' (that labour is bought and sold like any other commodity, that its status is thus, as one prominent Guild Socialist put it, 'exactly that of manure', and that the wage-bargain is consequently of the essence of slavery), and the uselessness of political action as a method of reform. Only industrial action can liberate the worker from his capitalist chains, and once freed he must reorganise production (having fought off the efforts of the collectivists to re-enslave him) in self-governing guilds.

Now this theoretical analysis clearly makes no sense to-day, whatever truth it may have had fifty years ago. The idea that the worker is an impotent wage-slave, contemptuously and ruthlessly exploited, bears no relation to modern conditions; nor does the belief that no help can ever come from the state. Steadily over recent decades, the individual worker has gained in strength vis-à-vis his employer, and the Trade Unions in relation to society as a whole. The best evidence for this gain lies on the one hand in the constant complaints of individual employers that they can no longer 'discipline' their workers, and on the other hand in

---

[1] v. Chapters XVIII and XX for a full discussion of the relation between planning and public ownership.

the widespread admission that even under a Conservative Government the Trade Unions remain effective masters of the industrial
scene.[1] A generation ago, victimisation or arbitrary dismissal
came as naturally to individual employers, as collective campaigns
for wage-cuts to the employing class as a whole; to-day the first
is a rarity, the second a complete impossibility. It is clear that
a revolutionary change in the balance of power has occurred,
which both makes nonsense of the original syndicalist case and
constitutes at the same time a partial fulfilment of the objective.

Of course the particular forms of workers' control proposed
would in any event have been impracticable, having been outmoded by the mass-production revolution and the trend towards
large scale and technical complexity. These make any craft or
guild organisation, based on analogies with the Middle Ages,
quite inappropriate to-day. Their cost in terms of efficiency and
the standard of living would be enormous -- like all Utopian
schemes, Guild Socialism had a purely static quality, and took
no account of the dynamic problems of economic growth and
technical innovation.

An important advance has been made, and the desire to improve the worker's status has been partially fulfilled by other than
the traditional means. Nevertheless, the objective is not yet fully
realised, and is rightly engaging attention to-day.[2] But it must,
if confusion is to be avoided, be divorced from the theories and
policies with which it was historically linked in socialist doctrine.
We now need, for obvious reasons, a form of organisation which
is consistent with efficiency and innovation, as well as with
democracy; and this the traditional ideas do not provide.

(4) The welfare objective: the abolition of primary poverty,
and the guarantee of a general subsistence minimum by means
of universal social services. To the great majority of British socialists, who never embraced any particular theoretical creed, this

[1] v. Chapter I. This is increasingly true in the U.S. also. Even in those industries
traditionally considered the citadels of capitalist power, Trade Union strength is now
overwhelming. In steel, a trial of strength between Unions and employers has twice
recently (1952 and 1955) resulted in the almost complete victory of the former. In
coal, John L. Lewis can call a 10-day 'memorial holiday' to give the mine-owners
an 'opportunity' of examining their safety precautions; and they can do nothing
to stop him. In the auto industry, the U.A.W. not merely forces the employers to
accept the principle of the guaranteed annual wage, but compels the smaller firms
almost to plead for mercy – American Motors argued publicly last year that it was
U.A.W.'s 'responsibility' to take the company's marginal position into account.

[2] v. Chapters XIV and XV.

practical, non-doctrinal, humanitarian attack on poverty was much the most powerful inspiration from the earliest days of the Labour Party. It appealed equally to the ethical or religious desire to help one's fellow-men, and to the Fabian instinct for social improvement along efficient collectivist lines.

Just as it was the most deep-seated instinct, so it was, in its historic form, the first objective to be substantially fulfilled when Labour came to power. Primary poverty has been largely eliminated; the 'Beveridge revolution' has been carried through; and Britain now boasts the widest range of social services in the world, and, as a result, the appellation 'Welfare State'. It is true that considerable areas of social distress, not mainly due to primary poverty and of a character not always foreseen by pre-war socialists, still remain. But that is a new and different question.[1] The historic objective has, in Britain, largely been attained; and the traditional means of universal, indiscriminate social services are in any case not always the most appropriate to the more subtle social problems which remain.

(5) The objective of full employment, to be achieved by government planning, and notably by fiscal and monetary policies. This cannot continue to be a major item in a distinctively socialist programme, so long as it is carried out by the Conservative Government. Of course, if unemployment due to deficient home demand were to reappear, then the full employment theme would provide all the dynamic needed to sweep Labour back into power with an unambiguous programme. But while the Conservatives decline to be so incompetent, the objective must be considered as achieved; and I personally believe, and argue later, that the deflationary tendencies of the inter-war period were exceptional, and that the years ahead are more likely to be characterised by inflation than unemployment.[2]

IV *The Need for a Restatement*

This gives a rather high proportion of traditional objectives either substantially achieved, or now irrelevant to the end in

[1] Which is discussed in detail in Part Two.

[2] This does not mean that British Governments can always guarantee permanent full employment if severe crises occur abroad. But these would present a problem different both in character and in magnitude from the pre-war unemployment problem.

view; and of traditional means or policies which have either been fully exploited already, or else are no longer appropriate ways of reaching the objective, or else are impracticable under modern conditions, or else have been replaced by more efficient means. Surely the verdict must go against the traditionalists, and in favour of revisionism.

Herzen, we are told, used to say of Heine and his friends that their minds were so lofty, and they found the study of contemporary conditions so uncongenial, that 'to understand the moan of humanity lost in the bogs of to-day, they had to translate it into Latin and arrive at their ideas through the Gracchi and the proletariat of Rome'.[1] Similarly to-day, conservative or indolent-minded people on the Left, finding the contemporary scene too puzzling and unable to mould it into the old familiar categories, are inclined to seek refuge in the slogans and ideas of 50 years ago. But Keir Hardie cannot provide,[2] any more than can the Gracchi, the right focus with which to capture the reality of the mid-twentieth-century world.

[1] Quoted by Edmund Wilson, *To The Finland Station* (Secker and Warburg, 1940), p. 163.

[2] As, indeed, with his remarkable blend of idealism and practical shrewdness, he would have been the first to realise.

IV

<hr>

THE MEANING OF SOCIALISM

I *The Psychological Resistance to Revisionism*

IT is surely time, then, to stop searching for fresh inspiration
in the old orthodoxies, and thumbing over the classic texts
as though they could give oracular guidance for the future.
The first need now, in R. H. Tawney's words, 'is to treat sanctified formulae with judicious irreverence and to start by deciding
what precisely is the end in view.'[1]

The need for a restatement of doctrine is hardly surprising.
The old doctrines did not spring from a vacuum, or from acts of
pure cerebration performed in a monastery cell. Each was the
product of a particular kind of society, and of minds reacting
to that society. Since this external factor was not constant and
unchanging, the doctrines changed through time. And as society
has changed again since before the war, so again a restatement of
objectives is called for. The matter can be put quite simply.
Traditional socialism was largely concerned with the evils of traditional capitalism, and with the need for its overthrow. But
to-day traditional capitalism has been reformed and modified
almost out of existence, and it is with a quite different form of
society that socialists must now concern themselves. Pre-war anti-
capitalism will give us very little help.

The traditionalists may comfort themselves by reflecting that
this will not be the first time that socialism has been restated;
nothing is more traditional in the history of socialist thought
than the violent rejection of past doctrines. Marx expended

[1] *Socialist Commentary*, June 1952.

prodigious energy in flaying the Utopian and Owenite brands of
socialism that held the field before him. The Fabians used less
vitriolic pens, but were as vehement in rejecting Marx as Marx
had been in rejecting Owen. Neither owed anything significant
to previous doctrine. Thus even revisionism is hallowed by an
appeal to the past; and the common-sense view that the more
is achieved, the less relevant traditional dogmas become, need
not be thought heretical.

But it will, nevertheless, be unpopular. I am not thinking simply
of the fact that people dislike new ideas, and hate to be jolted
out of the old, familiar habits of mind: but of a more subtle
reason why revisionism has, historically, always been resented.
This is because many working-class militants, and still more
some middle-class people who have espoused the workers' cause,
feel their whole status and psychological security to depend on
preserving a traditional, proletarian philosophy of class-struggle.

For the middle-class socialist, this is because he may think that
he must prove himself more royalist than the king – that he
must be combatively traditional and doctrinal in order to be
accepted as a good comrade, to win the approval of the workers,
and feel that he really 'belongs' to their party; in politics, as in
religion, the most rigid attachment to dogma is often to be found
amongst the converts. And for the working-class activist, devoting
his entire energies to the socialist movement, both his social status
and emotional certainty depend on the conviction that militant
struggle is necessary; it is only on this assumption that his life
makes sense. Revisionism, by casting doubts on the need for militancy, or suggesting that the class-struggle is now rather out-of-
date, challenges both his social and emotional security; if
class-conscious anti-capitalism is obsolete, what is his status as
a militant, and what his purpose in life? Hence the anger with
which criticisms of militancy or class-struggle are often greeted.

Bernstein, the great socialist 'revisionist', discovered this more
than 50 years ago. Arthur Rosenberg wrote that 'the practical
advantages of the revisionist theory for the labour movement
were far greater than those of official radicalism. . . . Nevertheless
the majority of the International refused to acknowledge [its]
logical justification and rejected it with impassioned vehemence.
For the majority of the workers the gesture of protest and isolation with respect to the bourgeois state had become a vital

necessity. Popular Marxism . . . endowed [them] with self-reliance, consolation, and hope for the future, almost reminding one of a religious movement. If they had accepted the proposals of the revisionists, however, [they] would have been compelled to renounce their Utopian belief in the future and their vitally necessary class sentiment.'[1] This instinctive clinging to class-consciousness can still be found in the Labour Movement to-day.

And there is now an additional psychological reason for resenting revisionism, stemming from the very success of the socialist movement. M. Raymond Aron has correctly observed that 'Socialism has ceased in the West to be a myth because it has become a part of reality'[2] – not, of course, a complete reality, but sufficiently so to be no longer a myth. Labour Governments have been in power, and have found responsibility harsher and quite different from anything they expected; while full employment and social security have destroyed the rationale of much of the old emotional enthusiasm.

Revisionism draws attention to this new reality. It is an explicit admission that many of the old dreams are either dead or realised; and this brutal admission is resented. It is resented, first, because it destroys the old simplicity, certainty, and unquestioning conviction. 'The will to Socialism', wrote G. D. H. Cole before the war, 'is based on a lively sense of wrongs crying for redress'.[3] And when the wrongs were so manifest, we all knew what to do, and where the enemy was, and what was the order of battle; it was exhilarating to fight for such clear-cut and obviously righteous aims. But now the certainty and simplicity are gone; and everything has become complicated and ambiguous. Instead of glaring and conspicuous evils, squalor and injustice and distressed areas, we have to fuss about the balance of payments, and incentives, and higher productivity; and the socialist finds himself pinioned by a new and unforeseen reality.

And the objective has become not only less clear-cut, but also, after the reforms described in the first two chapters, less urgent; hence it no longer excites the same crusading spirit. But people want something to crusade about; and even the partial fulfilment

---

[1] *Democracy and Socialism* (Bell, 1939), pp. 314-15. The next sentence is not without interest to-day. 'If content, and not external form, is considered, it must be admitted that the revisionists were actually much better Marxists than their "radical" opponents.'

[2] *The Century of Total War* (Verschoyle, 1954), p. 355.

[3] *The Simple Case for Socialism* (Gollancz, 1935), p. 15.

of a dream leaves a feeling of lassitude and anti-climax. 'Oh, how I should like to begin all over again!' cries Olof in Strindberg's play at the moment when the Reformation triumphs; 'it was not victory I wanted – it was the battle!'; and many socialists, deep down, feel much the same.[1] A people enjoying full employment and social security has lost its dreams, and lost the need to struggle; and the activists in consequence feel restless and frustrated.[2] That is why they resent revisionist thinkers who compel them to face the new reality, and try to delude themselves instead that all the old enemies – capitalist barons, Wall Street, exploiting profiteers – are still there, waiting to be attacked. 90% of resolutions at Annual Conference to-day are Quixotic tilts at objects still hopefully seen as 'outrageous giants of that detested race'; unfortunately, there are too few Sancho Panças to point out that they are really only windmills.

II *The Confusion between Ends and Means*

If we are to reformulate socialist doctrine, the first task is clearly to decide what precise meaning is to be attached to the word 'socialism'.

This is not an easy question to answer. The word does not describe any present or past society, which can be empirically observed, and so furnish unimpeachable evidence for what is or is not 'socialism'. Thus statements about socialism can never be definitely verified; and we cannot treat it as being an *exact* descriptive word at all. There is therefore no point in searching the encyclopaedias for a definitive meaning; it has none, and never could.

This can easily be seen by considering the numerous and, as the previous chapter showed, often inconsistent meanings attached to the word by people who have called themselves 'socialists'. Marx, defining it as the 'nationalisation of the means of production, distribution, and exchange', meant something quite different from Proudhon, who defined it as consisting of 'every

---

[1] *Master Olof* (Act III). Olof's later cry to his brother has the same pathos: 'Then we are enemies! I need them, since the old ones are gone.'

[2] In Sweden, as early as 1946, the Socialist leader Per Albin Hansson said: 'We have had so many victories that we are in a difficult position. A people with political liberty, full employment, and social security has lost its dreams.'

aspiration towards the amelioration of our society'. Sir William Harcourt, declaring in 1892 that 'we are all socialists now', evidently had a different version from his contemporary Bradlaugh, to whom socialism meant that 'the State should own all wealth, direct all labour, and compel the equal distribution of all produce'. And any history of socialist thought will provide dozens of different definitions, some in terms of ownership, some of co-operation, some of planning, some of income-distribution; and it soon becomes simply a matter of subjective personal preference which is chosen as the 'correct' one. Many definitions, moreover, are so vague as to be virtually meaningless; one can read almost anything, for example, into Sidney Webb's definition: 'the economic side of the democratic ideal'.

The confusion has become worse inasmuch as the word is also charged with a high degree of emotional content, and so has acquired a range of purely persuasive meanings. It is either used to denote or win approval, as in Hitler's National 'Socialism' and 'Socialism' in Eastern Europe, or when Left-wing weeklies attack a policy which they dislike as not being 'Socialist'; or pejoratively, as when Right-wing Americans speak of 'creeping Socialism'.

But the worst source of confusion is the tendency to use the word to describe, not a certain kind of society, or certain values which might be attributes of a society, but particular policies which are, or are thought to be, means to attaining this kind of society, or realising these attributes. To rescue the word from these confusions, and the debasement referred to above, one must begin by asking what, if anything, is common to the beliefs of all, or almost all, of those who have called themselves socialists. The only constant element, common to all the bewildering variety of different doctrines, consists of certain moral values and aspirations; and people have called themselves socialists because they shared these aspirations, which form the one connecting link between otherwise hopelessly divergent schools of thought.

Thus the word first came on the modern scene with the early nineteenth-century Owenites, whom Marx contemptuously termed 'Utopian' socialists.[1] They based their 'socialism' explicitly on an

---

[1] To be precise, the word first occurs in *The Co-operative Magazine* in 1827, and was used to describe the views and demands of the original London 'Co-operators'. 'They based their demands on moral grounds, on the doctrines of Robert Owen, and on the theory of labour value.' (Max Beer, op. cit., p. 187.)

ethical view of society, a belief in a certain way of life and certain moral values. The means by which they thought this 'good society' could be attained are irrelevant to-day; and in fact they were quickly challenged by other socialist schools of thought, since when a continuous debate has proceeded, with no agreement, about what constituted the most suitable means. This debate would have no particular interest to-day, but for the fact that all the protagonists tried to appropriate the word 'socialism' to describe the particular means which they themselves favoured.

Thus Marx appropriated it for the collective ownership of the means of production on the false assumption, analysed in Chapter II, that the pattern of ownership determined the character of the whole society, and that collective ownership was a sufficient condition of fulfilling the basic aspirations. And generally the word came to be applied to policies for the economic or institutional transformation of society, instead of to the ultimate social purposes which that transformation was intended to achieve; so one often hears socialism equated not only with the nationalisation of industry, but with government planning, or redistribution, or state collectivism. This of course is quite unhelpful, for although people may agree on ends, they may legitimately disagree about means. Moreover, the means most suitable in one generation may be wholly irrelevant in the next, and in any case (still more significant) a given means may lead to more than one possible end, as indeed has happened with each of the policies just mentioned.[1]

Thus if, for example, socialism is defined as the nationalisation of the means of production, distribution and exchange, we produce conclusions which are impossible to reconcile with what the early socialists had in mind when they used the word: such as, that Soviet Russia is a completely socialist country (much more so, for instance, than Sweden) – even though it denies almost all the values which Western socialists have normally

[1] The use of the term 'ends' and 'means' might seem to imply a Utopian or 'blueprint' view of society – a belief that society might, or could, settle down to a stable, unchanging state, analogous to the classical 'stationary' state of economics. And of course most early socialists did hold this view. But as used in the text, the word 'end' is to be understood simply as describing principles or values, such as equality, or justice, or democracy, or co-operativeness, which might or might not be embodied in, or determine the character of, a particular society: and the word 'means' as describing the essentially institutional changes required to realise, or at least promote, these values in practice.

read into the word. Similarly, if socialism is defined as economic collectivism or State control of economic life, then Nazi Germany would correctly have been called a socialist country. But in neither case would the end-result be described as socialism by most socialists; the means of nationalisation and planning have proved adaptable to more than one purpose, which shows how unwise it is to identify the means with the end.

Not only is it unwise, but it is also semantically and historically incorrect. The various schools of thought which have called themselves, and been called by others, 'socialist' – Owenites and Marxists, Fabians and Christian Socialists, Syndicalists and Guild Socialists – have differed profoundly over the right means; and no one means has a better title to the label 'socialist' than any other. The one single element common to all the schools of thought has been the basic aspirations, the underlying moral values. It follows that these embody the only logically and historically permissible meaning of the word socialism; and to this meaning we must now revert.

III *The Basic Socialist Aspirations*

These ethical and emotional ideals have been partly negative – a protest against the visible results of capitalism – and partly positive, and related to definite views about the nature of the good society; though of course negative and positive strands are often inter-twined.

Perhaps one can list them roughly as follows. First, a protest against the material poverty and physical squalor which capitalism produced. Secondly, a wider concern for 'social welfare' – for the interests of those in need, or oppressed, or unfortunate, from whatever cause. Thirdly, a belief in equality and the 'classless society', and especially a desire to give the worker his 'just' rights and a responsible status at work. Fourthly, a rejection of competitive antagonism, and an ideal of fraternity and co-operation. Fifthly, a protest against the inefficiencies of capitalism as an economic system, and notably its tendency to mass unemployment. The first three formed the basis of socialism as 'a broad, human movement on behalf of the bottom dog'.[1] The

---

[1] Cole, *A Short History of the British Working-Class Movement*, Vol. III, p. 22.

first and last were censures on the material results of capitalism;
while the other three stemmed from an idealistic desire for a just,
co-operative and classless society.

(I have listed only the social and economic aspirations. But of
course underlying them, and taken for granted, was a passionate
belief in liberty and democracy. It would never have occurred to
most early socialists that socialism had any meaning except
within a political framework of freedom for the individual. But
since this political assumption is shared by British Conservatives
as well as socialists, no further reference is made to it.)

As thus formulated, even these basic aspirations are not all
equally relevant to present-day society. Some are expressed in
language adapted to conditions that no longer exist, and in particular are too negative in character. This is natural, for they
were, in large part, a reaction against the actual results of pre-war
capitalism; and with two million unemployed, widespread poverty
and malnutrition, and appalling slums set against a background of
flamboyant wealth amongst the richer classes, it was natural that
the negative desire to abolish evils should outweigh more positive
and detailed aspirations.

But to the extent that evils are remedied and injustices removed, negative statements become less and less appropriate.
And they are seen to be inappropriate by the electorate, a growing
section of which has no recollection of unemployment, or poverty,
or dole-queues, and finds Labour propaganda which plays on
the themes and memories of the 1930s quite incomprehensible.
To a population which has lost its fears, and now has every hope
of a rapidly rising standard of living, a negative protest against
past wrongs is merely a bore.

Thus even when we go back to the basic aspirations, we still find
the same, welcome, difficulty that the pace of change has over-
taken the doctrine, and a re-formulation is needed. Of course if a
Tory Government were to re-create all the old evils, matters
would be simple. New thinking could be set aside 'for the duration', and negative statements would again suffice. But it is not
likely that the Tories will act so recklessly, or that mere periodic
counter-attacks to regain lost positions will remove the need for
a map of the new terrain.

How should we re-formulate these aspirations to-day in such a
way as to preserve their basic emotional and ethical content,

yet discarding what is clearly not germane to present-day conditions? Of the original five, the first and last are rapidly losing their relevance in a British context. Such primary poverty as remains will disappear within a decade, given our present rate of economic growth; and the contemporary mixed economy is characterised by high levels both of employment and productivity and by a reasonable degree of stability. In other words, the aspirations relating to the economic consequences of capitalism are fast losing their relevance as capitalism itself becomes transformed.

But the remaining three more positive ideals, described above as stemming either from a concern with the 'bottom dog', or from a vision of a just, co-operative and classless society, have clearly not been fully realised. No doubt we should phrase them differently to-day, but their basic content is still perfectly relevant. We have plenty of less fortunate citizens still requiring aid; and we certainly have not got an equal or classless society, nor one characterised by 'co-operative' social relations.

iv *The Co-operative Aspiration*

I propose to discuss the co-operative aspiration first, in order to get it out of the way – not because I think its content less important, but simply because I find it impossible to reach a definite conclusion about its relevance in contemporary conditions.

Most people would agree that Britain to-day is a markedly less competitive society than it was a century ago. This is especially true of industry; and it was industrial competition which drew down the strongest strictures of the early anti-competitive socialists. Such competition is now both more limited in extent, and less fierce in character; and business attitudes generally have taken on the more restrained and amenable character described in Chapter I.

But the change goes wider than this, and reflects a deep-seated change in the accepted ideology – from an uncompromising faith in individualism and self-help to a belief in group action and 'participation', and collective responsibility for social welfare. The consequence is a pronounced tightening of the conventional rules of competitive behaviour. A century ago competition was virtually unrestricted. It justified colonial aggression, child-labour, sweated workshops, violence against labour leaders, a callous ruthlessness towards competitors, and even interference with personal liberty. All these to-day would be excluded from the bounds of what was conventionally, and often legally, permissible. The moral consensus of opinion has altered; and the aggressive instinct has been civilised and circumscribed.

There is now probably no country in the world where competition is less aggressive, or individual exertion more suspect. The worker who exceeds his norm or works too hard, the employer who embarks on a price-offensive, are thought guilty at the least of not playing the game, and probably of flouting the principle of fair shares and showing disloyalty to comrades. To a large extent, security has replaced competition as the guiding rule of economic conduct. At any rate, it could scarcely be denied that the intensity of competition was significantly less.

The *extensive* frontier of competition may, it is true, have widened. But this, ironically, is partly the result of action and pressure by the Left, since it follows from the progressive equalisation of opportunities for advancement. This inevitably increases competition; and indeed the absence of competition for the highest posts is incompatible with democracy, and consistent only with a hierarchical caste or feudal society offering no possibility of social mobility.[1] Thus the antithesis of competition is not always co-operation – it may be social ossification, and the denial of individual rights. This clearly raises an awkward potential conflict of values.

The extent of competition, or at least of the individual pursuit of differential rewards, may have widened in another respect. A century ago it was mainly the entrepreneur whose income fluctuated with individual effort or hard work. But since then, as the last chapter pointed out, there has been a growing tendency for incomes to take the form of differential rewards for differential effort. The purpose of such differentials may be partially frustrated by the counter-force of group solidarity; but their existence must do something to foster individualistic attitudes and the motive of personal gain. But here again there may be a conflict of values, since differentials may be good for economic growth and the

[1] *v.* Chapter VIII.

standard of living. Once again, the antithesis of competition might be not co-operation, but economic stagnation.

Thus matters look a good deal less clear-cut than when the co-operative ideal was first formulated over a century ago. On the one hand, the excesses of competitive individualism have been significantly moderated; on the other hand, competition is seen to have certain compensating advantages, not previously much discussed. However, let us consider the implications of endeavouring to realise the ideal more fully. There appear to be two spheres in which it might be relevant: personal motives and relations at work.

First, people should work not for private material gain, but for the social good – either because they will then find a greater self-fulfilment and so be more contented, or because they will work better and harder, or simply because it is held to be ethically good that self-regarding instincts should be suppressed, and other-regarding instincts encouraged.

This is partly a factual statement, that people *do* work harder and feel happier if certain incentives are present: and partly a normative statement, that people *should* work for certain motives and not for others. Unfortunately the first is difficult to prove or disprove, and the second hard to express in concrete, practical policies.

It is clear that under the right circumstances the consciousness of working for a common purpose can be an extremely strong incentive, capable of eliciting exceptionally hard and contented work. In British aircraft factories after Dunkirk, in voluntary societies or charitable bodies, in village development schemes in India, or co-operative farms in Israel, people do appear to find a fulfilment and satisfaction in working for a common goal, and in consequence work better, and feel fewer grievances.[1]

But it is equally clear that people can work both well and contentedly for personal material gain under a system where rewards vary with individual effort. This is the case, for example, in a progressive and efficient private firm operating an elaborate system of bonus payments and incentives.

Evidently both motives can, under the right conditions, work extremely well. So far as the second is concerned, the essential

---

[1] *v.* W. Arthur Lewis, *The Theory of Economic Growth* (Allen and Unwin, 1955), Part III, Chapter 1, for an excellent discussion of this point.

condition in the normal case is probably an efficient management, pursuing an enlightened labour policy.[1] But the difficulty is to create the conditions under which the 'social' motive can operate effectively for more than a short emergency period. It is certainly not enough to tell people that they are working for the public good, nor even that they should in fact be working for the public good. They must see it, and feel it, themselves; and it is not easy to create the institutional framework within which they will.

This may be seen from the experience of nationalisation. The miners and railwaymen are in fact working for the public good as well as for themselves, and for an extremely urgent public good; and there are no shareholders or private profits to 'expropriate' any of the fruits of their labour. Yet this appears to make only a limited psychological difference; and neither industry has a contented atmosphere. This might be a matter of scale and distance. The villager working on a community scheme, and building a new road for his village, can see the result with his own eyes, can see his own personal contribution as being significant, and can see that his own community is in fact deriving the benefit. The miner cannot see the total result of his efforts, which is reflected merely in periodic output figures announced from Hobart House: he may think that his own contribution to the total result is insignificant; and he may be vague as to how the benefits are distributed. Thus he feels, it might be argued, no sense of personal indispensability; the scale is too large, and the distances too remote.

Yet there might, for all we know, be a quite different explanation – that the average miner and railwayman are not sufficiently interested in the public good or the total result. It could plausibly be maintained that in these two industries, much more, for example, than in mass-production factories, the worker is exceptionally well aware of his personal role and contribution – the crew of a train for obvious reasons, and the miner (at least at the face) because of the institution of the checkweighman. Yet this awareness, and such 'social' incentive as may follow from it, may be outweighed by other incentives or emotions – local group solidarity, resentment over wages or conditions, dislike of the local management, disappointment (in the case of the railways) with

[1] v. Chapter XIV, Section III, for a further explanation of this point.

the form of nationalisation and the performance of the Transport Commission; and so on.

All it seems possible to say in practice is (a) that people can work hard and contentedly for personal (or family) gain,[1] (b) that people can work badly and discontentedly even when they are working for the common good, (c) that no doubt they work best of all when both motives are present, but (d) if it is desired, on moral grounds, to effect a general conversion from self-regarding to other-regarding motives, this will be hard to achieve, since it might require either a change in the basic 'social character' or the creation of a largely novel institutional framework. This conclusion was of course reached at an early stage by the Soviet rulers, who quickly gave up the struggle and simply introduced the old 'capitalist' incentives, under the new label of 'Stakhano-vitism', in an extreme and indeed brutal version.

One cannot say that either of these means to a general con-version is strictly impossible, only that they are rather unlikely. A change in social character, altering the underlying balance between self-regarding and other-regarding instincts, cannot, I suppose, be ruled out as a matter of theory. Social anthropology and group psychology have shown that motivation and behaviour are not immutable, or biologically given, but to some (unknown) extent 'culturally' determined. But of course we know too little about the determinants to say anything very useful when it comes to practical policy.

Nor is it much easier to alter the institutional framework in such a way as to give more outlet to *existing* social motives. Clearly public ownership is not enough. We might even require a com-plete devolution and fragmentation of economic activity down to a local scale. Of course this simply will not happen, and could not work, in an advanced industrial economy. It is not merely that the result would be a catastrophic fall in living standards, but that one cannot turn back history in this way, or reverse the under-lying social and technological trends. Some devolution within the present framework is no doubt possible; and enlightened

---

[1] Indeed, material incentives for the worker are exceptionally strong to-day, since both the psychological expectation and the physical possibility of rising to an entirely new plateau of consumption, characterised by the ownership of expensive consumers' durable goods and reached with the help of hire-purchase, now exist on a wide scale. So strong are these incentives that Trade Union leaders, who would like to reduce overtime, often cannot persuade their members to forego it.

managements, by increasing attention to group activity and to
fostering a social spirit, will gradually do something to encourage
the desired incentives. But I cannot see what *national* policy a
Labour Government could have for inducing a general and deep-
seated, as opposed to local and marginal, change in personal
motives.

The second sphere in which the co-operative ideal is relevant
(though it is closely linked with the first) is that of relations at
work. The early socialists wanted people to work, not as separate
individuals, but communally and co-operatively, organised in
groups (co-operative guilds or communes) inspired with an
altruistic collective purpose. To-day, since self-governing guilds
are now impracticable, we should no doubt interpret this in terms
of joint consultation or joint participation, that is, of groups within
a large industrial unit (whether public or private) identified with,
and working co-operatively for, the purposes of that unit.

But we now see that the difficulty is often not, as the early
socialists thought it would be, to resolve a clash between individual
and collective instincts, or to persuade people to form groups and
adopt group standards. The human instinct towards gregarious-
ness is so strong that groups form automatically, in industry as
elsewhere, and quickly establish their own informal leaders and
standards of behaviour.

The difficulty is that these natural, self-created groups may be
far from expressing the co-operative ideal. It is not merely that
groups may develop (as anyone with experience of small political
or religious or refugee groups will know) extremely disagreeable
characteristics – intolerance of dissent, excessive conformity,
arbitrary cruelty in the exercise of their ultimate power to
ostracise (in modern language, send to Coventry) : but even if they
do not, their purpose and function may be in no way communal
or altruistic so far as objectives and institutions *outside* the group
are concerned. On the contrary, their function and behaviour
may be wholly selfish, and the element of identification or co-
operation with the firm or industry entirely lacking. Thus they
may, as industrial research has demonstrated, serve to restrict
output, not to expand it: to worsen relations with management,
not to improve them: to foster resentment and discontent, instead
of harmony and a sense of common purpose.

The problem is to harness the group instinct in such a way as to create the desired social and co-operative atmosphere – to cause the natural groups to identify themselves with the larger unit in which they work. Unfortunately we scarcely know in detail how this is to be done. It does not follow automatically either from nationalisation, as the mines and the railways show, or from setting up joint consultation, which may simply impose a formal and rootless group on top of, and at cross-purposes with, the real groups below.

Indeed if we examine industry, we find a bewildering variety of experience which makes it exceedingly hard to draw conclusions.[1] We can find firms with a loyal and contented labour force, yet with no formal 'participation' of any kind: others with elaborate schemes of joint consultation, yet with a sullen, unhappy labour force: and yet others where good relations do seem to depend on the existence of joint bodies. All we can say is that institutional change by itself is not enough: and that whether joint participation does or does not create a co-operative atmosphere depends on social forces on the exact nature of which industrial psychologists are not agreed – at any rate not to the extent that any clear national policy emerges.

This does not mean, of course, that there is no case for altering relations within industry, or for giving the worker more power. There is such a case. But it rests not on propositions about fraternity or social contentment, which our present knowledge does not justify, but on statements about social justice, the rights of workers, and equality. It is therefore subsumed, and so discussed in later chapters, under the aspiration towards social equality.

To sum up, the co-operative aspiration has at least been partially fulfilled, in that society is much less aggressively individualistic and competitive than a century ago; and indeed the trend toward 'sociability' is now so strong that we are more likely to be deprived of solitude than company. On the other hand we do not yet live in a co-operative Utopia. Most people still work mainly for personal gain, and not for the social good; and the ideal of communal, co-operative participation has scarcely begun to be realised in industry.

Now there are one or two specific directions in which a clear choice exists between more or less competition – most notably

[1] *v.* Chapter XIV for a further discussion of this point.

in education, separately discussed in a later chapter. There are
one or two further directions in which a less clear choice exists
between more or less communal activity, e.g. housing development and town planning. Furthermore, the *sense* of co-operation
in industry may spread as management grows more progressive
and enlightened; and a gradual increase in equality will itself, as
is argued in Chapter VIII, still further diminish the intensity of
competition. But beyond this, at our present state of knowledge,
we cannot go. We cannot assert definitely what would be the
effect either on personal contentment, or attitudes to work, or the
quality of our society, of a wholesale effort to suppress the motive
of personal gain, or to elevate collective at the expense of individual relationships: nor can we even begin to see a feasible
institutional framework within which these changes could be
brought about: nor can we be sure that even if they were practicable, they might not lead to serious losses in other directions, such
as privacy, individuality, personal independence, equality of
opportunity, or the standard of living.

While, therefore, I realise that as a matter of verbal precision
the co-operative ideal is certainly embraced by the word 'socialism', and while I accept that it would clearly be in some sense
'better' if there were a more general awareness of a common
social purpose, I do not feel able, in what is intended to be a
reasonably definite and practical statement of socialist aims, to
include this as part of the goal. I shall no doubt be corrected by
those with clearer views.

v   *The Welfare and Equality Aspirations*

The two remaining aspirations – the concern with social
welfare, and the desire for an equal and classless society – still
have a perfectly clear relevance. The first implies an acceptance
of collective responsibility and an extremely high priority for the
relief of social distress or misfortune, in contrast to the much lower
priority which it would receive in a 'free' economy guided mainly
by an individualistic philosophy. This is the contemporary
version of the traditional welfare and social-service philosophy
of the Labour movement, and of the instinct to side automatically
with the less fortunate and those in need.

There is plenty of residual social distress in Britain. It is now caused less by primary poverty, though this can still be found, than by secondary poverty, natural misfortune, physical or mental illness, the decline in the size of the family, sudden fluctuations in income, and deficiencies in social capital. These last, for all the high level of average personal spending, are still appalling – ugly towns, mean streets, slum houses, overcrowded schools, inadequate hospitals, under-staffed mental institutions, too few homes for the aged, indeed a general, and often squalid, lack of social amenities.

The relief of this distress and the elimination of this squalor is the main object of social expenditure; and a socialist is identified as one who wishes to give this an exceptional priority over other claims on resources. This is not a matter of the overall vertical equality of incomes; the arguments are humanitarian and compassionate, not egalitarian. It is a matter of priorities in the distribution of the national output, and a belief that the first priority should always be given to the poor, the unfortunate, the 'have-nots', and generally to those in need; from which follows a certain view about collective social responsibility, and thence about the role of the state and the level of taxation. This represents the first major difference between a socialist and a conservative.

The second distinctive socialist ideal is social equality and the 'classless society'. The socialist seeks a distribution of rewards, status, and privileges egalitarian enough to minimise social resentment, to secure justice between individuals, and to equalise opportunities; and he seeks to weaken the existing deep-seated class stratification, with its concomitant feelings of envy and inferiority, and its barriers to uninhibited mingling between the classes. This belief in social equality, which has been the strongest ethical inspiration of virtually every socialist doctrine, still remains the most characteristic feature of socialist thought to-day.

It is significant that these aspirations are not now primarily economic in character. The worst economic abuses and inefficiencies of modern society have been corrected; and this is no longer the sphere, as it has been for the greater part of the life of modern socialism, in which reforms are most urgently required. It is true, of course, that Britain still faces a serious economic problem – the problem of external solvency. But this is a problem common to both parties; and so far as specifically socialist policy is concerned, the battle is not mainly on this front.

It is also obvious that these ideals are much less pertinent to Britain, than to Britain's relations with the outside world. It is in the backward nations that the real poverty exists; and the inequality between those nations and Great Britain is far more glaring than the inequality between rich and poor in Britain. That is why the most obvious fulfilment of socialist ideals lies in altering not the structure of society in our own country, but the balance of wealth and privilege between advanced and backward countries. This I do not discuss, for this book, as I made clear in the Preface, is about the British domestic scene; and even within Britain these ideals are not yet fully realised. But socialists must always remember that inter-national now surpass inter-class injustices and inequalities.

VI *Is Socialism Still Relevant in Britain?*

The ideals have so far merely been stated. They have not been justified in detail, nor any evidence adduced to show that their further fulfilment would definitely improve our society. All that has been argued is that they constitute 'socialism' in the only legitimate sense of the word, and that they are not embodied in our present society to such an extent that most people would describe it as socialist.

A few people would, it is true, so describe it – not explicitly, but by implication. That is, they take the view that we are at, or anyway in sight of, the final objective. This of course is a plausible view only if we select those more modest aspirations which have largely been fulfilled, and define these, and these alone, as socialism. Thus if we were to say, as G. D. H. Cole once did before the war, that 'the Socialist has two main enemies to fight – poverty and enslavement',[1] it would follow that we now nearly have socialism in Britain, since we have very little poverty or enslavement.

Examples of such definitions can be found. Perhaps the most striking is the Frankfurt Manifesto of the reborn Socialist International in 1951, in which (after a preamble so vague as to be almost meaningless) the whole emphasis is placed on democratic planning, which is regarded as the basic condition of socialism.

[1] *The Simple Case for Socialism*, p. 19. I do not of course mean that Professor Cole himself defined socialism in this way.

The purposes of planning are defined as 'full employment, higher production, a rising standard of life, social security and a fair distribution of income and property' – purposes which (at least if one omits the one word 'property') are either not peculiar to socialists, or else are largely achieved already in Britain and Scandinavia.

Now it is true that the planned full-employment welfare state, which has been the outcome of the first successful spell of Labour government, is a society of exceptional merit and quality by historical standards, and by comparison with pre-war capitalism. It would have seemed a paradise to many early socialist pioneers. Poverty and insecurity are in process of disappearing. Living standards are rising rapidly; the fear of unemployment is steadily weakening; and the ordinary young worker has hopes for the future which would never have entered his father's head. There is much less social injustice; the economy works efficiently; and the electorate, as the Labour Party discovered at the last election, is in no mood for large-scale change, and certainly not for the complete overthrow of the present system. Many liberal-minded people, who were instinctively 'socialist' in the 1930s as a humanitarian protest against poverty and unemployment, have now concluded that 'Keynes-plus-modified-capitalism-plus-Welfare-State' works perfectly well; and they would be content to see the Labour Party become (if the Tories do not filch the role) essentially a Party for the defence of the present position, with occasional minor reforms thrown in to sweeten the temper of the local activists.

Yet this is not socialism. True, it is not pure capitalism either; and it does fulfil some part of the traditional socialist aspirations, and to this extent has socialist features. Yet it could clearly be a great deal more socialist than it is – not, as people sometimes think, because it now has only 25% public ownership and is not fully planned down to the minutest detail, any more than Soviet society *is* more socialist because it has 100% public ownership and complete state planning: but simply because the traditional socialist ideals could be more fully realised than they are. To put the matter simply, we have won many important advances; but since we could still have more social equality, a more classless society, and less avoidable social distress, we cannot be described as a socialist country.

The detailed case for fulfilling the remaining aspirations, that is, for moving towards socialism, is argued in Parts Three and Four, where the two aspirations are considered separately; while Part Five discusses their economic implications.

But one may at this stage briefly summarise, without attempting to justify, the reasons for wanting to move forward, and to alter what is admitted to be a prosperous and generally tolerable society; and the value judgments which underlie this wish. Lord Attlee recently remarked, looking back on his early days, that 'I joined the socialist movement because I did not like the kind of society we had and I wanted something better'. Why should anyone say the same to-day?

There are, I believe, three answers. First, for all the rising material standards and apparent contentment, the areas of avoidable social distress and physical squalor, which were referred to above, are still on a scale which narrowly restricts the freedom of choice and movement of a large number of individuals. Secondly (and perhaps more intractable), we retain a disturbing amount, compared with some other countries, of social antagonism and class resentment, visible both in politics and industry, and making society less peaceful and contented than it might be. Thirdly, the distribution of rewards and privileges still appears highly inequitable, being poorly correlated with the distribution of merit, virtue, ability, or brains; and, in particular, opportunities for gaining the top rewards are still excessively unequal.

This significant residue of distress, resentment, and injustice affords a *prima facie* justification for further social change – as I think, and shall argue, in a socialist direction. It may not justify the same *saeva indignatio* as mass unemployment and distressed areas before the war – rather a purposeful, constructive, and discriminating determination to improve an already improved society. But the belief that further change will appreciably increase personal freedom, social contentment, and justice, constitutes the ethical basis for being a socialist.

PART THREE

THE PROMOTION OF WELFARE

V

THE PURPOSES OF SOCIAL EXPENDITURE

1 *From Beveridge to the Conservatives*

THE first ideal was defined as the acceptance of collective responsibility and an exceptionally high priority for social welfare. I deliberately treat this first, for although the subject-matter might seem more prosaic than that of the next section on class and equality, I believe it to be more urgent, and more important, in terms both of justice and contentment.

This ideal raises the whole question of the role of the social services. It would, until recently, have been generally accepted that these had one simple purpose, namely the relief of poverty. But this, of course, is a purpose open to many different interpretations, and capable of justifying widely varying degrees of mean or generous provision. The history of the social services is the story of the gradual liberalisation of the definition of poverty: of the progress from a rigid destitution approach to a wider concept of a national minimum standard of life. After receiving its first great impetus from the Liberal Government of 1906, this progress continued, though erratically and not without opposition, until it reached its culmination in the Beveridge Report and the subsequent Labour legislation.

It was the Beveridge Report which gave the most complete and explicit statement of the philosophy of the national minimum. The social services had one prime object: the abolition of want. This object was to be achieved by isolating, not simply destitute individuals as the Poor Law did, but those entire categories of persons, or periods in an individual's life, which were commonly the most vulnerable to the onset of poverty. A presumption of

need having been established, benefits were to be paid to these
categories as of right, without a means test, at a flat-rate subsistence level unrelated to income; and the insurance principle
was made a cardinal part of the scheme precisely because it
symbolised the citizen's 'right' to receive a corresponding benefit.
National Assistance, relying on a test of means, was to be purely
a defence of last resort for those few who 'fell through the meshes'
of the main proposals.

For once a report was followed by effective action. Between
1946 and 1949 the whole field of social insurance and allied services was re-organised, co-ordinated and extended in a series of
major legislative acts; and people hailed the arrival of the
'Welfare State' as though finality had been attained, and the
social services had reached their ultimate form.

Yet within a few years, for a variety of reasons,[1] there was a
strong reaction against the Beveridge approach; and on all sides
there were demands for a new view of the fundamental purposes
of social expenditure.

The Conservatives have been the first to respond with a clear-
cut statement of purpose. This is set out in a book by two prominent Conservative politicians, one of whom later became Minister
Health. 'Given that redistribution is a characteristic of the social
services, the general presumption must be that they will be
rendered only on evidence of need, i.e. of financial inability to
provide each particular service out of one's own or one's family's
resources. Otherwise the process is a wasteful and purposeless
collection and issue of resources, which leaves people in the
enjoyment of the same facilities as before.'[2] Or again, as Mr.
Powell put it on a later occasion: 'Upon this view the ascertainment of need is the essential preliminary to meeting need, though
that ascertainment may take other forms than those which have
given the term "means test" its emotional and political content
to-day. A means test and a pure social service go together.'[3]

Now one can accept that redistribution of some kind is a
characteristic of the social services, since it is rather unlikely
that every citizen will pay in tax the exact amount which he
receives in benefits – though even if he did, the operation would

---

[1] Which are described in detail in the unabridged edition.

[2] Iain Macleod and J. Enoch Powell, *The Social Services: Needs and Means* (1952).

[3] *The Listener*, 17 April 1952.

not necessarily be 'purposeless', for his pattern of consumption might be different as a result; his children, for example, might receive more education than if neither taxes nor benefits existed.

But the redistribution might perfectly well be horizontal – from bachelors to families, the healthy to the sick, the young to the old, the employed to the unemployed, *at every income level*. All these transfers would normally be described as social services; all would redistribute income; none would be a 'wasteful and purposeless collection and issue of resources, which leaves people in the enjoyment of the same facilities as before'; yet none would require a means test or evidence of need.

It is only if redistribution is narrowly defined as being from those above to those below a subsistence line, and if a social service is then defined as entailing such redistribution, that the conclusions about evidence of need and financial inability follow; and that a means test becomes, not just a disagreeable necessity, but the central feature of social service policy. But of course there is no reason at all why a social service should be defined in this way; and most people would not in fact so define it. The definition is wholly arbitrary, and indeed is no more than a recommendatory statement describing what these authors think that a social service should be like. And this recommendation is in effect for a return to the 'poverty' approach which underlay the Poor Law in the last century, and, more recently, the concept of the national minimum.

Ignoring, then, the statements which purport to be definitions, but are not, what is to be said of this view? First, a means test as applied to the basic cash benefits is disliked for very real, and not merely 'emotional and political', reasons. It is undignified, humiliating, and highly inimical to working-class saving. It is resented as implying charity, and an open confession of lost independence and inability to support oneself; and indeed this resentment is itself a reassuring sign of civic sturdiness.[1] Because it is so unpopular, it fails to achieve its object, since many people even now refuse to apply to the Assistance Board, preferring to suffer in silence.[2]

[1] This resentment is particularly strong amongst war pensioners, who feel that the nation owes them, regardless of their means, a return for services rendered on the battlefield.

[2] cf. P.E.P., *Planning*, No. 349, 1 December 1952, 'Social Security and Unemployment in Lancashire'.

Secondly, this approach offends against the principle of social equality, since it publicly isolates the lowest and poorest section of the community and relegates them (or so they feel, whether logically or not) to the status of dependants on the public purse. Thirdly, it assumes that the social services are exclusively concerned with redistributing income to those in *financial* distress; whereas in fact, as is made clear later, there are many urgent objects of social expenditure which have little to do with direct financial need.

Lastly, it is offensive because it implies that social expenditure must always, on grounds of principle and not simply of cost, be reduced to the barest minimum. The socialist view, on the contrary, as was argued in Chapter IV, is that the relief of social distress should be given an exceptionally high priority; and this calls for a much more generous, less niggling and cheese-paring, attitude than is implied by an insistence on a test of means for every single social service.

II   *The Sociologists' Approach: Free Universality and Social Equality*

Should we then go to the opposite extreme, and say that all benefits, whether in kind or cash, should invariably be both free and universal, with no obligation ever to prove need? The principle of complete 'free universality' is urged on the assumptions first that the rationale of the social services is to promote social equality, and secondly that 'free universality' is a necessary condition of social equality. Let us discuss the second assumption first.

Universal benefits, it is said, symbolise the fact of social equality by conferring on everyone a badge, as it were, of citizenship. They eliminate any public distinction between social classes, between rich and poor, the eligible and the non-eligible. 'The strongest argument for showering benefits upon rich and poor alike,' writes Mrs. Barbara Wootton, 'is that nobody need then know who is poor and who is not.'[1] And Professor Marshall writes of the 'equality of status' that comes with universal services. 'Even when benefits are paid in cash, this class fusion is outwardly

[1] *Political Quarterly*, Vol. XXIV, 1953, p. 66.

expressed in the form of a new common experience. All learn what it means to have an insurance card that must be regularly stamped, or to collect children's allowances or pensions from the post office. But where the benefit takes the form of a service, the qualitative element enters into the benefit itself, and not only the process by which it is obtained. The extension of such services can therefore have a profound effect on the qualitative aspects of social differentiation.'[1] The labels 'ex-elementary schoolboy' and 'panel patient' disappear, class differences are blurred, and society become more homogeneous.

It seems rather doubtful whether the fact that everyone now has an insurance card, and repairs to the local post office, really does much to foster social equality. These cash benefits are too small in relation to the total incomes of better-off people to make much difference to how they live or feel – indeed the rich scarcely bother to draw them. 'Showering benefits upon rich and poor' will not prevent everyone knowing who is poor and who is rich; the only way of doing that would be to abolish the poor and the rich. And that requires much more than universal subsistence benefits.

When we turn to services in kind, however, we find a more direct link with social equality, especially in the spheres of health and education. If the state provides schools and hospitals, teachers and doctors, on a generous scale and of a really high quality, comparable with the best available for private purchase, then the result will be, not indeed a greater equality of real incomes, but certainly a greater equality in manners and the texture of social life. In Sweden, for example, scarcely anyone, whatever his income, uses private schools or hospital facilities – partly, it is true, for historical reasons and because wealth is more evenly distributed than in Britain, but also because the state schools and hospitals achieve such an impressively high qualitative standard. And the fact that people of every class go to the same school and use the same hospital facilities (and also, to a far greater extent than in Britain, live on the same new housing estates) is an immensely important influence in creating a sense of social equality and lack of privilege.

But in order to achieve this aim, these services need not necessarily be provided free to all, or without a test of means;

[1] T. H. Marshall, *Citizenship and Social Class* (Cambridge, 1950), pp. 56-7.

nor need they even be universally used. It is much more a matter of relative standards. Social differentiation is inevitable if standards in the state system are conspicuously and notoriously inferior to those in the private system. But as the gap is narrowed and facilities become genuinely comparable in quality, the mark of inferiority attaching to the public services will disappear, whether or not these are provided entirely free, and whether or not they are *universally* used; though naturally they will be more and more used as their relative standards improve.

Thus in education, despite the continued existence of parallel state and private schools, the inferior status attaching to the former is less marked than a generation ago, and the phrase 'ex-elementary schoolboy' has almost disappeared from the public vocabulary – not because state education has become more free or universal, but because its qualitative standards have risen rather nearer to those prevailing in the private sector. On the other hand a wide status gap still exists between the two, and would whatever the system of payment in the state schools, simply because the gap in standards remains very wide, and the private schoolboy in fact enjoys an incomparably superior education.

Again, in housing, the term 'council-house' is beginning to lose its pre-war social connotation, not because a higher proportion of the population lives in council-houses, still less because larger housing subsidies were for some time granted without an income-test, but simply because the standard of new municipal housing has risen relative to that of new private housing; indeed for some years after the war there was little difference between the two. And if, in the future, large blocks of sub-standard private house-property were to be municipalised, as the Labour Party proposes, we should find a pattern of social inequality in housing which bore no obvious relation to the size or distribution of housing subsidies, but depended solely on physical differences in housing standards.

The same process has been at work in health. People who use the National Health Service are not now opprobriously designated 'panel-patients'; large numbers of middle-class people use the service, and no superior status attaches to those who stay outside. Yet the service is neither free nor universally used. Private practice still continues; and a number of charges are made, subject to relief after a test of means.

It appears, then, that while social equality of course requires universal *availability* of the public service (though not necessarily completely universal use), it does not always require universal *free* availability. And there is all the difference, from the point of view of avoiding social differentiation, between a test of means which determines the right to use a service, and one which determines only the question of payment. Thus if beds in state hospitals were to be provided only for national assistance beneficiaries, or if old-age pensions were to be paid only subject to a means test, the sick or the elderly would be denied the right of unconditional *access* to the service; they would first have to apply to the State, and produce evidence of destitution. This would lay a clear mark of social inferiority on those who applied, who would openly confess themselves as incapable of self-support. The test of means is here both a denial of access unless certain conditions are satisfied, and a means of isolating the poorest section of the community.

But granted the right of access, an income-test to determine the question of completely free access – one, that is, which requires the state to apply to the citizen for a recovery of charges, and not the citizen to apply to the state for the right to use the service – need neither offend against social equality, nor cause humiliation, provided that two conditions are fulfilled. First, the benefit or service must not be so essential, and so large in relation to the recipient's means, that he may reasonably consider he has a social right to it, so that both his real income and self-esteem would be severely affected by a test of means. This rules out an income-test both for the basic cash benefits, which often constitute almost the whole of the recipient's income, and for the central, essential health and education services. Secondly, the income-line should be set as high as possible. If only paupers are excluded from the need to pay, there is more danger of inferior feelings arising than if only surtax-payers are compelled to pay. The income-test applied to University awards, for example, which exacts no payment below a certain level, then a graduated payment, with full payment only above £2,000, cannot be said to cause social inequalities – especially as tutors and fellow-students have no means of detecting who is grant-aided and who is not.[1]

[1] A graded payment of this sort was of course the policy of the Webbs. (*v.* Joan S. Clarke, 'The Break-up of the Poor Law', in *The Webbs and Their Work*, ed. Margaret Cole, Muller, 1949.)

Thus the link between free universality and social equality is rather tenuous. On the one hand, social equality is not necessarily threatened by an ascertainment of means, subject to certain conditions. And on the other, the provision of free and universally available services will not enhance social equality if they are much inferior to the corresponding private services. They will then simply not be used by better-off people; and class differentiation will be in no way diminished.

Social equality mainly requires the creation of standards of public health, education, and housing so high that no marked qualitative gap remains between public and private provision. It will then matter little whether or not occasional charges are imposed, subject to the above conditions. While as for universal use, this will either follow automatically (or perhaps be enforced by a growing equality of incomes); and even if it does not, and some diehard snobs continue to prefer their private doctors, this will really be of little moment. But the important point is that 'universality' must follow *from* social equality, and cannot itself create it.

III   *The Main Purposes of Social Expenditure*

I conclude that to set the principle of free universality against the Tory insistence on a stricter poverty approach is not the right answer: not, obviously enough, because the declared purpose of fostering social equality is wrong, but because this is not the right way to achieve it. The right way, in the field of social expenditure, is a generous, imaginative, long-term programme of social investment which will make our state schools and hospitals, and all the services that go with them, the equal in quality of the best which private wealth can buy.

But in any event, social equality cannot be held to be the ultimate purpose of the social services. This must surely be the relief of social distress and hardship, and the correction of social need; though naturally measures directed to this end will often also enhance social equality, which in any case remains an important subsidiary objective.

Now this central purpose will not be attained by adopting the Conservative view, since this presumes that unavoidable social distress (that is, distress not due to the irresponsibility of the individual concerned) is a function, if not of primary poverty, at least of financial hardship; hence the insistence on a test of means. But social distress and need to-day are a product not solely of primary poverty or an absolute lack of means, but also, and indeed increasingly, of other more varied and subtle causes, which operate far above a subsistence level of income.

This does not mean that primary poverty can be neglected, or that rising material standards do nothing to reduce the area of need. While any primary poverty remains, it must have the first priority. Moreover we must remember that *standards* of poverty change through time. Poverty is not, after all, an absolute, but a social or cultural, concept. Even in the most basic terms of health and nutrition, there can never be some constant, eternally valid yardstick by which to judge what constitutes 'subsistence' – standards rise here, as they rise in respect of less essential consumption. But in any event we should not behave like medical officers of health, concerned only to provide sufficient food and clothing to ward off starvation and ill-health. We are surely concerned with happiness and social justice also. This demands a relative, subjective view of poverty, since the unhappiness and injustice which it creates, even when ill-health and malnutrition are avoided, lies in the enforced deprivation not of luxuries indeed, but of small comforts which others have and are seen to have, and which in the light of prevailing cultural standards are really 'conventional necessities'.

Thus any view of poverty other than a clinical one, requiring only that the poor should come up to the right point on the calory chart or sickness graph, requires that standards of subsistence should rise with economic progress. If the opposite view were adopted, the poor would grow steadily poorer relative to the rest of the community; and this hardly seems consistent with humanitarian, let alone socialist, ideals.

But even if primary poverty, however defined, were finally to disappear, we should still be left with a large residue of need and hardship. First, hardship may be caused by what is loosely termed secondary poverty: that is, ill-health, malnutrition, or deprivation of essential needs, due not to an absolute deficiency of income but to unwise spending. Even Conservatives recognise the possibility of unwise spending, and accept it as a justification for basic health and education services.[1]

But it is sometimes thought that once these have been provided, little more need be done, especially as secondary poverty will gradually disappear with the rise in real wages. This is too optimistic. Whatever the level of real wages, children may be deprived of essential health provision by the genuine ignorance of their parents; it is rather an old-fashioned view to think always in terms of the neglectful or inebriate father, pouring his child's free orange juice into his gin. Wartime investigations of why only 38% of mothers regularly took up free cod-liver oil for their children showed that overwhelmingly the biggest reason was not a vicarious dislike of its taste, but sheer ignorance that it was beneficial; similar investigations of the diphtheria immunisation scheme revealed that less than one-third of the parents interviewed had any knowledge either of the disease or its causes.[2]

But quite apart from ignorance, secondary poverty due to unwise spending appears still to be disturbingly prevalent. It arises most commonly from a maldistribution of income within the family. There are many families whose total income would be quite sufficient, were it to be pooled, but where the housekeeping allowance granted by the husband to the wife is insufficient, to support a reasonable subsistence standard. This may occur in families of any size owing simply to the selfishness or thoughtlessness of the husband. But it occurs with particular frequency in large families, where the *additional* allowance made by the husband for each additional child is often not enough to defray the extra cost.

Family allowances on the existing scale are not an adequate answer. They were introduced to prevent the average standard of life of a family from falling as its numbers grew with no equivalent rise in wages; and if family income were normally pooled, they might at least go a long way in this direction. In practice, however, 'the idea of an average family standard of life was misleading. The financial burden of having an extra child was not . . . shared equally by all members of the family, *but fell with especial severity upon the mother and upon previous children.* Some husbands behaved

---

[1] Thus conceding, despite their strictures to the contrary, that the man in Whitehall does sometimes know best.

[2] *v.* Sheila Ferguson and Hilde Fitzgerald, *Studies in the Social Services*, Ch. V.

like employers. They did not increase their wives' "wages" as the size of the family increased.'[1] It is this changing distribution of relative income between husband and wife as the size of the family grows which explains the common phenomenon that the larger the family, the lower the expenditure on necessities relative to that on drink and tobacco.

Such secondary poverty, where dependent children are involved, at the mercy of other people's decisions, is clearly a communal responsibility (though mis-spending by adults is not – it is not the duty of the state to deal with every quiet inebriate). It justifies a high priority for a wide range notably of family social services: amongst services in kind, maternity and child welfare, and amongst cash benefits those, such as family allowances, which offset the financial hardship of bearing additional children.

A second cause of hardship, again unrelated to primary poverty, is the decline in the size and cohesion of the family group. In 1911, of women aged around 50 who had been married for 25 or 30 years, over 70% had four or more children, over 40% seven or more, and only 5% none. Of the corresponding group in 1951, only 25% had four or more children, 5% seven or more, and nearly 11% had none.[2]

The effect of this demographic change is exaggerated by simultaneous social changes. Spatially, families are much more scattered than they were two generations ago, as a result partly of increased occupational mobility, but mainly of housing developments – the growth of suburbs and new housing estates well away from the older property areas in the centres of large cities, and now of course new towns at an even greater distance. Fifty years ago, different generations of a family often passed all their lives in a small neighbourhood, within easy walking distance of each other; to-day, they are characteristically scattered over an area which makes mutual visits an annual, or at any rate not a daily or weekly, event.

But this disintegration of the family would probably have occurred in any case, owing to a change in social attitudes towards what constitutes a 'proper' family unit. The family used to be seen as the entire group of different generations; and the size of the

[1] Michael Young, 'Distribution of Income Within the Family', *British Journal of Sociology*, December 1952.

[2] Ferguson and Fitzgerald, op. cit., Ch. I.

Victorian household was not due solely to the larger number of children, but also to the larger number of grades of relatives which made it up. To-day, the family is seen simply as the parents and their dependent children. These, and these alone, constitute the proper household unit; and the presence of other relatives is resented, and even thought to be psychologically harmful. Hence the prejudice against sharing a home with in-laws: the belief that grown-up children should leave home and fend for themselves: and even the vague conviction that for adult relatives to live together is somehow wrong.

'As we have narrowed the home,' Margaret Mead has written, 'and excluded from it the grandmother, the unmarried daughter, the unmarried sister, and – as part of the same process of repudiating any sharing of a home with another adult – the domestic servant . . . each home has been reduced to the bare essentials – to barer essentials than more primitive people would consider possible . . . The mother is a nutritionist, a child psychologist, an engineer, a production manager, an expert buyer, all in one.'[1] And the converse is the greater loneliness of the other relatives who once shared the home, and now live separately.

Whether these changes are on balance good or bad, I do not know. But they certainly have implications for social service policy, for they greatly reduce the possibility of inter-family help. 'Middle-aged people had fewer young relations to help them in the crises of life. Young adults who were forming their own families . . . tended to have a good many aunts and uncles but fewer of the really near relations – brothers and sisters – who were more likely to help in emergencies. Moreover, as the families with dependent children were small, fewer families had older, reasonably responsible, children who could help with babies and the two to five year olds.'[2] But the most obvious manifestation of the change are the lonely elderly, with, as compared with 50 years ago, possibly no unmarried daughters to look after them, fewer married children, or even nieces and nephews, to pay them visits, and fewer grandchildren to keep them happy and occupy their minds.

Thus we see a steady contraction in the possibilities of mutual family aid at times of crisis or difficulty: during confinement,

---

[1] *Male and Female* (Gollancz, 1950), pp. 334-5.
[2] Ferguson and Fitzgerald, op. cit., p. 2.

the illness of a young mother, chronic sickness, and above all old age. And this has nothing to do with primary poverty, nor is it confined to the working class. Before the war, it is true, with domestic servants cheap and plentiful, and hotels or nursing-homes available at moderate prices, better-off people could manage with reasonable ease. But even they cannot always now, under conditions of high taxation, the decline in the purchasing power of fixed incomes, and the prohibitive price of domestic labour. Only the very rich can now cope entirely unaided with family problems, sickness, loneliness, and old age.

A substantial social provision, extending far beyond the conventional poverty line, is therefore required, not indeed to release the family from all its obligations, but to shoulder communally those obligations which even the most devoted family to-day, in view of its size and physical dispersion, cannot fulfil unaided. This calls for more nurses, nurseries, orphanages, small houses and service flats for the elderly, institutional facilities generally, and (perhaps most important of all) more domiciliary and home-help services.

The third cause of social hardship is the maldistribution of income relative to needs, both through time and between persons. This arises either because income is not fully adjusted to an accession of needs, as in the case of people bearing families: or because income actually falls just at the moment when needs are greatest, as during sickness: or because even when needs are perhaps declining, income declines more sharply still, as on retirement. The result is twofold. At every income level, families and old people are badly off relative to single people and those in work. And amongst the working class, as the Rowntree-Lavers study showed, even though only a very small fraction are living in poverty at any given moment, a much larger proportion pass through periods of poverty at some time during their lives.[1]

This general lack of correlation between needs and income is visible today in most advanced countries – in Sweden and America as well as in Britain. Everywhere the young single worker, and to a lesser extent the young childless couple and the parents still at work but whose children have grown up, are conspicuously privileged groups, with money to spare and few responsibilities; while parents with children, and old people living on their

[1] *Poverty and the Welfare State*, p. 80.

pension, with greater responsibilities or fewer resources, are just as conspicuously under-privileged. And this is not only unjust as between persons; but the fluctuations in living standards within the individual's lifetime – what Professor Titmuss has called 'disharmonies over the life-span' – also lead to conflict and stress. 'Concepts and standards of living cultivated by relatively high earnings before marriage may be shattered by the lower standards resulting from marriage and parenthood. The prosperities of late middle life may make the hardships of living on old age pensions seem harder than they really are.'[1]

Thus hardship must be seen not as an absolute concept, but as relative both to expectations and previously realised real income. This is particularly true to-day when, as a result of certain contemporary social habits which are reflected in heavy fixed-expenditure commitments, any given fall in income produces a much greater proportionate fall in freely-disposable income. Most people now undertake substantial commitments fixed in advance – mortgage payments, insurance premiums, hire-purchase commitments, education outlays, and the like.[2] If their income falls, they could no doubt afford a perfectly adequate standard of life if they cut these commitments – sold the house, allowed the insurance policy to lapse, defaulted on their hire-purchase payments. But if they do none of these, their uncommitted income may be drastically reduced, and genuine hardship follow, even though their total income remains well above a subsistence level. Thus changes in income are magnified in their effects on current expenditure; and it becomes more than ever important to consider not absolute income only, as the poverty approach requires, but also fluctuations.

Of course taxation and social services already redistribute income in the right direction.[3] But by socialist standards much more should be done, on grounds of justice as well as welfare, to raise the real incomes of the old, the sick, and those with young families relative to the rest of the population. And, as we shall see,

[1] 'Social Administration in a Changing Society', *British Journal of Sociology*, September 1951, p. 196.

[2] The Oxford Savings Surveys show that 75% of families have contractual savings of some sort (life assurance, superannuation, repayment of mortgages), and 25% have some hire-purchase debt. (*Bull. Inst. Stat.*, May 1955.) This last figure is probably growing rapidly.

[3] More than Professor Titmuss allows in the article just quoted.

the existing maldistribution is worse at the lower than the upper end of the income scale; and corrective measures will increase social equality between classes, as well as social justice within classes.

IV *The Neglected Special Cases and the Need for a New Orientation*

Lastly, there are the 'special cases', which fall into no large categories extending across the whole population, but where distress is due to specific, unavoidable, individual misfortune. The parents of backward children, the relatives of mental deficients, serious psychiatric cases, neglected children and children of broken homes, the blind, the tubercular, the chronic sick generally – it is amongst such groups that perhaps the greatest suffering of all remains.

Yet they always tend to be neglected, to be put at the bottom of the queue, and suffer the first cuts in expenditure. They are neither vociferous, nor numerous enough to count electorally. Even since the war, in the excitement of building the Welfare State, too much attention was paid to universal benefits, and too little to the relatively few, but often desperate, special cases. Thus schools for backward children, for example, were given a very low priority, and mental hospitals an even lower one – it only requires a few brief minutes inside a typical mental hospital to be appalled at existing conditions, and at how much needs to be done.

These are also cases especially hard hit by the smaller size and increased dispersion of the family, and by the lack of relatives to help or nurse them. And of course their need is such that the concept of a subsistence means test is totally inappropriate. These misfortunes are in no way related to primary or even secondary poverty; and people with normally perfectly adequate incomes may find the facilities they need far beyond their means (if indeed they can find them at all). There is no objection to recovery of payment in full or in part where this can clearly be afforded; but it is out of the question to make the *provision* of the necessary facilities conditional on a prior means test, least of all one at a very low income level.

How little all this has to do with poverty can be seen from the case of broken or problem families. These will not be automatically cured by paying subsistence cash benefits, or raising the level of real wages, or even by housing everyone in brand-new well-planned municipal estates. No doubt a proportion of the trouble can be traced to bad material conditions, but much of it will persist however completely poverty is eliminated; and there may be nearly as many problem families on the new housing-estates as in the old slums.

It is said by the experts[1] that the first requirement for more adequate treatment of many of these cases is a major administrative reform, designed to co-ordinate existing overlapping, and consequently wasteful and inefficient, services; this appears to apply especially to the case of the problem family.[2]

But this may come only as part of a wider re-orientation of outlook. In the past, social problems have been seen essentially as 'category' problems, and mainly also as problems of material deprivation. This was the philosophy underlying the Beveridge Revolution: that one isolated broad categories where need could be presumed without individual investigation, and then met the need by generous cash payments. The objective was the elimination, not of distress, but of want; and want was assumed to be due to causes common to the entire population. And at the time this was clearly the right approach; indeed it will remain a highly relevant one for many years to come.

But if our present rate of economic growth continues, material want and poverty and deprivation of essential goods will gradually cease to be a problem. We shall increasingly need to focus attention, not on universal categories, but on individual persons and families: not on the economic causes of distress, but on the social and psychological causes. We shall want the advice, not of the economists, but of psychiatrists, sociologists, and social psychologists. We shall rely less on broad, sweeping measures of expenditure than on concentrated measures of aid to limited groups, based on patient, empirical social research into the real nature of the need. And the aid will often take the form, not of cash payments, nor even of material provision in kind, but of individual

[1] *v.*, for example, 'Can the Family Survive?', by Peggy Jay, *Family Planning*, July 1955.

[2] A change in the law relating to adoption appears also to be urgently needed.

therapy, casework and preventive treatment. The tone of social expenditure may be set less by old-age pensions, than by the Family Planning Association, child care committees, home visitors, almoners, and mental health workers.

The Labour Party is perhaps not yet fully alive to this gradual change in the pattern of need. It still tends to think exclusively in the traditional Beveridge categories; while the Conservative 'test of means' approach is of course quite irrelevant to these problems. Yet the change is the inevitable corollary of the social revolution described in Part One. This, allied to a rapid rate of growth, is gradually giving us victory over the old enemies of poverty, unemployment and glaring injustice. But as we conquer these, we find that so far from Utopia coming steadily into view, new and more subtle social problems, hitherto concealed by a natural obsession with material standards, now come to the surface and demand attention. And these new problems will not be cured simply by doubling the standard of living in twenty-five years, or even by greater equality, highly desirable as both these objectives are. This is a field in which 'Keynes-plus-modified-capitalism' wholly fails to provide an adequate answer; and a determination to accord these social problems an over-riding priority should be a characteristic, even more than a belief in equality, of a socialist outlook.

v   *The War and the Social Services*

The first signs of a wider view of the social services came with the experience of war. The war was in any case a major agent of advance in the social service field. This was due partly to the mood of national unity: partly to the revelation, which evacuation provided to the middle classes, of the appallingly low standard at which many city-dwellers lived:[1] and partly to the urgent new needs created by evacuation and war mobilisation.

But the significant change was less the actual growth of new services, than the gradual realisation that social needs did not

[1] People have forgotten to-day the profound shock administered by the physical condition and behaviour of some working-class evacuee children. But the bitter controversy and mutual accusations over, for example, the widespread manifestation of enuresis amongst these children did at least demonstrate to middle-class people that an acute social problem of some kind existed.

arise solely from destitution, but were to be found at all levels. For these far-ranging additional needs manifested themselves at a time of full employment, when *economic* distress was less widespread than ever before in British history. The lack of correspondence between poverty and social need therefore stood out with exceptional clarity; and it was this experience which gave birth to the new and wider concept of the role of social services.

Thus it was believed in 1939, for example, that only the poor would need government aid if their homes were bombed, and that the rest could look after themselves; the responsibility for the bombed-out was therefore laid on the Assistance Committees. Naturally the belief and the arrangements both disintegrated with the first heavy raid on London. Again, when evacuation was first under debate in Whitehall, the Treasury refused to sanction money for providing temporary lavatory accommodation at rural reception stations, holding that this was not a legitimate object of social expenditure; this attitude also failed to survive very long. The issue of free milk and subsidised meals in schools, previously restricted rigidly to 'necessitous and under-nourished' children, was soon extended to all children as the obvious fact was realised that all were equally affected by the growing shortage of food. A last and characteristic instance was the treatment of unmarried mothers; originally only those who were destitute were thought either to need or deserve support, and the responsibility was again laid on Public Assistance Committees; gradually it was realised that here was an urgent, widespread and inevitable wartime social problem, with tragic consequences at every income level, and that aid must be given to all who needed it, whether destitute or not.[1]

By the end of the war, 'it was increasingly regarded as a proper function and indeed obligation of Government to ward off distress and strain among not only the poor but almost all classes of society'.[2] Of course war, with its accompaniment of physical destruction and social disturbance on a havoc-making scale, enormously extends the range of problems which even the better-off individual cannot meet himself. It would be quite wrong to suggest that the area of government responsibility should be as

[1] These examples are taken from the two social service volumes in the Official History of the Second World War: *Problems of Social Policy*, by Richard M. Titmuss, and Ferguson and Fitzgerald, op. cit.

[2] Titmuss, op. cit., p. 506.

wide, or even nearly as wide, in peacetime. But the basic philosophy is the right one in peace as well as in war.

VI   *The Social Services and Social Equality*

Four main areas of need were isolated above; and if these are agreed, the priorities in social expenditure more or less sort themselves out. The first three – secondary poverty, the altered position of the family, and fluctuations in needs through time – point above all to old people, those with large families, and those whose earnings are interrupted by sickness. Moreover the residue of primary poverty is also concentrated in these groups.

The first priorities are therefore fairly clearly ordained. They are on the one hand the traditional cash benefits to these groups – old-age pensions, sickness and disability benefits, and family allowances; and on the other, certain welfare services in kind already mentioned *seriatim* in the text. The other essential priority is to meet the needs of the 'special cases'; this will not require a vast outlay – it is much more a question of the *will* to be generous to numerically (and electorally) insignificant groups.

These are the expenditures required to meet social distress, hardship, and need. But of course additional expenditures are required to fulfil the allied purpose of increasing social equality. This was discussed earlier in relation to health and education. But there are also other ways, relevant to what might broadly be termed social policy, in which expenditure and/or tax reliefs can increase social equality by making available to poorer people essential facilities or advantages which better-off people can quite well buy for themselves. Legal aid is an obvious example.

But the main manifestation of inequality in this respect is the better provision which the rich are able to make, either from their private means, or through tax-concessions, or from the terms of their employment, for those periods in life in which needs rise sharply relative to income. That is, the elderly, the sick, and those with large families in the wealthier classes come off comparatively better than people similarly circumstanced in the poorer or working classes.

In the case of families, those with large incomes derive a relatively greater benefit, both in amount and duration, from tax allowances, than the wage-earner from family allowances; the former, unlike the latter, both extend to the first child and continue until the child's full-time education is complete. Moreover most middle-class people receive annual or periodic increments of salary which partially offset the extra cost of rearing children during the critical years from 25 to 40. Most wage-earners, by contrast, are earning the same at 40 as at 25.

In the case of sickness, the disparity arises because firms now commonly make up salaries in full for weeks or even months of sickness; but they seldom make up wages. The worker thus suffers a sharper relative drop in his income just when his needs are greatest. In the case of old age, the difference is due to the existence of private superannuation schemes, which are available to some employees but not to others.

Some of these disparities can and should be corrected by Trade Union action; while so far as fiscal policy is concerned, they point to the same priorities as the earlier considerations. But one question needs a rather more detailed discussion, namely private superannuation. For not only are two-thirds of the working population not covered by this, but of course individuals cannot choose whether to be covered or not – it depends on the organisation in which they work. The result is a growth, on completely haphazard lines, of two distinct classes: those who must subsist on the State pension, and who consequently suffer an extremely severe drop in their incomes on retirement, and those covered by superannuation schemes, who suffer a much less severe reduction. This offends against both social justice and social equality; and indeed it could easily lead to a greater inequality in old age than during working life.

Then what is the solution? We cannot base the entire national provision for old age on the principle of flat-rate subsistence pensions, partly because private superannuation has already spread so far, and also because it would in any case be illogical. If the object is to keep the standard of living in old age in a reasonable relation to that previously experienced, then pensions must vary with previous income.

No doubt the most logical solution would be to reorganise the entire National Insurance pension scheme, making both contributions and benefits variable. But the opposition to this is so strong that it hardly seems practical politics for the next decade;

and meanwhile something must be done. The obvious solution would therefore be, as has recently been proposed in Sweden by a Government Committee, a universal, compulsory scheme super-imposed on the existing national insurance scheme. Under the Swedish proposal, contributions would vary with annual income, and the pension with 'life salary' (i.e. the cumulative total of income earned during working-life).[1] (The pension would also rise automatically with increases in the real national income, and with any fall in the value of money.)[2] The next Labour Government would be wise to study this possibility at an early stage in its career.

[1] For a variant on this, *v.* Brian Abel-Smith and Peter Townsend, *New Pensions for the Old* (Fabian Society, 1955).

[2] But the scheme would be financially self-supporting – indeed, during the early years of build-up a large 'buffer-fund' would be created; and even after the build-up, each year's expenditure is to be fully covered by that year's income.

PART FOUR

THE SEARCH FOR EQUALITY

VI

—◆—

THE DETERMINANTS OF CLASS

1 *The British Paradox*

TWO developments have occurred which compel us to reconsider our approach to the second basic socialist aspiration, that towards social equality and a 'classless' society. First, it appears that after the redistribution of the last two decades, certain of the traditional socialist arguments for more equality no longer apply. This is discussed in the next chapter.

Secondly, we have moved some way towards equality of *incomes*, yet we still seem far from a *socially* equal and classless society. 'England', wrote George Orwell in 1941, 'is the most class-ridden country under the sun.' Matters have improved a little since *The Lion and the Unicorn* was written. Yet despite the levelling of incomes since before the war, we still retain in Britain a deeper sense of class, a more obvious social stratification, and stronger class resentments, than any of the Scandinavian, Australasian, or North American countries. In fact we almost take our class system for granted, so completely does it permeate our social attitudes. But the foreign visitor or even the returning traveller, less accustomed to the phenomenon, is still shocked and surprised by its extent.[1]

[1] And the phenomenon is also evident in our relations with other, and especially Asiatic and African, peoples. A recent (and poignant) testimony to it is Sherpa Tenzing's account in his autobiography of his agonised indecision as between climbing Everest with the British in 1953, or waiting to climb it another year with the beloved Raymond Lambert and the Swiss. 'I would rather have gone back to Everest with the Swiss. . . . With the Swiss and the French I had been treated as a comrade, an equal, in a way that is not possible for the British. They are kind men; they are brave; they are fair and just, always. But always, too, there is a line between them and the outsider, between sahib and employee.' (*Man of Everest*, Harrap, 1955, pp. 224-5.)

And indeed its stubborn persistence in the face of torrential social changes induced by two World Wars and six years of Labour rule is surely puzzling. Britain now presents an unusual paradox to the world: of a society characterised by an exceptionally mature political democracy, growing economic prosperity, and a social order which apparently metes out social justice in a reasonable degree: yet still with an unreconstructed class system, productive of deep collective resentments. The apparent invulnerability of this system to changes in the sphere of income suggests that the classless society will not be reached simply by more redistribution of wealth. We now need a wider interpretation of the goal, and, as a preliminary, a closer analysis of the nature of class, than we needed in the past.

II *What People Mean by Class*

When people speak of class, they are assuming that society is divided into a limited number of strata, one above the other. Each stratum can be called a social class. Societies differ in respect of the number of strata, the distance between them, and the precision of the dividing lines. These latter are rarely completely clear; but this does not make class divisions any less real – we are, after all, fully aware of differences in sex despite the existence of hermaphrodites.

This stratification derives from, and is reflected in, socially recognised relationships of superiority and inferiority. 'Social classes may be described as portions of the community, or collections of individuals, standing to each other in the relation of equality, and marked off from other portions by accepted or sanctioned standards of inferiority and superiority.' 'By class is meant two or more orders of people who are believed to be, and are accordingly ranked by members of the community, in socially superior and inferior positions.'[1]

These socially-recognised relationships express themselves in the way a man is collectively treated and regarded by other people, as well as in the way he treats and regards them. They therefore

[1] These two almost identical definitions are deliberately taken from two sociologists who disagree about the *determinants* of class: Morris Ginsberg, *Sociology* (Butterworth, 1934), p. 159; and W. Lloyd Warner, *The Social Life of a Modern Community* (Yale University Press, 1941), p. 82.

have both an external aspect, reflected in social attitudes – whether these are free and egalitarian, or deferential and condescending: and a psychological aspect, reflected in the strength or otherwise of subjective feelings of equality, superiority or inferiority.

This recognised web of relationships is the one incontrovertible fact about class. When we turn to consider how it is built up, what are the criteria of these socially-recognised distinctions, and what factors determine the individual's position in the hierarchy, we enter a realm where sociologists still disagree.[1] There is no one theory of class to which socialists can appeal when discussing how to have less 'class' than we now have. Moreover, almost all the evidence available from field research is American in origin; virtually no field-work has been done in Britain, and the examples in this chapter have necessarily to be taken largely from American studies.

This perhaps does not matter very much; for the object of this chapter is not to present a precise and detailed analysis of all the determinants of class, which in any case would be impossible at our present state of knowledge, but simply to emphasise the main determinants, and especially the fact that class-consciousness and social inequality rest on other factors besides income. These other factors may even be more important than income. But in any case they are certainly not always correlated with income (or with each other) – which means that the discussion inevitably gives an impression of indeterminacy; although in fact I believe, as I argue at the end of the chapter, that the picture is, for historical reasons, unusually determinate in England: that is, that the influences on the social hierarchy, being few and strong and rather closely correlated, are exceptionally clear. But even in England we must disentangle the separate influences, lest we mistakenly believe that more social equality is simply, or even mainly, a matter of more redistribution of wealth.

III   *The Marxist Theory of Class*

Most sociologists adhere to an 'objective' theory of class determination; that is, they assume that social class is more or less

[1] For an excellent account of the present state of the controversy, *v.* 'Social Stratification – a trend report', by D. G. MacRae, *Current Sociology*, Vol. II, 1953-4.

automatically determined by certain objective and identifiable criteria, normally of an economic character.[1]

The earliest such theory was of course the Marxist. Marx held that the forms and conditions of production were the fundamental determinants of the class structure and class attitudes. Specifically, the stratifying influence was to be found in the ownership or exclusion from ownership of the physical means of production, from which it followed that in the last analysis there could only be two classes – owners (bourgeoisie) and non-owners (proletariat), all intermediate groups gradually vanishing from the social scene. The determinants of class are seen as not merely economic, but almost technological; and a class is simply a functional group having a particular (ownership or non-ownership) relationship to the means of production. Other social and ideological class differences will, of course, emerge in the course of time; but they are essentially secondary and derivative, merely a 'superstructure' built on the base of productive relationships.

Now this analysis might be plausible on three conditions, which may have been fulfilled in the past, but are certainly not fulfilled in advanced industrial countries to-day. The first is that productive relations and the division of labour should be of a technically simple character, so that the population falls into a few clear-cut economic groups, each possessing an unambiguous relationship to the means of production. But in fact the last century has witnessed a rapid growth of service occupations (professions, administration, entertainment, and so on) which have no contact at all with the physical means of production. Even within manufacturing industry, the growth of scale and the increasing technical complexity of production have enormously multiplied the number of (especially managerial and technical) skills, so that the labour force no longer constitutes a clear-cut proletarian class. (Automation of course will reinforce this trend.) Thus so far from polarisation having occurred, we see a growing proliferation of middle, neither proletarian nor capitalist, classes: and of classes whose social attitudes are not determined by a direct relationship to the physical means of production.

[1] The words criteria and indices are often used in this chapter as though they were synonymous with determinants, since it is assumed that class is in fact determined by collective evaluations of certain objective criteria which thus become indices. But of course people may (*v.i.*) *quote* criteria other than those which appear objectively to be the determinants.

The second condition is that economic relationships, and hence the class structure, should be basically dominated by the criterion of the presence or absence of ownership. But Chapter II has already demonstrated the increasing irrelevance of ownership to economic power, income-distribution, the degree of exploitation, and all the other factors which might determine class attitudes.[1]

Thirdly, Marxist sociology presupposes, though Marxists do not admit it, a scarcity economy, in which men's lives and therefore social attitudes are ruled by the relentless pressure of material want and deprivation: for the majority, by poverty and resentment of poverty, and for the minority of rich by the inevitable counterpart – the fear of violent dispossession. Only in such a society would social relationships be wholly determined by purely productive relationships, and social aspirations by purely material drives.[2] But in the advanced industrial countries to-day, with their abundant and rapidly-growing economies, matters are beginning to look very different. Not only are social attitudes less and less dominated by crude economic resentments, but the decline in the hours of work, combined with the higher standards and greater variety of consumption-goods, are gradually weakening the significance for class evaluations of work relationships, and magnifying instead the impact of consumption and leisure relationships.

Of course class attitudes are still heavily influenced by the relations of production; a miner does not feel the same as a member of the Coal Board; industrial disputes have not died out (though increasingly the issues are non-pecuniary ones); and people still worry about their material standard of living. Marxist sociology (if fairly freely interpreted) therefore still has something to offer. But it clearly does not provide a sufficient, all-embracing theory of class.

IV *Income, Occupation, and Style of Life as Determinants of Class*

Most sociologists before the war, while rejecting the Marxist theory as too narrow, nevertheless preserved a broadly economic

[1] *v.* Chapter II, Section IV.

[2] It is therefore not surprising that Marxism always seems most plausible in times of depression – witness its sensational revival in the 1930s, and equally rapid decline since.

approach. They took, as the main index of class, occupational or economic status in the widest sense, deriving this from a number of variables: amount of income, source of income, degree of security, extent of independence, degree of initiative and control, type of work (manual or non-manual), non-pecuniary privileges, and so on.[1]

Most people would agree that 'economic status' in some sense was a main, if not the prime, source of class differentiation. It often occurs to people first when assessing someone's class location, and it appears to justify and explain the tripartite social division into working, middle, and upper classes. But its apparent simplicity and reliability are rather deceptive; and on examination it appears as not one criterion, but an amalgam of separate and sometimes conflicting ones.

In particular, income is not exactly correlated with some of the other factors; and these are often the more powerful influence on occupational prestige. Thus when people are asked to rank occupations according to the social status which they carry, the answer by no means corresponds with the structure of income distribution; professors, dockers, secretaries, judges, miners and many other groups occupy different positions on the two scales. The outstanding divergence is shown by the 'white-collar' class in industry. This class often earns less than the wage-earners, yet its occupational prestige is higher on account of the (often irrational) kudos conferred by non-pecuniary privileges: payment by salary and not by wage, later hours of work, different canteens, pension schemes, greater security, non-manual character of work, etc.

Indeed generally the 'middle-class' professions to-day, especially those which are paid by salary, are middle class much more by virtue of their non-pecuniary status than their income status, which is (relatively) much lower than it used to be. Conversely, some industrial workers, and most small traders (shopkeepers and the like), have made an advance in their income status which is in no way reflected in the prestige of their occupations. It is clear that we must treat income and non-pecuniary occupational status as two distinct and separate factors.

But in recent years, largely under the influence of social-anthropological studies of small towns, some sociologists have

[1] v. Ginsberg, op. cit., Ch. VI, for a clear statement of this view.

reacted against too exclusive an insistence even on very broadly-defined economic criteria. These studies[1] appear to show that social stratification is not always exactly correlated either with income or occupation, but rests partly on vaguer criteria of an individual's 'way of life', social habits and manners, and general pattern of consumption.

Thus Lloyd Warner found that in Yankee City class position was assessed in terms of type of house, dwelling area, style of clothes, kind of entertainment, etc., and that in consequence people's expenditure was strongly oriented towards winning social approval.[2] And these evaluations by no means coincided with income position; 'many people in classes below the two upper classes earned more money.'[3] Similarly in Plainville, Abram Kardiner found that the two main classes were divided more sharply and objectively by 'manners' (a conglomeration of cultural factors embracing house, car, food, dress, speech, and public behaviour) than by any other criterion. And again he found a low correlation with income: 'many lower-class families (perhaps a third) are richer than many upper-class families (perhaps another third)',[4] but their incomes do not suffice to hoist them over the class barrier.[5]

Detailed studies of consumption patterns show that the distribution of new and fashionable goods, which confer obvious social prestige, is often quite random from an income point of view.[6] An individual's pattern of consumption cannot be deduced from his position in the income scale; nor can his income be deduced from his pattern of consumption, which is dictated rather by a

[1] v. Lloyd Warner's study of Yankee City (Newburyport, Mass.), op. cit., and Abram Kardiner's of Plainville, U.S.A. (*The Psychological Frontiers of Society*, Columbia University, 1945.) Unfortunately no similar studies exist for Britain.

[2] op. cit., Chs. VI and XV.   [3] ibid., p. 287.   [4] op. cit., pp. 298-9.

[5] There is plenty of evidence that income is less and less the main socially-accepted criterion of high status. Certainly this is realised by rich men in America – consider the sad case of the corporation executives who, instead of being proud of the wide publicity which their salaries received when the U.S. Treasury decided to publish all salaries exceeding $75,000, fought this publicity and eventually, in 1949, succeeded in changing the law so as to discontinue publication.

Similarly in England rich people often become quite irritated if very high incomes are attributed to them. Of course this may be due to a fear lest details should come to the sharp ears of the Inland Revenue, or to anxiety about the possible reaction of workers or shareholders. But there is more to it than this; wealth as such is simply not esteemed (though it may still be desired!) as much as it used to be.

[6] v., for example, the study of the distribution of air-conditioning plants in an American suburb: 'The Web of Word of Mouth', by William H. Whyte Jr., *Fortune*, November 1954.

process of fashion leadership operating within his particular social group (and often transmitted in almost subterranean fashion by the children – 'Mummy, why can't we have a dish-washer too?').[1]

The most symbolic index of 'style of life' is of course dwelling-area: Kensington or Bermondsey; Edgbaston or Nechells; Woodstock Road or St. Ebbes; council-house or owner-occupier; East Side or West Side; uptown or downtown; the right or the wrong side of the tracks – these are the shorthand symbols often used for identifying an individual's class position. And this aggregation of individual differences in 'way of life' into distinct social and geographical units shows that consumption habits can give rise not merely to a continuing series of status rankings, but also to broad social strata.

These observations have led to a new emphasis in discussions of class. Veblen has come back into fashion; and great stress is once again laid on the *social* quality of consumption. The purpose[2] of expenditure is seen as not merely to satisfy wants or individual tastes, but also to meet the social standards of the group: not merely to give intrinsic pleasure and private gratification to the spender, but to validate, re-affirm, or enhance his social standing. Thus the criterion for consumption ceases to be the 'efficient' expenditure of funds as the mythical 'economic man' might see it, and becomes the expected social judgment of the group. Hence, in Veblen's phrase, the 'punctilious discrimination' in the choice of food, drink, service, ornaments, apparel, house, and amusements;[3] and to-day one would add car, television set, and domestic capital generally.

But we must not lean too heavily on Veblen. The significance of consumption in his theory was that it was taken as direct evidence of 'pecuniary strength'. Its social function was to demonstrate the wealth of the spender, and this required that it should take a conspicuous, ostentatious, and even wasteful form. It was, in effect, an external symbol, or demonstration, of a class structure already given by economic factors. A Veblenesque theory

---

[1] The distribution of TV sets has (at least until recently – they have now become much too common) been an example of this on housing estates in England. But TV in England has always had the peculiarity of showing a downward kink, so far as prestige is concerned, at a certain point in the social scale.

[2] Of course the purpose may be sub-conscious. This is an example, in Robert Merton's terminology (*v. Social Theory and Social Structure*, Ch. 1), of a latent as opposed to a manifest social function.

[3] Thorstein Veblen, *The Theory of the Leisure Class* (Huebsch, 1924), p. 74.

thus requires first that wealth is the one indispensable basis of esteem, and secondly that wealth is judged by the amount of conspicuous consumption.

But neither of these is the case to-day. (And neither was ever as true in Britain as in some other countries.)[1] Status is now assessed not solely by wealth, but also by the pattern of consumption; and this is judged not simply as a reflection of wealth, but as having an independent social value of its own. Thus the highest expenditure, while it may still demonstrate the greatest wealth, does not *ipso facto* confer the highest status; consumption has become not only an independent variable in social evaluations, but one which often fails to coincide with wealth. It follows that 'lavish display' and 'conspicuous waste' are no longer the socially relevant objectives of consumption. Indeed, perhaps we have gone to the other extreme. Ostentation is now usually considered vulgar; and the approval of the group is won not by exceeding, but on the contrary by adhering to, its collective standards of what is fashionable and in 'good taste'.[2]

However that may be, style of life and consumption habits exert an exceptionally strong influence on social judgments in Britain, because variations *between classes* are much greater than elsewhere. This is largely due to the fact that contemporary British society still bears deep marks of the hereditary, aristocratic society from which it descends. Thus different social classes can be instantly distinguished by their dress (especially men's clothes; though only a very insensitive person can share the now popular view that one cannot tell a woman's background by her clothes), eating (and even drinking) habits, taste in furniture, type of house, style of entertainment, sporting tastes, and leisure activities generally. And these contrasts are the more obtrusive owing to being articulated in a rather stratified pattern of social life, typified at the top by the social circle surrounding the Court, the elaborate ritual of 'coming out', and London society generally.

But part of the reason why these differences make so strong an impact is that they are associated with, and exaggerated by,

---

[1] Least of all amongst the upper classes, who never judged status solely by wealth, and despised the *nouveaux-riche* when they indulged in ostentatious, Veblenesque behaviour. Status was quite simply a matter of lineage. But the industrial bourgeoisie had a much more Veblenesque attitude.

[2] Veblen's second index of pecuniary strength, the conspicuous abstention from labour, also attracts more disapproval than approval to-day.

the most supremely unmistakable of all symbols of social standing – differences of accent and vocabulary. In no other country is it possible in the same way to assess a person's class standing the moment he opens his mouth; and this fact exaggerates to an extraordinary degree the importance of 'style' as a determinant of class. Even in 1956, Eliza Doolittle is not looked on in Britain as a completely absurd period character; but abroad *Pygmalion* is always regarded as a wildly improbable British farce.[1]

Now these differences are not merely a consequence or derivative of other, economic, class determinants. They are not precisely correlated either with income – the oldest and most 'socially-esteemed' section of the aristocracy may (and often does) legitimately envy the wealth of top business executives or self-made financiers – or with economic power, as can be seen by considering the cohorts of elegant, well-bred young men swarming unimportantly through the merchant banks and discount houses of the City. There is, of course, a link through time; the *nouveau-riche*, himself by now ennobled, will send his son to Eton and Oxford, where he will have no difficulty in acquiring the necessary social polish. But at any given moment a pecuniary and a stylistic index may give different results.

The closest correlation in England, so far as accent, social manners, and style of life are concerned, is with education, and to a lesser extent with occupational prestige; though outside the upper, public-school-educated groups the pattern of consumption is more nearly, though not exactly, correlated with income. This interacting triad, at the top of the social scale, of education, style of life, and occupational status is unquestionably a more important cause of social inequality than income; if we understand this, we shall be less puzzled by the relative failure of income-redistribution to diminish class-consciousness.

v *Power as a Stratifying Influence*

The last determinant to be considered is 'power'. There is evidently some sense in which power is a status-conferring attribute, with a strong influence on collective feelings of superiority

[1] And is there any other country in which articles on 'U' and 'non-U' words (*v. Encounter*, October 1955) would be treated not just as an engaging frivolity, but as describing a serious (and to many people, for all their humorous denials to the contrary, subjectively important) aspect of social class?

and inferiority. But it is, unfortunately, an ambiguous concept, with many possible meanings. Naturally we are not concerned with its purely individual or random manifestations, with the hypnotist or the sadist, but only with those which are common to entire social groups. But even here one cannot easily attach a precise or unique meaning to so many-sided a concept; we can only pick out a number of separate aspects which seem significant for the class system.

First, the direct 'face-to-face' power of individuals over the lives and fortunes of other individuals, where both sets of individuals can be aggregated into social categories. This is most obviously characteristic of industry, where a clear hierarchy exists in respect of power to sack, demote or promote, pay higher or lower incomes, move people from one place to another, organise work in a particular way, and generally influence, if not determine, the income, nature of employment, and occupational status of employees. This hierarchy is not, as the Marxists suppose, related to an index of ownership, but simply to location in the organisational structure.

There has now grown up, following the rapid extension of the activities of the state, a parallel hierarchy of bureaucratic power in the political-administrative sphere. A large class of public officials, charged with interpreting and executing government regulations, wields a power over the lives and fortunes of individual citizens quite comparable with that traditionally imputed by socialists to the businessman; power to issue or withhold materials, permit or forbid the building of a factory, dispossess or decline to 're-possess' a landowner, keep people incarcerated in mental institutions, grant or withhold assistance payments, and so on. Indeed, such power-hierarchies are becoming more and more common with the growth in organisational scale; even the professions are now becoming bureaucratised, with the result that power-positions become codified and consolidated as compared with an era when professional people worked on their own account.[1]

These power hierarchies are undoubtedly a source of social stratification, and again one which does not exactly coincide with

[1] An increasing number of professional (and even academic) people now work in large-scale organisations – in private business, nationalised industries, government bodies, large hospitals, research foundations, and so on.

other sources. It may well be that a Dorsetshire landowner, perhaps a Lieutenant-Commander married into the aristocracy, has a higher income and occupational prestige, and certainly a more elegant style of life, than the Ministry of Agriculture officials who refuse to restore his land. The businessman seeking a licence from the Board of Trade may have twice the income of the young Principal who decides his application. The personnel manager in a large firm has a degree of 'face-to-face' power which is quite disproportionate to his income. Thus power as a stratifying factor cannot be subsumed under a simple wealth criterion.

Secondly, the 'remote' power to take decisions affecting not merely the individual, but entire categories of persons. With the growth of scale and the inevitable concentration of decision-making, a relatively small class of high executives in both public and private industry, and also in the Trade Unions, now wields a strategic power occasionally over the life of the nation, frequently over an entire industry, and continuously over the hundreds or thousands of employees of a firm.[1] Such power, being inevitably wielded to some extent in secret, and without collecting the voices of the people most affected, has a quality of remoteness and detachment which makes it a particularly fertile source of resentment, and hence, since the disparities between controllers and controlled are so wide, of deep class consciousness.

Now such immense power of *fiat*, although inseparable from the mass organisation typical of an advanced industrial country, may be more or less autocratic and irresponsible according to the institutional framework, the social climate of opinion, the balance of power between conflicting groups (e.g. employers and Trade Unions), and the degree of intervention by the state. And it was suggested in Chapter I that in private industry in particular it was now less irresponsible, and altogether more circumscribed by checks and balances, than was the case a generation ago. Nevertheless it still commands a wide area of social life, and still gives rise to marked hostilities – not only in private industry, but equally in other large-scale organisations, notably the nationalised industries and the large Trade Unions, where an alarming gap, marked by heavy suspicion on both

[1] The fact that this power resides as obviously in the public sector and the Trade Unions as in private industry shows how far removed the problem is from the traditional 'capitalist economic power' of pre-war socialist theory.

sides, sometimes opens out between leadership and rank-and-file.

Again, this power is not exactly correlated with income. The heads of nationalised industries, top civil servants, and Trade Union leaders are paid salaries in no way commensurate with their position in the power hierarchy. (The case of Trade Union leaders is a fascinating example of the 'scatter' of high status attributes: in terms of lineage they might be considered working class, by income-standards or occupational status they are middle class, as judged by power they are indisputably upper class.) Even within industry, with the growth of specialisation, the new organisational or technical classes in the middle ranks of management may wield nearly as much power of this kind as higher-paid top executives, and certainly more than wealthier men in small-scale enterprises.[1]

Political power can also have an influence on class attitudes, but in a democracy only, I think, if one party remains in office for a long period. If the pendulum is swinging each five years, I doubt if the political factor exerts an independent influence, since political power is not then thought of as an attribute of any one class. But if one party remains in power (say) for twenty years, then attitudes become adjusted to that fact, and political power is conceived as being an additional attribute of the class on which that party is predominantly based.

Thus in Britain before the war, when Conservative Governments seemed the normal thing, collective feelings of superiority and inferiority were intensified by the belief that political power was an additional, semi-permanent attribute of a class which already appeared to possess all the other attributes of a ruling class. Conversely, in Sweden, the fact that a Socialist Government now seems the natural order of things has a profound effect in weakening collective class feelings, since at least the attribute of political power is differently located from the other attributes of the 'upper class'.

It creates, in other words, a definite 'scatter', and prevents a concentration, of 'top-class attributes'. The worker knows that

[1] 'Organisation people don't make the big money. But though it may be the automobile dealer and the owner of the local bottling franchise who drive the Cadillacs, it is the organisation man who now makes the decisions that most affect the lives of others. "Those fat cats around here are falling over themselves entertaining Charlie", says the wife of a plant engineer. "They could buy and sell us twice over, but he's going to decide the location of the new chemical plant." ' (Quoted from 'The Transients', by William H. Whyte Jr., *Fortune*, May 1953.)

even though his income, occupational status, way of life, and whatever else, may be lower than those of his employer, yet ultimately his political power is greater; and the employer feels the same. Thus political power counterbalances the influence of other class determinants, and hence diminishes the likelihood of strong, coagulated class feelings. But this will occur only if the period of one-party rule is sufficiently prolonged to cause a definite adjustment in psychological attitudes.

There are still other aspects of power of great interest from the point of view of class, such as social power in a small community.[1] This is still immensely strong in English rural and country towns, where there exists a subtle and elaborate, but precise and universally recognised, hierarchy of social power, again not exactly correlated with income. But this sort of power is essentially a matter of rural or small-town class relationships; and in industrial Britain the nationally significant determinants of class must be sought in urban influences and attitudes. Moreover local power of this sort is much weaker now than fifty years ago, and it is doubtful if it would survive as an important independent influence on social stratification if the other determinants were not so strong.

It is therefore the first two manifestations of power which seem, under contemporary conditions, to be the most significant. They do not, of course, exhaust all that can be said about the relation of status to power; there are many quaint discrepancies tucked away in odd corners of the social map. Members of Parliament, for example, presumably on account of a certain limited access to power, achieve a social esteem which, although by no means high, is certainly higher than could be explained by their income, and is perhaps not wholly justified by their way of life and consumption habits.

But such deviant cases are not very common; and power now has its main impact on social stratification through either the 'face-to-face' or the remote strategic power characteristic especially of large-scale industry. This is a major influence on the degree of social inequality, and again one which will not be much affected by measures of income-redistribution.

[1] This was strongly emphasised by the Lynds in their Middletown studies, especially in relation to the position of the X family. (v. Robert S. and Helen M. Lynd, *Middletown* (Harcourt, Brace, 1929), e.g. p. 301, and *Middletown in Transition* (ditto, 1937), e.g. p. 91.)

VI *The Subjective Theory of Class*

But suppose that class is not objectively determined at all? Some sociologists now favour a 'subjective' theory of class, on the grounds that in practice people appear not to think and act alike, or to fall into social classes, merely because they have similar occupations or incomes or whatever it may be; nor does their account of the class system, when questioned, base itself on any such objective criteria.[1]

On this view, people belong to the class which they think they belong to, or are thought to belong to. Class is simply what people say it is; and the final criteria are the subjective evaluations and self-placements of the society itself, as expressed in such phrases as 'they belong to our set', 'they don't fit in with our crowd', 'we don't know her family', 'I never saw her socially in my life', 'they are ordinary people like us', 'you feel at home with them', etc.

'Classes are psycho-social groupings, something that is essentially subjective in character, dependent on class-consciousness (i.e. a feeling of group membership), and class lines of cleavage may or may not conform to what seem to social scientists to be logical lines of cleavage in the objective or stratification sense'.[2] This being so, one unravels the class system simply by asking people questions. 'In the final analysis', writes Lloyd Warner, 'individuals were placed by the evaluations of the members of Yankee City itself.'[3]

It is not quite clear what is meant by calling this a subjective view of class. Such a view, if the word is used in its normal sense, would appear to imply that a person belongs to a social class because he says, or thinks, that he does. This proposition is not often advanced, since it would almost imply that an individual can select which class he wishes to belong to, in which case the word class would surely lose all meaning. Surveys show, for example, that most people (though not, of course, the upper classes, nor occasionally, for opposite reasons, middle-class Labour M.Ps.) assess themselves as middle-class. But if a person says that

[1] *v.* Lloyd Warner, op. cit., Ch. V.
[2] Richard Centers, *The Psychology of Social Classes* (Princeton University Press, 1949), p. 27.
[3] op. cit., p. 90.

he is middle class, yet others whom he also considers middle class refuse to accept him as a social equal, or to mix with him socially, then his self-placement is not confirmed by society. The indispensable factor of social recognition is lacking; and his self-judgment is not a statement about actual stratification, but a personal aspiration. Thus merely because a group of people say that they are middle class, one cannot treat them as socially homogeneous if in fact they are manifestly scattered all over the social map.

But all that appears to be meant by the 'subjective' view is that people belong to a class if they say or think they do, *and are recognised by others as so doing*. This seems quite consistent with the definitions of class given at the beginning of the chapter; and there seems nothing in any 'subjective' view as such which casts doubts on the common-sense list of determinants given above.[1]

It is true that the method of asking people questions may give apparently different results if people are asked not merely *what* class they place other people in, but *why*. The answers to the first question may coincide with the results of applying the objective criteria, but the answers to the second may bear little or no relation to any objective indices. People may allege that they base their class judgments on a, b, and c; but we might observe that the stratification resulting from those judgments bore little relationship to a, b, and c, but was closely related to x, y, and z. Then factors a, b, and c are evidently rationalisations of the real determinants. No doubt such rationalisation is quite common.[2] But it in no way affects the possibility of unravelling the class system by an objective approach.

It therefore seems reasonable to conclude that class location

[1] The classification elicited by the 'subjective' method of asking people questions, and the objective method of applying external criteria, must of course correspond if the objective criteria are correctly chosen. Thus Lloyd Warner found that with the aid of certain objective criteria he could 'determine very quickly the approximate place of any individual in the society', even though he placed individuals finally according to the evaluations of Yankee City itself (op. cit., p. 90); indeed, the correspondence was so close that he could have abandoned the 'subjective' evaluations altogether. It is true that this particular correspondence has been criticised as being true only of the upper classes in American small towns (*v.* 'Social Status and Social Structure', by Seymour M. Lipset and Reinhard Bendix, *British Journal of Sociology*, June 1951). But this is only a criticism of the list of criteria; the correspondence would be equally true of a working-class area provided the criteria were correctly chosen.

[2] Kardiner gives an example from Plainville, where much lip-service was paid to morals as a criterion of class, although it did not in fact appear to determine class divisions in the slightest degree. It could hardly be said to be a determinant in Britain, in view of the frequent appearance in court of members of the upper class.

is broadly determined by certain objective factors: that these factors will naturally vary through time, and between societies: but that the factors listed above, although they do not always coincide, appear to be the most influential in the advanced industrial countries of the West. At the same time, class attitudes may be subjectively explained or rationalised in rather different terms; and subjective collective evaluations are of course a necessary condition of people being *conscious* of class at all – without them, class would be not a social reality, but merely a formal construction of the social scientist.

VII   *Do Classes Exist and Do They Matter?*

Class, in the sense both of class-consciousness and the existence of clearly-defined classes, is an exceptionally marked phenomenon in British life. These two are not necessarily the same thing. We might have class-consciousness, but no classes. Professor Marshall has pointed out that in a socially heterogeneous community 'we may say that there is a national class system, in the sense, only, that class is a feature of the lives of all nationals, but that there are no national classes'.[1] The lines of class might be diagonal and criss-crossing, and the resulting sub-classes intermingle and overlap to an extent which, while it left plenty of scope for class feelings, did not allow the clear delineation of national social groups.

Whether national classes exist or not will depend on how far the separate determinants make a few broad and deep incisions into the social body, as opposed to innumerable shallow cuts; and how far these deep incisions coincide to form a single set of national divisions. Of course the coincidence will never be exact, as was made clear when the separate determinants were under discussion. But it does not follow from the existence of *some* overlap that every individual is merely an indeterminate bundle of conflicting social attributes, some belonging to a higher order and others to a lower, with no definite class location. If all the separate determinants are influential, it only requires a reasonable tendency towards coincident breaks and clusters for national classes to emerge.

[1] *Citizenship and Social Class*, p. 95.

This tendency is certainly evident in Britain. The hierarchies of education, occupational prestige, and style of life all show pronounced and visible breaks; and these breaks broadly coincide. They do so partly because they are causally related; a segregated three-tier system of education[1] imposes a corresponding pattern on the other two criteria. And inheritance is an additional factor making for correspondence. Of course ambivalent cases exist. But the correlation is sufficiently close to impart a strong significance at least to the tripartite division of working, middle, and upper classes. People accept this division subjectively as a reality; it influences their behaviour towards other people, and their social judgments. And it is objectively real in the sense that it would emerge, without asking people for their subjective evaluations, from the external application of at least the three criteria mentioned above (though not necessarily of the income criterion).

Even a somewhat more refined sub-division is not meaningless. People often employ a five-class framework when making social judgments (upper, upper middle, lower middle, upper working and working). This division also seems to have a genuine subjective and objective reality; people who speak in these terms are not saying things which their listeners fail to understand; and the factor of social recognition is clearly present. The indeterminate cases, of course, will now be more numerous. But even if they form quite a substantial minority, the 'tone' of social relationships will still be set by the majority whose class position is fairly unambiguous.

But why does the existence of classes and class-consciousness matter? It would matter rather obviously if it gave rise to a continuous, violent class conflict. But there is no necessary reason why it should. Of course different classes will always have divergent interests. They must compete over the distribution of class privileges, and each has a direct interest in preserving or improving its superior or inferior position. The consequence is a real class rivalry, either manifest or latent according to historical circumstances. '

This rivalry is normally articulated in the political system. Except in those countries with deep religious or regional divisions,

[1] That is, public, grammar, and secondary modern (plus occasionally technical) schools.

political parties are usually horizontally based, each party drawing its main support from particular class strata in the population. In Britain, for example, Labour and Conservative voters
are more accurately divided by the median line of class position
than by any other single factor. This is not to say that class
location alone determines political opinions, or that the correspondence is other than ragged and untidy. It is notorious that
some 'middle-class' electors habitually vote Labour, and a great
many 'working-class' electors vote Conservative. This proves
(according to taste) that some people either do not know where
their true interests lie, or that they know and act irrationally
nevertheless,[1] or that they know but are quite rationally influenced by non-class factors.

Naturally a two-party system cannot reflect, say, a fivefold
class division. Yet even a more refined class construction appears
to be mirrored in political *attitudes*. If the entire upper one-third
of the population is sub-divided into broad social categories, and
these are arranged in descending series according to income and
occupation, then the lower the category, the higher the ratio of
Labour to Conservative voters.[2]

But the fact that classes have divergent interests, which are
expressed in political terms, does not mean that violent class
conflict is endemic in our society. The Marxist theory of class
conflict was based on a theory of 'internal contradictions': 'the
basis of the class struggle is the contradiction between material
productive forces and existing relations of production'. No doubt
this contradiction has existed at certain periods of history; no
doubt also, even when it has not, class conflict can be all too easily
induced by unbearable material conditions, or economic instability, or extreme contrasts between poverty and wealth. But
neither the inner contradiction, nor any of these other factors, is
present in Britain to-day; and the various changes described in
Part One may be taken as excluding the likelihood of any explosive

---

[1] It is clear that no rational interpretation can explain *all* political behaviour. One
cannot, for example, explain Communist or Fascist attitudes in terms which do not
also explain the propensity of these parties, not shared by more moderate parties, to
daub slogans on walls.

[2] *v.* John Bonham, *The Middle Class Vote* (Faber, 1954). Mr. Bonham's total
'middle class', defined as all those in non-manual employment and numbering with
their families some 10 million voters, divided 3 : 1 in favour of the Conservatives
in 1951. If clerks, small shopkeepers and similar groups are excluded, the ratio
becomes 5 : 1; and if only well-to-do proprietors, managers and the higher professions are included, it becomes 12 : 1.

conflict. The dispute over the distribution of class privilege will remain pacific and tolerant, held firmly within the limits of democratic procedure.

But this greater equanimity of class relations does not necessarily lead to a *pro rata* diminution in class-consciousness, or even a blurring of class lines; and the reason why class matters in Britain is that a high degree of class-consciousness and a strongly-etched class hierarchy, such as we still have, at once implies and involves a correspondingly high degree of social inequality. Subjectively, it involves particularly strong collective and individual feelings of class position, which are at least potential causes of antagonism and resentment. Objectively, it implies wide gaps in respect of the various class determinants – income, power, style of life, and so on; and this in turn leads to an exceptional degree of cultural differentiation, and lack of uninhibited social intercourse between the different classes.

Now this state of affairs is not immutable. Nobody supposes, it is true, that class-consciousness can be wholly eliminated in any society. Nor is there any unit of measurement by which one society can be judged to be twice as class-conscious as another. Yet clearly subjective class feelings, and freedom of social intercourse, can be either greater or less; and on this basis descriptive and comparative statements about different societies are not meaningless. Thus it is not absurd to say that Elizabethan England was less of a class society than feudal England, or contemporary New Zealand than Egypt, or Illinois than New England, or Sweden than Great Britain.

Differences in the degree of class-consciousness and social inequality between different countries would appear to depend, according to the argument of this chapter, broadly on the following influences. (In practice of course these are mixed up; they are distinguished only for convenience.) First, the technological factor: the stage of economic development reached, and in particular whether the system of production is sufficiently primitive to give rise to a few clear-cut economic classes, each functionally related to the means of production, and to deal out goods in such meagre quantities as compared with people's aspirations that social attitudes are dominated by crude economic resentments.

Secondly, the mobility factor: the degree of vertical mobility between classes, and the area of free social movement. Clearly the greater the mobility, the greater the degree of social equality and free social intercourse; and the less the social system will be frozen into clearly defined and sharply separated strata.

Thirdly, the distance factor: the extent to which the various determinants of class make deep incisions, the social distance between these incisions, and generally the length of the status ladder in each of the separate spheres. These determinants, as listed earlier, are monetary wealth, occupational prestige, education, style of life and consumption habits, and power (of which the middle three appear in Britain to be the most important and the most closely correlated). To a greater or lesser extent, the scatter or concentration of these determinants is under social control; and a society therefore has it within its power, if it so wishes, at least to influence the degree of class-consciousness and inequality.

The discussion of class does not of course exhaust the subject of social equality. Even if national classes were to wither away, a status hierarchy of some sort would still exist; for any society must have some structure of conventional and accepted rankings. It is conceivable that such a status hierarchy might be as rigid and unequal as the class hierarchy which it supersedes. This is perhaps unlikely in practice; it is hard to believe that the disappearance of broad class demarcations, and their replacement by a continuous series of status gradations, would not diminish social inequality.

But if it does not, or if it still leaves too great a gap between the top and bottom of the status scale, this will make little difference to the direction of policy. In any given country, either a clear class stratification, or extreme status inequalities, are likely to rest on the same broad set of social factors; and whether one is interested in class-consciousness as such, therefore, or in inequalities of status in some more general sense, the programme of action for an egalitarian will be much the same.

VII

THE CASE FOR SOCIAL EQUALITY

1 *The Economic Welfare Argument*

IT still has to be shown that more equality would be a good thing. This cannot now be demonstrated by certain economic arguments which were often used before the war.

At any time up to 1939, the case for greater equality, at least of incomes, seemed self-evident. By making the rich less rich, the poor could be made less poor; and to all those with a social conscience this seemed a sufficient and conclusive argument. It appealed to every humanitarian sentiment, and to ordinary feelings of justice and compassion; while on the intellectual plane it was reinforced by the powerful influence of utilitarian thought. Poverty in the midst of plenty seemed obviously repugnant, and great wealth a disgrace because it appeared the cause of great poverty. To take some caviar from the rich, and distribute it in bread to the poor, was a clear moral imperative.

But we have now reached the point where further redistribution would make little difference to the standard of living of the masses; to make the rich less rich would not make the poor significantly less poor. If we distributed all surtax incomes amongst the working class, the latter would gain by at most a few shillings a week per head; and nobody supposes that even this is possible in practice. The main prop of traditional egalitarianism has been knocked away by its own success.

Further redistribution therefore cannot be clearly justified by the once-popular argument that to take £1 away from a rich man, and to give it to a poor man, will manifestly increase economic welfare. It is not that the argument itself has become untrue, but simply that if we are considering vertical redistribution *between entire social classes*, there are too few pounds. When the pound taken from the millionaire has to be spread in farthings amongst 960 beneficiaries, the welfare criterion inevitably gives an ambiguous answer; and few people would judge that a clear gain would result.

There is the further difficulty that any practicable redistribution, now that the extremes of wealth are so much less marked, would never be simply between rich and poor, but would also affect much larger numbers of intermediate people; and here it would be singularly hard to measure the gains against the losses. Generally, the further away we move from extreme inequality, the harder it becomes to draw up any agreed balance-sheet, and the more likely people are simply to differ hopelessly about whether economic satisfaction would or would not be increased by further vertical redistribution.

The traditional welfare argument, therefore, while it still justifies selective measures of redistribution towards small groups whose average gain might be significantly large, no longer clearly justifies overall measures of vertical redistribution; and one cannot state unequivocally that a greater equality of income will increase economic welfare.

Then what is the justification for continuing to preach greater equality? Why should the much-taxed rich, who have already lost so much, be further milched, if the result is not to be a clear increase in welfare? Socialists have been slow to realise that these are serious questions (especially now that they are backed by plausible arguments about incentives and personal savings); they often continue to speak as though the egalitarian case still rested on a self-evident proposition about welfare.[1] But in fact if we want more equality, the case for it must rest on statements largely, if not entirely, unrelated to economic welfare.[2]

---

[1] cf. the statement in *New Fabian Essays*: 'The more evenly wealth is divided the more welfare it will promote' (p. 71).

[2] Another economic argument often used before the war has also lost its force: namely, that a greater equality of wealth, because it would raise consumption at the expense of saving, was essential to full employment. To-day the problem is to increase, not diminish, savings.

II   *The Persistence of Collective Resentments*

Nevertheless the case can still rest firmly, as I believe, on certain value or ethical judgments of a non-economic character: on a belief that more equality, even though carrying few implications for the sum of economic satisfaction, would yet conduce to a 'better' society. This I believe to be so for three reasons, relating respectively to the diminution of social antagonism, to social justice, and to the avoidance of social waste. These will be considered in turn. [1]

Extreme inequalities can obviously give rise to antagonism by evoking purely *individual* feelings of frustration, envy, and resentment. In the past, such feelings have usually been associated with glaring inequalities of wealth. Even economists have long realised that high consumption by the rich cannot be treated in isolation as merely giving a certain quantum of satisfaction to the rich consumers; it also has consequences for other people's states of mind. 'The affluence of the rich', wrote Adam Smith, 'excites the envy of the poor, who are often both driven by want and prompted by envy to invade his possession.'

In contemporary British Society the poor are no longer driven by want to invade the possessions of the rich; and I doubt whether at present levels of real wages they are individually much prompted by envy. Contrasts in wealth, taken in isolation, do not now seem to cause widespread resentment. The ordinary worker feels no very bitter antagonism to the ostentations of a George Dawson or a Lady Docker (though he feels a great deal to any suggestion of higher salaries for his Trade Union leaders).

But we observe a widespread persistence of *collective* manifestations of discontent, which occur when resentments are articulated in, and then fed by, overt, explicit group hostilities.

Such hostilities are most apparent in industry, where they express themselves in unofficial strikes, lack of co-operation, and a general atmosphere of suspicious antagonism. I do not, of course, mean to suggest that industrial relations are worse in Britain than in most other countries – they are not. And they are infinitely better than they were 20 or 30 years ago. But are they not worse

---

[1] I discuss here only those arguments which have an obvious application to present-day British society. The more abstract argument for equality, based on the notion of a "common humanity", is discussed in the next chapter.

than one would expect, considering the absence of the normal economic irritants? Traditionally, industrial antagonism is caused by
unemployment, poverty, falling real wages, or a wage offensive by
employers. None of these causes is present, yet a surprising amount
of unrest persists. This surely suggests that it has not an economic,
but a sociological origin; and it is significant that with a few
exceptions, such as the railways, there is little correlation between
low wages and bad relations. Rather, indeed, the reverse; those
industries the most susceptible to wild-cat strikes – coal, docks, and
the metal and engineering trades – are exceptionally high-wage
occupations.

A parallel phenomenon is apparent in the political sphere. A
country's political deportment, and the atmosphere of its debates,
will normally reflect – allowing, of course, for the vagaries of
national character – the degree of underlying social tension. Now
British Parliamentarians are well accustomed to receiving, and
graciously acknowledging, the admiring congratulations of
foreign visitors on the tolerant and friendly atmosphere of the
House of Commons, the gentlemanly conduct of debate, the inter-
party social intercourse, the absence of fisticuffs and unruly
scenes; and undoubtedly these agreeable features of our political
life are conspicuous by international standards.

But before we deduce from this the absence of serious social
tensions, we must consider whether these easy-going inter-party
relationships are not misleading, inasmuch as they distract
attention from the true locus of political bitterness, which is now
within the Left itself. The most angry quarrels in recent British
politics have erupted not in the Chamber of the House of Commons, but in upstairs committee rooms, at the annual Labour
Conference, and in local Party meetings.

These quarrels on the Left were particularly violent for some
years after 1951. It is difficult to argue that they were *about*
anything real, or that the so-called Right and Left were genuinely
divided by serious, clear-cut policy differences,[1] But this is
irrelevant; bitter or resentful feelings often fail to clothe themselves
in cool, rational statements of policy. It is the depth of the bitterness, and not its verbal formulation, which is significant; and this

[1] Consider the ludicrously disproportionate fury aroused in 1951 by a dispute as
to whether £300 millions more or less should be spent on armaments out of a national
income of £13,000 millions.

was abundantly displayed during the ugly, long drawn-out history of the 'Bevanite' dispute.

This bitterness is only a reflection of a curiously strong tendency within the Labour Party towards a suspicious, militant, class-conscious Leftism.[1] It is a tendency which goes too deep to be explicable merely in terms of the brilliant personality of its most recent mouthpiece – Mr. Bevan only articulated a resentment which was already there. Nor can it be explained away as an inevitable reaction to Britain's changed and vulnerable position in a world dominated by America, Russia, and the hydrogen bomb. Certainly anti-Americanism, and a vague semi-pacifism and semi-neutralism, are obvious symptoms of the mood; anti-Americanism in particular is an almost universal left-wing neurosis, springing from a natural resentment at the transfer of world power from London to Washington, combined with the need to find some new and powerful scapegoat to replace the capitalists at home, their utility in this role being much diminished under full employment and the Welfare State.

But the world situation cannot provide the basic explanation. The actual divergences between Left and Right on defence or foreign policy were often far too trivial to account for all the bitterness; moreover this would not explain why it should be concentrated in particular social groups and at a particular point in the political spectrum. Anti-Americanism and anxiety over nuclear weapons are no more the real explanation of militant Leftism, than anti-Communism is of American McCarthyism; in both cases these are simply rationalisations of some deeper discontent.

The persistence of so much political resentment in Britain is surely surprising. Of course it is less marked than in certain Continental countries, and than it was before the war – but so it should be. One does not expect all countries to run the same political temperature at all times. We should expect extremism to be rampant, and tempers high, in societies suffering from unemployment, or low living standards, or huge disparities between wealth and poverty. But we should not expect it in countries enjoying, as Britain does, full employment, social security, rising

[1] I use the terms Left and Right only as they are now conventionally, though oddly, applied. In fact if Left is taken to imply intellectually radical, and Right intellectually traditional, they should be transposed in their application to the two wings of the Labour Party.

real incomes, and (by historical standards) a marked equality in
the distribution of incomes. (Or we might expect it in countries
suffering from violent ethnic, racial, or religious tensions; but
Britain is fortunate in being immune from all of these.)

And it is significant that the Scandinavian countries, which
have broadly the same political and economic climate, can show
no similar degree of bitterness on the Left, and no parallel to our
militant Leftism. Is it just an accident that the one respect in
which they differ conspicuously from us is in the degree of social
equality and class stratification?

It seems at least conceivable that the persistence in Britain,
despite all the social and economic improvements of the last two
decades, and in the face of a naturally amiable and even sunny
national character, of so much resentment, so many unofficial
strikes, so many touchy, prickly, indignant and frustrated citizens
in politics and industry, with grudges against society and grievances
at work, sending telegrams and passing angry resolutions,
flocking to meetings not with badges, but with chips on their
shoulders, peevishly waiting for someone to knock them off:
that this can be traced to underlying sociological causes, and
partakes, even if often sub-consciously, of that resentment against
social inequality which is characteristic of class antagonism.

III   *The Theory of Social Politics*

The possibility of a sociological cause has been rather neglected
in this country, where we still tend to assume that politics, and
industrial relations, should be interpreted in basically economic
terms. But whatever may have been true in the past, we must
now distinguish between what may loosely be called Economic
Politics and Social Politics. I do not mean that the distinction is
ever complete or clear-cut, only that there is a definite bias in one
direction or the other.[1]

Economic Politics are characteristic of any country or situation
to which a Marxist analysis might plausibly be applied. Thus they

[1] Some American writers, with broadly the same ideas in mind, have distinguished
between class politics and status politics. (*v. The New American Right*, ed. Daniel Bell,
Criterion Books, New York, 1955.) I am not sure that this is a wholly satisfactory
distinction. But the analyses in Mr. Bell's book of the social roots of McCarthyism
(especially the essays of Professors Riesman, Lipset, and Hofstadter) have greatly
helped to clear my mind on this whole subject.

are typical of periods of growing pauperisation, depression and mass unemployment, falling real wages, and a sharp polarisation of classes. It is at such times, when a direct clash of economic interest occurs between clear-cut productive classes against a background of material scarcity, that economic issues are the main determinant of political attitudes.

Social Politics are characteristic of periods of prosperity, rising incomes, full employment, and inflation, when attention is diverted from economic to social issues not only for the obvious reason that as living standards rise, and the problem of subsistence fades away, people have more time and mental energy to spare for non-economic discontents, but also for another reason.

Prosperity is typically associated with rapid economic change – either the sharp change from depression to boom, or the steadier change characteristic of any period of rapidly advancing technology. Such changes inevitably cause large shifts in relative incomes. As a result, the income hierarchy gets out of alignment with the class or social hierarchy. The latter, based on socially recognised evaluations having deep roots in the past and backed by a heavy weight of tradition, cannot adjust itself with sufficient speed to changes in the former. Consequently, some social groups feel that their position in the social hierarchy is not commensurate with their new and higher income status, while others feel that their worsened relative incomes are not commensurate with their traditional position in the social hierarchy. Such feelings are exceptionally productive of class tensions and resentment, although these will not be located, as they are under Economic Politics, in the worst-off, but in relatively well-off sections of the population.

Examples of the latter groups, which feel their social position menaced, not indeed by absolute poverty, but by the prospect of humiliating relegation as previous social relationships are disturbed by economic change, are certain sections of the European middle classes in the 1920s, threatened by inflation and turning to Fascism to protect their class position; or the old-family Anglo-Saxon upper class in the United States, left far behind in the economic race, steadily losing its erstwhile dominance to newer immigrant groups and the rising industrial middle class, and expressing its resentment in vehement support for the extremist wing of the Republican Party: or, in Britain to-day, certain salaried classes (e.g. teachers) or skilled groups (e.g. compositors,

or members of A.S.L.E.F. on the railways) whose differentials
have been narrowed by inflation, and whose relative income-
position is much worse both than it was before the war and than
the degree of skill would appear to justify: or, again, the lower
managerial grades in industry, who, having now lost much of
their income-advantage over the wage-earners, react by emphasis-
ing their social, non-pecuniary higher status.

Examples of the former groups, whose economic status has
risen without a corresponding promotion in the social scale, are
any *nouveau-riche* business class suddenly enriched by inflation or
full employment, from Texas oil millionaires to small shopkeepers
or sole proprietors, now highly prosperous but still socially insecure, feeling themselves slighted both by the gentry and the
intelligentsia, envying the self-assurance of the one and the
culture of the other, and growing resentful at their lack of social
recognition: or, as so often in the U.S.A., immigrant groups of
workers, for long excluded from the better occupations, who,
having now finally achieved a satisfactory economic status, yet
still encounter social snobbery and disdain from the native stock,
and turn angrily to McCarthyism to demonstrate their 100%
Americanism: or, again, certain fortunate sections of the working
class suddenly propelled by full employment towards an altogether
higher income status than any to which they had previously
aspired, yet still labelled and looked upon as 'working class'
or 'labour'; or, more generally, that section of the working
class whose earnings rise most rapidly at a time of rising
productivity.

Surely it is these last two groups which, in Britain, are now the
main source of both industrial and political discontent.[1] On the
industrial side, the industries with the worst relations, and the most
susceptible to outbursts of antagonism, are the coal-mines, the
docks, and sections of the engineering trades. It is significant that
the workers in these industries not merely enjoy exceptionally
high wages, well above the average for industry as a whole, but
have experienced a notable *relative* rise in the income structure
without, however, gaining correspondingly in social prestige.
The result is a marked discrepancy between the new economic
and the old social status.

---

[1] Though a subsidiary source is to be found in the penultimate one of the groups
mentioned earlier (e.g. skilled railwaymen and teachers).

May this not be the fundamental cause of these industrial discontents? Certainly this view finds support in such few sociological studies of these industries as have yet been made. 'The miner still believes', wrote Mr. Zweig, 'that both the public and the management are against him, and he has the nobody-likes-me feeling. He still remembers all the sayings against him and all the catch-phrases used by the snobbish "petty bourgeois". . . . He was, and as a matter of fact still is, looked down on. . . . Even his own son who has managed to get away from the mines might look upon his father as someone who was unable to do better. . . . Probably as this inferiority complex has developed it has by way of compensation become a superiority complex expressed in the aggressive attitude which the miners sometimes assume.'[1]

Another study speaks of 'the belief that the public regards the miner as an inferior type of being and almost a social outcast. These are strong words, but nothing weaker will convey the intensity of the miners' convictions. . . . Many of the apparently futile quarrels over wages are expressions of a feeling that the men's services, and hence the men themselves, are undervalued. . . . The absence of baths was seen as a social stigma rather than a physical inconvenience. In the same way, the proposal to employ Poles or Italians in the pits is interpreted as an insult; what they really resent is the suggestion that only unemployed foreigners can be conscripted to do the miner's work.'[2]

The same concern with social status emerges in the docks. 'The attitude of other people towards them has created widespread resentment among dock workers and provoked them to aggression and hostility which on occasion has led to outbreaks of violent or anti-social behaviour. . . . In spite of the improvements in wages and conditions which have taken place dock work still remains a relatively low-status occupation. . . . For their part, the dock workers have become more self-conscious.' Thus they excused themselves for being dock workers, and 'some of those with children at grammar schools admitted that they had told the children to do their best to conceal the fact that their fathers were dock workers.'[3]

This combination of a newly-won high income status, and an

[1] F. Zweig, *Men in the Pits* (Gollancz, 1948), pp. 17-18.
[2] *The Worker's Point of View* (Acton Society, 1952), pp. 11-12.
[3] *The Dock Worker* (Liverpool University Press, 1954), pp. 50-1, 55-6.

apparent obsession with low social status, is significant. And it is noticeable that even outside the mines and docks, a large proportion of disputes are not only in high-wage industries, but also are not concerned with wages or conditions at all. Rather they revolve around points of prestige and power: the failure to consult about overtime, the rights of shop-stewards, the dismissal of workers, the choice of foremen, and questions of discipline generally – all issues which appear to reflect a feeling amongst well-paid workers that their economic importance is not properly reflected in an enhanced social status and dignity.[1]

Militant Leftism in politics appears to have its roots in broadly analogous sentiments. Every Labour politician has observed that the most indignant members of his local Party are not usually the poorest, or the slum-dwellers, or those with most to gain from further economic change, but the younger, more self-conscious element, earning good incomes and living comfortably in neat new council houses: skilled engineering workers, electrical workers, draughtsmen, technicians, and the lower clerical grades. (Similarly the most militant local parties are not in the old industrial areas, but either in the newer high-wage engineering areas or in middle-class towns; Coventry and Margate are the characteristic strongholds.) Now it is people such as these who naturally resent the fact that despite their high economic status, often so much higher than their parents', and their undoubted skill at work, they have no right to participate in the decisions of their firm, no influence over policy, and far fewer non-pecuniary privileges than the managerial grades; and outside their work they are conscious of a conspicuous educational handicap, of a style of life which is still looked down on by middle-class people often earning little if any more, of differences in accent, and generally of an inferior class position.

It is, I think, this failure of social assimilation which creates antagonism, and explains its concentration in those groups which have risen or are rising economically, but whose social aspirations seem somehow blocked by our deeply-set class stratification.[2]

[1] Alternatively the disputes are inter-Union ones (as recently in printing, railways, and shipbuilding), and due to the resentment of skilled workers at their loss of (relative) economic status as a result of inflation.

[2] It is sometimes said that there is no particular significance in this concentration of militancy in the better-paid section of the working class, since the skilled artisan class has historically always provided the radical and militant leadership for the

Poised as we are halfway between extreme inequality and genuine equality, we seem to be getting the worst of both worlds. Again one reverts to the contrast with Scandinavia, where, in societies with less rigid class divisions, people of equivalent economic status have a relatively much higher social status; and one remarks again the freedom of those countries from any corresponding discontents.

Of course one cannot prove that this interpretation is correct. The explanation might be simpler – the dogged survival, for example, of bitter memories of past industrial conflicts and injustice, or merely a failure to eradicate Communist influence. But the *prima facie* evidence is surely strong.

IV   *The Ideology of Class Betrayal*

It is confirmed, I believe, by the persistence, amazing in the light of the changes described in Part One, of an unusual British phenomenon, the Ideology of Class Betrayal or Contamination.

By this I mean the touchy, defensive, almost neurotic fear that 'the class enemy' will somehow fatally weaken the working class, either by seducing its leaders away or insidiously corrupting their minds. This in turn sets up a defence mechanism, of which the most obvious manifestations are the deep hostility, couched in the language of class betrayal ('he's gone over to the boss's side'), shown to the worker who takes a supervisory or managerial post, and the antagonism towards Trade Union leaders, previously trusted figures, who 'go over' by becoming members of Nationalised Boards.[1] Even ordinary Trade Union officials are sometimes suspected of contamination if their way of life, their cars,

---

workers. But there is no evidence for this in British labour history. During the latter half of the last century, the skilled workers, typified by the Amalgamated Society of Engineers, stood throughout for extremely moderate policies; while the more radical New Unionism which sprang up in the 1880s drew its support from the unskilled and worst-paid workers. The exceptionally militant industrial action of the immediate pre-1914 years was again concentrated in relatively low-wage industries; while throughout the inter-war period it was the miners, then almost the worst-paid section of the working class, who were always the most radical element.

[1] One catches occasional hints of a parallel attitude on the other side, as when prominent socialist Old Etonians are labelled 'traitors to their class'. But whether due to the fewness of such hybrid creatures or the greater self-confidence of the upper classes, this attitude is not now very widespread.

or their incomes are thought to approximate at all closely (which they never do) to those of the employers.[1]

This attitude is absurdly irrational to-day, whatever might have been its justification 50 years ago.[2] It implies that the interests of labour and management must under all circumstances conflict, whereas everyone now recognises that although they may diverge (as over the wage bargain), they may also coincide (as over higher productivity). Nobody now rationally believes in a theory of irreconcilable conflict, or that anything which helps the management must *ipso facto* hurt the workers, or that the most efficient workers should not rise as fast and as far as they can, or that Nationalised Boards should be empty of Trade Union representatives; yet each of these beliefs is implicit in the ideology of class betrayal. (This ideology is thus wholly inconsistent with the reiterated claims, often made by the very same class 'patriots', that *more* managerial posts should be filled by workers, and *more* Trade Unionists be appointed to Nationalised Boards.)[3]

And even if the lines of labour-management conflict were more clearly drawn than in fact they are, such defensive fears would still be quite disproportionate in the light of the present massive strength of the working-class movement. They might be warranted if the working class had its back to the wall, and was in imminent danger of defeat – in such a situation all kinds of nervous and suspicious doubts are natural. And indeed an ideology of betrayal and contamination is historically characteristic of minority racial or religious groups fearing persecution, or the loss of their identity by absorption into some larger mass. So some Negroes in the U.S.A. have a touchy suspicion of anything

[1] It would be unthinkable in England for Trade Union leaders to be paid the sort of salaries which are quite normal in the U.S.A. Mr. Beck, for example, the head of the Teamsters' Union, in addition to a salary of $50,000 a year, lives rent-free in a $160,000 house bought by the Union, not to mention having a Union-owned Cadillac, plus caterers and gardeners as needed. 'It's a lovely place', says Mr. Beck. 'Downstairs I have an office and a bar, a movie-projection room, and a pool table. . . . There are two two-car garages, a swimming pool and a bath house.' (Quoted in *Fortune*, September 1955, pp. 84-5.) No doubt this is an extreme example; but the contrast in attitudes between the two countries is still violent.

[2] It is also extremely wasteful when it prevents, as it often does, ex-Trade Unionists who have worked their way through University from coming back to responsible positions inside the Trade Union movement. Such people are positively forced into 'bourgeois' occupations. The American Unions gain tremendously in effectiveness through not having such inhibitions.

[3] cf. the furious outcry amongst political militants against Sir Stafford Cripps when he once ventured to suggest that there were not sufficient trained and educated workers to make a success of workers' control.

which smacks of 'Uncle Tomism', and a nagging fear that their leaders or popular successes will be seduced into racial treachery by the white man's glamorous culture;[1] so in the face of anti-Semitism a section of Jews will aggressively over-emphasise their Jewishness; and so devout religious sects will lay down all manner of detailed prohibitions to prevent contamination by 'the world'.

But such desperate protective safeguards become absurd in a situation of strength; and there is something almost comical – though also highly damaging to the socialist ideal – about the entrenched and unassailable British working class displaying a deep sense of injury and betrayal when some of its members are rash enough to take the slogan of equal opportunity seriously.

Yet the persistence of this mood, despite its obvious irrationality, is significant. Reflecting as it does a deep-seated social insecurity and lack of confidence, it is eloquent of the strength of class-consciousness, and lends credence to the view that our class stratification is a direct incitement to social antagonism and resentment.[2]

v   *Socialism, Human Nature, and Social Contentment*

But it is sometimes said that one is doing something disgraceful, and merely pandering to the selfish clamour of the mob, by taking account of social envy and resentment. This is not so. These feelings exist, amongst people not morally inferior to those who administer such high-minded rebukes; and they are quite natural. It is no more disgraceful to take them into account than many other facts that the politician must attend to – such as the greed of the richer classes, who claim they must have higher monetary rewards and reduced taxation as an incentive

---

[1] cf. the sporadic attacks in the Negro press on Miss Eartha Kitt for her alleged preference for going out with white men rather than with members of her own race.

[2] There are some counterparts to these feelings at the upper end of the social scale, though for obvious reasons they are much less strong. One is a sense of guilt about the contrast between riches and poverty. Mr. Stephen Spender, speaking of his early political days, writes that 'I was driven on by a sense of social and personal guilt'. (*The God That Failed*, Hamish Hamilton, 1950, p. 271); and it was such a feeling that explained the almost mass appeal of the Popular Front and the Left Book Club in the 1930s to the comfortably-off classes. Of course it needed an unusual combination of circumstances to cause a guilt neurosis on so huge a scale; and the feeling is much less strong amongst the rich to-day – partly because unemployment and poverty have so largely disappeared, and partly, no doubt, because they feel they have expiated their guilt by (reluctantly) accepting surtax rates of 19s. in the pound.

to greater effort, patriotism being evidently not enough. If all envy (or all rapacity) could disappear by a wave of the wand, or by the peripatetic performance of Buchmanite plays, then well and good. But as it will not, it is a social fact of cardinal importance; and since it makes society less peaceful and contented, it is wrong not to try and adjust affairs in such a way as to minimise the provocation to it.

In fact, of course, the envy often takes a form which by no extreme of bigoted intolerance could be condemned as cupidity or selfishness, as when it is inspired by inequalities of educational opportunity. The upper and middle classes think it not reprehensible, but the mark of a good parent, to show anxious concern over a child's education and future prospects. They would be unwise, then, to censure the envy of working-class parents for the better education, the wider vistas, and the superior prospects of richer children than their own.

When discussing these aspects of social character, we are not dealing with necessarily immutable or ineradicable facts of 'human nature'. Social anthropology has at least shown that human temperament and social traits are not universal and eternal, but differ from one culture to another; and that these differences are not all biologically transmitted in the chromosomes of each particular race, as implied in theories of racial heredity, but are, partially at least, culturally selected.[1] There is, of course, some hereditary transmission of physical and biological traits; but it is not now thought that this can explain all the social and cultural differences between races disclosed by anthropological study, still less the changes through time in the social character of any one society.

This view is also supported by the group experiments of social psychologists,[2] which suggest that social influences may be decisive even in such basic spheres of behaviour as honesty and dishonesty – 'there are not honest-dishonest persons, but honest-dishonest situations':[3] and certainly that they determine whether group behaviour is aggressive or co-operative, resentful or contented, democratic or authoritarian. Of course one cannot make

[1] v. Ruth Benedict, *Patterns of Culture* (Routledge, 1935), or Margaret Mead, *Male and Female*.

[2] v. Kurt Lewin, *Resolving Social Conflicts* (Harper, New York, 1948), especially Chs. 5 and 7.

[3] Benedict, op. cit., p. 170.

precise and dogmatic statements about detailed cause and effect; and often, as in the case of the 'social' motives and relations discussed in Chapter IV, we cannot see how, or within what framework, a change in attitudes could be effected. But in this case, not only is it clearly possible to have either more or less social equality, but the evidence for linking cause and effect seems rather strong – especially in the light of the relative absence of corresponding collective resentments in Scandinavia, and the lesser social envy and class resentment in North America. This suggests some connection at least with the degree of social inequality and class stratification.

Thus the ethical basis for the first argument for greater equality is that it will increase social contentment and diminish social resentment. Such a statement could be purely descriptive; that is, there could exist such differences in the objective conditions under which individuals lived in two societies that they manifestly constituted a difference in the contentment of those societies. In practice, this degree of objectivity is lacking; and such a statement therefore becomes, partly at least, a value-judgment with a strong recommendatory force. It is justified, first, by the ethical premiss that a contented society is better than a discontented one, and secondly by the judgment that the contentment of the community is an increasing function of the contentment of individuals. It then rests on the hypothesis, which I have argued in this chapter, that some at least of our collective discontents can be traced to social inequality, and would be diminished if that inequality were less: and on the further hypothesis that the consequent gain in contentment would outweigh the diminution in contentment of the present privileged classes.

Because these are not purely factual or descriptive statements, but contain a strong value element, it does not follow that they are any the less significant. Any statement about the contentment or welfare of the community is of this kind – statements against, just as much as statements in favour of more equality. But some judgments have to be made, whatever the uncertainties. We have to have either more equality, or less, or the present amount; and politicians, in deciding which of these is the correct objective, must make some supposition about the welfare of the community. They have no excuse, merely because such statements can easily be shown to be of an ethical nature, for evading this responsibility.

It is to be noted that these statements are not statements about personal 'happiness'. We might diminish the extent of *collective* antagonism and resentment, and so increase social contentment, without increasing the sum of *personal* happiness in the community.

Most early socialists, it is true (and certainly Robert Owen), thought that the relation between socialism and happiness was direct and simple. They assumed that as society progressed in a socialist direction, it would more and more take on that Utopian quality described by William Godwin as 'most conducive to the extensive diffusion of felicity'; people would grow perfectly happy, all frustration and ill-will would fade away, and we should have an earthly paradise, a city of brotherly love. All unhappiness was attributed to social causes, and social change was believed to be a cure for any moral or psychological disorder.

Few people would take such a simple view to-day, if only on account of two difficulties. First, while it is not unreasonable to make the judgment (and indeed people do constantly make such judgments) that one society is more socially contented than another, in the sense of showing less social antagonism, collective resentment, and political bitterness, it would be rather difficult to say that individuals in one society were on the average happier than individuals in another. This is not because the word 'happiness' is necessarily ambiguous – on the contrary, people will often agree on whether a person is happy or not, and even that A is happier than B: but because of the utter impossibility of making judgments on this point about entire societies.

Secondly, even if such judgments were possible, we still know too little about the relation between personal happiness and the cultural-social background to be sure what influence changes in the latter will have on the former. Thus one might take an extreme early-Freudian view, and largely dismiss cultural factors altogether. We all know now that people rationalise, and that their overt and conscious reasons are a bad guide to their 'real' sub-conscious reasons. One might then argue that envy and resentment were only rationalised in social terms, and in reality were rooted in infantile experiences or sexual deprivation. Or one might adopt the attitude of those social anthropologists who argue that social traits are implanted by particular methods of suckling, weaning, and rearing new-born children, and are only indirectly dependent on wider social factors.

Such theories would imply in effect that a constant amount of discontent or frustration was endemic in society, or at least that the amount was impervious to social or economic reform. The only effect of such reform would be to alter the *direction* of the discontent, so that whereas previously it was externalised, and canalised into collective political and industrial antagonisms, now it became internalised in largely personal frustrations. In other words, if there were fewer political or social foes to act as the objects of psychological transference and compensation, new and purely personal objects would be found; but the amount of frustration would remain the same.

Even if this were true, I should not think that it destroyed the case for greater equality. For one thing, this can perfectly well rest on statements about social justice and social waste, discussed later in this chapter. But in any event collective resentments, articulated in group hostilities, have two especially undesirable characteristics as compared with purely personal ones. First, through the very fact of being collective, they feed on themselves, and become magnified and extended; and secondly they threaten, in a way which purely random personal frustrations do not, other exceedingly important values – democracy, social and industrial peace, tolerance, and even personal freedom.

But in fact I find it hard to accept the notion of a constant amount of discontent. I believe, on the contrary, that many of our collective resentments reflect – as does in certain countries the existence of a large Communist Party – a genuine and natural, even though largely sub-conscious, reaction against class stratification and inequality: and that these latter must breed tensions which manifest themselves in envy, resentment, and antagonism. As a famous psycho-analyst has written, 'existing gross inequalities, not only in possessions but in possibilities for education, recreation, maintaining and regaining health, constitute a group of factors replete with potential hostilities'.[1] Of course not all hostilities can ever be eradicated. But those which have a social cause can at least be reduced by social action; and this I believe to constitute the first argument for more equality.

[1] Karen Horney, *New Ways in Psychoanalysis* (Kegan Paul, 1939), p. 173.

VI   *Equality and Social Justice*

The second argument rests on a view of what constitutes a 'just' distribution of privileges and rewards. Being in essence a simple moral judgment, it is not susceptible of proof or disproof; it must be accepted or rejected according to the moral predilections of the reader. But there appear to me to be four respects in which existing inequalities offend against social justice; and this is wholly irrespective of whether or not they create resentment.

First, I suppose that most liberal people would now allow that every child had a natural 'right', as citizen, not merely to 'life, liberty, and the pursuit of happiness', but to that position in the social scale to which his native talents entitle him: should have, in other words, an equal opportunity for wealth, advancement, and renown. Complete achievement of this is, of course, an unattainable ideal; for the children of talented parents start with a pronounced environmental advantage. But subject only to this, all children can, if the society so decides, at least be given an equal chance of access to the best education.

This chance does not exist in Britain, since the wealthier classes can purchase for their children the overwhelming social privilege, denied to other children equally deserving but less fortunate in their parents, of a public school education. The point is argued in detail in Chapter X. Here it need only be said that the best public schools offer not only a superior education, but the further crucial advantages of the right accent, manners, and dependability of character: that these advantages are a major determinant of occupation, and hence of income, power, and prestige: and that their distribution is correlated almost exclusively with parents' wealth and class location, and only very indirectly with innate talent or performance. This seems to me, although I have personally benefited from it, an indefensible injustice, offending blatantly against the principle of equal opportunity.

Secondly, a similar argument applies to the distribution of wealth. An equitable distribution (ignoring deliberately eleemosynary payments) requires first that wealth should be a reward for the performance of a definite service or function, and secondly that all should have an equal chance of performing the function, and so of earning the reward. The highest rewards would then accrue to those who, because they possess skills or services in short supply, can contribute most to national prosperity or enjoyment; provided only that the possession of these skills and services should not be artificially (that is, to a greater extent than can be explained by innate differences in talent) restricted to a privileged few.

This last condition, for the educational reason just mentioned, is not completely fulfilled even in respect of incomes from work. But it is scarcely fulfilled at all in respect of incomes from property. A later chapter discusses whether the total of property incomes can be justified as the minimum supply price for an economic service. But even if we assume that it can, so that the first requirement is fulfilled for the total *amount* of property income, its *distribution* certainly cannot be defended by the second criterion, since no one can argue that all citizens have an equal chance of acquiring property, and so of earning the due reward for the service of supplying capital.

This would be the case only if all private property were 'earned', in the sense of representing the individual's own accumulated savings, the fruits of his personal effort and abstinence. But in fact the greater part of it has been inherited; and its distribution is related not to the owner's present or past performance, but to the accident of birth. There is thus no equal opportunity for acquiring it. And it is in addition, as we shall see, most unequally distributed, so that a small upper class of rich citizens all but monopolises the stream of unearned income.

This aspect of inequality is, surely, unjust. It confers on a particular group of fortunate heirs, and denies to the rest of the population, the massive advantage not merely of an additional source of income, and the possibility of capital gains and spending out of capital, but also of security and freedom to take risks; and this they enjoy through no merit of their own, and with no corresponding obligation. And the injustice feeds on itself inasmuch as private capital also makes possible, by the better education which it permits and the subtle social advantage which it confers, a higher occupation and work-income than might have been gained on merit alone.

Thirdly, the greater the inequality, the heavier the concentration of power. Liberals as well as socialists have always disliked the possibility that one individual, or a small group, should wield a dominant and irresponsible power over the lives and fortunes of other individuals. No one has any obvious moral right to such untrammelled power. The temptation to abuse it is great; and it is in any case distasteful and humiliating to adult people to be completely subject to the whims and moods of a single superior. Yet such undemocratic disparities of power may easily follow from large social inequalities (though they may follow from other causes also). They may derive simply from great concentrations of wealth, as with the large private landlord, owning numerous tied cottages, or even whole villages, and perhaps the sole source of local employment and parochial patronage. But authoritarian power to-day stems less commonly from monetary wealth or private ownership than from position in a bureaucratic hierarchy.[1] The top executives in public and private industry wield, in particular, a degree of 'remote' power, and their managerial subordinates a degree of 'face-to-face' power, which, although diminished as compared with before the war, still appears excessive. I believe that social justice would be improved if it were to be still further diminished, and the power of the worker at the point of production correspondingly increased.[2]

Fourthly, rewards from work. No socialist (except for Shaw,[3] and he not in later life) has disputed the need for a degree of inequality here, both because superior talent deserves some rent of ability, and because otherwise certain kinds of work, or risk, or burdensome responsibility will not be shouldered.[4] Thus one should pay differentially high rewards to the artist, the coal-miner, the innovating entrepreneur, and the top executive. But

---

[1] *v.* Chapter VI,   Section V, for a fuller discussion of this question.

[2] Though this would still leave many other problems of power to be dealt with, which have nothing to do with social inequality in the ordinary sense of the term.

[3] 'Socialism is nothing but an opinion about . . . how wealth should be distributed in a respectable civilised country. . . . The only satisfactory plan is to give everybody an equal share no matter what sort of person she is, or how old she is, or what sort of work she does, or who or what her father was.' (*The Intelligent Woman's Guide to Socialism and Capitalism*, Constable, 1928, pp. 1, 19.)

[4] Shaw dismissed all such considerations rather cavalierly. On incentives to work: 'Nobody wants her to work harder than another at the national task. On the contrary, it is desirable that the burden of work . . . should be shared equally by the workers. If those who are never happy unless they are working insist on putting in extra work to please themselves, they must not pretend that this is a painful sacrifice for which they should be paid' (op. cit., p. 72). The problem of 'dirty work' was dismissed with analogies to titled surgeons and physicians, students dissecting dead bodies and analysing the excretions of live ones, the bearing and nursing of children, and even 'ladies and gentlemen who attend to their own motor-cars' (pp. 74-5).

it is not clear that these considerations justify the present pattern of work-rewards, either in principle (that is, with respect to the overall spread from top to bottom) or in practice (that is, with respect to whether the right people are receiving the higher and lower incomes).

In practice, they certainly do not. A definite proportion of people even in high *earned* income-brackets have found their way there by a rather easy route, and not solely by merit. This is not now generally true of large-scale private industry,[1] nor of course of the public service. But it is still to some extent true of small-scale private industry, where nepotism is by no means dead. It is still more true of City institutions, where many of the most lucrative posts even now are filled by titled semi-nonentities, or retired soldiers and sailors, wholly innocent of financial expertise; and the most coveted lower posts, after inquiries on the 'old boy net', from amongst those with a suitable college or family background. So long as this continues, the pattern of work-rewards can properly be described as unjust, in that it denies an equal opportunity of attaining certain of the top rewards.

But supposing this were not the case, and that the recipients of different incomes were selected in an orderly manner, would the present overall spread of incomes still be justified? It is clear that some differentials are actually too *narrow* for economic efficiency. But these are normally what may be called the 'horizontal' ones, that is, the differentials within a given occupation or broad income-group. Thus we probably need larger differentials for miners as against other wage-earners, skilled against unskilled workers, foremen against non-supervisory labour, graduate against non-graduate teachers, the more efficient against the less efficient businessmen, and so on.

So far as the vertical spread is concerned, I feel rather agnostic. There are two uncertainties. First, how much should be allowed as rent of ability? This is a pleasantly ambiguous concept (though Shaw characteristically defined it as 'the excess of its produce

[1] Though the words 'now' and 'generally' should be emphasised. A random sample of British companies in 1936 showed 172 directorships (8% of the total, and 15% if the largest companies only are taken) as held by titled persons. Almost half of these had either inherited their title, or acquired it by prowess in the fighting services or sport. One large insurance company had, out of sixteen directors, two dukes, one marquis, one earl, one baron and three knights. (P. Sargant Florence, *The Logic of British and American Industry*, Routledge, 1953, p. 206.)

over that of ordinary stupidity').[1] It could be taken as a non-economic, normative concept, expressing not the money rent which the community *needs* to pay in order to elicit the ability, but the individual's 'worth' (in some sense) to the community. But if this were made the sole criterion (which of course it never has been, since only those abilities for which a popular demand exists have ever in practice commanded high rents – those of motor tycoons and film stars, not poets or philosophers), it is quite certain that we should get not more equality, but a degree of inequality which would be furiously (and rightly) resented by everyone.[2] This is because the scatter of human ability and inventiveness is far wider than any known scatter, in modern societies, of monetary rewards; the 'worth' to society of a Stevenson, a Faraday, a Ford, a Rutherford, or a Fleming, measured in terms of their contribution to future living standards or the abolition of disease, is not merely twenty times greater than the 'worth' of the rest of us, but some hundreds or thousands of times.

But if we reject 'worth' in this vague sense as the proper criterion, on the grounds that (assuming it to be biologically transmitted) it seems unjust and unwise to reward or penalise people to quite such a prodigious extent for inherited characteristics,[3] we are left with rent of ability as an economic concept: that is, the additional reward which exceptional ability can in practice command from the community.

How large this should be is of course impossible to lay down in general terms. If we believe in equality, we can only say that

[1] *Fabian Essays* (1931 ed.), p. 9. But he adopted a rather ambivalent attitude to the question of whether these rents should actually be paid, arguing that occasional freak incomes might not matter provided that they accrued to the possessors of lucrative personal talents, such as, he explained, himself. But these talents should not be allowed to make others rich. 'To allow Cleopatra to make money out of her charm is one thing: to allow a trader to become enormously rich by engaging 500 Cleopatras at £10 a week or less, and hiring them out at £10 a day or more, is quite another.' (*The Intelligent Woman's Guide*, p. 333.)

[2] 'We support and encourage Ability,' wrote Shaw, 'in order that we may get as much as possible out of it, not in order that it may get as much as possible out of us. . . . This is the sole safeguard for the existence of men of Ability. Give them and their heirs the entire product of their ability, so that they shall be enormously rich whilst the rest of us remain just as poor as if they had never existed; and it will become a public duty to kill them, since nobody but themselves will be any the worse, and we shall be much the better for having no provocation to the sin of envy.' (*Socialism and Superior Brains*, Fabian Tract No. 146, 1909.)

[3] The question of a 'just' distribution of rewards, assuming equal opportunity and a perfect selection by merit alone, is further discussed in the next chapter, Section V.

we shall balance the possible loss to equality against the possible gain from exploiting the ability. The balance of loss and gain will depend on the supply price of different grades of ability; this raises the whole question of incentives, about which we still know very little. Some danger point must evidently exist at which equality begins to react really seriously on the supply of ability[1] (and also of effort, risk-taking, and so on), and hence on economic growth. Where exactly this point lies, no one knows. I do not myself believe that we have yet reached it. The matter is discussed in detail later; but I am not convinced that the present 20 : 1 spread in post-tax incomes is really essential to incentive.[2] I therefore think that we should move slowly forward, concentrating on gross rather than net incomes, eschewing increased taxation on marginal earnings, and always preferring an increase in the lowest incomes to an attack on the highest: and after the next step forward pause, and scrutinise the repercussions, if any, on economic behaviour.

But I do not regard the re-alignment of work-incomes as being a particularly urgent task for a Labour Government, partly because they constitute a distinctly lesser 'injustice' than the three others discussed above, and partly because a decision here is not a decision about incomes or wealth as a whole. Some 40% of surtax income accrues not from work, but from property; and the higher the total income, the higher the proportion which comes from property. Measures to redistribute property will therefore greatly diminish the inequality of wealth, and will also indirectly alter the pattern of work-incomes by reducing the differential social and educational advantages which now follow from the possession of large inherited fortunes.

In any case inequity in respect of work-rewards often resides less in the distribution of direct money emoluments, than of certain privileges and advantages which conventionally go with them. Thus industry is riddled with non-pecuniary differentials far larger than can be justified on grounds of incentive: for

[1] At which, in practice, the ability begins to emigrate on a large scale to Canada and Kenya.

[2] Of course any nominal spread of this sort, such as emerges from the tax tables, underestimates the true spread owing to the wide possibilities of tax avoidance. If one were to allow for perquisites and business expenses which in fact go to raise the recipient's personal standard of life, and for tax-free capital gains made possible by his business situation, the real spread of 'rewards' from work would be much greater than 20 : 1.

example, in respect of holidays, sick-leave, working hours, and often superannuation.

This is only one aspect of a wider inequality, noted already in Chapter V, namely, that wealthier people, either through the terms of their employment or through tax allowances, are relatively better able to cope with the financial problems of rearing large families, of sickness, and of old age, than poorer people who depend mainly on the social services. Thus even if one could defend the present vertical distribution of direct money emoluments on the hypothesis that the entire population consisted of healthy young bachelors and spinsters, it is much harder to defend the distribution of total resources in periods of need in the light of the great variations in need between families. I believe that the vertical inequality in the distribution of these resources amongst the elderly, the sick, and those with large families constitutes a definite social injustice.

VII   *Equality and Social Waste*

The third objection to extreme social inequality is that it is wasteful and inefficient. If the determinants of class make deep incisions, and the space of free social movement is restricted, as is the case in Britain (mainly on account of the distinct layers traced by a segregated educational system), two undesirable consequences follow.

First, social intercourse between the classes is markedly inhibited, both by external differences in 'manners' and behaviour, and by subjective consciousness of class. One of the strong attractions of (for example) American society is the extraordinary social freedom, the relaxed, informal atmosphere, the easier contacts, the natural assumption of equality, the total absence of deference, and the relative absence of snobbery and of that faint, intangible but none the less insistent sense of class that permeates social attitudes in Britain. One does not ask that all Englishmen should suddenly take to calling each other 'Bud', or altogether abandon their well-known national posture of reserved hauteur; but it would be agreeable if they should intermingle rather more freely and with rather less restraint than they do to-day, and if our social system generally were less fragmented and sub-divided. But this is naturally a matter of personal taste and temperament; and possibly more reserved or inhibited Englishmen may not like the idea of a more mixed-up, egalitarian, informal pattern of social life.

However, the British class system also involves a definite social waste, since it selects its leaders badly. If social mobility is low, as it must be in a stratified society, and people cannot easily move up from the lower or middle reaches to the top, then the ruling élite becomes hereditary and self-perpetuating; and whatever one may concede to inherited or family advantages, this must involve a waste of talent.

Opportunities for rising are, it is true, more ample than they used to be; and any really outstanding working-class child now can, with an effort, reach the top. But even on the simplest grounds of efficiency this is not enough. In our highly complex and professional industrial society, the problem of leadership is not one merely of finding the tiny minority of brilliant geniuses; for there are far more responsible top positions than geniuses to fill them. We cannot be content with correctly distributing all the (as it were) alpha material, but must make the best use of our beta resources also. And here matters are far from satisfactory. Clever working-class children are still denied access to the public schools, while the less clever but still potentially useful have only a rather uncertain access to the grammar schools;[1] and there is certainly no perfect correspondence between natural talent and type of education. Moreover, as was observed above, inherited property, nepotism, and class favouritism all prevent a fair and effective competition, on merit alone, for the highest posts.

It follows that we are still not extracting the best from our population, or making the most exhaustive use of scarce resources of human ability. This is a definite social waste, and one directly related to a stratified social system which, by placing a premium on lineage, and barriers in the way of vertical mobility, prevents a genuine equality of opportunity.

VIII *How Much Equality?*

How far towards equality do we wish to go? I do not regard this as either a sensible or a pertinent question, to which one

[1] *v.* Chapter X.

could possibly give, or should attempt to give, a precise reply. We need, I believe, more equality than we now have, for the reasons set out in this chapter. We can therefore describe the direction of advance, and even discern the immediate landscape ahead; but the ultimate objective lies wrapped in complete uncertainty.

This must be the case unless one subscribes to the vulgar fallacy that some ideal society can be said to exist, of which blueprints can be drawn, and which will be ushered in as soon as certain specific reforms have been achieved. The apocalyptic view that we might one day wake up to find that something called 'socialism' had arrived was born of revolutionary theories of capitalist collapse. But in Western societies change is gradual and evolutionary, and not always either foreseeable or even under political control. It is therefore futile and dangerous to think in terms of an ideal society, the shape of which can already be descried, and which will be reached at some definite date in the future. Countries like Britain do not leap from one fully-fledged social system to another, but are, on the contrary, in a state of permanent transition.

Moreover, as was pointed out in Chapter IV, socialism is not an exact descriptive term, connoting a particular social structure, past, present, or even immanent in some sage's mind, which can be empirically observed or analysed. It simply describes a set of values, or aspirations, which socialists wish to see embodied in the organisation of society. One must confine oneself to saying, therefore, that society at any given moment either does or does not sufficiently embody these values; and if it does not, then further changes are required. But exactly what degree of equality will create a society which does sufficiently embody them, no one can possibly say. We must re-assess the matter in the light of each new situation.

We can thus only venture very general statements of the objective. I feel clear that we need large egalitarian changes in our educational system, the distribution of property, the distribution of resources in periods of need, social manners and style of life, and the location of power within industry; and perhaps some, but certainly a smaller, change in respect of incomes from work. I think that these changes, taken together, will amount to a considerable social revolution.

On the other hand, I am sure that a definite limit exists to the degree of equality which is desirable. We do not want complete equality of incomes, since extra responsibility and exceptional talent require and deserve a differential reward. We are not hostile, as our opponents sometimes foolishly suggest, to 'detached residences in Bournemouth where some elderly woman has obviously more than a thousand a year'.[1] I do not myself want to see *all* private education disappear: nor the Prime Minister denied an official car, as in one Scandinavian country: nor the Queen riding a bicycle: nor the House of Lords instantly abolished: nor the manufacture of Rolls-Royces banned: nor the Brigade of Guards, nor Oxford and Cambridge, nor Boodle's, nor (more doubtfully) the Royal Yacht Squadron, nor even, on a rather lower level, the Milroy Room, lose their present distinctive character:[2] nor anything so dull and colourless as this.

But where en route, before we reach some drab extreme, we shall wish to stop, I have no idea. Our society will look quite different when we have carried through the changes mentioned earlier; and the whole argument will then need to be re-stated, and thought out afresh, by a younger generation than mine.

[1] *The Tablet*, reviewing *New Fabian Essays*, 31 May 1952.

[2] On the condition, of course, already fulfilled in the case of Oxford and Cambridge, that entry into these eminent institutions is not a matter simply of lineage.

VIII

IS EQUAL OPPORTUNITY ENOUGH?

1 *The Conventional Objection to the Equal Opportunity Society*

SOME radicals, however, would be content with the strictly limited objective of equal opportunity. If everyone, they argue, has an equal chance of scaling the heights, if every worker carries a managing director's brief-case in his knapsack, why worry about the length of the climb, or the unequal distribution of rewards? The essential thing is that every citizen should have an equal chance – that is his basic democratic right; but provided the start is fair, let there be the maximum scope for individual self-advancement. There would then be nothing improper in either a high continuous status ladder (e.g. of income or consumption patterns) or even a distinct class stratification (e.g. a segregated educational system), since opportunities for attaining the highest status or the topmost stratum would be genuinely equal. Indeed the continuous traffic up and down the ladder would inevitably make society more mobile and dynamic, and so less class-bound.

Conservatives like to claim that this is the doctrine of modern Tory radicalism (although it also commands support on the Left amongst those to whom the lack of opportunity was the most inexcusable injustice of pre-war capitalism); and the 'ladder' concept has now become the ideological myth of the 'progressive' British Tory, who allegedly finds his ideal in those societies, such as Australasia, Canada, and above all the

United States, which appear to embody it most completely.[1]

But I deliberately stress the words 'myth' and 'allegedly', for I do not believe that such a society in any way resembles the true ideal of most Conservatives. Consider its most obvious implications – completely free, competitive entry into industry: an end to all nepotism and favouritism: a diminution, if not the virtual elimination, of inheritance: the abolition of fees in public schools: and generally the extrusion of all hereditary influences in our society – and contrast these with actual Conservative policies in these various spheres, and with their emotional attachment to precisely the most traditional and hereditary features of British life.

It is in fact a complete illusion that British Conservatives really want a mobile equal-opportunity society on the American pattern. They may say they do, in order to wear the mantle of reformers, and to lend some plausibility to their reiterated claims to be the party of adventure and initiative; and because in praising America they appear to be praising free enterprise and capitalism. But a moment's thought will show that the sweeping reforms required to create such a society would be anathema to them, and that their true ideology is poles apart from the restless, egalitarian ideology of contemporary America. This indeed comes much closer, though this is not always understood in England, to the egalitarian ideas of the Left than to the more static, conservative instincts of the Right.

From the point of view of the reformer, the equal-opportunity society has much to commend it. It avoids the deeply-felt injustice of hereditary status – the resentful feeling that the top rewards are reserved for the pre-selected few, that the well-born fool has a better chance than the poor-born genius, and that the son can hope to rise no higher than his father, but is condemned to fill that station to which it shall please God to call him. It allows more intercourse between the classes; and by lowering the barriers and stimulating movement in both directions it at least diminishes *collective* feelings of superiority and inferiority. And, lastly, it provides an admirably efficient method of selection for

[1] Perhaps one should add, to give a patriotic flavour, and because the more romantic Tories so continually perorate about it, Elizabethan England, of which Professor Trevelyan writes that 'class divisions, recognised without fuss on either side, were not rigid and were not even strictly hereditary. Individuals and families moved out of one class into another. . . . English society was based not on equality but on freedom – freedom of opportunity and freedom of personal intercourse.' (*English Social History*, Longmans, 1942, p. 162.)

the highest posts; the fools are weeded out, only the fittest can survive, and the consequent high calibre of the men at the top must be beneficial to economic progress.

But it is fashionable in some quarters to inveigh against a 'competitive ladder' society on socio-psychological grounds. A number of psychologists, sociologists, and social anthropologists assert that it must lead to new and alarming evils.[1] Its basic features will be a marked degree of social fluidity, such that the individual knows he could attain a higher status (as he cannot in a feudal society); an exceptional ease of invidious comparison, since there are no rigid barriers between the different levels; and a general determination to rise, since rewards at the top far exceed anything available lower down, and since both social prestige and psychological self-validation depend upon success in the competitive struggle. Thus every individual, spurred on by his invidious comparisons and the glittering prizes ahead, will both aim at a higher status and, because the door to self-advancement seems wide open, think he can attain it. Hence will be bred a universal, restless itch to rise in the social scale.

But the resulting accent on emulation and ambition, it is said, so far from increasing contentment, must certainly diminish it, and lead to general insecurity. Whereas in a hereditary system competition is severely limited, now it becomes quite general. And as the area of competition and the scope for self-advancement are increased, so the ratio of failure to opportunity must increase. A hereditary society, denying the opportunity to rise, avoids also the sense of failure at not having risen; but if all have the opportunity, and only 10% succeed, 90% are conscious of having failed, and suffer a loss of self-esteem. And the more unequal the rewards, the greater will be the frustration from failure, the more ruthless the competition, the more bitter the intolerance shown to rivals. Moreover acquisitiveness is intensified inasmuch as higher status depends, in Veblenesque fashion, on high consumption standards, and so on making money.

[1] This view is expressed or implied, with varying degrees of emphasis or moderation, by Karen Horney, *The Neurotic Personality of Our Times* (New York, W. W. Norton, 1937); Abram Kardiner, op. cit., Chs. XI, XII, and XIV; Robert S. Lynd, *Knowledge for What?* (Princeton University, 1945), Ch. III; Ruth Benedict, op. cit., Chs. VII and VIII; Margaret Mead, *Keep Your Powder Dry* (William Morrow, 1942), Ch. IX; Robert K. Merton, op. cit., Ch. IV; and amongst English writers, T. H. Marshall, op. cit., Ch. III. It has now found its way into some Left-wing political writing; cf. *Socialism* (Socialist Union, 1953).

Such is the society – restless, insecure, aggressive, and acquisitive – that results from the pursuit of equal opportunity, if these writers are to be believed.[1] The inevitable consequences are increased discontent in the lower ranks of society,[2] psycho-somatic diseases on a wide scale, and a maladjusted neurosis-prone community.[3] The United States is already in the grip of these ailments, and Britain is showing distinct symptoms of infection.

II　The Myth of Aggressive Competition

Surely we are faced here with a positive mountain of irrelevance and exaggeration, even though an element of truth lies buried under it.

First, there is no evidence to justify definite statements to the effect that psychoses, neuroses, and psycho-somatic diseases are more common to-day than in previous epochs. Alarming figures are quoted of the amount of absenteeism due to mental illness, the incidence of stomach-ulcers, the number of mental patients, and so on; but of course comparable figures can rarely be quoted for earlier periods. In fact such little comparative evidence as exists does not support these conclusions; according to a recent American study, there has been no increase in the incidence of

---

[1] The most extreme (and jargonish) version of this case is to be found in Kardiner. 'The whole community is permeated with the struggle to achieve prestige-status. . . . The presence of social mobility, or the absence of fixed statuses, increases the vigour with which these tangible forms of self-validation must be pursued. . . . This common goal makes for social instability because there is a constant turnover from underdog to overdog and vice versa. Anxiety is mobilised on the part both of those who have status-prestige and those who have not. . . . Those who fail feel self-condemnation and self-depreciation which is translated into hatred and envy of those who succeed. . . . This explains the abandoned destructiveness of contemporary society.' (op. cit., pp. 341-2, 364-5, 410, 453.)

[2] 'When the race is to the swift, the slow, who are always in a majority, grow tired of their perpetual defeat and become more disgruntled than if there were no race at all. They begin to regard the prizes as something to which they are entitled and of which they are unjustly deprived. They declare that no man ought to be made to race for his bread and butter, and the argument is not without force.' (T. H. Marshall, op. cit., p. 127.)

[3] 'The strains involved may be seen in suicides and in the mounting tide of entrants into our mental hospitals.' (Lynd, op. cit., p. 231.) 'A neurotic development in the individual arises ultimately from feelings of alienation and hostility. . . . Among the factors in Western civilisation which engender potential hostility, the fact that the culture is built on individual competitiveness probably ranks first.' (Horney, New Ways in Psycho-Analysis, pp. 172-4.)

the psychoses over the last 100 years despite the alleged increase in competitiveness, status struggle, and insecurity.[1]

Even if one could demonstrate an increase in mental disorders, it still need not be due to external social or economic factors. A strict Freudian, for example, would presumably argue that the proneness of society to nervous disorders varied only with the degree of restraint imposed by the prevailing cultural *mores* on the individual's basic biological drives.[2] But of course the fact is that the psychological sciences are not yet sufficiently mature to warrant any dogmatic statements about the social causes of neuroses.

But suppose we forget the flamboyant talk of mental ailments, and confine ourselves to the more modest proposition that personal insecurity and discontent may well be due to social causes, it would still not follow, even if they could be shown to be more widespread than 100 years ago, that this was *necessarily* due to social causes, still less to the particular social factor of mobility and competitiveness. It might be due to climatic, or dietetic, or racial, or religious, or a host of other possible influences.[3] Switzerland, for example, which enjoys only a placid degree of competition, is said to have the highest divorce and suicide rate in the world.

[1] Herbert Goldhammer and Andrew Marshall, *Psychosis and Civilisation: Studies in the Frequency of Mental Disease* (Glencoe: The Free Press, 1953). This finding does not prove anything definite about the incidence of the neuroses, for which scarcely any reliable past data exist. Whether one deduces anything from it about neuroses depends on which of two conflicting views is held – that these two classes of mental disorder are the product of largely the same set of causes (e.g. some total 'stress' factor to which social life subjects people), or that they have a quite independent aetiology.

[2] Freud allowed no great importance to social or cultural factors; even so standard a work as *New Introductory Lectures in Psycho-Analysis* contains virtually no reference to them. Neuroses are explained in terms of instinctual biological trends, which are at the most modified by culture and environment. Indeed, so far from accepting that the culture determined the neurosis, Freud tended to believe the opposite. 'Since he is convinced of the universality of the role played by allegedly instinctual drives, Freud feels entitled to explain cultural phenomena too on that basis. Capitalism is seen as an anal-erotic culture. . . . Qualitative differences in different cultures are accounted for by the nature of the instinctual drives which are characteristically expressed or repressed.' (Horney, op. cit., p. 169.)

[3] Norman Douglas's Mr. Keith was an enthusiastic exponent of a dietetic theory of human psychology. 'The best way to begin improving oneself was to keep one's bowels open, and not trouble about those of anybody else. The serenity of outlook thereby attained would enable a man to perceive the futility of interfering with the operation of natural selection. . . . Had the tribe of Israel been careful in the matter of dietary their sacred writings, a monument of malnutrition and faulty digestive processes, would never have seen the light of day. . . . We owe not only Magna Carta, but our whole Empire, to our costive habits of body.' (*South Wind*, pp. 281-4.)

At any rate, to prove the full anti-competitive thesis, it would at least need to be shown that contemporary Anglo-Saxon society, by virtue of its increased fluidity, did now lay an exaggerated stress on ruthless competition and egocentric aggression. Then, if certain specific assumptions are made about the greater frequency and social causes of personal frustration, a *prima facie* case might be said to exist.

This evidently cannot be shown of Britain. Earlier chapters have already suggested that whatever may have been the case in the heyday of Victorian capitalism, or even in the 1920s, British society and industry to-day, so far from being a breeding-ground for aggressive self-assertion, are psychologically oriented towards security, group solidarity, safe markets, and a quiet life with long week-ends, regular golf, and a place in the country.

However, Britain is not really a suitable test-case, for we still retain a rather static, rigid pattern of social relations. It is to the U.S.A. that we must turn for evidence: to a society undeniably fluid and dynamic, ostensibly parading to the world an ideology of competitive free enterprise, and allegedly the archetype of the aggressive, acquisitive society with all its attendant discontents. If this picture of the U.S.A. is accurate, it might indeed suggest that social mobility was inseparable from ruthless competition and so, in turn, from aggression and insecurity.

But I believe this picture to be largely mythical, even though some credulous Americans themselves accept it. It is not that insecurity is absent, but that it is mainly due to causes other than aggressive competition and an ethos of individualistic struggle for pre-eminence. These now represent neither the true prevailing ideology, nor the actual pattern of behaviour.

First, whatever business spokesman may assert at annual conventions, unrestricted free enterprise is no longer the effective ruling ideology. Political attitudes are a good guide to ideological trends; and it is now a quarter of a century since a party genuinely wedded to unrestricted free enterprise gained a popular majority. Twenty years of New Deal and Fair Deal, of anti-business bias and 'creeping socialism', have been followed by a Republican Administration still committed to social security, which has maintained the New Deal virtually intact, and even so cannot command a majority of the popular vote without the help of President Eisenhower. The disciples of extreme *laisser-faire* are confined to the Right-wing of the Republican Party; and the natural bias of the electorate is, as in Britain, towards a position a little left of centre. Perhaps the most symbolic event in recent American history was the successful opposition, even under a Republican régime, to the private-enterprise Dixon-Yates contract, lest it impinge too heavily on the publicly-owned T.V.A.

I do not mean that the current ideology is positively *anti*, only that it is no longer ardently *pro*, unrestricted free enterprise. Many American business leaders, more sensitive to shifting opinion than some sociologists, have observed the change, and become so alarmed at the decline of faith that they have launched a massive advertising campaign to rally their support. This is surely significant. If the free enterprise creed were still in the ascendant, there would be no need to set up Americans for the Competitive Enterprise System Inc.: no need for 8,000 outdoor posters, 136,000 car cards, and 3 million radio 'listener impressions' on the Free Enterprise theme: no need for General Motors to produce a full-length Hollywood film on the merits of the profit system: or for General Electric, Procter and Gamble, Republic Steel and many other firms to make free distributions of Free Enterprise comics.[1]

'All in all, the Free Enterprise campaign is shaping up as one of the most intensive sales campaigns in the history of industry – in fact, it is fast becoming very much of an industry itself. At the current rate, it is accounting for at least $100,000,000 of industry's annual advertising, public relations, and employee-relations expenditures. And it is not worth a damn. Even those who batten on it concede the failure. "Chief, what this needs is the hard sell. The message hasn't got across. We haven't hit 'em where they live. Joe Doakes has been tone deaf." '[2] Joe Doakes has been tone deaf because the Great Depression killed his faith in *laisser-faire*, and instilled in him an ineradicable attachment to a New Deal, social-security political philosophy.

This change in the climate of opinion is reflected in a change in the psychology of the business leaders themselves. Andrew Mellon or Andrew Carnegie, violent, splenetic, reactionary,

[1] *v.* William H. Whyte, *Is Anybody Listening?* This whole book, by one of the shrewdest commentators on the changing social climate of U.S. industry, should be read by anyone who still believes in the myth of American individualism.

[2] op. cit., p. 7.

merciless to competitors, ruthless towards trade unions, glorying
in their boundless power, and arrogantly contemptuous of public
or governmental opinion, belong to a dead past; and the few
survivors, such as Mr. Sewell Avery of Montgomery Ward, only
emphasise by their isolation, and their reputation as eccentric
oddities, the completeness of the change. The typical business
leader to-day is of an altogether different mould: quieter, more
civilised and unassuming, less confident about free enterprise
and faintly anxious to justify himself, a frequent visitor to Washington, an Eisenhower supporter, versed in economics, an adroit
negotiator on excellent terms both with competitors and Union
leaders, and quite content to accept state action, if need be, in the
interests of full employment.

The contrast is most evident in the field of labour relations.
I refer not merely to the obvious fact that Trade Unions have
now won almost universal recognition, but to the obsession of
business executives with personnel and labour problems. Top
management spends half its energies worrying about these problems, and searching for more and more 'progressive' personnel
ideas; and the talk is all of participation, co-operation, human
relations, the morale of the labour force, good communications,
group activity, and social engineering. Autocratic management
is taboo; teamwork is the universal maxim; and Elton Mayo
replaces Henry Ford as the symbol of management's attitude to
labour. But the contrast is also evident in respect of business
competition, which, although still significantly sharper than in
Europe, is now held within bounds which would not be recognised
or tolerated for a moment in a really aggressive, individualistic,
free-enterprise culture.

We find an analogous change in the psychology of consumption.
Fifty years ago the U.S. was a genuinely acquisitive, Veblenesque
society; and it is still assumed to be by the writers whom I have
quoted. A previous chapter has already cast doubts on the accur-
acy of this assumption.[1] In a Veblenesque society, expenditure
must be as conspicuous and ostentatious as possible in order to
provide irrefutable evidence of superior wealth; and right down
the scale, keeping up with the Joneses in fact means pushing as far
ahead of them as possible. To-day, it means literally what it
says – simply keeping up.[2] To push conspicuously ahead is no

---

[1] v. Chapter VI, Section IV.   [2] Sometimes, indeed, keeping down.

longer meritorious. To own a Cadillac when the rest of the group have Buicks, to be the first to buy an air-conditioning plant, to be too blatantly chic, generally to be extravagant and ostentatious and to parade superior wealth – these are to court unpopularity, to offend the canons of the group, and to be condemned as showing off. The wheel has turned full circle; William Randolph Hearst would now attract, not envy and acclaim, but pity or censure as a deviant, non-adjusted personality; cultural conformism has replaced the self-conscious desire for ostentatious eccentricity; and where once the whole object of expenditure was to attract 'invidious comparisons', to-day it is to avoid them.[1]

One final example may be quoted: the educational system, always an accurate mirror of underlying cultural attitudes. There are no schools in the world where less emphasis is laid on rivalry and competition, and more on co-operation and adaptability. This may be observed both in the curricula, with their classes in 'life-adjustment', 'group living' and 'social integration', and the studied effort to teach the pupils how to 'get along' with their fellows: and in the system of promotion. Promotion by talent or competitive examination has almost everywhere given way to 'social promotion' by age-groups, lest the brilliant child be encouraged to be too ambitious, and the stupid child depressed by open proof of his inferiority.

Generally, present-day American society is characterised by close behavioural conformity, an anxious desire for approval, an acute sensitivity to personal relations, a 'socialisation' of tastes and preferences, and a marked tendency to suppress idiosyncrasies.[2] This is in striking contrast to the picture of a society dominated by ruthless, masterful ambition, a lust for power, a desperate urge to compete, and a reckless, self-regarding individualism. The change appears to have begun in the early 1930s;[3]

---

[1] If we are to believe Miss Mitford, a parallel change has occurred amongst the British aristocracy. 'It has become a matter of policy to appear very poor. The lords are retrenching visibly, and are especially careful to avoid any form of ostentation: for instance, only 5 of them saw fit to attend the last coronation in their family coaches. Coronets on luggage, motor cars, and so on are much less used than formerly.' (*Encounter*, September 1955.) But this may be more 'a matter of policy' than a change in psychology!

[2] *v.* David Riesman, *The Lonely Crowd* (Yale University, 1950), *passim*, for examples of this tendency.

[3] Though the trend towards cultural conformism was of course evident long before then amongst immigrant groups. But there it was to be explained by the problem of assimilating ethnically heterogeneous groups into a stable and homogeneous society.

and it has developed so rapidly since that the America of the roaring 1920s now belongs to a wholly departed epoch.[1]

Not that American society, or any 'conformist' culture, is immune from social tensions. The emphasis on orthodoxy and communal activity[2] may well breed deep tensions and anxiety, and cause acute misery to the eccentric through the social obloquy which he incurs. Indeed it could be argued that such a society[3] causes greater emotional strain, insecurity, and worry than a more self-confident, individualistic, non-conformist culture.

Be that as it may, the relevant point is that these conformist, communal tendencies must, when judging American society, be set against the opposite competitive ones (such as those which operate so strongly within the junior executive class). Taking the two together, it does not appear that a fluid, equal-opportunity society, such as the U.S. is assumed to be, need necessarily engender the atmosphere and cultural pattern described in the previous section. Certainly such a pattern may exist in a society, and has done in past societies; and no doubt when it does it might – though we can scarcely know – give rise to all the atrocious evils alleged against it. But it cannot be said to follow inescapably from, and to be a sweeping indictment of, the objective of social mobility and equal opportunity.

III   *Advantages of the Equal Opportunity Society*

Moreover even if one did concede that greater mobility necessarily led to greater insecurity, and hence to some increase in (as it were) the *gross* amount of social discontent, it would still not follow that it brought an increase in the *net* amount of

---

[1] One reason for the inaccuracy of the picture presented by some of the writers mentioned above is their extreme ignorance of developments in the other social sciences. Thus Kardiner quotes profusely, as though it were incontestable evidence, from some of Laski's most obsolete political writings; while Lynd, writing in 1939, quotes a long list of economic facts and statistics none of which refers to a later year than 1929, and all of which were out of date by the time he wrote (op. cit., pp. 74-6).

[2] cf. the intensive, round-the-clock group activity in any American suburb – both recreational (*kaffeeklatsching* and parties) and organisational (civic clubs, church groups, and every kind of society). Indeed, it is the absence, not the excess, of individual effort which alarms the English visitor.

[3] Which is essentially characterised by a 'Someone Isn't Using Amplex' psychology.

discontent. People sometimes forget that social immobility has serious drawbacks, and that a greater fluidity brings in its train significant advantages, some of which were briefly mentioned at the beginning of the chapter.

Thus one could only wholly eliminate the alleged ill effects of greater mobility by wholly eliminating their cause, which lies fundamentally in the existence of differential rewards, which act as incentives, combined with an equal opportunity for attaining them. Only if one or other or both of these were eliminated would the discontents completely disappear.[1] 'The neurotic development of boundless ambition, for instance . . . is unthinkable in a culture which does not know individual competitiveness, and which offers no rewards for outstanding individual achievement. This holds true also with regard to neurotic strivings for prestige and possessions.'[2] No doubt. But the price to be paid for this condition of well-adjusted bliss is rather a heavy one – 'no rewards for outstanding individual achievement'.

More moderate critics would not, of course, go quite so far as this. But even their arguments tend in the same direction – the suppression of competition, and the denigration of incentives to self-advancement. The shop-steward who refuses a managerial post is praised; measures to restore price-competition are frowned on; piece-rates and monetary incentives are played down – all to an extent which comes perilously close to advocating an ossified and feather-bedded society, enjoying every conceivable protection against any nerve-racking competition whatsoever.

Now this might, in another age, be the right way to attain the ideal society. But it most emphatically is not to-day. It would entail a catastrophic sacrifice of economic progress and efficiency, which do demand, however hopeful one may be about the development of new incentives, *some* differential rewards and *some* competition for them. Certainly, as I argued in the previous chapter,

---

[1] In fact they would not disappear even then, on the argument of the most anti-competitive psychologists. 'Competitiveness not only dominates our relations in occupational groups, but also pervades our social relations, our friendships, our sexual relations, and the relations within the family group.' (Horney, op. cit., p. 73.) This extends the difficulty far beyond the sphere of business or professional competition, into a sphere where it would be innocent to believe that competition did not ante-date 'free enterprise', and optimistic to believe that it will follow the state and wither away under socialism. It is not obvious that the sex war derives from a fight for markets, or will disappear however 'socially-integrated' and 'participant' our society becomes.

[2] ibid., p. 176.

existing inequalities are greater than can be justified on these grounds; equally, as I argue in a later chapter, there is no call to become obsessed by the question of economic growth. But if any connection between differentials and efficiency is granted, and if we admit that whatever may be the position 20 years from now, we shall face many extremely urgent claims on resources for several years ahead, then we cannot dispense entirely with the spur of competition. Sociological Utopias, like earlier philosophical ones, tend to be wholly static in character, and to assume that the problem of production has been solved, so that all can laze in the sun without rivalry. But for the moment at least we might have to pay a heavy price, in terms of urgent wants foregone, for the elimination of all competitive endeavour.

Secondly, the absence of equal opportunity and social mobility is both a denial of democratic rights, and a positive cause of discontent. From the moment when the Industrial Revolution broke up the stable pattern of eighteenth-century society, and spatial mobility and social awareness suddenly increased, and still more from the moment when a working-class political movement came into being, and education became general – from that time on, unequal opportunity became resented, and itself a cause of social frustration. The masses were no longer willing to accept that there was some divine ordination about the existing social hierarchy. Convinced that they too had a right to rise, they challenged the social order which denied them the opportunity; and the persistence of that order became a positive source of mass resentment.

The gradual (though in Britain still very partial) evanescence of this resentment, as the upward routes were smoothed and broadened, should be set against the alleged increase in insecurity. But often it is not, the reason being, I think, that anti-competitive writers frequently make the wrong time-comparison. If one compares an equal-opportunity society with a stable hereditary one – the U.S. to-day, say, with Britain in the eighteenth century – it may be, for all I know, that the change is all for the worse, and hostile tensions greater. But this is hardly a relevant or interesting comparison, since no one proposes a reversion to a hereditary stratification. If, however, we compare an equal-opportunity society with one which aspires to equal opportunity, but is denied it by existing social relationships – with Britain, say, in 1906 –

then surely we would judge that the former showed fewer resentments and frustrations than the latter.

This is partly due, thirdly, to the fact that other social benefits
inevitably follow in the wake of greater social (and therefore
political) mobility. This latter was not, in Britain, a sudden
isolated arrival on the scene, but was part (and to some extent
the agent) of a broad movement of social reform which brought
such simultaneous gains as greater equality, better social security,
the spread of education – in fact, a general improvement in the
condition of the masses.

It is not clear that this whole process can be said, on balance,
to have increased insecurity. The same movement of reform
brought both the Welfare State and more equal opportunities.
Possibly the latter have intensified insecurity. But the whole practice and ideology of the former pull hard in the opposite direction
– towards security, social responsibility, co-operation. Taking the
two together, can one really assert that they have led to a net
increase in insecurity, ambition, and acquisitiveness? Most
people would surely judge that these characteristics were more
evident in mid-Victorian England, when opportunities were much
less equal, than they are to-day.

Fourthly, wider opportunities must tend to diminish class
feeling and stratification. This is the mobility factor referred to in
Chapter VI. If people from the bottom can rise to the top, the
relative status of those at the top is inevitably affected. A hereditary upper class maintains its towering and unchallenged status
by virtue of being impenetrable from below. But as soon as the
heights are invaded by social climbers, and those still at the
bottom can claim relatives or acquaintances amongst those at
the top, the prestige of the latter must obviously decline. Increased
mobility, especially when, as in Britain, it comes as part of a broad
movement of radical reform, will tend to diminish inequality in
respect of all the determinants of social class. Admittedly it will
not do so, as I argue later, to the extent that socialists desire – at
least not in Britain, where, as opposed to newer societies, class
stratification goes too deep to be uprooted merely by equalising
opportunities. Nevertheless it must have some effect in the right
direction.

IV *Inequality of Opportunity in Britain*

I conclude that the case often made against the mobile equal-opportunity society both exaggerates the evils, and underestimates the compensating gains. Certainly too strong an emphasis on equal opportunity may, under certain conditions to be discussed below,[1] lead to an excessive degree of competition, and hence of resentment and insecurity. But it will do so only if these conditions are present; and they need to be accurately defined. There seem no sufficient grounds for a sweeping condemnation on principle of any such society, regardless of whether these conditions are fulfilled or not.

In Britain, moreover, whatever may be the case elsewhere, a more equal spread of opportunity would bring some exceptionally notable gains at unusually little risk. This is because our national temperament and social habits constitute a reasonably adequate safeguard against too malignant a growth of neurotic, aggressive competition: because our economic situation imparts a particular importance to efficient selection for the highest posts: and because, having developed slowly from a traditional and hereditary society, we are still so far from granting an equal chance to every child.

The previous chapter quoted a number of examples of how unequal opportunities still are. A recent pioneer study now enables us to support this criticism by detailed figures.[2]

The authors of this study measure the degree of social mobility, as opposed to social inertia and class self-recruitment, by means of an 'Index of Association'. A situation of 'random' or 'perfect' mobility, in which there was no link between parental and filial status, and every son had an equal chance of arriving in any status category, would give an Index of Association of 1. This would mean that the actual number of sons of fathers in a particular category, who themselves arrived in that category, was exactly what would be expected on a purely random basis of selection. But if, say, the actual number of sons of fathers in a category who themselves arrived in that category was 20, whereas the expected number on a random basis was 15, the ratio of actual to expected recruits would be 20 : 15, and the Index of

---

[1] *v.* next section.

[2] *Social Mobility in Britain*, ed. D. V. Glass (Routledge and Kegan Paul, 1954).

Association 1·3. Thus the higher the Index, the higher the degree of self-recruitment and maintenance of parental status.[1]

An Index of Association of unity, implying a situation of perfect mobility, is naturally very unlikely, since parental background will always exert a strong influence. What would be significant would be not that the Index was higher than unity for the population as a whole, but if it had strikingly different values for different social groups.

This is precisely what it does have in Britain. For the whole group of males covered by the sample, the Index was 1·44. But when the group was divided into seven status categories according to occupation, it was found to be 13 for the top category (professional and high administrative) – that is, the number of sons of parents in this category who entered it themselves was 13 times as large as it would have been on the basis of random mobility: 5·8 for the second category (managerial and executive): it then fell below 2 for categories 3 to 6, and only rose again to 2·2 for category 7 (unskilled manual).[2]

This suggests a very restricted opportunity for children in the lower to rise into the upper categories, and especially into the top one. The extent of self-recruitment and maintenance of parental status is extremely high in those occupations with the greatest prestige, even though a considerable amount of mobility is apparent lower down. Moreover no significant changes have occurred in the seven Indices for many years; perhaps the 1944 Education Act will eventually make a difference, but the lack of a sustained improvement is disturbing. Sons in the top two categories still enjoy a marked advantage, while sons of 'lower' lineage still find it hard to rise into the 'middle-' and 'upper-class' professions. These figures show that Britain is, even now, far removed from offering equal opportunity; and this remains an essential socialist objective.

v   *Why Equal Opportunity is Not Enough*

Yet there is a reason why it is not a sufficient objective in Britain, or one which absolves us from responsibility for a direct

[1] op. cit., Ch. VIII.   [2] ibid., Tables 11A and 11B, pp. 199-200.

attack on other inequalities. It is a reason which is only partly concerned with insecurity or ferocious competition, and is mainly related to other considerations. It stems from the danger that under certain circumstances the creation of equal opportunities may merely serve to replace one remote élite (based on lineage) by a new one (based on ability and intelligence).

Now some degree of 'éliteness' is inevitable in any society – and indeed desirable, for we are not trying to create a mediocre mass society, in which everyone is levelled down to a uniform denominator. Thus we can hardly imagine a society in which University education, for example, does not create a degree of élite feeling. But provided the society has an egalitarian ambience and no deep class divisions, the élite need not be divided by any large gap from the mass of the population, who will therefore not feel markedly envious or inferior – indeed the term élite can scarcely be said to apply. This is the case in Sweden or the United States, where there is little trace of an élite psychology because there are no glaring status differences between top and bottom, and no sense that the leaders belong to a different and superior class. All have shared broadly the same school education, there are no sharp differences of accent or style of life, and no deep consciousness of social inferiority or superiority.

But too much 'éliteness', and too great a detachment and remoteness from the rest of the population, are clearly undesirable. Yet this might easily be the case in Britain even with equal opportunities – generally on account of our traditional and deeply-embedded class stratification, which, although no doubt jolted, might not be sufficiently disturbed by the greater mobility: and particularly because we have a segregated, privileged system of schools. A concentration on equal opportunity alone would mean that we retained the present (highly unequal) educational and prestige relationship between the public, grammar, and secondary modern schools, but simply ensured that selection for the first two was open to all and genuinely by merit – that is, we should throw open the doors of Eton to competitive examination.[1]

The implications of such a policy are discussed in detail in

[1] I concede that I begged this question when briefly discussing education in the context of the social services (v. Chapter V), and assumed that we should adopt the wider goal of social equality, and seek to equalise the standards and status of different types of school.

the chapter on Education. Here I will only say, anticipating, that the gulf between the different educational tiers is so wide that even with equal opportunity an excessive gap between élite and non-élite would still persist. It might persist in any event simply because the child population was physically separated into different schools at an early age. But, in addition, the gulf between Eton (even with competitive entry) and a secondary modern school would still be such as to impart to children and parents alike an intense consciousness of an educational order of merit.

Nor is this simply a matter of snobbery and social prestige (though it would not necessarily be less significant if it were). It also reflects very real objective differences. Not only is the education in public and grammar schools immensely superior, but the Eton boy, even though he came from a working-class home, would still end up a quite different person from the secondary modern boy in his accent, dress, manners, outlook, and entire style of life. Thus the juvenile population would remain divided into separate, superior or inferior, social classes.[1]

This segregation during the formative years necessarily intensifies inequalities in after-life. Not only are the contrasts in social manners carried on into adult life, where they remain a conspicuous index of class location: but because educational background is increasingly the main determinant of occupation, and hence of other status criteria – income, power, and occupational prestige – divergences in adult status are significantly widened by being superimposed on prior divergences in educational status.

Given that these divergences are so wide, the mere fact that opportunities of joining the élite are equal will not cure all the frustrations and resentments due to social inequality. For one thing, neither parents nor children will feel that the chance was really equal when it presented itself at so early an age as 11. However elaborate the provision for subsequent transfer, those who fail at 11 will always maintain that if only the selection had occurred later, the results would have been quite different; and they will resent being given an inferior docket for life at an age

---

[1] Chapter X gives further evidence for the thesis that our educational system, if we concentrate simply on making opportunities equal, will still tend to create an excessively privileged élite.

when, looking back, they feel they were not fully developed, **nor** old and mature enough to realise what was at stake.

Even if all the failures could be convinced that they had an equal chance, their discontent would still not be assuaged; indeed it might actually be intensified. When opportunities are known to be unequal, and the selection clearly biased towards wealth or lineage, people can comfort themselves for failure by saying that they never had a proper chance – the system was unfair, the scales too heavily weighted against them. But if the selection is obviously by merit, this source of comfort disappears, and failure induces a total sense of inferiority, with no excuse or consolation; and this, by a natural quirk of human nature, actually increases the envy and resentment at the success of others. This is the kernel of truth in the anti-competitive theories discussed above: that *if the inequality of rewards is excessively great*, the creation of equal opportunities may give rise to too intense a competition, with a real danger of increased frustration and discontent.

Now whether, for the population as a whole, this additional discontent outweighs the compensating gains, no one can tell. The point is simply that equal opportunity, if still combined, as it might be in Britain but is not in Scandinavia or North America, with a marked stratification between an élite and the rest of the population, will not remove all the discontents which extreme inequality creates, and in particular cases may even intensify them.

And there is a more general argument on grounds of justice. People do not want to be ruled even by a select élite. They feel that such disparities cannot be justified on any grounds, and that the whole system is basically unfair. And there is much in what they feel. Admittedly, from the point of view of social justice, an aristocracy of talent is an obvious improvement on a hereditary aristocracy, since no one is in fact denied an equal chance. Yet I do not believe, as a personal value judgment, that it can be described as a 'just' society.

It implies that very unequal rewards and privileges are distributed solely on the basis of, if not one, at any rate a particular group of traits of human personality;[1] for any selection must in practice be based on a limited number of more or less known

---

[1] My views on this point owe much to discussions with Mr. Michael Young.

and measurable aspects of character. Let us suppose that intelligence is made the main criterion. Why should this trait be singled
out for such exceptional treatment? One might hold this to be
palpably unjust on the grounds that superior intelligence is
largely due to parental status, through a combination of heredity
and beneficial upbringing: and that no one deserves either so
generous a reward or so severe a penalty for a quality implanted
from outside, for which he himself can claim only a limited
responsibility.

But whether inbred or not, why should this one trait, or even
a group of traits, alone determine success or failure, riches or
poverty, a high or low prestige? Why should no marks be given
for saintliness, generosity, compassion, humour, beauty, assiduity,
continence, or artistic ability? These questions denote no anti-
intellectual bias – matters would be in no way improved if we
chose some other trait to be the sole criterion for exceptional
rewards. It is the injustice of isolating, as a basis for extreme
inequality, certain selected ones out of the multiple strands that
go to make up the human personality, which constitutes the
fundamental ethical case against any élite or aristocracy.

Of course the practical reasons for rewarding outstanding
ability generously are obvious enough; and any society would
be foolish not to offer such rewards as will attract the ability
into the service of the community. But if this requires such large
differential privileges as to create a distinct élite, differently
educated and socially select, it must be regarded as an unpleasant
concession to economic efficiency, and not as being intrinsically
just. In practice, however, I do not believe, after studying the
experience of the U.S. and Scandinavia where the selection is
highly efficient yet social equality much greater, that the inequality and class segregation, which would characterise an élite
of ability in Britain under our present educational system, could
possibly be justified by any considerations of efficiency.[1]

Judged by the third argument for equality, that it reduces
social waste, an élite of talent of course scores much more heavily,
since it eliminates the waste involved in a hereditary, non-
competitive selection for the highest posts. Yet if children are
divided into separate streams at 11, and the streams flow through
such very different country as they do in Britain, it would still

[1] This point is further discussed in Chapter X.

not eliminate the waste associated with restraints on uninhibited social mixing, and the resultant loss of goodwill and breadth of personal experience.

One particular consequence of this, to which attention is often drawn, has disturbing political implications. If the best brains in the working class, creamed off by scholarships and grants, are steered into a distinct and superior educational stratum, the working class will increasingly lose its natural leaders, and have to rely either on the second-rate, or on people who, having been subjected to a quite different educational experience, may now be untypical and remote from working-class psychology. Society's educational talent-scouts will spot the future Bevins and Morrisons at an early age, and rush them off for training as members of the élite; and the Trade Unions will be led by the indifferent residue, and the Labour Party entirely by Old Etonians. This cannot be good for the quality of democracy; yet it follows inescapably from an élite system of education.

This is one aspect of the wider point that an élite must by its very nature be aloof and detached from the mass of the population. It may therefore grow impatient, or ignorant, of what people really want, and be inclined to give them what it thinks they ought to want. We should be saddled with a system of government, efficient and benevolent no doubt, but essentially paternalistic in outlook. There is intrinsically an illiberal and superior quality about élite government, which should make it instantly suspect to a socialist, and indeed to any democrat.

The conclusion must be that in Britain equality of opportunity and social mobility, though they lead to the most admirable distribution of intelligence, are not enough. They need, not to be played down, as some sociologists would have us do, but to be combined with measures, above all in the educational field, to equalise the distribution of rewards and privileges so as to diminish the degree of class stratification, the injustice of large inequalities, and the collective discontents which come from too great a dispersion of rewards. The limited goal is not, from a socialist point of view, sufficient.

IX

SOME ARGUMENTS AGAINST EQUALITY; AND THE AMERICAN EXAMPLE

1   *The Threat to Economic Efficiency*

THIS chapter discusses some common criticisms of the objective of greater equality, and also considers the United States as a test-case of the factors affecting social equality.

The most fashionable criticism runs in terms of the likely effects of equality on the growth of output and living standards, via its adverse reaction on incentives, the supply of savings, and economic efficiency generally. But this criticism is of only limited relevance to the issue of more equality as it is treated in this book. The influences making for class inequality were listed in Chapter VI as the mobility factor, and a number of distance factors. So far as the former is concerned, it is evident that greater mobility would be positively good for efficiency, since by weeding out those whose only pretensions were inherited wealth or lineage, it would strengthen the calibre of the country's economic leadership. Of the various distance factors, it is hard to see that a greater equality of educational standards, style of life and consumption habits, or occupational prestige could do much harm. Sweden and America both combine much greater equality in each of these respects with a degree of productive efficiency at least comparable with our own.

The obviously relevant distance factor is the distribution of wealth. We may at once concede that greater equality will tend to diminish personal savings. But to maintain large inequalities simply in order to guarantee a certain flow of personal saving seems rather a lop-sided approach; and I therefore take this to be an argument, not for surrendering the objective, but for taking counter-measures to ensure sufficient savings from other sources. This is discussed in Chapters XVI and XVII.

On incentives to effort and innovation there is not much to be said in general terms. As I suggested earlier, our present knowledge of economic psychology hardly justifies dogmatic statements – if we were not aware of this already, we should have learned it from the falsification of so many post-war prophecies about the effect of high taxation on incentives. Moreover the whole question of incentives is at least as much a cultural as an economic issue; conventional notions of what constitutes a reasonable reward are not immutable, and for all we know may be quite different in ten years' time from now.

We can be reasonably sure, it is true, that some methods of redistributing work-incomes would have a bad effect – notably, much higher taxation of marginal earnings. But this does not much weaken the socialist case. The largest inequalities stem not from the distribution of earned incomes, but from the ownership of inherited capital; and a desire to redistribute earned income is not one of the most urgent socialist objectives. In so far as we do want more equality of earned income, we must simply proceed slowly in the manner suggested in a previous chapter.[1] But the whole question of combining equality with a rapid rate of economic growth is fully discussed in Part Five.

II *The Threat to Culture*

The second criticism is more fundamental, being based not on economics or practical expediency, but on a denial of the basic value judgment that greater equality will lead to a 'better' society, even assuming no unfavourable effect on output. This approach, which is based essentially on the belief that equality and culture are mutually antagonistic, has a long history; but as a basis for discussion I shall take its most recent expression by M. Bertrand de Jouvenel.[2]

An egalitarian distribution of wealth, writes M. de Jouvenel,

[1] *v.* Chapter VII.
[2] *The Ethics of Redistribution* (Cambridge University Press, 1951).

will give an 'optimum' position only in relation to subjective wants, by which he means economic satisfactions in the utilitarian sense. The demand for equality is thus based on the assumption that incomes are to be regarded solely as a source of individual consumer-satisfaction; and in this narrow sense an equal distribution might give us an economic ideal. But it will not give us an ideal society as judged by non-economic considerations, since the process of redistribution must involve heavy losses in other directions: notably, the disappearance of all those artistic and cultural activities now kept alive by the patronage of the rich, and of all those socially valuable leisure occupations which depend on a comfortable surplus of income over needs (good conversation, hospitality, prolonged travel abroad, unpaid voluntary work). It is not enough that the State should make alternative provision, since, besides being less efficient, this would involve an altogether undesirable enlargement of the role of government. Once we take these non-material losses into account (though, to be fair to economists, they have long been subsumed under the heading of external economies of consumption by the rich), we can be fairly sure that a greater equality of wealth, so far from promoting, would positively menace what most people mean by the 'good' society.

Now these are seductive arguments, especially to socialists, always neurotically afraid of being thought analphabetic vulgarians, or materialists who care nothing for cultural values. And indeed if we accept the inevitability of cultural losses, this argument might be thought, depending, of course, wholly on the individual's scale of values, to destroy an egalitarian case based solely on utilitarian economics. But it was made clear in Chapter VII that the real case for more redistribution was not now based on a utilitarian calculus, or on statements about economic satisfaction or welfare – indeed, I categorically disclaimed any certainty that further redistribution would increase economic welfare. The case rests, just as much as M. de Jouvenel's counter-argument, on non-economic value-judgments, and on a view of what constitutes a 'good' society. A denial of economic utilitarianism leaves this case wholly intact. One would simply have to measure a cultural loss against a gain in social justice or contentment.

In weighing these losses and gains, two points would appear to be relevant. First, if we accept for the sake of argument the inevitability of a cultural loss, what degree of counter-loss in respect of justice and contentment – that is, what degree of inequality – are we asked to endure in order to escape the cultural loss? Secondly, is it in fact the case, so far as mid-twentieth-century Britain is concerned, that there need be a cultural loss at all?

First, how much inequality is supposed to be needed? It might be rather a large amount – if, for example, cultural activity were an increasing function of inequality. Thus it might be that culture was at the margin of expenditure by the wealthy, in which case if the masses could be squeezed to make the wealthy wealthier still, there might be an exceptionally sharp proportional increase in cultural spending – with slavery, presumably, as the logical conclusion. 'It is very difficult indeed', remarked a famous Greek scholar, 'to overrate . . . the advantages of having slaves, if men desire to keep a fine edge on their aesthetic faculties.'[1] Unfortunately not many cultural enthusiasts are as frank as Mr. Clive Bell, who writes that 'civilization requires the existence of a leisured class, and a leisured class requires the existence of slaves. . . . On inequality all civilizations have stood. The Athenians had their slaves: the class that gave Florence her culture was maintained by a voteless proletariat: only the Esquimaux and their like enjoy the blessings of social justice.'[2]

Now it is perfectly reasonable for those who believe this, and who place culture supreme above all other values, to advocate as unequal a society as they choose; though not many people to-day would share their scale of values. But the trouble is that most contemporary anti-socialist writers are less forthright, and fail to make their scale of values clear. In particular, do they demand on behalf of culture at the very least a return to the pre-war spread of incomes: or do they, conceding that culture must be balanced against other 'goods', merely oppose any further moves towards equality? One might take rather a different attitude according to which of these two positions they adopted.

But in any case, is it true that greater equality will necessarily involve a cultural loss? The answer presumably depends on a comparison between the proportion of their surrendered wealth which the rich were previously spending on culture, and the

[1] J. P. Mahaffy, *Social Life in Greece* (Macmillan, 1925 ed.), p. 441.
[2] *Civilization* (Pelican Books), pp. 175, 179.

proportion so spent by the transferees – the state, or the workers, or whoever they may be.

In certain past ages, the former proportion might well have been high – but surely not in Britain to-day. Only a rather insignificant fraction of surtax incomes is directed towards art or culture, or indeed towards any intellectual activities whatever; the bulk goes on expensive cars and houses, holidays in Cannes, servants, gin, hotels and restaurants, dances, lavish parties, and the like. There is no need to be censorious about such activities, which are no doubt often bracing. But they hardly uplift the cultural stand-ards of the community; and we should not be asked to underwrite them on the pretext of subsidising art. Cultivated foreign visitors, charmed by the civilised hospitality of Cambridge Common-rooms, may think their reception typical of the lives of the English wealthier classes. But indigenous critics have no such excuse.

Indeed Britain can perhaps claim in recent times to have had one of the most illiterate wealthy classes in history.[1] At any rate, private patronage in the century up to 1939, when the more rapid income-redistribution began, could hardly be said to have had a uniformly splendid record; one thinks of much of what it built, of the innumerable Georgian buildings in London it failed to save, of the art-treasures it allowed to flow to New York and Chicago, and of the furious revolt against existing society of so many of the outstanding artistic figures of the period.[2] Of course one can never generalise about different forms of patronage – in some periods private patronage has been wholly beneficial.[3]

[1] Mr. Clive Bell would agree on this at least. 'The proportion of the existing leisured class which could be described as "highly civilized" is absurdly small.... We may suppose that the future could devise some method which would exclude from the leisured class at least two-thirds of those whose names now swell the peerage and whose portraits enliven "the weeklies".... Take every two-thousandth baby and you will almost certainly get a better result than you get from the present system.' (op. cit., p. 181.)

[2] Would any of the following, for example, have considered the preservation of the existing social system in Britain as being essential to culture: Carlyle, Ruskin, Browning, Matthew Arnold, William Morris, Whistler, Meredith, James Joyce, or D. H. Lawrence? Though Sir Alfred Munnings and Professor A. E. Richardson no doubt would.

[3] No doubt the eighteenth century was such a period, though not all contemporary observers thought so. John Wesley, who lived through the middle of it, always referred to the rich as the 'great vulgar'. 'There is so much paint and affectation, so many unmeaning words and senseless customs among people of rank, as fully to justify the remark made seventeen hundred years ago, *Sensus communis in illa fortuna rarus*.' (Quoted in *John Wesley*, by C. E. Vulliamy, p. 248.)

But we are concerned with contemporary Britain; and here, surely, the cultural loss from a further transfer of wealth would be so small that the transferees and the state would have to do very badly not to be able to compensate for it.

Why should the transferees not make up some of the loss? Indeed they must do so, if we accept the causal linking of culture and inequality; for this presupposes that cultural spending is an increasing function of a surplus of income over subsistence needs. This is presumably true, to some extent at least, of beneficiaries as well as losers. People sometimes deny this, pointing to the high proportion of incremental working-class income spent on drink, tobacco, gambling, and so on. But for reasons given in Chapter XI, it is certain that this proportion will now rapidly decline.[1] And even to-day it is clear from attendance figures at art galleries and concerts, the number of books borrowed from public libraries, the sales of periodicals, and the week-end crowds at Longleat and Luton Hoo, that some of the recent extra income and leisure has been well spent.[2] Much of it, moreover, is spent on travel (abroad as well as to the sea), which must have some broadening effect on people's minds.

But even if there is a net loss so far as private individuals are concerned (e.g. in respect of the upkeep of historic houses), what is the difficulty about public bodies stepping in to fill the gap? M. de Jouvenel says that they will spend less 'efficiently' than private individuals. I cannot see why. No doubt public patronage has as patchy a historical record as private patronage – from the Greek temples and many of the masterpieces of the Renaissance at one extreme, to the arid consequences of Louis XIV or Stalin at the other. But it performs at least tolerably well in Britain at the moment. The Arts Council, Covent Garden, the art galleries, the British Museum, the Edinburgh Festival, much of the serious theatre, ancient monuments, many historic mansions, and to a growing extent even the Universities, all subsist on, or are aided by, public funds; and the State has not shown itself notably Philistine or unduly interfering as a patron. Innumerable grants

[1] *v.* p. 221.

[2] Nor are Teddy-Boys, often deplored as the first awful outcome of the egalitarian welfare state, a convincing argument on the other side. Certainly they include delinquents amongst their number. But they represent the first awakening of a genuine working-class interest in sartorial elegance; and they are also steeped in what is now becoming a genuine popular culture amongst the young – the study of jazz.

are made for cultural foreign travel, which most of the recipients could certainly not otherwise afford. The Festival of Britain, which gave more splendid openings to young architects than they had enjoyed for a long time past, showed that the State can even initiate, as opposed to merely supporting, artistic endeavour of the highest quality. There have been many errors, notably in the sphere of town and country planning, and many omissions.[1] But there seems no clear case for saying that the state will do, or is doing, either much worse or much less in the role of patron than the British wealthier classes who would suffer from further redistribution.[2]

The final fear is lest an extension of public patronage may whittle away our liberties. Now there may easily, under certain circumstances, be a real danger in the growth of state bureaucracy; this is discussed in a later section. But it can hardly be taken seriously in the field of culture. Public patronage is invariably decentralised to independent bodies moving on the loosest possible rein, indeed on virtually no rein at all. It is vigilantly scrutinised by Parliament, and over-vigilantly by a section of the Press. All parties agree that public monies should not carry with them state control over their expenditure. Generally, it is hard to see the Arts Council or the University Grants Committee as the thin end of the totalitarian wedge – rather, indeed, the opposite; for by helping to create a more literate and sophisticated electorate, they make us less likely to succumb to the wiles of a would-be dictator.

I therefore see no reason to think that the cultural loss from a further move towards equality, if indeed it is positive at all, cannot be offset by public action. And indeed, as I shall suggest in Chapter XXI, the more completely we conquer the old social and economic enemies, the higher a priority we should give to cultural activity by public bodies – the more imaginatively we should plan, and the more generously we should spend, to beautify our country and civilise our way of life. No one can say that British capitalism has set a very high standard for British socialism to improve on.

[1] v. Chapter XXI, Section V, for a discussion of some of these.

[2] The arrival of the Welfare State and greater equality in Britain has in fact coincided with a marked renaissance both in music and the plastic arts (though not in literature).

III *The Threat to Liberty*

It is sometimes said that equality must threaten personal liberty. This is often argued on wide political grounds, relating to the possible tyranny of the 'mob' or the 'masses', who are, it is said, Mill, de Tocqueville, and Acton being called in aid, characteristically indifferent to freedom and hostile to non-conformity. And indeed it is clear that popular rule, or the participation of the masses in politics, is no guarantee of political liberty, and that 'democracy' in this sense and personal freedom are by no means synonymous. Thus it is easy, even in recent history, to find bitterly anti-libertarian movements which enjoyed genuine mass backing, as, for example, Fascism and McCarthyism, or which were mainly based on working-class support, as Communism and the Peronista Labour Unions. Similarly it may be true (though rather natural) that the working classes are sometimes less liberal than more educated classes – e.g. they may be more anti-Semitic or anti-Catholic, or racially prejudiced, or intolerant of dissent.

But this has little to do with the point under discussion. We already enjoy in Britain a form of political democracy which is strikingly stable, which in no way partakes of mob rule or mass violence, and which, based as it is on a long liberal tradition, is exceptionally tolerant of dissent. Even if we attained a greater degree of equality, we should still retain our Parliamentary institutions, our liberal tradition, and a national character strongly attached to personal freedom. There therefore seems no good reason why our political liberties should be curtailed. We have, after all, more social equality than 100 years ago, yet most people would judge that our liberties were also greater; it is not clear why the trend should suddenly be reversed. And so far as personal illiberalism is concerned, a more equal spread of education will obviously improve matters.

It might, however, still be argued, not that equality represents a positive menace to freedom, but that inequality represents a negative protection of freedom against certain imminent dangers. These dangers might stem from the inevitable growth of a state bureaucracy impinging heavily on the lives of individual citizens; or, more generally, from the potential tyranny of voluntary groups (whether social, political, or religious). One possible defence against such threats, it is said, is the possession of private means. This enables at least a few fortunate citizens to finance what may be a long and expensive campaign against, for example, the threat of dispossession by a Government Department, or even a threat of expulsion by a strongly-organised voluntary body. Crichel Down comes obviously to mind; but history provides many examples of men fighting and winning battles for personal liberty and the right to dissent solely because they had the financial resources to sustain them.

This is a serious point, though with only a limited application to the case presented in this book. It is scarcely relevant at all to most of the inequalities which have been discussed. Even in the one relevant sphere of wealth-distribution, it does not require that we preserve all our millionaires on the off-chance that one of them may fight an occasional battle for freedom, any more than on the off-chance that one of them may prove an enlightened patron of the arts. But it is an argument against carrying equality of wealth to a bitter extreme in which no one can ever be even temporarily self-sufficient, or have access to private resources on which to maintain himself while declining to conform.

This is not, in practice, an acute dilemma in this country, for British socialists have never wished to press matters to this extreme, or to destroy all moderate fortunes. It was, after all, a Labour Chancellor, Mr. Dalton, who raised the death-duty exemption limit from £100 to £2,000, and the Labour Party subsequently pressed successfully for its further increase to £3,000; while socialist literature on the death duties has never been very hostile to estates of, say, £20,000 and under.

Clearly amounts of capital such as these do offer the possibility of maintaining independence for a considerable period, and so of sustaining dissent or non-conformity, or a struggle against bureaucratic injustice. On the other hand, they are not inconsistent with reasonable socialist objectives. Although, therefore, there is a genuine libertarian argument (quite apart from more obvious economic ones) against a total flat equality, it in no way precludes the degree of equality suggested in this book.

IV *Factors Affecting Social Equality in the U.S.A.*

It would hardly be denied that the United States had more social equality, and less sense of class, than Great Britain. I therefore take it as a test-case of the factors affecting social equality. I should have preferred to take Sweden, which in other ways comes much nearer to a socialist's ideal of the 'good' society: that is, it gives a higher priority to social welfare and the social services, it has a greater equality of wealth, it enjoys a more harmonious and co-operative pattern of industrial relations, it is characteristically ruled by socialist governments, and its cultural record is exceptional. But the choice of the United States is dictated by the fact that it is the only country about which a sufficient sociological literature exists to justify more or less definite statements.

This choice inevitably lays one open to misunderstanding. I must therefore make it clear that the analysis of social equality in America implies nothing about whether the U.S. is or is not a 'good' society, or a better society than Britain, in other respects such as foreign, economic, cultural, racial, or civil liberties policies. A high degree of social equality is, unfortunately, quite compatible with exceedingly reactionary policies in all these fields. Nevertheless, since socialists are concerned with social equality, it seems foolish not to study the American experience.

The facts about America are hardly in dispute. Objectively, class differences in accent, dress, manners, and general style of life are very much smaller; and one cannot, strolling about the street or travelling on a train, instantly identify a person's social background as one can in England.[1] Subjectively, social relations are more natural and egalitarian, and less marked by deference, submissiveness, or snobbery, as one quickly discovers from the cab-driver, the barman, the air-hostess and the drug-store assistant.[2]

---

[1] I suggest the following experiment to any sceptic: immediately after a visit to America, to travel first-class from Kemble to Paddington by the 9.4 on a Monday morning, and to follow this up with a walk through Shoreditch; alternatively, merely to stand (and listen) outside a large factory, or cinema, or football match, and compare it mentally with the same experience in the States.

[2] Bagehot once called England a 'deferential country'. No one could apply that phrase to the U.S.A.!

The consequence is much less sense of class stratification, and in particular of a three-class hierarchy (working, middle, and upper). Margaret Mead, in her classic study of the American character, writes that 'the American system is really a classification based on a ladder, up which people are expected to move, rather than upon orderly stratification or classification of society, within the pigeon-holes of which people are born'.[1] Thus the 'upper' classes are merely those 'whose only possible social movement is downwards. . . . They have no distinguishing manners and no distinguishing morals and no distinguishing occupation or lack of it. . . . If a member of the upper class of Baltimore should turn up in shabby clothes in Billings, Montana, he would find it very difficult to document his position. . . . Former residents of Baltimore might be able to identify him if they had known him personally, but not by his bearing and accent, as would be the case in England.'[2]

At the other end of the scale, there is less envy and resentment at high incomes, since those who enjoy them are not thought to belong to a different or superior class, or to have inherited them from their parents: less distinctive working-class psychology, either individually or collectively:[3] less belief in inevitable class conflict: and no parallel to the ideology of class betrayal described in Chapter VII. Workers who take managerial posts are not condemned as traitors to their class. Trade Union leaders are not thought to be in danger of contamination if they have large cars, and smoke cigars, and draw huge salaries. The Unions are not thought guilty of treachery if they co-operate with management to boost sales or raise productivity, or even accept a wage cut to save a firm from bankruptcy; nor are they suspect if they send their officials to Harvard and Yale for training, and employ large numbers of university graduates.

What accounts for the difference? Evidently not two factors which socialists might traditionally have looked for first: neither more public ownership and a less 'capitalistic' distribution of

[1] *Keep Your Powder Dry*, p. 58.

[2] op. cit., p. 62. Of course one must exclude freak old-world survivals like the Creoles of New Orleans; some older regions in New England are also exceptional.

[3] And the contrast never fails to amaze Americans; cf. this typical comment from a very sympathetic account of a T.U.C. Conference: 'Labour observers from the United States have also been impressed, as Americans in England usually are, by the extent and the depth of the class-consciousness that still prevails among industrial workers.' (*New York Times*, 4 September 1952.)

economic power, nor a more equal distribution of incomes.[1] This does not prove, of course, that these two factors have no relevance in Britain. The determinants of class feeling are not the same in every country, but vary with the cultural and historical background; and in Britain, more than in most countries, class tension and hostility are concentrated in industry, and appear to derive from work-relationships. This difference may be due to the greater efficiency of American industry, or the higher real wages, or the atmosphere of equal opportunity; and it may be that industrial class feeling in Britain, receding as other egalitarian measures take effect, will prove to have been only a rationalisation of quite different discontents.[2] But for the moment it is much stronger in Britain, and might be thought to provide a *prima facie* case for changes in the industrial structure.

Similarly with respect to incomes. Any given degree of income inequality may induce more or less resentment, and be considered more or less unjust. In Britain, the resentment and the injustice are both greater. This is due partly to the American Horatio Alger and 'rags to riches' tradition, which, by offering a greater hope of reaching the top, thereby diminishes the resentment against those already there: and partly to the fact that a higher proportion of large incomes in Britain, being unearned and derived from inherited property, do not have the excuse of being a reward for personal effort or ability.

A popular view is that the difference between the two countries is due simply to the greater vertical mobility in the United States. But recent studies have shown that vertical mobility *as such* is not significantly greater, and that sons of manual workers have only the same chance as in Britain (and other European countries) of rising to higher, non-manual occupational status.[3]

This does not mean, however, that the question of mobility is

---

[1] Income distribution appears to be very similar in the two countries (*v.* A. M. Cartter, 'Income Shares: Great Britain and United States', *American Economic Review*, December 1954.)

[2] *v.* Chapter XIV for a further discussion of these various possibilities.

[3] *v.* Glass, op. cit., and for a summary of the evidence, S. M. Lipset and N. Rogoff, 'Class and Opportunity in Europe and the U.S.', *Commentary*, December 1954. There appear to be two reasons why so many major countries exhibit a consistent upward pattern of mobility: first, they have all experienced for the past three decades a pronounced growth of white-collar relative to manual occupations, which of course creates the possibility of upward movement; secondly, in all of them the high-status categories have been bearing proportionately fewer children than the low-status categories, thus leaving still more room for upward movement.

irrelevant. Although vertical mobility is no greater in America, horizontal and geographical mobility both are. There is, as compared with Europe, an exceptionally large and persistent movement of population into the cities, due to the steady decline in the size of the (extremely large) agricultural labour force. The urban American economy thus offers ample opportunities, not necessarily for rising in the social scale, but for changing occupation, for starting afresh in new surroundings, for leaving home in search of wealth and fame. This favourable 'opportunity structure', arising from a major structural change in the economy, does make for a more fluid and mobile society, with a weaker link between parental and filial status.

In any event, whatever the facts about relative vertical mobility, the accepted image of it is strikingly different in the two countries. Americans *believe* in the 'office-boy to president' mythology. The level of aspiration is therefore higher, the hope of achieving the aspiration greater, and the individual's life-perspective generally more buoyant. This of course is immensely significant for social attitudes and morale. The difference is no doubt partly due to the greater spatial fluidity just mentioned. But it is also due to the egalitarian ideology which causes top executives to boast, not of their lineage, but of their humble origins; in Britain, by contrast, self-made men often try to play down their social origins, and feel embarrassed and inferior at not having been to a public school.[1] Thus in America the prevailing ideology emphasises, whereas in Britain it tends to conceal, the extent of vertical mobility; and this helps to foster the picture of a land of equal opportunity.

The mobility factor therefore accounts for some part of the difference between the two countries. Historical factors naturally account for a further part. They account, for example, for the fact that in the U.S. the traditional-conservative, as well as the liberal-radical, ideology has been egalitarian from the start, whereas in Britain it has consistently been (and still is fundamentally) anti-egalitarian. The assumption, sanctified by the famous words of the Constitution, of a natural human equality, has had a profound influence in orienting American social attitudes in an egalitarian direction; and the results may be observed

[1] Thus the autobiographies of successful American businessmen have such titles as *The Story of an American Workman*; cf. the frequent (and often rather misleading) advertisements put out by large companies boasting that all their top executives started at the bottom and worked their way up.

far outside the sphere of class relationships – in the relations between the sexes, for example, or between voters and politicians, parents and children, teachers and pupils, officers and other ranks.

This difference again reflects the fact that the U.S. never developed a stable, hereditary ruling-class, or those prestige-symbols, characteristic of a ruling-class, which still persist in Britain even though the precise class structure which gave them birth has largely passed away. Such symbols either do not exist at all in America; or, if they do, they are imitative and artificial, and have little social significance. To take some examples at random, there are no titles of any kind; a few 'prestige' schools exist, but carrying a social weight and snob appeal in no way comparable to those of the major English public schools; no distinct ruling-class style of architecture has ever emerged, but only lavish imitations of Tudor mansions, French chateaux or Renaissance palaces; there are debutantes, and even a Social Register, but they are not taken seriously outside a very narrow circle.

Another major difference lies in the more amorphous character of American society, and particularly its greater ethnic hetero-geneity. The second-generation American never developed a proletarian class-consciousness, because he was never a prole-tarian – the lowest-status jobs were always taken over by Negroes, or by the next wave of immigrants.[1] Virtually no second-genera-tion whites, for example, have ever done domestic service. This particular influence is no doubt weakening with Negro emancipa-tion and the decline of large-scale immigration, but not before it has fufilled, as it were, its historic function of inoculating the American worker against a proletarian class outlook.

There are, however, other reasons for the differences which are not peculiar to the U.S.A., and which do carry a moral for socialists in Britain. The first and most important is the educa-tional system, which has none of the fissiparous effect on society produced by the British system. The first reason for this is the absence of any segregation at 11+ in the state school sector. Public secondary schools are 'comprehensive'; and the huge majority of the population therefore share the same educational experience up to the time when they leave school.

[1] In Professor Hofstadter's phrase, immigration acted as an 'automatic built-in status elevator'.

It is true that private schools exist, possibly even in the same proportion to the whole as in Great Britain. Yet they create no national educational élite as do the British 'public' schools. The figures for private-school pupils are in fact rather misleading. Far more of these schools than in Britain are simply parochial, especially Catholic, schools; and of the remainder, a high proportion are concentrated in small geographical areas – in traditional New England, the 'social register' areas of New York State and Florida, and certain parts of the South. And the figures are misleading in another way, since a much larger number of private-school pupils than in Britain attend a private school for only a part of their educational lives, and spend the remainder in state schools.

In any event, there is much less social gap between the average public and private school. Educational standards (in most areas) are more nearly comparable than in England; and there is no wide gulf in social prestige – few private schools, for example, are at all widely known by name. And, most important, there is little difference in the school leaving age; the great majority of high-school pupils remain until 17 or 18, and one of the major causes of the wide status gap in Britain is thus avoided.

The consequence is that employers are much less interested in an applicant's school (as opposed to college) background, and seldom ask what school he went to. Different schools carry little weight in terms of job selection; and the school system does not, as it does in Britain, largely determine adult occupation, and hence access to other high-prestige criteria – income, power, and occupational status.[1]

Secondly, the pattern of consumption is markedly more equal than in Britain. 'Prestige-goods' are widely distributed, and there is less conspicuous contrast between the standard of living of different income-groups. To take the most obvious example, almost every family owns a car; and this is significant not only because a car is the most conspicuous of all consumption goods, but also because universal car-ownership leads to the universal

[1] A further reason for the lack of correlation, as compared with Britain, between school and occupational status is that not only is the number of children who have had a 'segregated' education relatively less, but the number of non-manual jobs is relatively greater. Thus a high proportion of non-manual jobs are filled by ordinary high-school pupils; and the tiresome British correlation (grammar or public school = non-manual job, secondary modern = manual), so strongly productive of class feeling, is largely avoided.

consumption of other conspicuous or semi-luxury goods – holidays, hotels, middle-class habits of shopping, etc. But the lack of external class-distinctions can be observed in many other spheres: e.g. clothes, eating-habits, drug-stores, the ownership of consumer durables, and so on.

This greater equality in consumption habits and style of life is not due to a greater equality of incomes. No doubt it has many and varied causes: the egalitarian tradition which hindered the emergence of obvious class differentiation in matters such as dress: the influence of the mass media of communications: the American trend towards conformism: the gadget-minded and novelty-oriented American character: and above all, as I shall argue in Chapter XI, the fact of an absolutely higher standard of living. But whatever the exact cause, it is a factor of profound importance in creating a sense of social equality.

A third factor is the diminishing importance of economic class pressures in a high-consumption society. This is the 'technological' factor referred to in Chapter VI. In such a society, as poverty disappears, so does the driving pressure towards economic conflict. Any desired consumption-good becomes more and more easily accessible; and economic envy is diminished. Leisure increases relative to hours of work, and the importance of consumption factors relative to that of productive relationships. The 'service' grows relative to the manufacturing population, and technical and non-manual relative to unskilled manual labour; and the outlines of distinct economic classes become increasingly blurred. All this has conspicuously occurred in the U.S.A., with the result that social attitudes are less dominated than in Britain by consciousness of economic class.[1]

None of this is to be taken to mean, as I have already pointed out, that America is a superior society. Social equality can quite well be combined with a reckless foreign policy, an illiberal attitude to civil liberties, an unenlightened tariff policy, an excessive tenderness to business interests, large-scale unemployment, social intolerance, and all manner of reprehensible things.

Nor does it mean that there is no labour-management conflict in industry – on the contrary, there is; and the Unions often wage

[1] Interesting evidence of the influence of this factor is to be found in the Lynds' Middletown studies. They found that between 1925 and 1935, the consciousness of economic class differences had noticeably *increased* as a result of the depression (*Middletown in Transition*, pp. 450 seq.).

it more militantly and violently than their British counterparts. But because it exists, it does not follow that a whole theory of sociology can properly be built around it. And in the U.S. it is much less significant for social attitudes as a whole. It goes both less deep, since it does not dominate the whole social orientation of the individual; and less wide, since it does not determine attitudes outside the strict productive sphere as it does in Britain (e.g. political attitudes – witness the absence of a Labour Party, and of any serious pressure to establish one).[1] The economic class conflict exists, but is not carried over into 'off-duty' or 'after-hours' relationships.

Nor does greater equality mean that America can show no violent social conflicts and resentments; it is only that these can normally be traced to ethnic or racial, and not to direct class antagonisms. Nor, again, does it mean that one cannot speak at all in terms of social classes:[2] or that there are no prestige-symbols, expressive of social standing:[3] or that there are no social gradations (as of course there must be in any society).[4] It is simply that class distinctions are less pervasive and less hereditary, social attitudes less class-conscious, the atmosphere more natural and unrestrained, the social ladder as a whole much shorter, and social envy and resentment less – in sum, social equality is greater.

The reasons for the difference tend to confirm the analysis of Chapter VI. The technological factor (the stage of economic development) is evidently of great importance. The mobility factor is significant for the image of it which exists in the public mind. But because this image is different in Britain, and because

[1] And the pressure is weaker to-day than 40 years ago; similarly Trade Union attitudes are less 'class-conscious' now than then.

[2] Thus Lloyd Warner divided Yankee City into six classes – upper-upper, lower-upper, upper-middle, lower-middle, upper-lower, lower-lower. But it is doubtful if these divisions would be thought to have much significance if American thought were not oriented in European terms. 'It is possible to describe the American system without mentioning class. . . . If our European observer could be eliminated, I think that is the way it would be done. An observer from a country without a feudal past, or an observer from a country still in the feudal state, would find . . . our temporary crystallization of status to have so little form as to be unworthy of primary mention.' (Mead, op. cit., p. 66.)

[3] e.g. East side and West side, uptown and downtown, silk-stocking class, station-wagon class, Scotch and Bourbon, Cadillacs, University Clubs and fraternities (in some areas), Groton, Ivy League, the Stork Room, the Social Register. But many of these (e.g. the Social Register) are a pure joke; and none carry the social weight of their British counterparts.

[4] In fact, Lloyd Warner (rather unconvincingly) lists 89 'social positions or statuses'!

in addition we descend from a still deeply influential traditional and hereditary past, the 'distance' factors will need to be objectively more favourable to equality than in America. It is clear in any event that greater social equality in Britain will require a more egalitarian educational system, and a greater equality in the pattern of consumption. But it will also, for the reasons described above, call for a further redistribution of inherited wealth, and an equalisation of power and privilege within industry. These four central distance factors are discussed in this order in the succeeding chapters.

X

THE INFLUENCE OF EDUCATION

I *Limitations on Equal Opportunity*

THE school system in Britain remains the most divisive, unjust, and wasteful of all the aspects of social inequality. First, it denies even the limited aim of equal opportunity. Before the war, it did so to an extent which now seems almost fantastic, so that a high proportion of children had no access to secondary education of any kind. Of boys born between 1910 and 1929, only 14% of those from state elementary schools achieved a secondary education, compared with 89% of those from private primary schools. Taking the occupational status categories described in Chapter VIII, a boy from categories 1-3 had five times the chance of a grammar school education as a boy from categories 6-7 (and thirteen times the chance of reaching a University) – and this without reference to boys educated at independent schools.[1] Part of the cause of this deplorable situation was directly economic – even when a working-class child did win a free grammar school place, his parents often could not afford to take it up. But mainly it was due to governmental apathy and meanness.

The 1944 Education Act set out to make secondary education universal; and formally it has done so. Yet opportunities for advancement are still not equal.

First, the intention was, since it was recognised that the grammar schools would retain their superior quality and hence

[1] *v.* Glass, op. cit., Ch. V.

their differential advantage as an avenue to the better occupations, to throw open this advantage, by abolishing fees and standardising entry procedures, to all social classes on equal terms. This aim has not yet been fully realised. The class distribution of the grammar school population is still markedly askew. An investigation in 1951 showed that the middle class was still heavily over-represented:[1] the upper working class, with one-third of grammar school places, now reasonably well represented: but the lower working class, with only 15% of places, still heavily under-represented.[2] And not only do proportionately more middle class children enter the grammar schools, but once there they do much better. Children from professional and managerial families account for 15% of the total population, 25% of the grammar school population, and 44% of the sixth-form population. 'From the children of [such] parents at one extreme to the children of unskilled workers at the other there is a steady and marked decline in performance at the grammar school, in the length of school life, and in academic promise at the time of leaving.'[3]

These contrasts are much larger than can be explained on genetic grounds. No doubt the proportion of high-I.Q. children is greater amongst the middle class than amongst the working class; but given the far higher absolute numbers of the latter, one would still expect them to show significantly better results than they do. The explanation must be looked for partly in social influences – the less educated parents, the more crowded (and noisy) homes, the smaller opportunities for extra-curricular learning, of working-class children: and partly in financial factors – a child continuing at school is still a heavy financial strain on working-class parents, and one which could at least be mitigated, and early leaving thus discouraged, by more generous maintenance payments and an extension of family allowances. But, for the present, equal opportunity is subject to definite limitations.[4]

But the question of grammar school places is relevant only

[1] That is, over-represented from the point of view of equality and justice – not necessarily, as things now are, from the point of view of efficiency.

[2] *v.* A. H. Halsey and L. Gardner, 'Social mobility and achievement in four grammar schools', *Brit. J. Sociology*, March 1953.

[3] *Early Leaving* (H.M.S.O., 1954).

[4] This is quite apart from the notorious inequalities of opportunity deriving from the unequal *geographical* distribution of grammar school places.

to the above-average child. Matters are much worse when we
turn to the average child. The least we can ask for is that all
ordinary children, irrespective of social background, should
enjoy a good primary and secondary education in decent buildings, with classes of reasonable size, and up to a reasonable age.
This the children of better-off parents enjoy in the independent
schools. But many working-class children, owing to the appallingly
low quality of parts of the State educational system, are still
enjoying nothing of the sort.

The handicap arises mainly from overcrowding and bad
buildings. The deficiencies on these two counts are by now notorious. The Select Committee on Estimates wrote in 1953 that 'at
every point they were confronted with overcrowding, lack of
schools, a shortage of teachers, and often rapidly deteriorating
and even dangerous school buildings. . . . The condition into
which many of the older schools in the country have fallen is the
worst feature. Some of them are no better than slums.'[1] No doubt
matters are gradually – though very gradually – improving; and
the situation will be greatly eased when the population 'bulge' has
finally left the schools in the early 1960s.

But one cannot speak of even an approach to equal opportunity
until the average size of class in State schools has been substantially reduced: the 'all-age' schools, which still deny a proper
secondary education to over 700,000 children, have been re-
organised: the black-listed slum schools have been closed down:
the many structurally sound but grimly forbidding Victorian
Gothic schools in industrial towns have been improved: the school-
leaving age raised: and County Colleges opened as envisaged
in the 1944 Act. This is, of course, simply a matter of money and
resources, on which something is said later in the chapter.

II   *The Need for Reform of the Public Schools*

But even when these improvements have been made, we shall
still not have equality of opportunity so long as we maintain a
system of superior private schools, open to the wealthier classes,
but out of reach of poorer children however talented and deserv-

[1] *Eighth Report from the Select Committee on Estimates* (*Session* 1952-3), pp. vii and ix.
Cf. also Peggy Jay, *Better Schools Now!* (Turnstile Press, 1953.)

ing. This is much the most flagrant inequality of opportunity, as it is cause of class inequality generally, in our educational system; and I have never been able to understand why socialists have been so obsessed with the question of the grammar schools, and so indifferent to the much more glaring injustice of the independent schools.[1]

That these schools are superior, and notably the 'public schools',[2] is beyond dispute. As compared even with grammar schools, let alone most secondary modern schools, their staffing ratio is higher, the academic quality (and often the devotion to teaching) of the staff superior, their surroundings more agreeable, their extra-curricular facilities more ample, and (most important for good teaching) their holidays longer. It is sometimes said that these advantages are confined to some thirty or so of the major public schools, and that the remainder are in no way education-ally superior to good grammar schools. I doubt this (except for a tiny handful of famous grammar schools). But even if it were true, the minor public schools would still confer a crucial *social* advant-age, namely, better prospects of a high-paid or high-status job. This advantage is attributable partly to the widespread belief (whether well-founded or not is irrelevant) that public school products are more dependable and self-reliant: partly to the still important though intangible factor of the right accent, bearing, and manners: and partly to the fact that persons now in authority, and responsible for selecting and promoting, have commonly themselves been to public schools, and so have a natural bias. This bias may often be unconscious (though loyalty to the old school is by no means defunct); but it is none the less real for that. The consequence is that boys even from minor public schools have significantly better occupational prospects at any given level of educational attainment; and the attachment of parents to these schools is not just irrational 'snob' prejudice.

Granted that this is an obvious injustice, what is to be done about it? There are three possible courses of action. First, the State might proscribe private education altogether, on the

---

[1] *Challenge to Britain* contained no proposal whatever for altering the present system. There have been a very few exceptions to the general indifference (cf. H. D. Hughes, *A Socialist Education Policy*, Fabian Society, 1955).

[2] By which is meant here the independent boarding schools, and not the entire membership of the Headmasters' Conference. Foreign readers should note the quaint solecism whereby public schools mean exclusive private schools.

grounds that the purchase by wealthy citizens of so overwhelming a social advantage is clearly inequitable. This is not the right solution. It is out of tune with the temper of the country, and is therefore not likely in any event to be politically practicable. It is not sensible to stifle all private educational experiment; this may be sometimes crankish, but at other times is genuinely progressive. And a flat proscription is undesirable on libertarian grounds. Once incomes have been distributed as the government of the day thinks fit, it is generally right, save in war-time or post-war periods of national crisis, that citizens should be left free to spend them as they wish, provided only that no nuisance is caused to others. And the interference with private liberty would be intolerable; the closing of all independent schools would naturally encourage a strong demand both for private tutors and places in schools abroad; and the resulting inequalities would compel the extension of the ban to these facilities also.

The second approach is the sanguine one. Some optimists expect the public schools to wither quietly away as redistribution bites further into the higher incomes, and as the State schools improve their standards. This is excessively hopeful. Whatever happens in the State system, the independent boarding schools will long retain a real advantage in educational standards, social prestige, and job prospects; and recent years have shown that middle-class parents are prepared to make very substantial sacrifices to obtain this advantage for their children. Moreover our tax system permits fees to be paid in many other ways than out of current taxed income – not only out of capital, or tax-free capital gains, but by tax-free covenants taken out by relatives, or insurance policies taken out at birth. The next Labour Government might alter matters somewhat. But all the public schools now have long waiting-lists; and in the light of middle-class parental psychology, I can see little sign that they are likely to be starved out by penury.

A drift away from the private preparatory schools is rather more likely. These offer, on the average, a lesser relative educational advantage; in the nature of things they have little influence on ultimate job-selection; and although some of them are appalling breeding-grounds of snobbery, they carry less social prestige than the public schools. It is therefore quite possible that middle-class parents might gradually desert them as standards in the primary schools improve.[1] This would be wholly desirable. The educational loss would be infinitesimal, if indeed positive at all; and a pronounced social gain from mixing the classes would result. But in England at least no change at the primary level can ever be wholly decisive, either for class attitudes or the diffusion of opportunities; and the problem of the public schools remains.

The third and most sensible approach is to work for a gradual integration of these schools into the State system of education. This is no more than a reversion to the proposals of the Fleming Committee, which, recognising even in 1944 the injustice of the present system, recommended that the independent schools should initially offer 25% of their places to non-fee-paying pupils from State elementary schools, the proportion to rise stage by stage 'with a view to the progressive application of the principle that schools should be equally accessible to all pupils and that no child otherwise qualified shall be excluded solely owing to lack of means'.[2]

Unfortunately this recommendation was not implemented after the war. In some areas no attempt whatever was made to follow it up, in others local authorities compromised with a much lower figure than 25%. The reasons for this failure are well known. Local authorities, naturally reluctant at a time of rapidly rising rates to incur the heavy additional fee expenditure involved, always disliked the scheme. Many parents of working-class children were also hostile; and indeed it is far from clear that the social and psychological effects of applying the proposal on a very small scale are at all desirable – the 'guinea-pig' children will either be unhappy, or become *déclassé*; and in any case the effects on the social structure would be infinitesimal. And both the grammar schools and Labour educationalists were naturally unfriendly to the removal of the best pupils from the State system in order to bolster up the private sector.

But this is quite a different matter from applying the scheme on a really large scale; and the next Labour Government must simply choose between sending no State-aided pupils to the public schools at all, which would be a public confession that it had lost

---

[1] Although a condition of this occurring might be a change in the Common Entrance examination; this is now attuned to the syllabus of the private preparatory schools, which is different in many respects from that of the State primary schools.

[2] *The Public Schools and the General Educational System* (H.M.S.O., 1944), pp. 65-6.

interest in socialism and equality;[1] and sending a really large number. Clearly it must do the latter, and announce that its policy requires the grant by the public schools initially of 25% 'free' places, rising rapidly to 50%, and later to at least 75%; the ultimate objective being 100% competitive entry, regardless of whether the children had previously been to State or private schools.[2] The corollary would be financial assistance, and public representation on governing bodies.

Would this raise insoluble social and educational difficulties?[3] So far as the public schools themselves are concerned, the answer is surely no. We already have a large number of 'direct grant' schools, including some of the most famous grammar schools, operating a 25% or 50% 'free place' system with great success. They find neither that the publicly-appointed governors make an interfering nuisance of themselves: nor that selection by an external test gives worse results than the school's own internal methods of selection: nor that social divergences arise between aided and fee-paying pupils. No doubt in major public schools, where the latter are drawn from a narrower social class, such divergences would be more obvious. But then half the object of the scheme is to present social contrasts under a single roof, in order ultimately to narrow them.

Unlike the limited post-1945 experiment, this reform must in the last resort be the responsibility, both financial and administrative, of the central government. Otherwise the local authorities, with an eye on their rates and fearing the extra cost, will simply decline to co-operate (or else select only their problem children).

Could such a reform be carried through voluntarily? It is always better to act by agreement if this is at all possible. Although the public schools are not now under any great financial strain, many headmasters, and notably those from the better and more famous schools, have a distinctly bad conscience about their

[1] Incredibly enough, the Labour Party made this confession at the last election – unless some stray pieces of nationalisation were thought to be a substitute for reforming the strongest remaining bastion of class privilege.

[2] The allotted places need not all be completely free; payment could (and should) be assessed according to a graduated income scale of the kind already applied to State university awards.

[3] For an excellent discussion of some of the problems involved, v. Hughes, op. cit. One obvious problem would be the age of entry, since the break between primary and secondary education is now 11 in the State sector and 13 in the private sector; some adjustment would be necessary here.

present methods of selection; and they might be inclined to co-operate. It would certainly be worth while to make a bid for an agreed scheme first; and if a majority of the public schools came in, this might be sufficient. But if a majority declined, the community must then assert its right to deal with what is a flagrant restriction on equality of opportunity.

By this solution the public schools, while retaining their distinctive character, teaching cadres, and genuine educational assets, would steadily grow more socially heterogeneous; and they would cease to cause that interaction between parental status, educational opportunity, and filial status which now creates such social 'inertia', and restricts the upward movement from below. No doubt middle-class children would remain for some time over-represented, as they are in the grammar schools, by virtue of genetic or environmental advantages. But the over-representation would at least be based on genuine differences in intelligence, and not on the adventitious possession of private means; and in any event it would be much less marked than now.

III *The Case against an Élite School System*

We should then have an educational system which was exceptionally just and fair, in the limited sense of offering equal opportunities regardless, so far as this is ever possible, of birth or wealth; and exceptionally efficient in that the ablest pupils would be creamed off and given a superior training. We should largely have attained the goal of the equal-opportunity society.

But I argued in Chapter VIII that this was not a sufficient goal for socialists in Britain. Equal opportunities for self-advancement, superimposed on a segregated educational system, would still leave too wide a gap between the new élite and the average citizen. Of course the gap would be less, owing to the freer vertical movement, than under the present system; and the selection for the élite more just. And of course some degree of educational 'éliteness', resting on the Universities, the sixth forms, or simply the fact of staying at school until 18, is inevitable. But here the prestige-gulf between the public schools and the rest would still be such as to create an élite much too detached from the point of

view either of social justice, or contentment, or democracy.[1]
We can find supporting evidence for this view in the post-war
experience of providing equal opportunities even within a
segregated *State* system of education.

The implementation (though it is not clear that it was the
intention) of the 1944 Act was in terms of a tripartite secondary
school system – grammar, secondary modern and technical – the
three streams being divided out by a selection at 11 +. Although
there was supposed to be 'parity of esteem' between the three
types of school, it was recognised that the grammar schools would
long retain their superiority; and the 11 + examination, combined with the abolition of grammar school fees, was intended to
provide an equal opportunity for all children to enjoy this
superior advantage.

It was precisely because the advantage was so superior that the
11 + examination assumed such overwhelming importance, both
objectively and subjectively, in the years following the war.
Not only did the grammar school often start with a long-standing
prestige, while the secondary modern started with none; not
only did it offer an immensely superior education at a time when
the secondary modern school was being improvised, usually from
scratch, and in wholly unsuitable buildings: but it also represented
the main, if not the only, avenue to well-paid, non-manual, high-
status occupations. This reflects the fact that as the small man and
the self-employed give way to the large-scale managerial structure,
and as technical proficiency becomes increasingly essential, educational qualifications (which in this context mean a grammar
school background) become more and more the indispensable
condition of rising in the social scale.

We have here a microcosm of what a national élite system of
education, based on competitive entry, might look like. One
thing cannot be doubted, that it would be exceedingly unpopular.
The 11 + examination came to be bitterly disliked and resented.
It was thought that a child's whole future was decided on a
single day's test.[2] No doubt much of the dislike was based on
ignorance or exaggeration. The results were in fact never decided
on a single day's test. Immense care was commonly taken over

[1] *v.* Chapter VIII, Section V.

[2] The middle and upper classes, if they have girls of University age, are now
gaining an inkling of what the 11 + examination is like from the extremely competitive conditions of entry into women's colleges at Oxford and Cambridge.

borderline cases. There was always provision (though often imperfect) for re-testing and transferring 'late developers'. And the
better secondary modern schools began increasingly to provide
advanced courses and thus a route to the higher occupations.

But there was quite sufficient truth in these intuitive fears to
give them a genuine validity. Nor were they assuaged by the
seeming justice of the process of selection – indeed this may, as I
suggested in Chapter VIII, actually have exacerbated the resentments. At any rate the depth of these fears and subsequent
resentments, and the intense mental and nervous strain imposed
on parents and children alike by the knowledge of what was at
stake, strongly underline the argument of that chapter that equal
opportunity, if combined with marked educational and social
disparities, will not create a society which is contented and
deemed to be just.

There are also, of course, strong practical objections to segregation at 11. It is conceded that mistakes in selection are inevitable,
and indeed occur on a wide scale [1] The question is whether any
practicable provision for later transfer can adequately correct
them, given the upheaval involved in changing schools, the social
disgrace for children who are graded downwards, and the
pressure on overworked headmasters and Education Officers.
Nor is it clear that there is any logic in this particular tripartite
division – that there are in fact three clearly-marked types of
child, which can be neatly sorted and labelled in this way: or
even if there were, that the numbers in each could be accurately
pre-determined, as they must be if separate schools are to be built
for them. The whole business has a distinctly arbitrary air.

If we add to these drawbacks, inherent in the segregation of
grammar school children, the parallel drawbacks which would
attach to a still further selection for free places in the public
schools; and if in addition to the practical drawbacks we consider
the divisive and stratifying effect, wholly unknown in most other
advanced countries, of educational segregation at widely varying
levels of social prestige and advantage, then we must surely
incline, as socialists, towards a 'comprehensive' system of education, under which all children would ideally share the same broad

[1] How fallible the selection process is can be judged by the fact that 24% of the
grammar school population leave at 15, and only 17% avail themselves of the hard-
won opportunity of staying until 18. (v. Early Leaving.)

experience at least up to the official school-leaving age. Indeed if the argument of previous chapters is accepted, this would seem, if we had a free choice in the matter, a condition of creating an equal and 'classless' society.

IV Comprehensive Schools in Principle

In fact we do not have a completely free choice, since we inherit an elaborate non-comprehensive school structure, which cannot be forcibly dismantled. For this and other reasons to be discussed in Section VI, the Labour Party could never impose a comprehensive system rapidly on the entire country. Nevertheless we have some choice in the matter; and we must therefore consider the arguments commonly brought against comprehensive secondary education.

The most forceful opposition spokesman has been Dr. (now Sir) Eric James.[1] He bases his case on a passionate belief in the importance of 'leadership' – an importance greater than ever now that the range of social problems has become so wide and complex. The nurture of potential leaders, he argues, must be the first concern of the educational system; this requires their segregation into separate schools; and any egalitarian sentiment must give way to this over-riding aim.

No reasonable person would deny that leadership is important. But general statements do not advance matters very far. For instance, how wide a gap in status is required between the leadership élite and the rest of the community? How do we weigh the need for leadership against other social 'goods', such as democracy, or equality, or group participation? And, more fundamentally, can we so precisely delineate the qualities needed for leadership that we could, even if we so wished, build our entire educational structure round them?

Dr. James lists these qualities as high intelligence, an intensive academic education, integrity, courage, judgment, stability, tact, and perseverance.[2] But some of the most effective leaders in history have been illiterate, academically moronic, dishonest,

[1] v. Education and Leadership (Harrap, 1951).

[2] The qualities, evidently, of a successful headmaster.

unstable, neurotic, if not actually insane or epileptic. Even if we exclude 'bad' leaders and confine ourselves to 'good' ones, we still find a great many of the latter, indeed probably a majority, who have had no intensive academic education (and still more who have had no tact). In fact the above is just a list of 'optimum' leadership qualities so vague and general that almost anything can be read into it.

All we can say about leadership is that as an absolute concept it has little or no meaning. The quality of leadership is specific to particular situations; 'what makes for good leadership in one situation may actually militate against it in another';[1] and group psychology has not advanced to the point where we can be sure of how to elicit the leadership qualities required by different situations.

However, we have to make common-sense judgments; and surely all the evidence is against the view that the type of leadership required to-day is likely to be the type encouraged by an élite system of education. No doubt Plato and Arnold were all very well in their day; but it would be distinctly odd if educational systems adapted in the one case to an idealised oligarchy of philosopher-kings, and in the other to the needs of a far-flung British Empire, were equally well adapted to a democratic, egalitarian, mid-twentieth-century society.

Most people would, I suppose, agree that leadership to-day called for three attributes, apart from a list of desirable moral qualities: it must be characterised by good judgment in public affairs, it must be technically efficient, and it must be democratic. The first attribute, more than ever necessary by reason of the growing scope and complexity of public action so rightly stressed by Dr. James, does not obviously demand an intensive academic education. It requires a measure (no more) of brains and intelligence, a 'feel' for situations, a sense of the possible, great psychological intuition, and a knowledge of public affairs. It does not require exceptional academic attainments, as anyone who has been both in academic life and politics well knows, nor, so far as one can see, a special, separate education; indeed if anything one would suppose the opposite, both *a priori* and judging by the

[1] J. A. C. Brown, *The Social Psychology of Industry* (Penguin Books, 1954), p. 221. The whole of Dr. Brown's chapter on 'Leaders and Leadership' is highly relevant to this issue.

lack of this practical wisdom amongst so many contemporary intellectuals.

On the question of technically efficient leadership, there is often a misunderstanding. It is sometimes said that the selective education of the most talented children is essential to Britain's survival in a competitive and technical world. But what this survival calls for is simply a great deal more expenditure on research, applied science, technical colleges, and so on; and this does not require segregated secondary schools of the type suggested, as the example of the U.S. clearly shows. And there is a more general confusion here. Where Britain lags behind the U.S. is not in the calibre of the top academic or 'grammar school' section of the population, but in the *average* technical ability lower down the scale. From this point of view we positively need less concentration on an educational élite, and more on the average standard of attainment. It is here that Britain is always weakest; and America gains competitively far more from having eight times the proportionate number of students in (often second-class) Universities, than Britain gains from having public schools and grammar schools.

Lastly, the democratic quality of leadership. Dr. James argues that segregation along Platonic lines represents a 'profoundly democratic conception', since it provides equal opportunity without regard to birth or wealth.[1] Certainly this is more democratic than segregation without equal opportunity, such as we have at present. But this is scarcely the relevant comparison; and one cannot reasonably maintain that any system of segregating a particular group of children, however chosen, into superior schools offering superior prospects, is more democratic than a system in which all children share broadly the same education. And whichever is the more democratic conception, the latter is surely more likely to foster democratic attitudes.

We cannot, I think, yet be at all sure what system of education is most likely to generate the type of leadership which we require; indeed it is not altogether clear, in our rapidly changing society,

[1] op. cit., p. 31. But so far as Plato himself is concerned, most people would prefer Mr. Crossman's judgment. 'Plato's philosophy is the most savage and the most profound attack upon Liberal ideas which history can show. It denies every axiom of "progressive" thought and challenges all its fondest ideals. Equality, freedom, self-government – all are condemned as illusions which can only be held by idealists whose sympathies are stronger than their sense.' (R. H. S. Crossman, *Plato To-day*, Allen and Unwin, 1937, p. 132.)

what type of leadership we do require. But *prima facie* judgments, and a consideration of the experience of other countries, certainly do not point unequivocally to a Platonic élite.

One may be allowed to ignore other arguments, allegedly of principle but in fact rather emotional, such as that to object to an 'aristocracy of learning' is to display 'social prejudice', or a bias in favour of mediocrity, or 'a purely political' attitude, or an indifference to the needs of individual children and hence to the requirements of the community.[1] We may assume that neither set of protagonists is more prejudiced, political or callous than the other; but that they simply differ on how various values are to be weighed, how the community can best be organised, and how the needs of children *as a whole* can best be met. Nothing is to be gained by the use of prejudicial language.

v *Comprehensive Schools in Practice*

But many people still object to the idea of comprehensive schools, not necessarily on grounds of principle, but simply because they fear the results may be bad in practice. The most common fears are, generally, that standards will be lowered, and the clever child held back to the pace of the average child: and specifically that if the school is to cater adequately for advanced and sixth-form study, it must be vast in size – Dr. James mentions a figure of 5,000 – and so sacrifice any intimate, personal quality, and all chance that the headmaster will know all his pupils personally.

These are matters to be determined factually; and in this country, with (at the time of writing) only some 14 comprehensive schools as yet in being, there is naturally no conclusive evidence. But a careful study of the experiments to date affords at least

[1] James, op. cit., p. 44. It seems hard that socialists should have to bear the entire brunt of this disapproval, since many highly respectable non-socialists have also objected to an aristocracy of learning. Even so impeccably-constituted a body as the Fleming Committee regarded 'any segregation of the particularly gifted children of the country as altogether unfortunate. . . . If a school is to be a true community, it must contain children of varying intellectual qualities. . . . Any attempt to make use of the Schemes which we propose in order to segregate the abler children and to send them to boarding schools would be socially and educationally wrong.' They therefore rejected 'without hesitation' any idea of a competitive examination for the free public school places (p. 71).

preliminary evidence; and this does not bear out the fears expressed.[1] There is no sign of any levelling-down of standards, and some evidence even of the reverse. The main reason is that the comprehensive schools have not, as many feared (and some hoped) that they would, mixed children of different abilities in the same class, but have adopted a system of testing and differentiation designed to produce homogeneous classes of more or less similar standards of attainment.

This has shocked some comprehensive enthusiasts, who had hoped for a system of 'social promotion' on the American model, with virtually no grading by ability.[2] But both common sense and American experience suggest that this would lead to a really serious levelling-down of standards, and a quite excessive handicap to the clever child. Division into streams, according to ability, remains essential.

This does not mean, as some critics suggest, that the whole experiment is then a waste of time, since this selection by ability will reproduce all the evils alleged against the 11 + examination. This is to get the matter out of perspective. The object of having comprehensive schools is not to abolish all competition and all envy, which might be rather a hopeless task, but to avoid the extreme social division caused by physical segregation into schools of widely divergent status, and the extreme social resentment caused by failure to win a grammar (or, in future, public) school place, when this is thought to be the only avenue to a 'middle-class' occupation. That division and that resentment bear no relation whatever to the effects of grading *within* a single school, with the possibility of re-grading at any time simply by moving across a corridor. One has only to think of the present public schools, where it could hardly be maintained that the divisions and resentments created by failure to get into the sixth-form, or to become a prefect, are in any way comparable with those caused by failure to win a grammar school place.

So far as the sixth-form argument is concerned, the evidence is necessarily inconclusive. It is not true that all comprehensive schools will in fact be vast; most of those now projected are for

[1] *v.* Robin Pedley, *Comprehensive Schools To-day* (Councils and Education Press, 1955).

[2] Some of them, their heads perhaps a little turned by too much sociology, even insist on classes being known not by numbers, but by the teachers' names, lest any mark at all of superior or inferior status be conferred. This is simply egalitarianism run mad.

well below 1,500 pupils, and some for only 500–600. Even supposing the average size to be 1,000, it is not clear to the layman, given a reasonable devolution, that this must be disastrous. Many public schools are of a comparable size; and most of their products whom I know had little personal contact with their headmaster, for which they now seem none the worse. At any rate, the existing comprehensive schools appear to provide for advanced work at least as adequately as do most grammar schools; and this is a criticism which so far, at least, must be regarded as non-proven.

Much of the argument against comprehensive schools proceeds by analogy. The critics point to the low standards characteristic of many American high schools. These low standards are not in dispute. But there are many possible explanations besides the comprehensive character of these schools: for example, the anti-highbrow and anti-academic ('anti-egghead') tradition of American life, the acute shortage of teachers (especially male teachers), the low quality of many of the teachers (amounting sometimes almost to illiteracy),[1] the insistence on automatic 'social promotion' by age-groups and the lack of grading by ability, an excessive attachment to Deweyism and 'life-adjustment' education at the expense of more basic academic disciplines, the overwhelming preference for vocational courses, and so on.[2] All or any of these influences, none of which are or need be reproduced in English comprehensive schools, may be responsible for the lower standards.

This is confirmed by the experience of Sweden, which has recently embarked on the experiment of replacing a tripartite by a comprehensive system of education. (Indeed the comprehensive schools are actually to embrace primary as well as secondary age-groups.) This experiment appears to be proceeding most successfully. The size of school varies from 200 in rural areas to 1,200 in Stockholm; and no one suggests that a much larger size is necessary to ensure an adequate grammar school stream. Educational standards have been maintained. There is no disagreeable status gap or resentment between the different streams.

---

[1] *v.* 'Can Our Teachers Read and Write?' *Harper's Magazine*, November 1954. Of course it is not intended to suggest that these low standards are universal; but the average teaching standard is certainly lower than in England.

[2] The range of subjects taught is often distinctly bizarre – from driver education and consumer buying at one end, to the study of 'boy and girl friendships', 'one's own personality', and 'plans for marriage' (for senior pupils only) at the other. I have taken these examples from an actual high school prospectus.

And all the major political parties are supporting the experiment. Taking Sweden and America together, it seems clear that the results of comprehensive education are not uniquely determined by the fact of 'comprehensiveness', but depend mainly on the cultural traditions of the country concerned.

And surely the analogy of the pre-war public schools is relevant. Many of them then bore a close resemblance to a comprehensive school. They were often extremely large – certainly too large for the head to know each individual boy. They taught all faculties – they had, that is to say, the equivalent of grammar, secondary modern and technical streams. They took all intellectual levels, and not simply the top 15% or 25%; indeed with a few notable exceptions, such as Winchester, almost any child, unless an imbecile, could find a place. No doubt the average level of intelligence was higher, owing to the more favourable parental background; but the dispersion was probably not significantly less. Yet the educational results were excellent, even in lesser-known schools where no exceptional heredity factor was at work. It seems that many of the anti-comprehensive arguments are not consistent with a belief in the virtues of the mixed fee-paying public school.

VI *A Labour Educational Policy*

Were we starting *tabula rasa*, I should therefore strongly favour a non-segregated, comprehensive system of schools, with other schools, not indeed abolished, but existing merely as an oblique appendage to the national system, as they do in most other countries, and not as a separate, nation-wide top stratum, as in England. The social arguments for this solution seem to me irresistible, the educational arguments against it inconclusive.

We are not, however, starting *tabula rasa*, but with segregated schools already established and strongly entrenched; and even if they were not, we could still not drive straight on to the objective, for the ground ahead is studded with obstacles – the shortage of suitable buildings, the state of public opinion, and the fact of local educational self-determination.

Thus even within the state sector there can be no question of suddenly closing down the grammar schools and converting the secondary moderns into comprehensive schools. These latter require a quite exceptional calibre of headmaster, of which the supply is severely limited: a high-quality staff for sixth-form teaching – again a factor in limited supply: and buildings of an adequate scale and scope – and most secondary modern buildings, which would have to be converted, are quite unsuitable. Until and unless the proper supply conditions exist, it would be quite wrong to close down grammar schools of acknowledged academic quality. The result would simply be a decline in educational standards, and discredit on the whole experiment.

Not that this would be possible, in any event, so long as we have local autonomy in educational matters. Only a minority of education authorities at present favour a large-scale conversion to a comprehensive pattern; and no one proposes that the remainder should be coerced. It would, moreover, be absurd from a socialist point of view to close down the grammar schools, while leaving the public schools still holding their present commanding position. This would simply intensify the class cleavage by removing the middle tier which now spans the gulf between top and bottom. It is curious that socialists, so often blind to the question of the public schools, should fail to see that 'parity of esteem' within the State sector, combined with a continuation of independent schools outside, will actually increase the *disparity* of esteem in the system as a whole.[1]

What, then, can be done? First, a Labour Government should explicitly state a preference for the comprehensive principle, and should actively encourage local authorities – and such advice carries great weight – to be more audacious in experimenting with comprehensive schools in the light of the marked success, described in Dr. Pedley's survey, of the experiments to date.[2]

Secondly, where new comprehensive schools cannot or will not be built, the object must be to weaken to the greatest possible extent the significance of the 11 + examination, and the rigidity of the prestige and physical barriers inherent in the present tripartite stratification. This is partly a matter of money and

---

[1] At least until the esteem of the State sector is relatively much higher than it is to-day.

[2] But with the important proviso, in large cities which are divided into rather clearly-marked one-class neighbourhoods, that the catchment-areas are so drawn as to straddle neighbourhoods of different social standing.

resources. As new secondary modern and technical schools are built and staffing ratios improve, thus narrowing the gap in standards and general ambience, so the desperate, universal obsession with a grammar school place will weaken. It is partly a matter of facilitating later transfer, so that the 'last chance' atmosphere now attaching to the 11 + examination is dissipated. And it is partly a matter of severing the present direct and unique link between grammar school and superior occupation – by creating 'grammar school streams' in secondary modern schools, encouraging the taking of subjects in General Certificate, instituting 'special courses' of a more advanced nature, facilitating late transfer into the sixth-form at grammar schools, and so on. But perhaps the most important step, directly in fostering 'parity of esteem', and indirectly in encouraging these other reforms, would be the raising of the school-leaving age to 16.

All this is to some extent a second-best. Late transfers from one school to another are not in general satisfactory; and considering the leeway to be made up, the secondary modern school will not easily achieve parity of esteem. But these changes will at least increasingly break up the present rigid, tripartite pattern – the more so as local authorities experiment with bilateral and other new types of secondary school. Diversification is at least one route towards equality.

But we still face the problem of the independent schools. One important change for the better, as I suggested earlier, may be the gradual closure, as we achieve more equality of wealth, of private preparatory schools, and the disappearance of one early and influential source of class insemination. In the independent secondary schools, the existence of 75% free places will of course weaken their present stratifying influence.

The problem is then twofold. First, these schools must not be allowed to become the breeding-ground of a new, superior intellectual élite. This requires that we carefully attend to the admonition of the Fleming Committee, that the free places in these schools should not go only to the cleverest children, but should be spread amongst a wide cross-section, with a preference, naturally enough, for those who want, or seem apt for, a boarding-school education. And in the long run it requires, in my view, that some of these schools should be converted to other educational uses – as high schools for advanced tuition, short-term boarding establishments, junior universities, adult education centres, and the like.

But a huge gap in social prestige will remain for many years to come. Closing this gap is simply a matter of standards in the State sector, and hence ultimately of priorities in national expenditure. It is true that an air of unreality, even of absurdity, now attaches to this statement. This is because it has so often been made in the last few years, especially in perorations, where it was always sure of a round of applause; but nothing has ever been done to implement it. Only if performance really matches promise – only if, that is, the Labour Party gives education a much higher priority than in the past, and comes to see it as of far greater significance to socialism than the nationalisation of meat-procuring or even chemicals – only then will the reality take shape in the form of bricks and mortar, more and better teachers, a longer school life in ample, imaginative surroundings.

Gradually, the schools which children go to will become, as in the United States, not an automatic function of brains or class location, but a matter of personal preference and local accident. The system will increasingly, if the Labour Party does its job, be built around the comprehensive school. But even in the large non-comprehensive sector, all schools will more and more be socially mixed; all will provide routes to the Universities and to every type of occupation, from the highest to the lowest; and it will cease to occur to employers to ask what school job-applicants have been to. Then, very slowly, Britain may cease to be the most class-ridden country in the world.

XI

THE PATTERN OF CONSUMPTION

1 *Rising Average Income and the Pattern of Consumption*

THE second influence on social equality is 'style of life' and the visible pattern of consumption: that is, how wide are the contrasts, both in fact and in terms of how people feel, between the style and standard of living of different social groups.

Naturally this depends partly on the distribution of total real income. But it also depends on the distribution of certain especially conspicuous and significant items of consumption; and this need not vary directly with total income. One aspect of this, to which attention was drawn in Part Three, is the consumption of 'social' goods such as health and education. Equality here, whatever the distribution of total income, can have a marked effect on social attitudes and the general sense of class equality.

But this chapter is concerned with the pattern of personal consumption, and with the proposition, which has important implications for Labour Party attitudes, that *seen and felt disparities in personal living standards are a function not only of income-distribution, but also of the absolute level of average real income.* That is, the higher the level of average income, the more equal is the visible pattern of consumption, and the stronger the subjective feeling of equal living standards. This arises from the fact that some forms of consumption are more conspicuous and socially significant than others, and that the richer a country grows, the more equal the distribution of these particular forms of consumption becomes, almost regardless of the distribution of total income.

In a poor and backward country, such as contemporary Egypt or Persia, the unequal distribution of wealth is glaringly exposed to the public gaze by the fact that the rich alone have any 'discretionary purchasing power', i.e. surplus of income over subsistence requirements. They alone, therefore, can afford whatever luxuries are conventionally considered the prestige-symbols of a high standard of living – good housing, high quality clothes, excellent food and drink, cars, holidays, travel, restaurant meals, TV sets, and the like. The fact, conspicuous to all, that only a few rich can afford such expenditures, while the masses live at a bare subsistence level, induces an overwhelming sense of inequalities in style of life.

But as the national income rises, these 'luxuries' come increasingly within the reach of the masses, until in contemporary America, to take the extreme example, a high proportion of the population enjoys many of the 'luxuries' which until recently were considered the prerogative of the rich;[1] and the ordinary worker lives at what even two decades ago would have been considered in Britain a middle-class standard of life.

But why should this equalise the pattern of consumption? Why, with any given income distribution, should not the rich move on a further step, and maintain the gap between themselves and the masses by branching out into new and equally conspicuous forms of luxury expenditure, which would be just as much a symbol of wealth and social superiority as the old? One might expect each generation, as incomes rose, to develop its own pattern of ostentatious sumptuary expenditure, so that visible contrasts in living standards always remained the same.

The rich cannot, evidently, maintain their lead merely by consuming quantitatively more of existing goods. At some point they must come up against an effective frontier of consumption, set by the law of diminishing marginal utility. It is well known that as incomes rise, the proportion spent on staple foodstuffs falls; and even the biggest glutton soon reaches a point where additional quantities of food hold no attraction. The same relative decline can, after a point, be observed in respect of tobacco, alcohol, and fuel for heat and light.

[1] Or could enjoy if it so wished. In one particularly conspicuous case, housing, it does not always so wish; and the shiny car outside the shack is a familiar sight to the traveller. But the reason for bad housing is not solely economic; it lies partly in the (to an Englishman) peculiar contours of the American consumer's preference map.

But even more luxurious articles also have a limit. The *Tailor and Cutter* asserts that the well-dressed man-about-town needs 30 suits; and although this sets the physical frontier further back than most of us would have supposed, it does at least concede that some satiation point exists. A very rich man may want two, or even three, country-houses or large mansions; but he does not want 10 or 20, or even indefinitely larger ones. He man want two, or even three, Rolls-Royces; but again he does not want 10 or 20, or indefinitely larger ones. He may want to spend six months, or more, of the year at Cannes; but he cannot in the nature of things spend more than 12. He therefore finds it increasingly hard to maintain his lead simply by consuming greater quantities of existing goods and services.

But why cannot he maintain it by extending the number of goods which he consumes – by finding new forms of consumption to symbolise his superior wealth? The answer lies in the inherent nature of the modern mass-distribution economy, which will, I believe, after a certain stage of development, make it almost impossible to preserve large disparities in socially conspicuous consumption.

In a pre-industrial society, the possibility of extending the number of goods consumed scarcely exists; it is ruled out by the slow rate of technical innovation. But then the necessity for doing so hardly arises either; the incomes of the poor are static, and the superior living standards of the rich are not being challenged from below.

It is the Industrial Revolution, and the higher rate of innovation associated with it, which both poses the problem for the rich, and ultimately makes its solution impossible. Initially, it is true, although it jerks up the living standards of the masses and so shatters the long-standing consumption relationships between rich and poor, it also enables the rich to keep ahead by the purchase of new luxury goods. For a long time, in the early or middle industrial era, while mass production is still the exception yet the rate of technical innovation is high, the rich can acquire conspicuous new inventions which the masses cannot afford, even though their basic standard of living may be rising. This is the pre-mass-production era, when the rate of new invention has outstripped the techniques of widespread engineering application.

But this, although prolonged, eventually proves a transitory phase. When the Industrial Revolution finally matures into the modern mass-production economy, as it has in the United States and is about to do in Britain, the rich can no longer hold their lead in this manner. This is not because the rate of innovation and production of new goods slows down – on the contrary, it accelerates still further. But it is now outstripped by an even more rapid progress in engineering application, and in the development of productive techniques. The time-lag between invention and widespread application has steadily shortened from 100 years in the case of the steam engine to five years, or even less, to-day;[1] and it gradually becomes possible to mass-produce, at comparatively low cost, almost any conspicuous new invention.

This development coincides with a change on the side of consumption. Not only is it reflected in a rapid rise in incomes due to the rising productivity, but the masses, having by now satisfied their basic wants, are ready to branch out into luxury expenditure. They therefore provide a ready market for the new goods, and so are always stepping on the heels of the rich. And the trend is further reinforced by the development of consumer credit and instalment buying, which enables the working class to buy more goods than their financial assets unaided would permit. Consumer credit in the U.S.A. (excluding house mortgage loans) now totals over $30 billions, having grown (in money terms) by 500% since 1939; between 50% and 70% of sales of all consumer durables – two-thirds, for example, of all car sales (new and used) – are financed by credit.

It is thus a basic characteristic of the mass-production, mass-distribution and mass-credit economy, towards which we are now moving, that the rich will never be able to maintain an extensive lead in the consumption of new prestige-goods for more than a comparatively short period. Of course this would not be true if conspicuous new goods came out in a torrential rush – then no doubt the masses would fall behind. But even with the highest imaginable rate of innovation, new goods of this character, distinctive enough to be fastened on as symbols of high consumption and not simply improvements or small gadgets, will only appear at spaced intervals; and mass distribution will then quickly follow. Whereas the motor-car remained a remote symbol

[1] v. Wassily Leontief, *Scientific American*, September 1952.

of wealth in Britain for forty years, it is hard to imagine any new article holding this position in America to-day for more than five; one has only to think of the spread of cars and refrigerators before the war, of TV sets and washing-machines since the war, and no doubt of drying-machines, electric dishwashers, garbage disposal units and air-conditioning plants in the next few years.

These economic influences are reinforced by familiar sociological pressures. The element of emulation and fashion-leadership, and the dependence of social status on the pattern of expenditure, have already been discussed in Chapter VI. Naturally these are especially relevant in the case of any conspicuous or revolutionary-sounding new commodity; and social pressure therefore combines with high purchasing power to create a mass demand for such commodities as soon as they appear on the advertisement pages of the glossy magazines – or as soon as some of the neighbours are seen to own them. This 'socialisation' of consumption patterns may already be observed in this country on new housing estates, where TV aerials were for a time an obvious prestige-symbol.[1] And it helps to explain the amazingly rapid spread in America of any 'fashionable' new good – often more rapid than can be explained on cost and income grounds.[2]

II *Rising Consumption as a Socialist Objective*

Since the rich will not be able to preserve their consumption lead through the exclusive possession of conspicuous new goods, they must find an outlet for their higher incomes mainly in a *qualitative* increase in the consumption of existing goods, i.e. by buying ever more splendid or expensive varieties. But this form of outlay, however lavish, has a much smaller significance for social evaluations of comparative living standards.

This is partly because much high-quality consumption has a

---

[1] For a general discussion of the socialisation of consumption, *v.* Riesman, *The Lonely Crowd, passim.* For its economic implications, *v.* George Katona, *Psychological Analysis of Economic Behaviour* (McGraw-Hill, 1951), pp. 109 seq., and James S. Duesenberry, *Income, Saving and the Theory of Consumer Behaviour* (Harvard, 1949), pp. 20-32 (though the latter's sociology should be treated with some reserve).

[2] Thus Duesenberry found (op. cit., p. 104) that washing-machines and refrigerators spread much more rapidly in the U.S. during the inter-war years than could possibly be explained by variations in price or income, or by autonomous changes in taste.

domestic character; it is enjoyed in the privacy of the home, and as a badge of wealth or superior style it attracts too little public notice. Thus the rich will spend their higher incomes on buying Matisses or antique furniture, on entertainment, on jewellery for their wives, on expensive food and wines, on interior decoration, on acquiring books, or commissioning a fashionable portrait painter.

And even if these prodigal outlays do become known to the neighbourhood, they will inspire other people with little or no sense of inferiority. They come too low on the average person's scale of preferences ever to be accepted as critical symbols of a much superior (i.e. strongly desired and envied) standard of living. This can already be seen in the United States. For better or worse, the average American worker or bourgeois does envy a new car, a deep freeze, and a holiday in the sun, and feel poor and deprived if he cannot have them. But he does not much care for French Impressionists (except for some simpler ones in reproduction) or Louis XV furniture or fine old silver or vintage port. He therefore does not feel their absence (provided he can afford the car, the deep freeze and the holiday) to be a serious reflection on his social status or living standards, nor their presence in other houses a mark of an altogether superior style of life.[1]

To the extent, moreover, that refinements in quality do matter for social evaluations, they can, with modern techniques, be only too easily copied and so lose, not indeed their superior intrinsic value, but at least their 'snob' glamour for the average citizen. At the extreme, mass-produced 'antique' furniture and prints of old masters, of a quality which fully satisfies the mass of citizens, are now available to all who want them. Bourbon is almost as palatable as Scotch, South African as Spanish sherry, and tinned as fresh asparagus; even in Britain a Montague Burton suit is a (just) passable imitation of one from Huntsman, while in America,

[1] Despite the fact that he can observe these domestic luxuries more directly than ever before through the medium of the films, TV, and the glossy magazines. But this does not, I think, increase the amount of social envy, mainly for the reason given in the text, reinforced by the further fact that familiarity breeds a certain contempt. When they had no idea of what went on behind the curtain, the less well-off no doubt suspected it was something much to be envied and desired. But now they know it is only books and pictures and candles at dinner, they cannot see what all the fuss was about; there seems nothing here, to people owning a car and a deep freeze, which represents a distinctively higher standard of living. Thus the influence of the films and TV is partially to de-glamorise luxury consumption, and drain it of its pristine mystery and allure.

although a Cadillac costs very much more than a Chevrolet, the outward difference is only marginal (indeed to an Englishman hardly visible), and anyway next year's Chevrolet will look very much like this year's Cadillac.

Of course these marginal differences are immensely significant for small status gradations. But that is not the point at issue; and they certainly do not give rise to a sense of broad class divisions or wide disparities in living standards.

Thus the rich cannot, once this stage is reached, preserve a conspicuous consumption gap even if they desperately wish to. But there are, in any case, certain social pressures, characteristic of a mature industrial culture, which tend to mollify their desire to do so. First, from a mixture of social motives combined with the limitations just discussed, the very rich will often give up the struggle at a certain point, and limit the rise in consumption altogether. Instead they give huge sums to charity or education, preferring the 'psychic income' which comes from playing the role of benefactor; so we have the phenomenon of the trusts and foundations associated with the names of Nuffield, Rockefeller, Carnegie and Ford.

In addition, as was suggested in Chapter VI, conspicuous consumption becomes positively unfashionable, and may even give way to conspicuous under-consumption.[1] This latter has always characterised a section of the European intelligentsia – the battered car, the tatty tweed jacket, the cult of beer and the cheap Italian restaurant. But it is now percolating into the ordinary middle and upper classes – certainly in England, and even in America.[2] Ostentation is becoming vulgar; rich men tend to disclaim their wealth; and a general modesty in consumption becomes the fashion. This naturally reinforces the trend towards equality in outward style of life.

This trend has now gone a long way in the United States. Every visitor is struck not only by the lack of glaring objective contrasts between the living standards of different social classes,

---

[1] *v.* Chapter VI, Section IV.

[2] I recently visited a high school in Florida, where I was not surprised to find that 400 of the pupils had cars (nor even that 50 were married), but was definitely surprised to see a number of battered 25-year-old Fords amongst the shiny new cars: even more so to be told that the owners of the former held a much higher status (as measured by the exact criterion of number of dates per week) than the owners of the latter, who were considered rather ordinary and plebeian.

but also by the general *consciousness* of equal living standards – the feeling that everything is within reach, and nothing wholly unattainable. This is one of the basic causes of the greater social equality, and the absence of deep class feeling.[1]

The trend is now beginning to be apparent even in Britain. The percentage of working-class expenditure available for purposes other than food, housing, fuel, and light rose from 5% in 1904 to 30% in 1937–8, and must now be higher still. The average worker to-day possesses a substantial margin not only for the traditional working-class 'luxuries' – the average household in Britain spends about £110 a year on alcohol and tobacco,[2] and another £50 a year on gambling; it spends more on alcohol than on rents, rates, and water rates, and twice as much on tobacco as on heat and light – but also for relatively new 'luxuries', such as the cinema, newspapers and periodicals, and books. Every household in Britain contains on the average two people who go to the cinema once a week; *Picture Post, Illustrated, John Bull, Everybody's, Woman,* and *Woman's Own* have a combined circulation of more than 10 million (out of a total of under 15 million households); and every second household contains one member who borrows a book from a Public Library once a week.[3]

But these expenditures, although they represent an absolute rise in living standards, do not create much atmosphere of greater equality, since they are either not accepted as significant symbols of high consumption, or else they are traditional *working-class* luxuries. It is when we enter the field of middle-class luxuries, i.e. genuine prestige-symbols of high consumption, that the trend becomes significant. From 1949 to 1954 television licences multiplied tenfold, and at the present rate of increase a majority of households will own sets by 1960. The number of private cars on the road is now 4 million, and at the present rate of increase one household in four will own a car by 1957. (The first miners' car rally was recently held in Yorkshire.) Half the population now leave home for at least a week's annual holiday, of whom

---

[1] Of course the greater equality of consumption patterns as compared with 30 years ago is also due to the marked redistribution of income which has taken place. But this is probably a less important factor than the rise in the absolute level of average income.

[2] Though these two items have shown very divergent trends in real terms. *Per capita* consumption of tobacco is 2½ times as high as 50 years ago, of alcohol only half as high.

[3] Many of these facts are taken from T. R. Fyvel, *Socialist Commentary*, March 1955.

two-thirds go to the seaside, 2 million to holiday camps, and
$1\frac{1}{4}$ million (three times the pre-war figure) go abroad.[1]

I do not, of course, mean that the whole of the working class
can now afford these luxuries – far from it. So far this is only a
trend – we are still only at the threshold of the new era of abundance; and there are many workers on £7 or £8 a week, and even
more social service beneficiaries, who are still acutely worried by
the problem of subsistence. But the trend is now quite definite;
and it is significant that even these poorer workers are themselves
peering across the threshold; they have accepted the new standards as the social norm, and are already thinking of the day when
they too will acquire these goods.

All this must have a profound effect on the psychology of the
working class. Engels wrote as long ago as 1858 that it seemed 'as
if the English proletariat is actually assuming bourgeois characteristics to an ever-increasing degree; apparently this most bourgeois
of all nations finally wishes to have a bourgeois aristocracy and a
bourgeois proletariat besides the bourgeoisie itself'.[2] He would
have been even more horrified could he have gone canvassing
round new housing estates in 1955, or read the Gallup surveys of
what class people think they belong to. There are clear political
implications here for the Labour Party, which would be ill-
advised to continue making a largely proletarian class appeal
when a majority of the population is gradually attaining a
middle-class standard of life, and distinct symptoms even of a
middle-class psychology.[3]

But the immediate point at issue is the sociological significance
of the spread of high consumption. It must weaken the sense, as
of course it lessens the fact, of inferior or unequal standards of
life, and of class inequality generally. Quite apart from its direct
and obvious effects on economic welfare, therefore, about which
something is said below, higher personal consumption must form
part of any statement of the socialist goal on fundamental egalitarian grounds.

[1] Housing is still a notable exception to the egalitarian trend, though the disparities here, due partly to overcrowding and partly to the gradual decay of old
rented houses, or at least the failure to renovate them, are almost as marked within
the working class as between classes.

[2] Quoted in Rosenberg, *Democracy and Socialism*, p. 211.

[3] Though this process is still held back in Britain, as compared with newer societies,
by the survival of a strong class-consciousness amongst the working class (v. Chapter VII).

III   *Must this Create an Acquisitive Society?*

But one has only to say this, for a terrible outcry to be raised. It seems that this means accepting a Tory, or capitalist, or materialist, or even (worse still) an American, philosophy of life, or at any rate one that is somehow unethical and unsocialist. What appears to be meant is that the acceptance of the goal of higher material standards will at once require and encourage an accent on material gain, extreme individualism, and aggressive competition. It is therefore held to be inseparable from an acquisitive and antagonistic society, in which on the one hand social values of great importance – security, leisure, culture, stability, and so on – will be neglected; and on the other, personal character and social relationships will be coarsened and debased. Thus the pursuit of higher material standards inevitably involves the denial of the traditional socialist ideal of 'the city of brotherly love'.

Generally, I have never been able to see why high consumption and brotherly love should be thought incompatible – why should not the brothers be affluent, and the love conducted under conditions of reasonable comfort? But in any case this whole criticism seems to rest on a misunderstanding. First, as was pointed out in Chapter IV, the actual social results of competition depend entirely on the framework within which it is conducted. A century ago these results were deplorable, because the background was one of complete *laisser-faire*. But to-day competition takes place within a strict framework of legal and conventional rules designed to obviate adverse or 'anti-social' results. If these rules are thought to be inadequate, it lies wholly within the community's power to make them tighter.

It might still be said that to aim at higher consumption, and hence at rapid economic growth, must encourage aggressive, competitive relationships which are socially or ethically undesirable even though society is protected against any direct adverse results. But there is certainly no sign that such relationships are being encouraged in Britain to-day. Previous chapters have already drawn attention to the apparently ineradicable instinct in industry towards co-operation, group solidarity, and teamwork, and have suggested that Britain to-day is probably the

least competitive nation in the world. Yet we are already achieving a rate of growth which, if maintained, will double the standard
of living in twenty-five years.

Nor is there any sign that this pattern of behaviour is likely to
change. There is no reason to believe that an acquisitive and
individualistic pattern of behaviour is an essential condition of
rapid growth, which on the contrary appears to be consistent
with many different kinds of social relations and economic institutions. At the present time, rapid rates of growth are being
achieved in countries with the most diverse institutions, sets of
motives, national characters, patterns of ownership, degrees of
equality, and so on – in Russia, Germany, Britain, and America.
There seems nothing to justify the conclusion that because in the
heyday of capitalism an aggressively individualistic and competitive society did display a rapid rate of growth, therefore it
is the only one which can.

Indeed, the fact is that advances in productivity and technical
innovation to-day do not come characteristically from people
working competitively for individual profit, but from people working on a fixed salary in a large managerial structure; and not
from cut-throat competition, but often from co-operation – between firms, between industry and government and the universities, between management and labour. And rapid expansion
appears to be possible under any set of social conditions which
permits the creation of a sufficiently wide technological base, a
sufficient degree of scale, and an emphasis on research – provided
these are backed by a high level of demand and an accepted
ideology of growth. I therefore see no reason to accept the identification of a slow rate of growth with amiable sociability, and
a rapid rate of growth with violent competition.

However, even though rising consumption does not require a
highly competitive culture, it might still be attacked as likely to
foster the self-regarding motive of personal material gain, as
opposed to more altruistic motives. But I doubt whether the
acceptance or rejection of the goal of higher consumption by
politicians or intellectuals will make much difference to the average person's motives, which surely go too deep to be so easily
changed. Of course the action of politicians can (within limits)
thwart the motive of material gain, as by imposing heavy marginal
rates of taxation. But this will not alter the motive itself, which

will continue to exist whether consumption rises rapidly or slowly. To achieve a basic change in motivation would require a much more elaborate change in our society; and this, as I argued in Chapter IV,[1] we cannot see clearly how to achieve.

I therefore fail to see that to accept the virtues of rising personal consumption is in any way 'unsocialist', or will do anything in practice to lower the moral tone of society. Of course to accept them implies nothing about the priority to be given to home consumption as opposed to other claims on output – that is discussed in Section V. It simply means that we accept it as one out of many desirable aims of social policy.

IV   *The Paternalist Objection*

This objective is sometimes attacked, however, as being based on a fundamental delusion: namely, that it will increase welfare, or make people more contented. As soon as existing wants are satisfied, it is said, new ones will spring up in their place: the gap between possessions and desiderata never narrows: and rising personal incomes will therefore leave people just as dissatisfied as they are to-day – all this annotated with contemptuous remarks about a television-set-refrigerator civilisation.

I have never thought much of this argument, although in fact the case as presented earlier in this chapter was not based on the proposition which it seeks to deny. No doubt the gap between possessions and aspirations is never fully closed. But because no saturation point exists, it does not follow that the gap is always constant. If this were so, it would imply that individuals never felt economically better off as their real incomes rose, and generally that improvements in the standard of living had no effect on the economic welfare of either nations or persons (at least after a certain point – I suppose that even the most ethereal view of the unimportance of material goods would concede that relief from acute poverty and starvation would increase economic welfare).

But the fact is that people do feel economically better or worse off; and they distinctly like to feel better off. Thus working-class people will frequently say that they are much better off now

[1] Section IV.

than they were before the war; and middle-class people will admit that economically things are much easier now than a few years ago. And these are not meaningless statements. Indeed the sceptic need only study recent voting trends, or collect impressions of the last election, to convince himself that changes in the level of consumption do reflect themselves in diminished economic discontent. It would certainly be hard to explain the social and political history of the last 50 years if this were not so.

Naturally, as I have argued before in a different context, one cannot state dogmatically that rising material standards, or any other socio-economic change, will make people 'happier'.[1] I personally think that they probably will. But on certain possible views of the causes of unhappiness, they might simply alter the direction which it takes, causing it to become more personal, rather than being articulated in political or economic grievances. Even then I should still regard rising standards as wholly desirable; first, because, for reasons already discussed, it is preferable that grievances should take a personal rather than a collective form: and secondly because whatever the effects of rising standards on happiness, they clearly increase the individual's range of choice and area of cultural possibilities.

But there are some moral ascetics, especially amongst the more astringent type of intellectual, who would deny even this. They base an instinctive hostility to higher consumption not on a fear lest it may fail to make the masses happier (rather indeed the reverse), but on an aversion to the *form* which the higher consumption allegedly takes. They combine a belief in the moral virtues of abstinence, with a conviction that the working class wastes all its higher income on alcohol, tobacco, and gambling.[2] This mixture of puritanism and paternalism is curiously common amongst the British intelligentsia. The Webbs, of course, typified it to perfection: consider Beatrice's favourite phrase, 'the average sensual man' – how the adjectives sting!

A more recent example may be cited, chosen only because it is recent and not because it is worse than most. 'There is still much wasteful and unnecessary expenditure in a country like

[1] Chapter VII, Section VI.

[2] This is really a more refined version of the old 'coals-in-the-bath' argument.

Britain. . . . There is a surprisingly large amount of fat to be melted off the general mass of solid working- and lower middle-class families. The wastage here may well be far greater, in total, than in the small marginal "luxury" or "problem" groups which waste on a more conspicuous scale. The best-known surveys of recent years give the impression that the chief spending outlets of the British masses are pubs, pools, and prostitutes. . . . A certain sparseness and asceticism . . . is part of the good life, and it would hardly be claimed that the British consumer has attained it.'[1] Indeed it would not, and it is to be hoped that it never could be.

There is really little to be said about this attitude, except that one does not share it. These critics are entitled to their views, so long as they recognise that they represent a highly idiosyncratic set of values, which does not represent the general will or mood of the country: and that any attempt to express it in government policy, or to play down the objective of rising consumption on this account, would be a wholly improper and undemocratic exercise in paternalism.

In fact, of course, these strictures give a misleading impression of how workers spend their extra incomes. Naturally the figures show large increases in the money value of drink and tobacco expenditure. Much of the increase is due simply to higher tax; and these were, after all, the traditional working-class luxuries, and as such were bound to attract a high proportion of extra spending in the early stages of a rapid rise in incomes. But they are already approaching satiation point; and we can expect that future increases in income will mainly be spent in what everyone would agree were creditable directions – in giving children a better life, in improving health, making a more generous provision for old age, buying a house, travelling and going on holidays, relieving drudgery in the home by buying washing-machines, drying-machines, electric dish-washers, and the like.

Some of the increase will of course be taken out in leisure, and may even be spent on culture. 'In spite of all that is said', wrote Matthew Arnold, 'about the brutalising influence of our passionate material progress, it seems to me indisputable that this

[1] Michael P. Fogarty, *Economic Control* (Routledge, 1955), pp. 124-5. And on a later page: 'It is possible to say of some forms of expenditure, as, for instance, alcohol, that they are either immoral in themselves or liable to lead to immorality' (p. 132). People should speak for themselves.

progress is likely, though not certain, to lead in the end to an apparition of intellectual life; and that man, after he has made himself perfectly comfortable and has now to determine what to do with himself next, may begin to remember that he has a mind, and that the mind may be made the source of great pleasure. I grant it is mainly the privilege of faith, at present, to discern this end to our railways, our business, and our fortune-making; but we shall see if, here as elsewhere, faith is not in the end the true prophet.'[1]

But whether it is or not, I should still regard a sustained rise in material standards as wholly desirable – probably because it will increase personal contentment, but certainly on grounds of personal freedom, since rising standards inevitably widen the area of choice and opportunity: on grounds of social justice, which surely requires that the masses, for so long deprived of luxuries which others have enjoyed, should now also be admitted to the world of material ease, if only to see whether they do in fact enjoy it: on strict egalitarian grounds, since rising consumption increases the fact and the consciousness of social equality, and so contributes to the fundamental aims of socialism: and on grounds of democratic anti-paternalism, since this is clearly what the workers want. And anyone who tells them they are wrong, and that in fact they are simply becoming vulgarised, or Americanised, will be given rather short shrift, especially if he himself appears to have a good deal of material fat which might be melted off.

Generally, those enjoying an above-average standard of living should be rather chary of admonishing those less fortunate on the perils of material riches.

v *The Question of Priorities*

But since the open advocacy of higher home consumption is sure to be resented and misrepresented in certain quarters, the qualifications must be explicitly set out.

First, I am asking that it be granted, not an over-riding priority, but simply the status of an important socialist objective. Thus we might decide to give an over-riding priority, for a period,

[1] *Essays in Criticism* (Macmillan, 1895 ed.), p. 17.

to the under-developed areas, or to exports or investment. But let it then be recognised that the sacrifice required of British material standards is not a positive good in itself, which will strengthen the moral fibre of the masses and save them from the insidious temptations of Americanism, but the sacrifice of a definite socialist objective. Perhaps it may often be necessary to rate the claims of British consumption lower than other claims; but they should never be *automatically* put at the bottom of the list.

The second qualification concerns the distribution of the additional wealth. It is here that the difference between Conservative and socialist attitudes reveals itself. The Conservative, while accepting the aim of higher consumption, is content that it should fall where economic chance dictates – that it should remain with those so placed in relation to the productive process that they initially receive it. This means, in a free economy, that the benefits accrue in larger relative measure to the middle and upper classes than the workers, to capital gains than wages and salaries, to workers on piecework than those on minimum time rates, and generally, reflecting a belief in low taxation and the minimum transfer of income, to the working population than to social service beneficiaries. This follows inevitably from Conservative views on taxation, wages policy, and the role of the capital market. The socialist, by contrast, should favour a distribution according to a system of social priorities which will certainly require strict government intervention for its enforcement.

Generally, this chapter is a plea less for specific changes in Labour policy, than for a change in psychology and ideology. The Party must recognise that its identification in the public mind with austerity, rationing, and restrictive controls is highly damaging, and that we are in grave danger of allowing the Tories to run away with the kudos of being the Party of prosperity and high consumption. We should now proudly proclaim the fact, though it seems almost incredible that we should need to do so, that we want to see individuals happy, and rich, and enjoying what in the past have been solely the luxuries of the upper classes; and in the process we should take a long stride forward towards the classless society. No doubt the speed of our advance must depend on the urgency of other claims; but let us at least make our objective known.

XII

THE DISTRIBUTION OF WEALTH (I)

1 *Injustice of the Present Distribution*

THE third distance factor to be considered is the distribution of wealth, that is, of the individual's total command over economic resources, or spending power. But does this matter, it may be said, if rising real incomes, however distributed, will in any case gradually equalise the pattern of living standards, and if, moreover, further redistribution cannot be definitely expected to increase economic welfare?[1]

It matters for two reasons. First, in an old society like Britain there will remain, at each level of average real income, more socially significant and conspicuous differences in consumption than in newer societies like the U.S. and the Dominions. This is because we inherit from an aristocratic past certain important prestige-symbols of wealth and superior class, which cannot in their nature ever be widely distributed, and which have for historical reasons a social or class connotation to which no analogy exists in a new country.[2] It follows that a more equal distribution of wealth will be needed to produce any given degree of equality in visible living standards.

Secondly, and much more important, the present distribution of wealth in Britain is flagrantly unjust; and this is wholly irrespective of the visible pattern of consumption, the effect of redistribution on economic welfare, and even the presence or absence of resentment against the injustice. The only relevant factor is

[1] *v.* Chapter VII, Section I.

[2] This applies especially to housing. The contrast can be seen in the new towns, where much less outward class distinction in housing is visible, not because all houses are the same size, but because they are all new.

that the possession of great differential wealth still confers an enormous social and economic advantage, however it is spent; and the distribution of this advantage is a matter of social concern.

Inequalities of wealth may be considered unjust, first, if they stem from inherited property, and not from work. This offends against the principle that every citizen should have an equal chance of attaining the highest rewards,[1] and confers a differential advantage related solely to the accident of birth, and not in any way the 'fruit of the man's own labour'.[2]

Secondly, large inequalities even of earned income may be thought unjust, either if they reflect not simply differences in ability but also differences in opportunity – if, that is to say, there is an artificial 'rent' element: or if they are so large that people think it unfair to single out the one quality of economic ability for so huge a reward as compared with other personal attributes.

Thirdly, injustice may arise if certain incomes are too generously treated by the tax system as compared with other similar incomes – if the basis of taxation, that is to say, is a poor measure of the taxable capacity of individuals.

These three sources of inequality, and therefore of inequity, are all very evident in Britain. (And their presence, especially the first two, explains why it is that any given degree of inequality is more unjust, and probably more resented, in Britain than in the Dominions or North America, where inherited property is less important, and everyone thinks he has an equal opportunity of reaching the highest income-grade.)

First, the unequal distribution of property is still the major cause of inequalities in spending power. Its importance may be seen even from the figures of conventional property income. But of course these figures tell only a small part of the story, since the ownership of property confers far more substantial economic advantages than can be measured simply by the investment income to which it gives rise. It confers, most obviously,

---

[1] It also offends against another principle mentioned in Chapter VII, since it may lead to an excessive concentration of power.

[2] Not that this is a very sensible phrase even when applied to incomes from work. Most work-incomes are not the fruit of a man's individual effort, but of joint production to which many different individuals have contributed. How this joint output should be, and will be, imputed to individuals is a matter of personal judgment, the market structure of relative prices and incomes, relative bargaining power, and historical convention.

the advantage that very high levels of current spending can be sustained by the periodic judicious realisation of capital assets. The cost in terms of loss of future income is negligible at present surtax rates, the advantage enormous since expenditure out of capital bears no tax. The annual dissipation of only a small fraction of a large estate can easily fortify to the extent of two or three times the owner's post-tax income. Thus the equalising intentions of fiscal policy are frustrated, and the distribution of consumption becomes much more unequal than the distribution of post-tax incomes.

Moreover, those who already possess capital can, if they are prudent and skilful (or have a good stockbroker), make substantial capital gains, especially on the Stock Exchange. At current rates of increase in industrial profits and dividends, the sums involved are now extremely large, and a major factor in raising the spending power of property-owners relative to that of the rest of the community.

Furthermore, inherited property confers a number of advantages which cannot be measured in money terms, but are manifestly of great significance. It confers access to the best possible education and professional training. It confers security, especially against old age. It confers the freedom to take risks. And it confers a wider range of economic choice both between occupations, and between work and leisure.

How unequally these total advantages are distributed may be seen from the figures of the distribution of private capital. It appears that 1% of persons over 25 own 50% of all private capital in England and Wales, 10% own 80%, while 61% must be content with a residual 5%.[1]

The second source of inequality is the distribution of incomes from work. Even after taxation, the spread from top to bottom is still about 20 : 1; and this is wider than most socialists would consider 'just'. But in this case justice needs to be tempered with efficiency, and questions of incentives arise. This is an issue on which, as I argued earlier, we need to adopt a rather agnostic attitude. It probably rules out any further major redistribution of earned income by direct taxation, and nothing more is said about this possibility. But *gross* incomes from work could cer-

[1] *v.* Kathleen Langley, 'The Distribution of Capital in Private Hands', *Bull. Inst. Stat.*, December 1950 and February 1951.

tainly still be narrowed with a distinct gain in social justice, and no loss in economic efficiency.

Moreover the distribution of the top incomes between individuals is clearly unjust, since opportunities for attaining them are by no means always equal. Very high work incomes presumably arise because the supply of certain skills is scarce in relation to the demand. This scarcity may sometimes be absolute, and due to an unalterable shortage of innate talent. But often it is not; and the high incomes are not genuine rents of exceptional ability, but artificial rents of a monopolistic character. These may be due to a shortage of facilities for acquiring the best education and the necessary skills: or to restrictions on entry into certain professions: or to nepotism in the widest sense (selection from a narrow social circle).

A redistribution of property would do much to remove this rent element. For the rest, we need to reform the educational system in the manner described in Chapter X: to break down the institutional barriers to free entry into professions such as Lloyds and the Stock Exchange, and into industries now protected by restrictive agreements: and generally to create a pattern of social relationships less dominated by nepotism and the 'old boy net'. And such a widening of opportunities would not only lead to a fairer (and more efficient) selection for the most lucrative occupations, but would also, by reducing the monopoly element in their rewards, narrow the vertical spread of incomes from work.[1] As these matters fall mainly outside the scope of fiscal policy, nothing more is said on them in this or the succeeding chapter.

The third inequity is that the basis of British taxation provides only an indifferent measure of taxable capacity; and the burden of taxation is therefore not allocated fairly between individuals. This is so for a number of reasons, of which the outstanding are that capital gains are excluded from the definition of income, and bear no tax: that certain classes are greatly favoured as compared with others in respect of allowable expenses: and that a number of obvious loopholes exist for tax avoidance.

This might seem merely a horizontal inequity, as between

[1] Anyone who doubts the efficacy of wider social and economic changes in altering relative gross incomes need only consider the violent change in the relative income position of the salaried middle classes between 1939 and 1950.

different taxpayers of the same wealth. But it also has implications
for the vertical distribution of wealth, since it is in practice mainly
large incomes which are let off lightly. As the Minority Report of
the Radcliffe Commission pointed out, 'the tax base lags increasingly behind true taxable capacity as we move up the income
scale'.[1] A correction of these inequities would therefore not only
make matters fairer as between different large incomes, but
would also lead to a redistribution of the tax burden between all
large incomes and the remainder.

The most important of these tax inequities, the exemption of
capital gains, is intimately bound up with the first injustice discussed above, the unequal distribution of private capital. It is
therefore on this aspect of inequality that this and the next
chapter concentrate, since it is in principle the most indefensible,
and in practice the most important. Other aspects are dealt with
elsewhere.[2]

II *Alternative Methods of Redistributing Property*

The maldistribution of private property can be attacked from
a number of directions. First, existing property can be transferred
to the State by direct property taxation. This is discussed in the
rest of this chapter.

But property steadily increases in value with the growth in the
national income; and we want this increment to be better distributed than existing property is. Secondly, therefore, we need to
increase the ratio of public to private property in order to ensure
that more of these gains accrue in public, and fewer in private,
hands. Death-duties will help in this, provided they are treated
as capital and not as income. Generally, this requires that we
should increase public savings – by encouraging the nationalised
industries to make profits, and by running a Budget surplus: and
limit private savings, mainly by high taxation of company profits.

But so long as we have a mixed economy and achieve a rapid
rate of growth, private savings, mainly in the form of undistributed profits, will inevitably be high. Thirdly, therefore, we must

---

[1] *Final Report of the Royal Commission on the Taxation of Profits and Income* (Cmd. 9474),
p. 424.

[2] *v.* especially Chapters V, X, XV, and XVII.

limit the extent to which high (corporate) savings are reflected in an increase in the personal wealth of the rich. This can be done partly by limiting the extent of personal capital gains – either by capital gains taxation (discussed in the next chapter) or by corporate taxation (discussed in Chapter XVII): partly by distributing share-capital more equally (discussed in Chapter XV): and partly, of course, by direct measures to encourage working-class saving and investment.

III   *The Case for a Gifts Tax and Higher Death-duties*

The most obvious method of redistributing existing property is by death-duties. It is clear that these are not now high enough. Contrary to original expectations, they have not effected any large alteration in the pattern of property distribution. The figures show, it is true, a faint improvement over four decades. The top 1% of adult persons, who now own 50% of the capital in private hands, in 1936–8 owned 55%, in 1924–30 60%, and in 1911–13 70%. Similarly the top 10%, who now own 80%, before the war owned 85% . But so slow an improvement over so long a period is certainly not satisfactory. The offsetting forces of accumulation have proved sufficiently strong largely to counter the effects of the duties, which indeed have not done much more than prevent the maldistribution from getting worse.

Those who hope, moreover, that the post-1945 increases in the duties will steadily improve matters must remember that there are strong forces working in the opposite direction. First, avoidance, especially by gifts *inter vivos*, is only now growing to significant proportions. It was not until a few years ago that the rich seem to have woken up to the fact that the higher duties had come to stay, and their tax advisers to the easy loophole offered by the absence of any tax on gifts.[1] Since then the rich have increasingly been giving their fortunes away before death, and are likely to do so more and more. Owing to the five-year rule, the effects of avoidance on the yield of the duties are only now becoming apparent; but they must grow steadily more severe. Furthermore, with full employment and a rapid rate of growth, the average annual rise in capital values will be considerably greater than in

[1] If made more than five years before death.

the past; and higher rates of death-duties would be needed simply
to prevent the position from deteriorating.

The first task of the next Labour Government in this field will
be to reduce avoidance by a tax on gifts. There would be no point
in raising death-duty rates without doing this – the only result
would be still more avoidance, and a growth of gifts *inter vivos*
to the point where they made a complete farce of the duties, and
wholly frustrated their intention. Gifts during lifetime must
therefore be made liable to whatever rate and form of inheritance
taxation is decided on. Gifts are subject to tax in many countries.
In Sweden, for example, a person making gifts to his descendants
which amount in any 10-year period to more than the minimum
exemption limit for estate duty pays the normal estate duty on
those gifts (at rates which assume them to come from the highest
tranche of his estate). In addition, the recipient pays a tax on the
gift at rates which vary with his degree of consanguinity to the
donor. The object is solely to prevent the evasion of death duties;
and the two taxes are therefore exactly assimilated to the Swedish
Estate and Inheritance Taxes. A similar tax is urgently required in
Britain simply to make the present duties effective.

But given the sums still passing at death under the present duties
(when not avoided), and the likely rise in private capital values
under full employment, there is a strong case for increasing the
nominal rates as well. This is especially so because death duties
have, as compared with other forms of taxation, notable advantages. They are politically perhaps the least controversial of taxes;
the moral argument against large inheritance, on grounds of
equal opportunity and the equation of rewards with personal
effort, is now widely accepted; and the number of people affected
is very small.

Hardly anyone now seriously accepts the once-popular view
that whereas the taxation of income is legitimate, the taxation of
property is not, since it amounts to an act of confiscation which
denies the natural 'right' of a man to dispose of his own as he
wishes. This distinction between income and property was always
tenuous; and the argument was refuted once and for all by Sir
William Harcourt, the author of the death-duties, in his famous
Budget Speech of 1894. 'The State has the first title upon the estate,
and those who take afterwards have a subsequent and subordinate
title. Nature gives man no power over his earthly goods beyond

the term of his life. What power he possesses to prolong his will after death – the right of a dead hand to dispose of his property – is a pure creation of the law, and the State has the right to prescribe the conditions and the limitations under which that power shall be exercised.' Moreover, it is now more widely realised that the virtually complete freedom of bequest which the English law allows is not a natural and universal practice, but only one of many possible varieties of inheritance law.[1]

It was also at one time fashionable to attack death-duties for over-riding the moral claims of widows and children to the property of the deceased. If accepted, this criticism would, of course, require a quite different form of inheritance law from the British freedom of bequest, under which widows or orphans may be cut off without a penny. But in any case the argument commands little support to-day. Penniless widows normally had penniless husbands, while the widows of rich men usually have some property of their own. The 'children' who inherit have an average age of forty, by which time they have not only had the advantage of an expensive education, but might perhaps be considered as able to fend for themselves and earn a living. Moreover, while a decent provision for widows and young children is a very desirable motive for saving, it can only justify the passing of quite modest sums, such as will be possible however severe the duties in the upper ranges, and not enormous fortunes of hundreds of thousands of pounds.

On the economic side, death-duties have the overwhelming advantage of not being a serious disincentive to work and effort. The desire to leave property after death, as opposed to giving children a generous start during the parents' lifetime, is only one of many (monetary and non-monetary) incentives to effort, and certainly not the most important. It is impossible to believe that any significant number of active and ambitious men will be

[1] For a discussion of some quite different regulations of inheritance in other countries, v. Josiah Wedgwood, *The Economics of Inheritance* (Pelican Books, 1939), Ch. IV. In fact death duties are as old as the Roman Empire – though admittedly their introduction was not popular even then. When Augustus, in A.D. 6, first proposed an inheritance tax in order to defray the expenses of defence, 'the nobles of Rome', Gibbon tells us, 'were more tenacious of property than of freedom. Their indignant murmurs were received by Augustus with his usual temper. He candidly referred the whole business to the Senate, and . . . insinuated to them that their obstinacy would oblige him to *propose* a general land-tax and capitation. They acquiesced in silence.' And Gibbon even adds that the tax 'was most happily suited to the situation of the Romans'. (*Decline and Fall*, Vol. 1, Ch. VI.)

deterred from enterprise and effort by the fact that the state will take more, and their grown-up children less, of what remains after their death. Indeed it is hard to think of any direct tax which has less disincentive effect.

One would expect, it is true, a more serious effect on the supply of savings. While successful men exert themselves from many motives other than a desire to hand over large properties at death, it is much more plausible to argue that they will save less if death-duties are increased. The desire to leave money to one's family is a relatively stronger motive in the case of savings-decisions than in respect of decisions about effort, in which ambition, emulation, the desire for power and prestige, and the wish to enjoy a high current standard of living, all play a part. Faced with the prospect that 80% of his estate will pass to the State and not to his family, a wealthy man might well not bother to build up his possessions, but choose instead to dissipate them in current consumption.

Nevertheless, the point can be exaggerated. 'The desire to build up capital possessions', wrote Professor Pigou, 'is not a simple thing. It is made up of various elements blended in various ways among different men. One element is the desire to be able to exercise the constructive force, which a strong man may find in himself, in conjunction with a large-scale undertaking; another is the desire for that power in society . . . which great wealth confers; another is the desire for fame or notoriety: another the desire for a large income accruing without effort in later life: another the desire for posthumous glory in dying very rich: another mere inertia. . . . All these motives are concerned only with the lifetime of the man who contemplates saving under the stress of them: the fact that after his death his fortune does not also die is, so far as they are concerned, an irrelevant accident.'[1]

Some weight must be attached to these diverse motives for accumulation; moreover the increasing tendency to give capital away before death may, paradoxically, help to buoy up the family motive for saving. Nevertheless, any significant steepening

---

[1] A. C. Pigou, *A Study in Public Finance* (Macmillan, 1947 ed., pp. 142-3). But some of these motives are probably weaker to-day, with the change in social character, than in Victorian days – for example, the desire for posthumous glory in dying rich. Surely fewer people now gloat in anticipation over 'the majestic effect of that little paragraph in the morning papers accorded to Forsytes who die with a hundred thousand pounds'. (*The Man of Property*.)

of the duties must be expected to have some effect on the propensities to save and dissave; and given the precarious margin which separates full employment from inflation, even a small effect could be serious. Yet we must not be manœuvred into the farcical position where large property-owners can blackmail the State, by threatening to create inflation, into leaving them alone. We must therefore push on with higher property taxation, but accept, as a corollary, the necessity for simultaneous measures to discourage spending out of capital, and generally to encourage savings.

How high should the duties be raised? The socialist case against large inherited fortunes clearly requires a maximum limit on the amount of inheritance permitted. It is not easy to say exactly where this should be set. It should perhaps be set at, or even rather above, the amount which a successful and prudent business or professional man might reasonably hope to accumulate during his lifetime. Perhaps the limit might eventually be set at £50,000, with the rates increased between £25,000 and £50,000. Such an objective of course cannot and should not be achieved at a single fiscal blow. But the next Labour Government must certainly move the next stage; and it should be quite a long one.

If these figures were adopted, only 15% of estates now liable, or some 5,000 families annually, would be affected – only, that is to say, a tiny class of (mainly) hereditary rich. The hard-working professional and salaried classes would be untouched; and nothing would occur to prevent them from working and saving to pass on a moderate but helpful – indeed a generous – sustenance to their dependants. No widows would be left suddenly penniless; and the sums still passing would be ample, for example, to enable young married couples in the middle ranks of society to buy a house, and generally to make a comfortable start to their lives together. At the same time, no individual legatee would normally inherit enough to permit of a prolonged sumptuary existence either on unearned income or by drafts on capital.

This should be a sufficient answer to ill-informed critics who suppose that socialism is against all thrift and saving, or the continuity of family life, or the living standards of the middle class. Of course it is nothing of the sort. The socialist aim is the removal of extremes of wealth, not the reduction of all to the lowest common standard.

IV   *The Case for a Simultaneous Reform of Death-duties*

This, then, should be the broad objective. But it is not certain that a simple increase in the existing estate duty is the best method of achieving it. Estate duty grades the tax according to the size of the total estate. But this is not the only, though it is the simplest, form of inheritance tax. There are two obvious alternative methods of assessment. The tax might be graded according to the degree of consanguinity of the legatee to the testator (as it was under the Legacy and Succession Duties, abolished in 1949, and as it is under the Swedish Inheritance Tax), or according to the size of bequest received by each legatee (either the individual bequest, or the cumulative total of bequests from all sources).

The Succession principle does less injury than estate duty to the saving motive, since bequests to the nearest relatives (widows and children) are more lightly taxed than other bequests. But conversely it is less effective from an egalitarian point of view, since the largest bequests, being normally those to the nearest relatives, attract the least tax.

The principle of progression according to bequests received is logically the most sensible of all. Social justice requires attention less to the total size of the estate, than to the amounts received by the beneficiaries. But a simple estate duty presupposes complete indifference to the disposition of the estate, and an interest solely in its size. This is certainly illogical from a socialist point of view. We should be far from indifferent to whether a large estate passes wholly to a single individual, or in small parcels to many different individuals, or to charitable purposes (e.g. the upkeep of churches, bequests for which purpose still attract duty). On the contrary, we should be most hostile to the first disposition, much less so to the second, and not at all to the third. It follows that we should logically tax the first disposition at a higher rate than the second, and the second at a higher rate than the third. This is impossible under estate duty, but could be largely achieved by a duty graded according to the size of bequests accruing to any individual. Such a duty would not only accurately fulfil the essential objective (which is to prevent the receipt of large unearned sums by the legatee, rather than the transfer of large sums by the testator), but would also encourage the division of large estates into smaller parcels, and so help to disseminate property more widely by a natural process quite apart from the yield of the duty itself.

It is true that any form of assessment other than on the total estate raises administrative difficulties. Estate duty is a tax-collector's dream, since the provisions of the will are irrelevant. But once they have to be considered, complications arise – for example, where property is left in trust to be disposed of in various ways at later dates. Nevertheless the Inland Revenue informed the Colwyn Committee that such a duty was not administratively impossible; and there is a strong case for accompanying an increase in estate duty with some progression according to bequests received. Certainly any maximum figure would apply much more logically to total receipts of bequests, than to the total size of the estate.

But whether this reform is adopted or not, the problem will arise, once the duties are raised really high, of how they shall be paid. It might not be easy for the heirs to a large estate to make a sudden forced sale of virtually the whole estate in order to pay in cash; and even if market conditions permitted, it might well be socially undesirable. Here, as in other spheres, the corollary of greater equality, if certain benefits previously flowing from the expenditure of the rich are not to be placed in jeopardy, is a greater responsibility on the part of the State. Large historic mansions provide a pertinent example. The community has a strong interest in their proper upkeep, and the present rate of decay and destruction is appalling. Increased death duties must inevitably make matters worse. Suppose that an heir cannot pay the duties without disposing of a mansion and most of its contents, what is to be their fate? One must immediately be troubled at the prospect. Many undesirable or vandalistic things might happen, and must be prevented. The State should therefore be willing to accept payment in kind and with it the responsibility for the upkeep of the mansion, which it would no doubt in practice hand over to the National Trust with a suitable endowment.

The principle of payment in kind was introduced by Mr. Dalton in respect of land; and a few large tracts have already passed to the state. It should now be extended to real estate and quoted securities. In the case of land and real estate, several public or semi-public bodies already exist which could carry the new responsibility efficiently. In the case of securities, some new organisation would be needed. This would be a most interesting development. It is now generally agreed that there are definite drawbacks to the wholesale nationalisation of entire industries; yet socialists still want to see an increasing proportion of property income and capital gains accruing to the community, instead of to a small property-owning class. Payment of death-duties in kind, which would be a form of gradual and piecemeal public ownership, would help to resolve the dilemma.

The Government would need to establish a body of Death-duty Commissioners, analogous to the National Debt Commissioners, though with a different function. Whereas the purpose of the latter is to support the Government's monetary policy, and so to operate mainly in the gilt-edged and money markets, the former would act like an investment trust, seeking to maximise dividends and capital gains. Their capital should consist of the total cumulative yield of the duties, which should accrue to them whether payment was made in cash or kind. This would both require and facilitate a change in Budgetary accounting which is in any case to be desired on grounds of economic logic, namely, that death-duties should cease to be treated as an ordinary 'above the line' revenue item, and should be treated as a capital receipt.

This might have another incidental advantage. Many people fear that increasing equality may threaten the supply of risk capital, and that particular sectors of industry may find it hard to obtain new capital from the traditional sources. A later chapter discusses this point, and considers the possibility of a government investment corporation to provide funds to industry. Such a body, if set up, would find its task much easier if there already existed, in a government death-duty fund, a growing portfolio of gilt-edged and industrial stock, all easily marketable. Between them, these two novel approaches might make an interesting contribution to a more fluent movement of capital between different sectors of the economy.

However that may be, the project of accepting payment in kind would still constitute a fascinating social experiment, and one that will in any case become inevitable as we move to correct the maldistribution of private property.

XIII

— ◆ —

THE DISTRIBUTION OF WEALTH (II)

I   *The Tax Bias in Favour of the Property Owner*

FOR a steady advance towards equality, death-duties alone
will not suffice. They bite only slowly; and meanwhile
inherited property confers altogether too large an advantage on a small class of wealthy persons. Moreover, a tax on
inheritance does nothing to correct the inequities amongst the
living between those with property, whether inherited or accumulated, and those without; whatever one may think about
inheritance or the right *vertical* distribution of income, the British
tax system fails to distribute the burden fairly as between
property-owners and non-property-owners.

It fails to do so because it is based on income; and the definition of taxable income is not an adequate measure of true spending power, or taxable capacity, in any society in which private
property exists on a large scale.[1] Thus it makes no distinction
(except for the minor differentiation introduced by the existing
earned income allowance) between two individuals with the same
income, even though one has property worth £100,000 and the
other no property at all.

Clearly the spending power, or wealth, of these two individuals is by no means identical. The first, unlike the second, can
adopt a nonchalant attitude towards the future, and need make
no provision out of his income against the day of his retirement;
he is not faced with the risk that his income may fail, or be interrupted, on account of sickness or accident; and above all he can

---

[1] It will be obvious to the reader that the whole discussion of taxable income in
this chapter owes much to Mr. Kaldor's recent fiscal writings.

supplement his consumption by large amounts through the sale of capital assets, or from capital gains. The financial situation of the two individuals is thus in no way comparable, and in no way reflected in their actual incomes. An income basis of taxation therefore involves a bias in favour of property-owners, whose taxable capacity is under-stated as compared with those whose incomes are derived from work. This inequity calls for correction whatever may be decided about inheritance; though in practice corrective measures will also diminish the spending power of inherited property in the interval while death-duties are slowly doing their work.

Such measures could take the form of a direct annual tax on property and/or a tax on capital gains.

II *An Annual Property Tax*

The possibility of an annual tax on capital, which would be in the nature of a small continuous capital levy, has been curiously little discussed by socialists, or even economists.[1] It has obvious advantages. It would not have the unpredictable consequences of a once-for-all, large-scale capital levy; yet it would have a continuing influence on the distribution of property, and with no ill effect on incentives to effort and enterprise.

In what little discussion there has been, the writers have usually assumed that anything called an annual capital or property tax would have very moderate rates, and would in practice, however assessed, be normally paid out of income. This could not be so to-day. At present rates of surtax, even exceedingly modest rates of capital tax would quickly raise the total tax burden to above 20s. in the pound; and on all larger incomes the tax would necessarily be paid out of capital.[2] This was the case, as all commentators agreed, with the Special Contribution in 1948, which was a non-recurrent property tax, even though assessed on income. And of course if the object is to influence the distribution of property, the tax would make no sense unless it fell on capital.

[1] The only recent detailed discussion that I am aware of is in J. R. Hicks, U. K. Hicks, and L. Rostas, *The Taxation of War Wealth* (Oxford, 1941), Ch. XXII. The matter is also mentioned in Mr. Kaldor's recent book, referred to later.

[2] That is, if it was not avoided altogether (*v.i.*).

Previous discussions, which have assumed payment out of current income, therefore offer little help.

Should the tax be assessed on capital or investment income? (It applies, of course, only to private and not to business holdings of capital.) At first sight there might seem to be no difference, if it is assumed that the value of property is, in the long run, determined by the income it yields. But in fact there are many forms of capital which yield no money income, but a generous non-monetary satisfaction or 'psychic' income; such are cars, yachts, artistic treasures, valuable jewellery, etc. These would bear tax if the assessment were on property, but none if it were on money income; and it might be thought unfair that one man, who has invested heavily in such objects, should escape more lightly than another, who chooses to hold the same amount of capital in money-yielding form.

But of course this draws attention to what is the fatal objection to assessment on income: namely, that the tax would become wholly inoperative as soon as an individual's combined tax rates rose above 20s. in the pound. It would then pay him to withdraw his capital from income-yielding assets, and hold it in cash (or cars, jewellery, pictures, non-dividend-paying stocks, etc.), in which form it will attract no tax. By so doing he would, above that point, avoid any surrender of his property to the State, even though he would be compelled at the same time to dip into capital to maintain his previous level of consumption. But the object of the tax is not to compel dissaving, but to collect and redistribute property; and in that it would be frustrated just at the point where the large estates come into view. This problem did not arise with the Special Contribution, since it was unexpected; the assessments were on tax-returns already rendered, and no possibility of avoidance arose. But if the tax is annual, or even periodic, avoidance must, in the upper reaches, become wholesale.

A capital tax assessed on income would therefore not be a tax on capital at all, but merely a stiffer tax on unearned income. A regular tax which is to fall on capital must be assessed on capital. This raises the administrative problem of the valuation of private capital – not of individual estates at irregular intervals, as now for death-duties, but of all estates simultaneously, and moreover repeated every few years to keep pace with changes in capital values. It is hard for the layman to judge whether this is practicable – only the Inland Revenue can give a final answer. But such a tax, assessed on property, already exists in Sweden, where the administrative difficulties have not been found insuperable.

If practicable, it would be a useful, if modest, supplementary weapon in the attack on inequality. It would start, like the death-duties, only above a substantial minimum figure; and the rates, since it is only a supplementary measure, need be neither high nor steeply progressive – though they should, in view of the greater inequality from which we start, be higher than the Swedish rates, which rise only from 0·5% to 1·8% of capital. It would have negligible effects on the incentive to save, since the rates are low and it falls not on the margin of new savings but equally on the whole property, and none on risk-taking, since if assessed on capital it does not alter the relative attraction of high (risky) and low (safe) yields. Altogether it is worth more con-sideration than it has so far received in this country.

III *The Case for a Capital Gains Tax*

If taxable income is so poor a measure of the true spending power of the property owner, the question arises as to whether the present definition of income for tax purposes is either logical or accurate. Is the existing lack of correspondence between income and taxable capacity inevitable and incorrigible, so that no reform in the sphere of income tax can ever make matters better: or is it partly due to deficiencies in the concept of taxable income?

There is one glaring deficiency, namely the exclusion of capital gains from the definition of income. Income is defined by econom-ists as 'the maximum value which [a man] can consume during a week, and still expect to be as well off at the end of the week as he was at the beginning':[1] that is, the net 'increment of "spending power" or "economic power" in a period . . . the increase in the individual's command over resources in a period'.[2]

On these definitions, capital gains would appear to constitute income. They can be consumed during the week, while still leaving the individual as well off as he was at the beginning of the week (i.e. with his original capital intact). They confer a clear increase in spending power and command over resources. And indeed

[1] J. R. Hicks, *Value and Capital* (Oxford, 1939), p. 172.   [2] Cmd. 9474, p. 356.

not only economists, but ordinary investors also appear to regard them as income, and spend them without any sense of running down their capital. They should logically, therefore, be taxed as income, as they have been in the United States for many years.

Moreover apart from considerations of logic and equity between taxpayers, there is a clear redistributive case for taxing capital gains. They accrue only to those who already own property; and the present distribution of property, as was pointed out in the last chapter, is not only highly unequal, but also, since so high a proportion is inherited, the least defensible aspect of inequality. Thus all the evils inherent in the maldistribution of private capital are magnified by the exemption from tax of the gains to which that capital gives rise, and which still further increase the inequality of purchasing power; and a tax on these gains is therefore wholly to be desired on socialist grounds.

Moreover the quantitative significance of capital gains is, in an expanding economy, very considerable. The value of quoted Stock Exchange securities alone rose by £5,000 millions between 1950 and 1954. No doubt this was the product of an exceptionally strong bull market. But in a full employment economy, the real value of private property may be expected to increase by anything up to £1,000 millions a year.[1] There is no justification for leaving this huge accretion to private spending power untaxed, when incomes from work are treated so severely.

The economic arguments for and against such a tax have been exhaustively discussed in the Radcliffe Report, and will only be summarised here. The usual arguments brought against it are, first, that capital gains which occur as a result of inflation are not real, but illusory gains. This is true; but it does not follow that they should not be taxed. 'If the proceeds of the gain are spent the recipient derives the same benefit as he does in spending taxed income. If the gains are saved, the argument about their illusory character applies equally to all saving, and not merely capital appreciation. If a man regularly saves up a part of his earnings by adding to his savings deposits or paying premiums on a life assurance, it may equally happen that as a result of inflation the real value of his accumulated savings is shrinking. He is in no different position from another man who attains the same increase in the money value of his capital as a result of capital appreciation.'[2]

[1] v.i.   [2] Cmd. 9474, p. 366 (Minority Report).

Secondly, it is said that gains resulting from a fall in interest rates are also illusory, since they do not augment the investor's future income. This again may be true, but again is not an argument against taxing the gains. Holders of long-term bonds will still be at an advantage as compared with other savers (e.g. those who hold savings deposits), since in their case the fall in interest is offset by the capital gains on their existing holdings. In any case, what they lose on the swings they gain on the roundabouts; there is no visible long-run tendency for interest rates to decline, and periods of falling rates alternate with periods of rising rates, with no significant change on balance.

But of course a high proportion of capital gains are due neither to inflation nor to falling interest rates, but to the rising profits and dividend payments of private industry. This provides the answer to a third argument against taxing them, that they are irregular and not sought after by the recipient. They are, it is true, less regular than an annual salary or fixed-interest income – but so, if it comes to that, are many work incomes (e.g. those of writers and actors) which are nevertheless liable to tax. But in an expanding economy they will occur, not indeed steadily, but at least with sufficient regularity to be treated as income by the recipients; indeed wealthy people already regard them as a major, even though periodic, element in their total receipts. And it is absurd to say that they are not expected or sought after by the investor; a glance at any broker's investment circular will demonstrate that they are not merely sought after, but commonly provide the primary motive for investment.

The last criticism concerns the prospective yield. It is pointed out that the average yield of the American tax has not been large; and the Board of Inland Revenue estimated the likely average yield in Britain, assuming that gains were charged to both income and surtax and that the tax was based on realised gains, at only £75–£100 millions annually. But this estimate was based on a projection of the rate of capital appreciation in the inter-war period – a period which spanned at least one complete trade cycle, and one of the deepest depressions in economic history. Presumably no one now supposes that a 1931-type slump is likely to recur, or that the trade cycle continues in its classical form. On the contrary, all parties are committed to full employment and rapid growth; and estimates based on pre-war trends therefore have little value.

The Minority Report of the Radcliffe Commission has provided what may be a more realistic estimate. Basing itself on post-war trends of industrial production, gross profits and company reserves, it concludes that the annual appreciation of private capital will be of the order of £600–£1,000 millions. On this basis the annual net yield of the tax (i.e. allowing for a consequential decline in the yield of death duties), even if imposed only at income and not at surtax rates, would lie between £160 and £310 millions per annum.[1] This cannot be called a negligible sum.

What effect would the tax have on incentives and economic efficiency? It would tend somewhat, though not sensationally, to discourage consumption and increase savings. Capital gains are often realised in order to be spent, and it is well known that during a Stock Exchange boom luxury consumption is particularly heavy.[2] A tax on realised gains would increase saving both by diminishing the net realised gain to the investor and equivalently augmenting the Budget surplus, and (more doubtfully)[3] by encouraging investors not to realise (and spend) their gains so rapidly, but to allow the increase in the value of their property to accumulate as savings.

But it must clearly have an adverse effect on the individual investor's willingness to take risks, which now depends partly on the hope of tax-free capital appreciation. The effect on individual risk-bearing, however, cannot be treated in isolation. The effect on companies must also be considered. The present exemption of capital gains from tax causes Governments, for fear of the social and economic consequences of large tax-free gains, to take measures

[1] op. cit., pp. 378 seq. The Report also correctly points out that one of the reasons for the low yield of the American tax is that all accrued gains are wiped out when property passes at death, so that a high proportion of gains escape tax altogether.

[2] And conversely, as Lorelei discovered in the film *Gentlemen Prefer Blondes*:

'He's your guy when stocks are high,
But beware when they start to descend:
It's then that those louses
Go back to their spouses –
Diamonds are a girl's best friend.'

[3] Because the main effect might be to discourage switches between shares rather than realisations for spending.

directed against companies and logically designed to restrict the extent of such gains. This is part of the rationale of heavy corporate taxation, the differential tax on distributions, and generally of measures to limit dividends. These may well have *some* adverse effect, though the matter has been ridiculously exaggerated in the post-war years, on entrepreneurial decisions about expansion (both by reducing the internal funds available, and by raising the effective cost of making new issues). But the introduction of a capital gains tax would permit a reduction in the level of corporate taxation (or, if it were preferred, in the rates of taxation on earned incomes), and on balance the effect on risk-bearing and economic growth might be beneficial.[1]

Nevertheless, the individual investor's attitude to risk-bearing is of some importance (though probably less in relation to the Stock Exchange than to the small entrepreneur, who might be discouraged by a very heavy rate of capital gains tax, especially under conditions of inflation, from building a business up, and then selling it in order to move on to bigger things). This is not an argument for doing nothing; but it is an argument against aggregating gains fully with ordinary income, and so taxing them at the full progressive rates of surtax as well as income tax. This applies with particular force inasmuch as the gains, accruing as they do largely to the higher income groups, would often attract exceedingly high marginal rates of tax, rising to 18s. 6d. in the pound. Such rates would not only have too adverse an effect on risk-taking, but might also, by tempting property owners to dissipate their capital, have harmful results on savings. Gains should therefore be liable for income tax only, and not for surtax. The tax would then be a flat-rate one above the point where total income (including gains) became liable for the standard rate.

There is another reason why the tax should be at a flat, and not progressive, rate. If confined, as it must be for reasons explained in the next paragraph, to realised gains, it taxes in one year a capital appreciation which may have occurred over several years. The investor holding a number of easily marketable securities could easily, by timing his realisations, avoid an

---

[1] As a method of limiting the gain to shareholders, a capital gains tax is of course much more equitable than high business taxation, since it strikes equally at all gains. Company taxation, on the other hand, is wildly crude and haphazard as between individual gains. Moreover, capital gains arise on other forms of property besides industrial equities.

excessive burden of marginal taxation in any one year. But certain types of investor might be unable to avoid a bunching of realised gains in one year; and a progressive tax would fall on them with undue severity. This would arise, for example, in the case of a private business sold as a going concern, or in any case where the capital assets were not easily marketable, and could be disposed of only in large blocks.

The tax must be based on realised and not paper gains for overwhelming administrative reasons. There could be no question of an annual valuation of capital assets of such a degree of precision that exact changes in their market value over the year could be fairly computed. Moreover it makes no difference to the yield in the long run whether the tax is levied on realised or accrued gains, since if gifts and inheritance are treated as realisation, as they should be, the two must amount to the same thing over the taxpayer's lifetime – though of course the difference in timing might be very significant for the individual (e.g. for the man who neither switched nor over-spent his income – for him the tax would be simply a second death-duty).

On more detailed points, there seems little to be said for making a distinction, as the American tax does, between short-term and long-term gains. Realised losses should be allowed as an offset against realised gains (though not against other income), with provision for carrying forward. To reduce the administrative difficulties the tax should be limited, at least initially, to gains arising out of the sale of businesses, stocks and shares, and real property. There should be an exemption limit to exclude small gains and small amounts of property; and gains arising out of the sale of an owner-occupied house should be exempt if the proceeds are used to buy another house.

There is no reason why we should boggle at a capital gains tax. It is, as experience in the U.S. and elsewhere shows, perfectly practicable; though in the immediate post-war years, when the Revenue was under-staffed and over-worked, the administrative difficulties seemed, naturally enough, forbiddingly formidable. The yield would probably never be enormous; but the case for it, on grounds both of equity between individuals and equality between classes, is overwhelming.[1]

[1] Since the manuscript of this book was substantially complete, Mr. Kaldor has published his important proposal for shifting from an income to an expenditure basis

IV   *The Concerted Attack on the Maldistribution of Wealth*

The measures proposed in these two chapters, taken together, would greatly diminish inequalities of wealth, especially when combined with a policy for industry, to be discussed in later chapters, designed to prevent a large rise in share-values from occurring in the first place. None of them, by itself, will change the face of society overnight, as would a huge capital levy. But taken in conjunction they would steadily carry us forward towards a reasonable and equitable distribution of wealth.

I must underline, in conclusion, in an attempt to forestall (the probably inevitable) misunderstanding, that all these measures are designed to equalise wealth only by striking at property, and especially inherited property, and only by striking at large amounts of property. None of them affects earned incomes; and all are subject to exemption limits which would effectively exclude small and medium savings. Indeed to the extent that they gradually eliminate this central and most indefensible cause of inequality, the maldistribution of property, it will become possible both more actively to encourage the growth of small property, and to take a more favourable attitude towards the taxation of incomes from work;[1] the more so if other measures designed to remove the rent element in gross work-incomes are also successful. Socialists have no desire to penalise small savings, or enterprise and initiative; their aims are social justice and genuine equality of opportunity. Once these are achieved, and the dead hand of inheritance removed, we shall more easily be able to lighten the load of taxation on incomes from work, and restore to individual effort and enterprise some of the rewards which the unequal distribution of property now forces us to tax away.

---

of taxation, at least for surtax payers (*An Expenditure Tax*, Allen and Unwin, 1955). This would achieve, a good deal more efficiently, many of the objectives discussed in this chapter, besides having excellent effects on savings decisions. But any firm verdict must wait on an exhaustive discussion by the experts of the feasibility in practice of such a tax.

[1] For instance, one of the objections to-day to reducing the standard rate of income tax is that a significant proportion of the benefit accrues to large property incomes. This objection would disappear if property ceased to be a major source of inequality.

XIV

POWER AND PRIVILEGE IN INDUSTRY

I *The Status of the Worker*

THE last two distance factors to be discussed are inequalities
in the distribution of power, and in non-pecuniary occupational status. These factors, and especially the first, as was
made clear in Chapter VI, have many different aspects,
political, economic, and sociological.[1] But from the point of view
of socio-economic reform it is their incidence in large-scale industry which is most significant, on account both of the numbers
of people affected and the still powerful influence of work-
relationships on social attitudes.

It was suggested in Chapter I that the changes of the last two
decades – the seller's market for labour, the greater strength of
both the political and industrial Left, and the internal revolution
within industry – had enormously improved the position of the
worker relative to the employer; and that the latter now neither
could, nor commonly tried to, act in an arbitrary or authoritarian
manner. Nevertheless there are still great disparities within
industry, and perhaps especially in large-scale industry, of status,
privilege, and power.

The matter is sometimes argued, by writers such as Mr. Peter
Drucker, in rather wide sociological terms. The 'mass-production
world revolution', it is said, has actually depressed the worker's
technical status at work. The man on an assembly-line has no
individual function or responsibility comparable to those of the
craft worker in pre-industrial days. Indeed he can scarcely be
called a 'producer' at all. 'It is only a very small minority of

[1] *v.* Chapter VI, Section V.

artists and professional men who can produce at all by themselves. All the others are dependent upon access to an organisation to be productive.'[1] In the extreme case of repetitive work,
the worker has become 'just one more sloppily-designed machine'.[2]
And this decline in his personal responsibility at work has coincided with an increase both in his educational maturity, and
in the range of his responsibilities outside work; the result is a
rather glaring contrast between his status in the hours of leisure
and the hours of work.

It is hard to believe that there is no exaggeration here. The
mass-production revolution may have brought the assembly-line,
but it has also brought, if we look at the labour force as a whole,
a marked decline in the proportion of unskilled labour in the
total. In the U.S. it now constitutes less than 20% of the labour
force, while the semi-skilled have risen to 22%, and skilled
workers, clerks, and professional personnel to 42%. Automation,
requiring as it does a very high (almost 100%) ratio of skilled to
unskilled labour, will accelerate this trend; and the typical worker
of the future will be not the robot figure on an assembly-line of
Chaplin's *Modern Times*, but the highly-skilled instrument-reader
and repair-worker in a fully automatic factory.

However that may be, there is no disputing the second consequence of large scale: the tendency for decisions to be centralised, and power concentrated, in fewer and fewer hands. The
result is a degree of 'remote' power (to use the terminology of
Chapter VI), reflected lower down the scale in 'face-to-face'
power, which is much greater than would exist in a society of
small-scale units.

The case for redistributing this power, and transferring a
greater share of it to the workers at the expense of other groups
in industry, might be based on either of the two main arguments
for more equality postulated in Chapter VII: social contentment
or social justice.

II   *The Causes of Industrial Discontent*

If we argue the matter in terms of social contentment, we enter
a difficult sphere; for not only do the experts disagree in their

[1] *The New Society* (Heinemann, 1951), p. xvii.
[2] *The Future of Industrial Man* (Heinemann, 1943), p. 75.

diagnosis, but all the suggested reforms are open to exceptionally strong practical objections.

The diagnostic difficulty emerges as soon as we make comparisons between countries. I suggested in Chapter VII that we retained a degree of bitterness, sullenness, and resentment in industry which appeared surprising in the light of the absence of such traditional provocations to discontent as falling wages or unemployment. And we find that other countries largely escape this resentful atmosphere, despite having an organisation of large-scale industry very similar to our own; they do not, that is, have significantly more nationalisation, or industrial democracy, or workers' participation. This is the case both in Sweden, where industrial relations are unusually harmonious and strikes a rarity, and in the U.S.A., where, although the Unions are more militant than our own and disputes more violent, there is much less underlying, nagging class resentment and consciousness of irreconcilable conflict – much less hostility, for example, to high profits or even dividends. And the contrast is reflected in the fact that only in Britain of these three countries is there any sustained pressure for major industrial change, whether by nationalisation or workers' control.

In the light of the similar industrial and ownership patterns prevailing in these other countries, it is hard to believe that the contrast is not partly to be explained, as I suggested in Chapter VII, by their greater degree of social equality.[1] They have less sense of conflict because the worker feels there is a fair opportunity of rising into the ranks of management: because he does not suspect the boss of being boss on account of nepotism, or lineage, or inherited wealth: because he does not feel himself socially inferior to the manager – after all, he too drives to work in a car, and has even had much the same education, and is not marked off by a wholly different accent or style of life: and lastly because the management actually turn up to work at the same time, and claim fewer social privileges simply for being 'staff' as opposed to 'labour'.

This point is particularly important. Non-pecuniary status privileges are exceptionally widespread in British industry; and their persistence acts as a constant irritant. They can hardly all be

---

[1] It is also partly to be explained by their greater success in extruding Communist influence from their labour movements.

justified on grounds of discipline or incentives, since they are so much less conspicuous in American firms whose efficiency is beyond dispute. The contrast is shown most clearly when an American firm, using American managers and supervisors, embarks on an enterprise in Britain. The construction of the Esso refinery at Fawley is a well-documented case in point.[1] The report on this enterprise refers to the 'minimum stress on the symbols of inequality of status between supervisors and men'. The American staff kept the same hours as the men, 'mucked in' whenever it was necessary, treated the men as equals, and showed no trace of the snobbery so prevalent here amongst supervisory and black-coated staff. The manifest absence of social barriers, so far from prejudicing good order and discipline, appears to have been a major cause of good relations, and consequently of greater efficiency.

This status inequality calls for action on several different fronts. It can be lessened, indirectly, by social service and taxation policy.[2] It will in practice be weakened as the educational and other changes discussed in earlier chapters diminish the natural class sentiment now so strong in Britain, so that the managerial classes lose their present ingrained assumption of social superiority. And it can be weakened by Trade Union action. This requires that the Unions should steadily widen the agenda of collective bargaining, and increasingly direct their pressure, as they already do to some extent, towards 'fringe' benefits designed to equalise non-wage privileges: pension schemes, longer paid holidays, sickness benefits, and the like. The culmination will no doubt be to eliminate the ultimate social distinction between wage and salary, and at the same time the worker's greater insecurity, by means of the guaranteed annual wage.

But if this thesis is correct, that the deeper industrial resentments in Britain are not wholly due to causes internal to industry itself, but are partly a symptom of social inequality – if, that is, the orientation of these resentments towards work and production conflicts is partly a process of psychological transference or rationalisation: then the cure will be a long-term process, and will depend on our success in implementing the wider egalitarian measures discussed in earlier chapters.

[1] v. Construction of Esso Refinery, Fawley, British Institute of Management, Occasional Papers No. 6, 1954.
[2] v. Chapter V, Section VI.

Yet there are also causes internal to industry. Another marked difference between Britain and the U.S. is the greater attention paid in America to the whole question of labour relations and personnel management. This is treated as a central and specialised aspect of the management function, and is studied much more seriously and systematically than in Britain. The result is that management is, on the average, appreciably more imaginative, progressive, and enlightened in its labour policies; and relations are better in consequence.

Furthermore, workers in America are less suspicious of high profits and dividends, because they feel more certain that wages will obtain a generous share of any increase in productivity. And as a matter of fact they are right; wage increases are both frequent and absolutely large owing to the rapid rise in productivity, and the high-wage ideology prevalent even within management itself. But there is a further important influence. Ever since the famous 1950 U.A.W.-G.M. contract, Unions have increasingly asked, and management conceded, that wage increases should be pledged for some years ahead on the assumption of rising productivity (and often also pledged in the event of a rise in the cost of living). The worker therefore has less suspicious apprehension lest he be cheated out of the fruits of his labour; and being more certain that his own interests are well looked after, he is less hostile to the share of profits going to other groups.

III *The Importance of Local Management and the Unimportance of Ownership*

The greater industrial discontent in Britain does not, then, seem directly traceable to our industrial structure, so much as to our social system generally, the quality of management, and the absence of an *explicit* high-wage ideology. The significance of the management factor, and the lesser importance of the actual structure, are confirmed by the extraordinary variations in morale amongst British firms of broadly the same size and organisation.

Within the general picture, we have a number of firms enjoying excellent relations and a genuinely co-operative spirit between management and labour. This occurs where the management is both efficient and enlightened, and where in consequence not only are wage-rates above average, welfare facilities good, and the firm technically efficient and amply equipped with modern plant; but also (and probably more important) the personnel managers are highly trained, the supervisory grades competent, the workers' representatives given ample information about future plans and past performance, and an effective channel exists for raising grievances. In such firms morale is high even though dividends are generous, discipline strict, and formal joint consultation often absent.

These are essentially the firms which, like most American enterprises, pay the most careful attention to enlightened personnel management. A famous case-study was provided by the Fawley refinery already referred to. There was no attempt here at formal joint consultation or participation in management; discipline was firmer than is usual on a British site; the functions of shop-stewards were curtailed below their normal; and even wages and welfare facilities were not significantly better than the average.

Yet labour relations were exceptionally harmonious; and the reason lay in the enlightened labour policy of the management. There was an unusually high degree of co-operation with the Unions: a smooth-working machinery for raising complaints: a marked willingness to settle grievances quickly and on the spot: and a very high number and quality of supervisors who 'mucked in' with the men, worked the same hours, were always accessible, and took constant trouble to ensure the widest possible dissemination of information about what was being done, and why. Labour relations were, in other words, given the highest priority by a progressive and intelligent management, with the result that the worker felt himself to be a respected and responsible member of a team despite the absence of any formal joint machinery.

It is clear, then, that within any given framework, greater or lesser harmony is largely a function of the quality of management.[1] Where confidence in the management exists, and above all confidence that it will listen and attend to grievances, formal changes seem to be unnecessary. Where confidence does not

---

[1] One unfortunate consequence (though of course there are advantages also) of industry-wide wage negotiations is that the Trade Unions are less interested in the quality of local management than they would be under a system of plant negotiation.

exist, resentments occur. But it follows that these resentments, being due to essentially local frictions, may not be curable by action at the national or industry level – by nationalisation, or dividend limitation, or legal changes in the structure of industry. These may have an influence on Trade Union attitudes also at the national or industry level, and hence might be relevant, for example, to wages policy. But they will not have much influence on local tensions where, as is often the case, these are caused by managerial shortcomings.

Thus nationalisation is no panacea for bad relations. It has, it is true, removed particular grievances in particular cases, notably in the coal industry. But nobody could claim that morale in the public sector was uniformly high, or even better on the average than in good private firms; and in two industries, coal and the railways, it is quite exceptionally low.[1] This appears again to be mainly a matter of the calibre of management. These two industries were never famous in this respect; and even under public ownership they are well below the average for industry as a whole.

Indeed there are some features of nationalisation, as so far practised, which may be positively bad for industrial relations. One is the pressure towards centralisation, especially evident on the railways, where a highly centralised and uniform structure has replaced the previous regional traditions and variations. Another is the tendency to delegate responsibility for labour policy to an ex-Trade Union member of the Board, who has no experience or expertise in this specialised branch of management. A third is the generally low level of salaries as compared with private enterprise, and the correspondingly lower calibre in the middle ranks of management.

At any rate there is little reason to expect nationalisation to produce an automatic change for the better; though of course it may or may not be desirable on other grounds.[2] Does this mean, then, that the complaints of shop-stewards and working-class militants about dividends, bonus shares, and private profits have no significance? This must certainly often be the case, for they do not occur in well-managed private firms, whatever the level

[1] v. the 'Studies in Nationalised Industry' produced by the Acton Trust in 1952-3, and Hugh Clegg, *Labour Relations in London Transport* (Blackwell, 1950).

[2] v. Chapters XVIII and XIX.

of profits and dividends; and they often continue just as vehemently under nationalisation, though now articulated in different language. They must therefore often be a rationalisation of purely local discontents (a tyrannical foreman, a failure to consult, or general inefficiency).

Where they are not, they appear to reflect one of the other two factors mentioned above – the persistence of obvious class inequality, or a suspicion that wages are not rising as fast as they should. Neither of these will necessarily be removed by nationalisation. As Chapter II made clear, the pattern of ownership is not now a major determinant of the social structure as a whole; while the suspicion that wages are not getting a fair deal can, as the case of the railways shows, only too easily persist under public ownership.

IV *'Participation' and Joint Consultation*

The fact that morale so often depends on the quality of local management is also a difficulty when we turn to consider the proposals sometimes made by sociologists and industrial psychologists. There is the further difficulty here, it is true, that the suggested solutions have undergone rather radical changes over quite a short period. It was only comparatively recently that low morale was attributed to insufficiently subtle and detailed methods of incentive-payments: or to the lack of welfare or recreational facilities: or to poor lighting, or the wrong humidity, or the ceiling not being painted the right colour: or the absence of 'music-while-you-work'. All these prescriptions are now out of fashion; and the emphasis is all on giving the worker a sense of status and function, on encouraging the group rather than the individual, and on 'participation'.[1]

It is not easy to avoid a certain irritation when one hears the word 'participation'. Not only has it become a catch-phrase, bandied about as though it were a nostrum for every social evil, but those who preach it hardest appear to think that collective is always superior to individual action, and that we must all be herded into participating groups of one kind or another. 'Man

[1] For a reasonably moderate statement of this approach, *v.* Brown, *The Social Psychology of Industry.*

cannot find his fulfilment in selfish isolation. . . . He may limit
his creative activities to his home and his garden, but in so doing
he denies his responsibilities within his own community, and
indeed his concern with the whole of mankind beyond it. With
this denial, there comes, inevitably, a stunting of his personality;
a drying-up of the wells of human sympathy.'[1]

I have already suggested that there is another side to this –
that membership of a group can also stunt the individual personality, since groups themselves often develop distinctly undemocratic and selfish characteristics.[2] In any case, we surely do
not want a world in which everyone is fussing around in an interfering and responsible manner, and no one peacefully cultivating
his garden. Of course this inevitably pains some socialists, as it
did the old Chartist who, touring the North of England in 1870,
found the material condition of the workers much improved, but
'noticed with pain that their moral and intellectual condition
had deteriorated. . . . In our old Chartist time, it is true, Lancashire working men were in rags by thousands; and many of them
lacked food. But you would see them in groups discussing the
great doctrine of political justice or the teachings of socialism.
Now you will see no such groups. But you will hear well-dressed
working men talking of co-operative stores, and their shares in
them, or in building societies. And you will see others, like idiots,
leading small greyhound dogs, covered with cloth. They are about
to race, and they are betting money as they go.'[3]

And why not, indeed? If one believes in socialism not on paternalistic grounds, but as a means of increasing personal freedom
and the range of choice, one does not necessarily want a busy,
bustling society in which everyone is politically active, and spends
his evenings in group discussions, and feels responsible for all the
burdens of the world. As Bertrand Russell once wrote, 'the sphere
of individual action is not to be regarded as ethically inferior to
that of social duty. On the contrary, some of the best of human
activities are, at least in feeling, rather personal than social. . . .
Prophets, mystics, poets, scientific discoverers, are men whose
lives are dominated by a vision. It is such men who put into the
world the things that we most value, not only in religion, in art
and in science, but also in our feeling towards our neighbour,

---

[1] *Socialism: A New Statement of Principles* (Socialist Union), p. 35.
[2] Chapter IV, Section IV.   [3] Quoted in Beer, op. cit., Vol. II, p. 221.

for improvements in the sense of social obligation, as in everything else, have been largely due to solitary men whose thoughts
and emotions were not subject to the dominion of the herd.'

However, most of us are not prophets or mystics; and we may
at once concede that people working in an impersonal mass
organisation certainly want to be consulted and respected, and
to feel they matter, and possibly, though more doubtfully, to
'participate' (in some sense) in managerial decisions. It is clear
that the element of consultation, in particular, is crucial, and an
essential condition of the confidence mentioned above. A great
many strikes and much resentment would be avoided if management, not necessarily set up an elaborate machinery for joint
participation, but took the workers into its confidence, gave them
information, and ascertained their views.

But unfortunately none of this can be imposed from above.
In the good firm, it will occur automatically as part of an enlightened management policy, whether dignified as formal joint
consultation or not. In the bad firm, nothing will change simply
because an elaborate consultative machinery is set up.[1] The
managerial or worker attitudes which are the root of the trouble
will still persist; and the failure of the new machinery will become simply another source of grievance.

Effective consultation will spread only as a by-product of a
gradual improvement in the quality of management – and, a
very relevant point, of a gradual change in attitude on the part
of the Trade Unions. The failure is by no means always the fault
of management, but often of Union indifference, if not hostility,
based on a fear lest consultative committees may usurp the
negotiating function which is seen as the basis of Trade Union
power. In Sweden, for example, 'joint enterprise councils' are
widespread and effective. But they work only because *both* sides
in industry take an enlightened interest in 'enterprise economics',
and therefore take the whole business seriously. This is a very
desirable outcome, and the industrial atmosphere is better in
consequence. But industrial contentment cannot be increased by
edicts from Whitehall.

The conclusion is that the unequal distribution of power in
industry, in the sense of a failure to consult, is certainly an

---

[1] *v.* Chapter IV, Section IV, for a discussion of the problem of eliciting the 'right',
as opposed to the 'wrong', group attitudes.

indirect cause of resentment; but it is not the only one, nor is a major structural or legislative change a plausible solution. *Prima facie*, it appears that greater industrial contentment requires three things. First, an attack on social inequality and class privilege generally, partly within industry (in the matter of non-pecuniary status), but mainly in spheres outside. Secondly, a more effective assurance to the worker that he is not being 'done out' of wage increases which are his due; this can be achieved partly by more imaginative wage-bargains on the industry level, and perhaps occasionally in individual firms by collective production bonuses. Thirdly, the spread of more enlightened management and Union policies, of which one aspect, namely more effective consultation, will represent a genuine transfer of power.

v   *Industrial Democracy and Joint Management*

But structural changes designed to redistribute power, whatever their effects on morale, might still be justified on grounds of justice.

Historically, the aspiration towards a 'juster' organisation of industry has been enshrined in the demand for industrial democracy or workers' control. This has a long history in the Labour Movement, stretching back to Owen's ambitious Operative Builders' Union of 1832, and reaching a climax in the stormy decade before the First World War when even revolutionary syndicalism briefly caught the imagination of the British Unions; while Guild Socialism, a more prudent and pacific version, took a strong hold on the minds of younger socialist writers. But that was the high-water mark; and the tide receded rapidly after the First World War. Syndicalism looked less and less practicable with the growth of scale, and less and less desirable with its blunt exclusion of the State and the consumer. Guild Socialism deteriorated; Whitleyism never took root outside the public service; and the final blow came in the early 1930s when the Labour Movement itself, after a protracted debate, voted for the Public Corporation with no direct workers' representation on it.

If we wish to revive the issue, we shall not derive much help from the old literature. Guild Socialism, for example, as was pointed out in Chapter III, was ideologically rooted in a theory of 'wage-slavery' which has no relevance to present-day conditions, combined with a deep mistrust of political action characteristic of the pre-1914 decade; while on the organisational plane the notion of 'self-governing guilds' has been outmoded by technological change. The whole question needs to be thought out afresh.

The matter is often expressed in terms of a demand for 'democracy'. Unfortunately this is not, as East-West diplomatic notes make clear, an unambiguous concept. It describes neither a formal abstraction nor a single set of observable phenomena, but is a word loosely applied to a number of different theories of the State, of actual political movements fighting for particular aims, and of diverse historical political systems. Its connotation has therefore varied through time; and even within the 'Western democracies' to-day, different people would give different answers if asked to distil the essential meaning of the word into a policy which could then be applied to industry.

Thus some would stress simply the rights of free speech and criticism. Others would stress equal rights for all citizens, which might point merely to equal opportunities for promotion: or respect for minorities (which might be held to require the demise of the closed shop!): or active participation of citizens in government, which would point to a large extension of joint consultation: or the rule of law: or the existence of a legal opposition – a condition already fulfilled in industry by the Unions: or government by consent, requiring simply joint consultative machinery: or government by the people through elections, requiring some much more elaborate reform. Clearly no unique meaning can be attached to the word. Nor, even if it could, would it necessarily be either logical or sensible to apply it by analogy from political government to industry.

But let us consider the most popular recent version of the demand for industrial 'democracy': participation in management by the Trade Unions.

Joint management may mean anything from the elaborate proposals of the Union of Post Office Workers for a Joint Administrative Council appointed equally by management and the Unions,[1] to the less ambitious proposals heard at every Labour

---

[1] v. *Consultation or Joint Management?* (Fabian Tract 277, 1949). This scheme is not unlike the *Mitbestimmung* experiment in Germany, under which, in the coal and

Conference for the direct nomination by the Unions of representatives on Nationalised Boards. But the essence of the idea is always the direct representation of the official Trade Unions on the Board, and their active participation in the management function.

The central issue of principle is therefore whether the Unions should give up their independence in order to participate in management. To reject joint management, the argument runs, implies a continued acceptance of a 'two sides' conception of industry, with the authority of management wholly unimpaired, and the Unions still limited to their old concern with wages and conditions. This is not merely a betrayal of the hopes of the socialist pioneers, but a denial of democracy, of the ideal of an industrial fellowship with all ranks sharing in control, and of the basic right of workpeople to have a voice in the determination of their industrial destinies.

Now no one denies this right; but it does not necessarily point to Trade Union participation in management. As was shown above, democracy is a rather ambiguous concept, and the mere use of the word does not point to anything specific at all. The democratic rights of workers might be fulfilled in a number of different ways.

Furthermore, the concept of 'two sides' in industry, and of divergent interests generally, is not a reactionary or obsolete one, but merely a statement of the obvious. It is, for example, quite specious to argue that there is no fundamental conflict between the workers in an industry and the rest of the community, on the grounds that the workers *are* the community. They are no such thing; and their interests obviously diverge from those (for instance) of pensioners or salaried persons when it comes to questions of the level of either money or real wages. And even if there were no conflict between all workers and all consumers, inasmuch as both equalled the whole community, there would still be a conflict

steel industries at least, the Boards consist of equal numbers of management and workers' representatives, the latter partly nominated by the Unions. But of course the background and motives were quite different in Germany. The Unions were not concerned, when they pressed for *Mitbestimmung*, to raise the status of the worker or to establish industrial democracy, but to increase Trade Union control over large-scale industry. They remembered the political role played by heavy industry in the days of Stinnes and Thyssen; and their main anxiety was to diminish the politico-economic power of big business in post-war Germany. This particular argument obviously applies less strongly in Britain.

between workers in any one industry and workers generally, and between workers and employers in the same industry.

It is this last point which is often denied. It is said, for example, that the whole of industry now has one common objective, namely higher production, and that co-operation in achieving this objective should replace the old opposition. Now higher production is obviously a common objective, which justifies, indeed demands, a large measure of co-operation. But because two groups have one common interest, it does not follow that all their interests are identical; and between management and men there remain other conflicting interests, which this one common interest cannot wholly over-ride. These are most obvious in the sphere of wages, where there is a clear short-run conflict over the division of the final product and/or the level of prices. But they also emerge in other spheres, such as the question of discipline, the role of shop-stewards, the introduction of new machinery, the closing down of a plant, the numbers to be employed; there may be short-run conflicts of interest over all these matters, even though in the long run both sides have the same interests. Moreover there are many decisions affecting the workers which have nothing to do with higher production, but where interests are clearly not identical; this applies to all the non-pecuniary privileges mentioned earlier in the chapter.

There will thus always be potential conflicts between management and labour. The two sides exist, and must to a large extent remain two sides; and the workers' side must have an untrammelled Trade Union movement to defend its claims. These are harsh facts which cannot be spirited away by moral rearmament touring troupes, or luncheons of progressive businessmen, or syndicalist castles in the air. If the Unions were to abrogate their independent role and leave the workers without proper representation, it would be to King Street, and not to Caux, that the latter would turn.

Given that the two sides exist, there is thus some sense in which the management plays the role of government, to which the corollary is the need for an opposition to enforce popular control over policy, and to protect the rights of the worker. It is this opposition role of the Unions which Mr. Clegg has stressed in his important book *Industrial Democracy and Nationalisation*.[1] This does

[1] Blackwell, 1951.

not rule out joint consultation and co-operation at the plant or workshop level. But when we are considering the large organisation – the multi-plant firm or the whole industry – the role of opposition is the essential guarantee of democracy; and it is in order to carry it out effectively that the Unions need to remain independent. They may well – indeed they must[1] – exercise a growing *influence* on management. The more influence they have, the more effectively they carry out their role; and an extension of this influence will, in practice, prove the most direct way of extending the democratic 'right of workpeople to have a voice in the determination of their industrial destinies'. But the influence must be exerted from outside the managerial structure, and must not be allowed to destroy the Unions' essential opposition freedom.

It is sometimes said that the opposition function is now unnecessary, in view of the large transfer of power which has occurred towards the wage-earners. This is an exaggerated view. A transfer of power has, it is true, occurred on a momentous scale. But this does not mean that management has lost all power, and will automatically grant any wage-increase which seems reasonable, or at once submit, without the need for pressure, to other demands mentioned earlier in this chapter. Business executives (whether public or private) are certainly not ready to surrender all along the line, or settle conflicts automatically in favour of the workers. Even in a nationalised industry, where private profit is not at issue, management will stiffly resist wage claims in order to avoid the odium of a deficit or a price increase; on the railways, in particular, only the stubborn opposition of the Unions has kept wages at a socially tolerable level.

The increased power of the Unions is not an argument for their 'joining the government', and participating in management, for the basic reason that it depends in the last analysis on their doing no such thing.[2] This is because it rests finally on the threat of a withdrawal of labour, on the lesser threat of an awkward disturbance to production by (e.g.) a ban on piecework or overtime, and on the indirect but still powerful threat of vicarious pressure through the government of the day. None of these final sanctions could be easily applied by a body enmeshed in, and committed to,

---

[1] *v.* next section.

[2] Which of course is why one should not press the political analogy too far.

the responsibilities of management; and the power of the Unions would be gravely impaired if they ceased to be an external, independent force, freely able to choose their tactics, without too many binding commitments. Thus the extent of their power, so far from requiring logically that they should 'enter a coalition government', demands on the contrary that they should not.

Even in the more social-democratic climate of to-day, therefore, the divergence of interest and the need for an opposition remain. And of course this means that the practical and technical objections to Union participation in management are overwhelming. It was these which underlay the conclusion of the T.U.C. 1944 Report[1] that Union officers appointed to Nationalised Boards should resign their Union posts in order to avoid an irreconcilable clash of loyalties – to Union members on the one hand, and the Board and the community on the other – under the strain of which they would become both bad workers' representatives and bad executives, with everyone worse off in consequence.[2] If there are to be workers' representatives on the Boards of industry, they should be chosen not by the Unions, but directly by the workers in each firm.[3]

VI   *The Case for High-level Industrial Democracy*

If we reject joint management, we are left so far with three minimum conditions for a reasonable distribution of power and status within industry.[4] First, a more equal distribution of non-pecuniary privileges, and less social gap between staff and labour.

Secondly, effective consultation at the point of production, both in order to diminish and equalise face-to-face power, and because it is obviously just that the worker should be consulted about matters which determine his working life and conditions. This would improve contentment as well as justice; but, as was pointed out in Section III, it is not something which can be

---

[1] *Interim Report on Post-War Reconstruction.*

[2] The classic example of such a clash of loyalties, and of the harmful effects which follow, is the Dock Labour Board.

[3] *v.* next chapter for a discussion of this possibility.

[4] I am ignoring, of course, all the wider influences discussed in Chapter I – conditions in the labour market, the Government's labour policy, the psychology of management, and so on; though these may have more effect on the distribution of industrial power than the internal factors discussed here.

imposed from above, but must come gradually with a general rise in standards of enlightenment.

Thirdly, the maximum Trade Union influence, though exercised from outside and not inside, at the national level of the industry, so that 'remote' decisions are taken only after consultation with the workers' representatives. In some industries 'high-level democracy' of this sort already exists to a limited extent – in coal, for example, where the N.U.M. exerts a strong influence on the decisions of the Board, or in boots and shoes, or cotton textiles, where a high degree of co-operation prevails.

But I believe that an extension of this 'high-level industrial democracy', which in turn means a great enlargement of the range of Union interests, is one of the most important reforms now needed in British industry. I have already suggested certain respects in which the Unions should extend their interests – e.g. in the direction of greater attention to non-wage privileges, and a more ambitious perspective over wages and productivity.

But these extensions still fall broadly within the scope of the traditional British collective bargain; and it is this scope itself which is, under contemporary conditions, too restricted. It certainly could be widened, in the sense that the Unions have the power, after the changes described in Chapter I, to compel management to discuss a much larger range of subjects. And it is significantly wider in other comparable countries. Thus both the Swedish and American Unions take a much closer interest in, and wield much more influence over, questions of managerial efficiency, the industry's long-term development plan, the relation between wages and prices, the factors affecting productivity, the conditions under which automation shall be introduced, the size of the industry's labour force, and generally the economic problems and prospects facing their industry.

There is a faint, but still very faint, trend in this direction in Britain; and certainly many top Union leaders privately hold both strong and enlightened views on all these subjects. But generally the Unions have contracted out of responsibilities other than the traditional one for wages and conditions; or, rather, they have not widened their interests and influence to a degree in any way commensurate with the increase in their economic power. And indeed they scarcely could take on these additional interests without considerable changes in their own internal organisation –

e.g. an increase in the number (and probably the salaries) of their full-time officials, a large expansion in their research staffs, and perhaps a new attitude to the employment of University graduates. But if they were willing to accept this objective of 'high-level industrial democracy', the result would be a more significant transfer of economic power than any which could be accomplished by structural or legislative reform.

Of course they must stop, for the reasons set out in the previous section, at the point where they begin to lose their independence, or feel unable to press the workers' claims wholeheartedly, or if they seem in danger of being saddled with more responsibility than power. But the 'opposition' argument need not, as the experience of other countries shows, exclude a strong constructive influence at the decision-making stage. This would certainly increase social justice, and might possibly, through the knowledge that 'remote' decisions were now taken only after consultation with the Unions, also diminish suspicion and resentment.

XV

THE STRUCTURE OF PRIVATE INDUSTRY

I *The Functionless Shareholder*

THREE further questions relating to status and power in industry remain to be considered. Would either social justice or contentment be improved first by a reform of company law: secondly, by an extension of profit-sharing: thirdly, by statutory dividend limitation?

There are two schools of thought on the subject of company law. On the one hand, City writers defend the present legal position of shareholders, and indeed urge them to exercise their rights more vigorously. On the other hand, there are critics who, believing the existing law to be dangerously out of touch with reality, demand a major structural reform which will give legal expression to the rights of the workers and the community. I confess I feel rather neutral in this dispute, disagreeing wholly with the first school on grounds of principle, but doubting whether a major change is worthwhile in practice, or indeed whether the legal issue really much matters.

In principle I can see little to be said for the present law. It gives to shareholders, and to shareholders alone, the right to appoint directors, and to receive and approve the company's accounts. This right they possess because they, and they alone, are legally 'members' of the company by virtue of owning shares. No legal responsibility exists towards the workers, the consumer, or the state; and none of these has any legal rights.

This seems a somewhat unreal position. It can hardly be denied that industry is in practice a joint enterprise in which management and workers participate as well as shareholders, and indeed

participate rather more actively; and the law, by investing the
shareholders alone with legal rights, does not merely fail to
reflect the reality – it turns it upside down. As even a well-
known Conservative statesman has written, 'the human association which in fact produces and distributes wealth, the association
of workmen, managers, technicians, and directors, is not an
association recognised by law. The association which the law does
recognise – the association of shareholder-creditors and directors –
is incapable of production or distribution.'[1]

This legal position can hardly now be justified on grounds of
principle. The doctrine of the 'rights of property' has, it is true,
an old and honoured history in political theory, going back, in its
modern form, to Locke. And the Lockean doctrine of inalienable
private rights was, in its contemporary setting, a progressive and
even revolutionary philosophy. But political theories are not
eternally valid; and this doctrine can hardly be held to forbid
any change in the organisation of industry in the quite different
circumstances of to-day.[2]

When asking themselves what rights private property ought to
retain, when these conflict with other rights in society (such as
the rights of labour, or the consumer, or the locality), most
people would, I suppose, be influenced by two main considerations.[3] First, what function does private property fulfil to justify
its rights? Secondly, how is the property distributed, and do all
citizens have an equal chance of acquiring it?

A century ago, industrial property-ownership fulfilled a vital
economic function, being directly associated with active management. But to-day, over the bulk of industry, ownership and management have become divorced in the manner sufficiently com-
mented on elsewhere in this book. The owner, from being an
active entrepreneur, has become the familiar passive shareholder,
neither in fact controlling his firm, nor capable of doing so even
if he wished, since effective government by shareholders is now a

[1] Lord Eustace Percy, *The Unknown State* (1944).

[2] Yet by some people it still is, in a crude and bowdlerised form; cf. the debates in
the financial press during the take-over bid controversy of 1953-4, especially those
relating to the Savoy and Worcester Building Company episode (e.g. *The Economist*,
12 and 19 December 1953).

[3] We are not here concerned, of course, with personal property, used by a man
for his own comfort and enjoyment, but with property in the sense of ownership of
the means of production.

physical impossibility. They are both too numerous – some industrial giants have over 100,000 on their register, and most public companies have over 2,000 – and too geographically scattered.[1]

Nor, of course, have they any desire to govern. The majority are ignorant of business – 40% of shareholders are women – and the remainder too busy with their full-time jobs elsewhere. They hold shares because they want the income or capital appreciation, not because they want control. They spread their money between several different companies, instead of concentrating it as they would if they aspired to active management; and there is, moreover, a rapid turnover of shares in all large companies (much more rapid than the turnover of workers), instead of the stability of holdings which would denote a genuine and permanent concern with the fortunes of the firm.

None of this is denied by the shareholders' champions. The late Hargreaves Parkinson, the most notable of these, wrote that 'only a handful of shareholders attend annual meetings, or appoint voting delegates, and their function is mainly to be a rubber stamp for the decisions of the Directors. It must be admitted that, in the ordinary way, the stockholder is *not* an interested party, in the sense of one who takes an intelligent, even if discontinuous, interest in the company's affairs. As a rule, he neither understands them nor makes any attempt to understand them. . . . To-day, there is only one bond of union between shareholders – a common desire to obtain as high a dividend as possible.'[2]

Even the shareholders themselves seem subconsciously to sense the decline in their economic function; and they have become listless and apathetic to all attempts to organise them for the defence of their ancient rights.[3] 'The capitalist process, by substituting a mere parcel of shares for the walls of and the machines in a factory, takes the life out of the idea of property. . . . The holder of the title loses the will to fight, economically, physically,

[1] Companies can of course be found in which a small group of large shareholders own a sufficient proportion of the total voting shares – which may be only 20% or 30% in view of the atomisation of the remainder – to give effective control if they wish to use it. But these are exceptional cases.

[2] *Ownership of Industry* (Eyre and Spottiswoode, 1951), pp. 99-100.

[3] Perhaps they read too much of the great Marshall. 'The rights of property, as such, have not been venerated by those master minds who have built up economic science; but the authority of the science has been wrongly assumed by some who have pushed the claims of vested rights to extreme and anti-social uses.' (Alfred Marshall, *Principles of Economics*, Macmillan, 5th ed., 1907, p. 48.)

politically, for "his" factory and his control over it, to die if necessary on its steps. . . . Dematerialized, defunctionalized, and absentee ownership does not impress and call forth moral allegiance. Eventually there will be *nobody* left who really cares to stand up for it – nobody within and nobody without the precincts of the big concerns.'[1]

Matters have not moved quite as far as this in Britain – yet. But the decline in the will to fight and the self-confidence of the share-owning class is very visible. The nationalisation measures of 1945–51 met with scarcely more opposition than measures to limit the employment of children 100 years ago; and the political inertia of shareholders was the cause of bitter lamentation amongst their self-appointed champions. Later proposals (e.g. for nationalising steel and chemicals) of course aroused more opposition; but even then it was not only much less violent than might have been expected, but came wholly from management, with shareholders playing no part at all. Characteristically, the one tearing, vehement (and very successful) public campaign against a nationalisation proposal came from an individual and a firm both (exceptionally amongst large public companies) largely entrepreneurial in character – the late Lord Lyle, and Tate and Lyle.[2] But generally the attempts to arouse a fighting spirit amongst shareholders were a dismal failure, almost as though they had as little faith as their opponents in the validity of their claims.[3]

There has, it is true, been a certain revival of shareholder activity since 1951, expressed in take-over bids and the formation of stockholders' associations. But what is surprising is not how many, but how few, such efforts were made; for circumstances were exceptionally propitious. A prior period of dividend limitation, a marked gap between asset values and share values, heavy taxation of income but none of capital gains, a Conservative government, vociferous support from all the City Press, and

---

[1] Joseph A. Schumpeter, *Capitalism, Socialism, and Democracy* (Allen and Unwin, 1943), p. 142.

[2] Tate and Lyle at one time had six Tates among the 20 largest shareholders, holding between them 27% of all voting shares and six directorships, and three Lyles holding between them 15% of all voting shares and two directorships.

[3] They remained, for instance, as unmoved by Hargreaves Parkinson's stirring cry – 'The remedy is in his hands. Let him unite. He has everything to lose.' (op. cit., p. 104) – as by the efforts of the *Financial Times* in April 1949 to organise a Shareholders' Defence League.

undoubtedly a good deal of managerial flaccidity after 15 years of an inflated sellers' market – one would have expected, in a situation of this sort, much more shareholder activity than in fact occurred. As another shareholders' champion, surveying the take-over bid years, and lamenting the continued passivity of share-holders as 'Capitalism's Trojan Horse', wrote sadly at the end of the period: 'Progress has been made, but I should not be inclined to say that the overall record was an inspiring one.'[1]

But the doctrine of shareholder control, although clearly now untenable by reference to an active entrepreneurial function, might still be justified by reference to the risks involved in investment.

In the days before limited liability, these risks were indeed tremendous – they were risks of total bankruptcy.[2] But to-day they are very much less. The investor risks only that sum which he invests in the company concerned; and almost all investors minimise their risk by spreading their shareholdings between several different firms. Even if they did not, the risk, so far as most public companies are concerned, would not be great. There appears to be a declining long-run trend in the number of bank-ruptcies; and few large companies to-day can be considered really risky in the sense that shareholders may lose their whole invest-ment. A high proportion have some element of monopoly pro-tection in their market situation, a still higher proportion spread their own risks by multi-line production, and full employment and inflation constitute a further strong protection in the back-ground.

There remains, of course, a risk of capital depreciation (though much less now than formerly) – but so there does with gilt-edged

---

[1] Candidus in *Investors' Chronicle*, 19 November 1955.

[2] Their most famous victim was Sir Walter Scott. Scott knew himself to be a mine of wealth as a writer; he also had very expensive tastes. He was determined that he, and not his publisher, should be the main gainer from his talent, and, sanguine by nature but innocent in financial matters, he took the risk of putting large sums of money first into the firm of Ballantyne Brothers – of whom the one appears to have been a trickster, the other an ineffective and melancholy epicure, but both equally extravagant – and later into Constable (described by the young Disraeli as an 'osten-tatious braggart').

Eventually Constable went bankrupt, and Scott found himself liable for £40,000 – a far larger sum than he had ever put into the business. By the time he died seven years later, he had succeeded, by a sustained and almost frenzied effort of writing, in paying off 16s. in the pound.

It is ironical, in the light of this experience, that he bitterly attacked the early experiments in joint-stock organisation as 'madness' and 'the extremity of folly.' (v. Sir Herbert Grierson, *Sir Walter Scott, Bart.*, Constable, 1938.)

stock, which can fall rapidly in value if the rate of interests rises; yet no one suggests that bondholders should therefore have legal control over monetary policy. Similarly there is a risk of loss of income (though again much less than formerly), which justifies a claim to an income large enough to compensate the risk. But the risk of permanent loss of capital is negligible. Indeed in terms of risk the worker would seem to have at least as strong a case for legal control. Unlike the shareholder, he cannot spread his risk between different companies. If the firm in which he works goes bankrupt, or lays him off, he faces the prospect (even under full employment) of an involuntary change of work and employer, perhaps at lower wages and in worse conditions; while if he lives in a town dominated by a single huge concern, he may face either prolonged unemployment, or a domestic upheaval as he and his family are forced to move to a new and unfamiliar home. In the light of this, it seems rather impertinent, unless it is meant to be jocose, to press shareholders' rights to sole control on grounds of risk.

The decline in risk is again fully admitted by the shareholders' spokesmen. 'The risk that a sound company . . . will lose its earning power completely is negligible. Investors can, and do, largely disregard it. . . . Ordinary [shares] have a dynamic quality which, over a period of years, is usually expressed in a higher dividend and increasing market value. The "risk" on a really good ordinary share, therefore, is on balance a positive risk.'[1] Indeed such writers not only admit the decline in risk, but make it the basis of their contention that the ordinary share is now a suitable vehicle for those small savings which will gradually convert us into a 'property-owning democracy'. They cannot have it both ways. Either the risk is still considerable, in which case it becomes a cruel deception to urge the poor man to invest his exiguous savings in ordinary shares. Or the risk is negligible, in which case small savings may very properly be urged into industrial equities, but the claim to control on grounds of risk is unconvincing. Clearly the latter is in fact the case.

There is therefore nothing to-day in the nature of investment or the function of the capital market which gives the investor any natural 'right' to sole legal control. Investment entails no social responsibility, and should carry no additional social rights beyond

1 Parkinson, op. cit., pp. 26-7.

those, shared with all citizens, of protection against theft or confiscation. All it entails is an economic risk; all it is entitled to is an economic reward commensurate with that risk.

II *The Proposal for Government Directors*

But the question is: is it worth a major change in company law in order to alter the present position? This depends on the complications involved, and on the real benefits (as opposed simply to the gain in logic) which are to be anticipated. I have doubts on both these points after examining the proposals of the three main protagonists of reform – Mr. Drucker,[1] Mr. Goyder,[2] and Mr. Albu.[3] These writers deserve exceptional credit for their pioneering efforts to find a more logical industrial structure. Yet I doubt if the results of reform would be worth the effort.

The most common proposals are that first the government, and secondly the workers, should have the right to representation on the boards of companies.[4] On the first point, the Board of Trade is to be entitled by law to one share in every public company, carrying with it the right to nominate directors if the Minister so desires. Thus will public responsibility be ensured, and effective control provided over the whole economy.

But what is wrong with large public companies to-day, after the changes described in Chapter I, is not a lack of 'public responsibility', in the sense of a neglect of the wishes of the Government. Such companies, in frequent touch with government departments, are normally attentive to government policy (that is, if there is one), and try consciously to act in the public interest. And if they do not, there are more effective ways of ensuring compliance than the despatch of one or two strange directors, who, after a short dose of the firing-line, would no doubt long for the role of *embusqué* Cuthbert in Whitehall.

But general responsibility apart, it is argued that government directors are needed to ensure a more effective *planning* control over industry. There appears to be a confusion here as to the

[1] *The New Society* (Heinemann, 1951).

[2] *The Future of Private Enterprise* (Blackwell, 1951).

[3] 'The Organisation of Industry', in *New Fabian Essays*.

[4] In fact Mr. Goyder, although he does not want government directors, proposes an immensely elaborate new legal structure – so elaborate as to be quite impracticable.

nature of modern governmental planning. Except under conditions of wild inflation, it is not detailed planning down to the level of the individual firm that is required, but a much broader influence operating on whole industries, and often groups of industries.[1] And if under special circumstances firm-by-firm planning is called for, then physical controls are a better method than government directors. They are more flexible, and can be either imposed or taken off as required, and more efficient in that policy can be directed and co-ordinated at the centre, instead of relying for its execution on some hundreds of individuals scattered over the country.

The practical difficulties, moreover, are formidable. There is the familiar objection that government nominees on a private board must either 'go native' or remain suspect, and in neither case will do their duty properly. Similarly they must, whenever a dispute over policy occurs, either have recourse to their power of veto, or be content to be out-voted; efficiency of management will suffer in the first case, and the whole point of the scheme be lost in the second. And where are these hundreds of directors to be recruited? We already face a serious shortage of men who, combining proved business ability with progressive views, would make cheerful and effective nominees of a Labour Minister. This shortage bedevils labour relations in the existing public sector, and makes it exceedingly hard for a Labour Government to man a whole host of public bodies. It will be further aggravated by the extension, discussed in a later chapter,[2] of competitive public enterprise, which will call for men with precisely these qualifications. It would not be sensible to waste such scarce talent on an objective which can be much better achieved by other means.

Lastly, the proposal would arouse the maximum of political heat for the minimum of effective result. The Government would be portrayed as taking sweeping powers over the whole of industry, and for a completely unspecified purpose. Management as well as shareholders would everywhere be up in arms. And indeed there is substance in the contention that the State's relations with its citizens should be regulated by the law, so that everyone knows where he stands, and what behaviour is reprehensible and what is not, and not by a system of Government agents with no fixed terms of reference, and hence inevitably arbitrary in their decisions.

[1] v. Chapter XX.   [2] v. Chapter XIX.

III *The Proposal for Worker-Directors*

We are then left with the proposals relating to the legal position of the workers. First, it is suggested that the workers in a firm should become, if they so choose (and after a minimum length of service), legal members of the company, with the same rights as shareholders to receive financial information, and with some fixed proportion of total voting rights at annual general meetings. This could be achieved by the issue of a special class of non-interest bearing shares, as suggested by Mr. Goyder. Secondly, the workers should have the right to elect a proportion of the Board. It is not, of course, proposed that they should elect the entire Board – the objective is not to establish complete workers' control – but simply that they should be represented. Exactly what number would be a matter for debate. The German *Mitbestimmung* Law gives one-third of the seats to the employees' representatives; Mr. Goyder suggests that workers and shareholders should each elect two-fifths, and the management one-fifth. The employee-directors are not, for the reasons set out in the previous chapter, to be chosen by the Unions. In a single-plant concern they might be elected by the entire body of workers, and in the large multi-plant company by the workers' representatives on the joint consultative body.

The workers' moral (and logical) claim to such representation is, I believe, incontrovertible. The trouble is first that they seem to have little desire to exercise it, and secondly that such a reform, besides being subject to severe practical difficulties, cannot be guaranteed to produce any real benefit.

On the first point, the Trade Unions would be indifferent, if not actually hostile, to the change. They fear the creation of a parallel hierarchy of workers' representatives, neither chosen by nor responsible to themselves, possible rivals for the loyalty of their members, and dangerously likely to interfere in the proper Union function of negotiation. These fears may or may not be irrational, but they exist; and it is not easy to press a reform on behalf of the workers which their chosen leaders show no sign of wanting. Nor is there any sign that the rank-and-file much want the change. Most of them probably prefer to be left in peace, and not to take on added responsibilities; and even amongst the militant minority this is not an issue which is debated at Trade Union or Labour Party meetings, or stirs much interest.

The technical difficulties are manifest enough: the shortage of potential worker-directors of the right calibre – men combining a strong personality, some financial and technical knowledge, and ability in committee work: the danger of divided counsels on the Board and a consequent loss of entrepreneurial initiative: the ambivalent relationship of the worker-directors to the Unions, especially when wages come to be discussed: the risk that a large number of Communists may be elected, bent solely on disruption: and so on. These points are sufficiently familiar.

The economic effects are harder to assess, since one scarcely knows how the scheme would work in detail in companies of different size and structure (though it is only intended to apply to public companies). There are two issues: the effect on managerial efficiency, and on the supply of capital. The first would depend simply on the quality of the worker-directors, and the way in which they interpreted their duties on the Board – that is, how much weight they gave to efficiency and enterprise as opposed to representing the short-term claims and grievances of their constituents. The outcome is merely a matter of guesswork. But in the light of the fact that many critics are already concerned at the calibre of British top management, that this is a sphere in which unity and freedom of action are particularly essential, and that the qualities most likely to win votes are not necessarily those which make an efficient director, one can hardly be sure that no loss of efficiency will ensue.

The effects on the supply of equity capital can no doubt be exaggerated. I argue in Chapter XVII that the role of the shareholder as a source of new capital is consistently over-rated; and this book makes several proposals for limiting his net rewards – notably a tax on capital gains and measures to restrain dividend payments. But so long as we retain a large private sector, there is of course a limit to the risks which we can take with the supply of equity capital. For reasons set out in Chapter XVII, I do not believe that we have yet reached this limit so far as taxation, or indeed any known and definite method of limiting dividends, is concerned. But we should exert a much more adverse influence on the supply of new capital by causing complete uncertainty, such as these changes would create, than by any definite measures of taxation or dividend limitation. Investors would never know what policy a Board so constituted, and with a membership possibly changing every year, was likely to pursue; and while this might not always matter with established public companies, it could make it almost impossible for a private company ever to sell itself to the public – no one would know what to expect in the way of distribution policy, when the composition of the Board was due to change as soon as the company ceased to be private. And since this disturbance to the supply of new capital is wholly unnecessary in order to ensure a low dividend ratio, this being easily enforceable by taxation,[1] it surely constitutes some argument against the change.

Probably none of these difficulties is insoluble; and they might be worth enduring if a definite gain, either in contentment or social justice, was likely to result. But this seems rather doubtful.

If the diagnosis of the previous chapter is accepted, there is little reason to expect a gain in contentment or industrial morale. These seem to depend on the quality of local management and supervision, the degree of effective consultation at the point of production, the nature of the wage-bargain, and wider considerations of social equality. None of these will be much affected by the presence of a minority of worker-directors on the central Board of large public companies; and the instinctive indifference of the workers to the suggested change is thus perhaps well justified. Indeed the election of worker-directors might easily become a source of resentment of its own. If they seem to act in the long-term interests of the firm at the expense of the short-term demands of their constituents, they will quickly be accused of having 'gone over to the other side'; and the first time they are known to have supported the management on a wage-claim (or the first time one of their wives is observed driving round in a company limousine), the most violent recriminations will break out. It is much better that resentment should be directed at the existing management; Quisling accusations always create the deepest bitterness of all.

Will justice be improved? That is, will economic power become more equally diffused, and in some measure pass from the hands of shareholders or management into those of the workers, the State, or the consumer? If we recall the determinants of

[1] v. Chapter XVII, Section III.

economic power discussed in Chapter I, we shall not expect this to occur simply as a result of changing company law. Such power now scarcely depends at all on the legal structure of the firm. The shareholders, who retain the sole nominal power, have little real power; and the real power of the other parties in no way depends on their being represented on the Board. The State can exercise what power it chooses through taxation, or physical controls, or legislation. The power of the Unions depends on conditions in the labour market, their external influence on the firm or the industry, and the labour policy of the government. The power of the individual worker again depends partly on the employment situation, and partly on the degree of consultation at the point of production. And the power of the consumer depends simply on the degree of monopoly and the extent of inflation. None of these would be in any way increased by a change in company law.

It is easy to become bemused with constitution-making and legal formulae. But if we stick to the real object, which is a certain distribution of effective power, we see that a change in the law, logical though it might be, would make no difference to the underlying reality. Despite the existing law, the shareholders have little power, and the government and the Unions have much. It is therefore surely not worth so elaborate a reform, with all its intricate complications, if the result is to be no serious gain either in contentment or in social justice.

IV *Profit-sharing*

Is profit-sharing perhaps a compromise solution?[1] After an unhappy history in the inter-war period, this has recently attracted a marked revival of interest. Certainly the atmosphere is more propitious than it was before the war. The lead is being taken by the more progressive managements; and profit-sharing is no longer associated, as it often used to be, with bad personnel relations. The greater stability of profits under full employment

[1] By this is meant any scheme under which a company's annual surplus, after prior claims and charges have been met, is divided on stated terms between shareholders and employees, the payment to the latter taking the form either of cash, or shares, or payments into a fund (e.g. a pensions fund, or workers' share bank).

reduces the risk of collapse through insolvency; while the post-war schemes are more imaginatively framed than their predecessors, and the possible benefits somewhat larger. Since, in addition, Trade Union strength is now such that no firm could possibly hope to use profit-sharing as a means of cutting wages or weakening Union loyalties, the pre-war hostility of the Unions has largely disappeared; and some of the recent schemes have even been worked out with their co-operation.

What attitude, then, should the Labour Party adopt towards profit-sharing? The Conservatives seem suddenly to have discovered it as the new panacea for all our industrial troubles; and some socialists have reacted, by an instinctive reflex action, with an equal degree of suspicion. In practice, neither great enthusiasm nor deep suspicion seem justified.

Profit-sharing might serve one of three useful purposes. First, it may have some influence on the distribution of wealth, by guiding a larger share of profits than otherwise towards the worker, and a smaller share towards the stockholder. This influence is in practice small, partly because the amounts paid out under most existing schemes are, as a proportion of total profits, quite derisory; and partly because the worker's share in rising productivity depends far more on the skill of the Trade Unions in negotiating piece-rates, production bonuses, and wage increases.

Nevertheless, the influence, such as it is, is in the right direction; and there is no point in being haughty about gains which come without our having to lift a finger. From this point of view it makes no difference what form the profit-distribution takes; and a collective production bonus has the same effect as a more elaborate scheme.

Secondly, profit-sharing might be regarded as an alternative method of achieving the object of the Albu-Goyder reforms, namely to raise the legal status of the worker relative to that of the shareholder. This would be achieved if the distribution took the form of voting shares, and if these were issued in amounts which were significant in relation to the total outstanding voting capital. (Neither of these is true of most existing schemes.)[1] Those workers who chose to keep their shares would then automatically become members of the company, and gain the same

[1] Of course, the only true profit-sharing (and co-partnership) is to be found within the Co-operative Movement.

voting and elective rights as the existing shareholders, without the need for a complex change in company law.

This is a possible line of advance. The present schemes, pretentious as most of them are, have at least inserted the thin end of the wedge. This could be driven in further by a Labour Government. It is of course out of the question to impose a single uniform scheme on the whole of industry, laying down some universal ratio of profit-distribution. But the Government could both make it clear, through Parliament and the joint advisory councils, that it favoured effective schemes, of whatever exact nature, for the wider diffusion of voting shares amongst the workers,[1] and that its attitude to firms and industries would be influenced by their response to this appeal: and possibly also, as Mr. Gaitskell[2] and others have suggested, consider legislation compelling the distribution of some fraction of any *bonus* issue either direct to the workers, or to a trustee or eleemosynary fund.

It would certainly be logical that the workers, or their representatives, should thus acquire some legal rights in the company. But no sensational results are to be anticipated from this; for, as was pointed out above, the wage-earners seem as reluctant to accept these rights, as managements often are to accord them.

But thirdly, and in practice most important, profit-sharing may under certain circumstances increase industrial contentment. It will not, of course, induce a greater physical effort on the part of the worker – save in a very small concern, the link between the individual's effort at the margin and the company's total profits is remote to the point of being non-existent; and even if it were not, the infrequency of the profit-distribution would make it seem so.

But it might conceivably improve industrial relations by removing, or weakening, the suspicion that wages are not gaining their fair share of higher productivity. In view of the prevalence of such suspicions, to which the last chapter drew attention, this might seem a serious argument in favour of profit-sharing. And there is some evidence that companies operating such schemes have better-than-average labour relations, and indirect supporting evidence in the fact that those firms with the most progressive

---

[1] Though allowing companies reasonable latitude – enough to ensure, for example, that the result is not simply a decline in company saving; we do not want a direct transfer from undistributed profits to workers' consumption.

[2] At the 1951 T.U.C. Conference.

personnel policies in the past are now in the van of the profit-sharing movement. Nevertheless, elaborate schemes of the sort now becoming popular will certainly not work any miracles. Those firms which introduce them usually enjoy good labour relations anyway, so that they are less the cause than the effect of good relations. And in firms where relations are bad already, and no confidence between management and men exists, an elaborate scheme will not make matters any better, and may easily make them worse by introducing a new source of suspicion and misunderstanding. It can therefore only be a supplementary aid, useful if superimposed on a situation already basically healthy.

But if we forget elaborate profit-sharing devices, it remains true that any direct link between total wage-payments and the performance of the firm, provided that it is simple enough to be clearly understood, and that the amounts involved are significantly large, can often help to eradicate suspicion about the distribution of increased output. Some British firms already achieve this result by a collective production bonus; and in the U.S., and increasingly in France, the Trade Unions (though admittedly bargaining on a plant level, which makes things easier) often establish a link between basic wage-rates and future increases in productivity. If we were considering legislation, a legal sanction for some such link would be preferable to the imposition of a more complicated structural reform; though even here general legislation would be rendered exceedingly difficult by the heterogeneity of the private industrial sector. Trade Union action would be more effective. While mildly welcoming, therefore, the spread of profit-sharing, I should much prefer the Unions to develop a more ambitious attitude to the wage-bargain, so that wages not only in fact obtained, but were clearly seen and known to obtain, a generous share of the benefits of rising productivity.

v *The Shareholder's Claim to the Surplus*

The last point to be considered is the public supervision, at the *national* level, of profit and dividend policy. This is required for reasons not primarily connected with economic control, but in order to prevent the incomes of shareholders from being too large relative to other incomes.

The moral case for limiting the reward of shareholders is based directly on the egalitarian arguments presented in Chapter VII. Private property, besides being to a significant extent inherited, is still most unequally distributed,[1] and shareholdings more unequally even than total private property. The Oxford Savings Survey shows that only 5–7% of families hold any stocks and shares, and that even within this small number ownership is heavily concentrated.

Conservatives sometimes argue that dividends ought at least to rise in line with capital employed.[2] But, as is often pointed out, since in a progressive economy capital employed (as so defined) may be expected to rise faster than the national income, this would mean a continuous transfer from the rest of the community to shareholders. This cannot be considered acceptable.

In any case, the moral basis of the claim is highly dubious. Naturally if the additional capital comes from a new issue of paid-up share capital, the subscribers are entitled to a dividend income commensurate with the risks involved. But where it comes from ploughing-back, it is not clear that the shareholders' claim is justified.

It is argued that these reserves are the result of past abstinence; they represent monies which, had the shareholders been more grasping, might have been drawn out of the business year by year in higher dividends, but which instead have been ploughed back; and for this restraint a monetary reward is justified. Socialists have been rather impatient with claims to large property-incomes based on theories of abstinence ever since Nassau Senior, first proclaiming in 1836 that abstinence was an instrument of production, was attacked by Marx in one of his most acid passages. 'An unparalleled sample this, of the discoveries of vulgar economy! It substitutes for an economic category a sycophantic phrase – *voilá tout*. . . . All the conditions for carrying on the labour process are suddenly converted into so many acts of abstinence on the part of the capitalist. If the corn is not all eaten, but part of it also sown – abstinence of the capitalist. If the wine gets time to mature – abstinence of the capitalist. The

[1] *v.* Chapter XII, Section I.

[2] Defined as subscribed share capital, and capital and revenue reserves.

capitalist robs his own self whenever he uses [the instrument of production] . . . instead of eating them up, steam-engines, cotton, railways, manure, horses, and all; or, as the vulgar economist childishly puts it, instead of dissipating "their value" in luxuries and other articles of consumption. How the capitalists as a class are to perform that feat is a secret that vulgar economy has hitherto obstinately refused to divulge. Enough that the world still jogs on, solely through the self-chastisement of this modern penitent of Vishnu, the capitalist.'[1]

Ignoring the rather unreal picture conjured up by the word 'abstinence', with its suggestion of painful sacrifices borne with stoic fortitude, in what sense can one say that a growth in company reserves, as a matter of justice, or even of economics, properly 'belongs' to the shareholders? Suppose the expansion to be due to greater efficiency. It would, presumably, then be argued that this was made possible only by the more effective utilisation of the shareholders' property in the shape of the existing capital assets. But it is notoriously hard to impute a rise in output to any one factor of production. It might just as reasonably be said to be due to the efforts of labour or management; and indeed Trade Unions often base wage claims on precisely this argument. There can never be any scientific grounds for saying that an increase in net profits (even the residual increase after higher earnings have perhaps been paid to wage-earners) derives from a higher productivity of capital, as opposed to a higher productivity of labour or management.

Alternatively, the extra profits might be due not to greater efficiency, but to higher unit sales following an expansion of demand, or higher unit profits consequent on inflation or an increase in the degree of monopoly. In this event none of the parties could lay claim to the surplus on grounds of extra effort or efficiency; and the strongest claimant might be thought to be the consumer.

The truth is that there is little use in parading any of these arguments, since there exist no agreed criteria by which a growth in profits can be divided up amongst the contending parties. The only basis for the shareholders' claim is the purely legal one that under present company law all current profits 'belong' to them; and if they abstain from drawing them out in one year,

[1] *Capital*, pp. 608-9.

they are entitled to an income on them in future years. But this
legal attribution of profits has no obvious moral or economic
basis. Indeed the workers might equally well claim that they
had abstained, by their restraint in the matter of wages, from
appropriating the surplus in past years, and therefore deserved
the same reward in future years. In the end, the proper division
of the surplus depends simply on one's view of the right distribution of total income.

VI *Methods of Dividend Limitation*

If control over dividend policy is required primarily in order
to achieve such a distribution, and to remove from the hands of
private management the power to decide the share of net dividends in total income, this can be easily enough effected by fiscal
measures, both personal (e.g. a capital gains tax) and corporate.
The latter raises the whole question of profits taxation and the
supply of savings, and is discussed in detail in Chapter XVII. But
within limits the government has it within its power, by using
different methods of taxation, to enforce any desired ratio of
dividend distribution to total profits; and there is no need from
this point of view to go outside the sphere of fiscal policy.

But perhaps some statutory control is needed to improve
industrial relations? There is no definite evidence that this is
so. The persistence of industrial resentments appears to be due
to our lingering social inequality, to the average calibre of British
management, and to a suspicion, which is equally evident in
nationalised industry, that wages are not obtaining a fair share
of rising productivity. If, therefore, large dividend increases are
in fact prevented by taxation policy, it is not clear that statutory
limitation would make much difference.

However, we cannot rule out the possibility that it might be
desirable under certain circumstances[1] – if a practicable scheme
can be devised. This, unfortunately, is not easy. The only possible
solution in practice would be to allow an increase in dividends in
a certain ratio to the increase in profits. This would at least be
reasonably flexible. Not only could the permitted ratio be altered
if economic events required; but firms would fare differently

[1] e.g. as part of a national wages policy negotiated with the Trade Unions.

according to their current earnings performance. Those that showed the largest increase in profits could raise their dividends the most, and conversely. Thus expansion would be rewarded; and those companies which, by virtue of their expansion, were the most likely to need more capital from the market would be the most favourably placed for obtaining it.[1] At the same time share values would not become completely divorced from asset values, nor dividend yields from earnings yields.

But even this, although probably a workable and not wholly damaging scheme, would create problems for certain types of company – for example, the company which traditionally distributes a high proportion of its earnings, which shows a rising trend of profits, and yet has no need or desire to finance a large expansion of capacity: or the raw material-producing company operating overseas, subject to an exceptional degree of risk, often operating wasting assets, and traditionally distributing almost to the limit of its (sharply fluctuating) profits. These difficulties are probably not insoluble; but they would add both to the complexity of the scheme, and to the disturbance which it would create.

It is therefore clearly preferable to keep statutory limitation as a weapon of last resort, and to rely, unless the arguments for legislation seem overwhelming (and in terms of labour relations they are not), on measures of taxation.

But there is another influence to which too little attention is paid. It is sometimes thought that dividend and profit policy are inexorably determined by economic facts, or by the particular organisation of industry: that given private ownership, a competitive economy, and the pre-eminence of financial incentives, a particular (in this case generous) dividend policy is an absolute condition of efficiency and a rapid rate of growth.

There is not much evidence for this view in practice. On the contrary, attitudes to profits and dividends even in a privately-owned economy appear to be, partly at least, culturally and historically determined. What management thinks it normal and proper to pay out, and shareholders to receive, depends within very wide limits on the tradition, the social character, the balance of class power, and the general moral climate of the country

[1] A new issue of paid-up share-capital (as opposed to free or scrip issues) would of course entitle a company to raise its dividend disbursements *pro rata*.

concerned. Britain, the U.S., Germany and Sweden, all operate largely privately-owned and 'free-enterprise' economies. Yet the importance of the shareholder, the role of the capital market, and the attitude towards dividends, vary significantly between these four countries.

And these attitudes can change quite rapidly through time. In Britain, for example, they are quite different to-day from what they were in the 1948–50 era of Crippsian restraint; and the expectations of shareholders are significantly greater. It is not unlikely that they could change again. A gradual advance towards a more social-democratic society, and a further growth in the power of both management and workers relative to shareholders, might well, even with no change in the law or the pattern of ownership, diminish the expectations of capital-owners, and induce that culturally-determined moderation in dividend policy which now characterises social-democratic Sweden.

Indeed the whole discussion of this chapter and the last has served to emphasise the importance of wider social influences. A more equal distribution of industrial power seldom requires, or indeed can be obtained by, legislative change. It requires as an absolute condition the maintenance of full employment and a favourable political climate. Beyond this it depends much less on action taken in Whitehall, than on a change in the attitudes of both labour and management. The former is at least as important as the latter, and presumably more under the influence of a socialist party. The attainment of this part of the egalitarian goal is therefore largely in the hands of the Trade Unions. If they press successfully – and they largely have the power to do so – for the equalisation of non-wage privileges, the spread of effective consultation, and 'high-level democracy' at the national and industry level, they can help to create a social-democratic atmosphere in industry which will parallel and reinforce the other egalitarian changes suggested in this book.

PART FIVE

ECONOMIC GROWTH AND EFFICIENCY

XVI

INVESTMENTS, SAVINGS, AND INFLATION

1 *The Arguments for Rapid Growth*

IN considering what economic policy a Labour Government should pursue, the first thing to decide is how much weight to attach to economic efficiency and a rapid rate of growth.

One can imagine a society in which the problem of production might reasonably be treated as secondary, because the standard of living was already so high that people did not fret over-much about still further amelioration. This condition is partially ful-filled, for example, in the United States. Living standards are such that the public is quite happy to 'endure' (as it might seem to less fortunately-placed peoples) a colossal 'waste' of resources on 'frivolous' or at least non-essential production, such as adver-tising, or the mass manufacture of fripperies and titivating novel-ties of all kinds; and the whole notion of 'scarce resources' is hardly relevant. Under these circumstances it seems absurd to speak as though economic efficiency were the central issue; and, provided always that full employment was maintained, a reformer could turn his main attention to non-economic problems without worrying too much about the rate of growth.

Before the war, most socialists had visions of a similar state of abundance being quickly attained in Britain; and they were therefore rather indifferent to questions of higher productivity. This was a natural attitude at the time. Unemployed resources were at hand, and it was evident that if they could be drawn back into production an easy rise in living standards would result. Moreover incomes were most unequally distributed; and this offered the possibility of a clear improvement in working-class standards simply by the transfer of existing wealth. Nor did our exceptional dependence on foreign trade then seem to present a vexing obstacle. Food and materials could be had on the cheap; and there was no sign that the improvement in the terms of trade, which for two decades had sustained the British real income, was about to be reversed.

It was a world in which supply everywhere seemed to exceed demand; and every Labour week-end speech contained its quota of references not merely to unemployment at home, but to coffee being burned in Brazil, to crops destroyed in the U.S.A., to livestock slaughtered in the interests of restriction schemes. Ample scope clearly existed for raising living standards everywhere – it was only a question of so organising monetary demand as to ensure the full utilisation of resources, and of transferring wealth from rich to poor. It was thus not unnatural that socialists should repeat that 'the problem of production is solved: only the problem of distribution remains' – they were, after all, fortified by the authority of Keynes himself, who supposed, looking only a generation ahead, that it would be 'comparatively easy to make capital-goods so abundant that the marginal efficiency of capital is zero'.[1]

But to-day there are no such easy reserves waiting to be tapped. Employment could hardly be fuller than it has been since 1945; while the bulk of the population would not gain much materially from further redistribution. Improved living standards, or any other economic claims, can now be met only by higher production per head; and questions of growth and efficiency move into the forefront of matters to be attended to.

But how near to the actual forefront should they be placed? Some socialists, despite the changed conditions, still want to relegate them to a rather unimportant status. They invite us to stop worrying about hard work and economic matters, and to relax into greater leisure and more cultural pursuits.[2] I agree

---

[1] *The General Theory of Employment, Interest and Money* (Macmillan, 1936), p. 221.

[2] But they often confuse efficiency and effort (=hard physical work). Total output does not, in a modern economy, depend mainly on harder work or longer hours, but on technical and managerial standards and the quantity of capital equipment. Thus the average working week in the U.S. is shorter than in Britain, and hourly physical effort no greater. To stress economic efficiency does not entail a continual nagging about harder physical effort, or a guilt-feeling about shorter hours.

with them in principle, but not in timing; that is, I shall agree
with them two decades from now. But for the moment the total
claims on our already fully-employed resources are certainly too
great to permit indifference to the rate of growth.

First, we need more foreign investment to assist the rate of
growth in the under-developed countries. The post-war Labour
Government did a little – too little – in this direction; but further
progress has been infinitesimal since the Conservatives came to
power. The matter is sometimes argued in terms of the fight against
Communism; but of course the overwhelming argument for a
greater effort is moral and humanitarian. At present our net
expenditure on foreign aid is trivial. Some socialists have spoken
of 2%, or even 3%, of the national income as the minimum level
of aid which is compatible with a clear conscience in the matter.
But whatever the exact figure, a substantial increase in our export
surplus will be needed.

Secondly, the relief of hardship and distress at home. This was
discussed in Part Three, where it was made clear that a considerable rise in social expenditure would be required for several
years ahead; and even then many urgent requests for help might
have to be temporarily refused.[1]

Thirdly, the backlog of social investment. We are still plagued,
as a result of wartime and post-war scarcities superimposed on
twenty years of neglect, by a constricting shortage of social
capital – hospitals, mental homes, new schools, slum-clearance
housing, homes for old people, and the like. And if we set as our
objective the provision of public health and education not merely
at a decent standard, but at a standard comparable with the best
available to the richer classes, it is clear that we shall need a large
increase in expenditure.

Fourthly, higher personal consumption. The case for according
this, on socialist grounds, a high priority, was argued in a previous
chapter. But whether this case is accepted or not by writers and

[1] Even the remnants of primary poverty require for their relief something more
substantial than vague and patrician expressions of good-will, such as, for example,
those vouchsafed us by Sir Osbert Sitwell when he writes that 'it has always seemed
to me that there should be no poor, and that people should not have to trouble
about money' (*Great Morning*, p. 36). This rather takes one's breath away. However,
all socialists should applaud the immediately preceding sentiments. 'Avarice and
even carefulness have always to me seemed to be vices. I avoid the skinflint as though
he were a source of contagion. I even turn from the words that describe this mortal
sin, such nouns as parsimony, niggard, screw, scrimp, lick-penny, such verbs as stint,
scrimp, pinch and gripe.'

intellectuals, the people themselves are quite determined on a rapid improvement in their living standards; and governments will have to attend to their wishes.

Fifthly, our balance of payments position is still precarious; and we need a larger export surplus to buttress it more securely, quite apart from the claims of the under-developed areas.

And, lastly, not only might a rise in manufacturing investment be a condition of accommodating all these claims, but a rise in certain hitherto neglected forms of non-manufacturing investment (e.g. roads) is an urgent necessity.

This adds up to a considerable total of demands. I do not see how anyone can avoid the conclusion that a rapid rate of growth will be an important objective for many years to come: and that the next Labour Government will need to show both agility and determination in the economic field.

Now to give a reasonably high priority to economic growth is not, as some socialists curiously suppose, to accept a Tory philosophy – rather, indeed, the reverse. A majority of these claims would be rated higher by most socialists than most Conservatives – certainly the first three, and possibly the fourth; while the last two are conditions of the fulfilment of the others. A rapid rate of growth, therefore, at least for the next decade, so far from being inconsistent with socialist ideals, is a pre-condition of their attainment. And it is certainly also a pre-condition of attaining office; for if the Labour Party were to neglect the goal of higher production, it would be accorded, and deserve, the clear disfavour of the British public.

II *The Pressures towards High Investment*

It is a truism to say that growth depends on many and various factors, some economic, others political, sociological, historical, and so on. This is not a book about growth, and most of these factors are not discussed. I have selected only the most controversial issues, and notably those most germane to socialist policy.

First, a high rate of capital formation is clearly a condition of rapid growth. This requires three conditions: first, a sufficient incentive to invest on the part of business executives; secondly, adequate funds to finance the investment; thirdly, available physical resources, that is, sufficient communal savings.

A deficiency of any of these might, at different times, be the main limiting influence on investment. Looking ahead, from which direction is the limiting influence most likely to come? I find it impossible to believe that in an advanced industrial country, boasting a highly organised and sophisticated financial system, it will come (at least for industry as a whole) from a deficiency of actual finance, or risk-capital. If, against all expectation, it should do, there are plenty of counter-measures open to a determined Government; these are discussed in the next chapter.

In the inter-war period the limit was normally set by the reluctance of businessmen to embark on new capital expenditures. With heavy unemployment and a depressed market for goods of all kinds, profit-expectations were characteristically pessimistic; and since existing capacity was commonly under-utilised, the incentive to expand was weak. The unemployment of course reflected the underlying fact that savings were 'excessive', in the sense that the community was releasing more resources from private and public consumption than industry was willing to absorb in new investment.

But the inter-war period can now be seen, in the perspective of history, to have been markedly abnormal in this respect; and the prospect for the years ahead appears to be altogether different. We have now enjoyed more than ten years of consecutive peacetime full employment – not only in Britain, but in most other major countries also. This suggests that a world-wide change in the economic climate has occurred. Its causes are many and various: the higher consumption and lower savings associated with the equalisation of incomes, a more sensitive moral conscience about social expenditure, the enhanced power of the Trade Unions, the stabilising influence of large Budgets with 'built-in stabilisers', the more rapid rate of growth of world population, and a larger volume of international trade.

There is no sign that these influences are about to go into reverse; and the underlying pressures towards high levels of demand and employment may therefore be expected to persist. But even if these pressures should weaken somewhat, and the threat of deflation re-appear, their place will be taken by equally powerful political pressures. Electorates now believe that full employment can quite well be maintained, and are consequently in no mood to tolerate a failure to maintain it. Any Government which permitted appreciable unemployment for more than a short period would court certain defeat at the polls; and this acts as rather a strong inducement to governments deliberately to sustain, where this is necessary, a full employment level of demand.

And post-war experience, especially in the United States (where recessionary tendencies are naturally stronger than in Britain), supports the view that measures to maintain or restore demand are both practicable and broadly effective. The modern economist's income-analysis (to the surprise of some economists) actually seems to work. It is true that *predictions* about the behaviour of different components of demand are still inexact and unreliable; and it is not always possible to prevent the initial occurrence of minor recessions.[1] But the significant fact is that these can now be quickly corrected, since demand has proved to be malleable, and in a broadly predictable manner, by fiscal policy (on the side both of taxation and expenditure), changes in consumer credit regulations, and to some extent even by monetary policy. The prosperity of the United States since 1945, maintained in the face of unceasing prophecies of imminent depression, and without calling into play such reserve weapons as public works programmes, is proof at once of the strong 'autonomous' pressures towards full employment, and the power of the modern state to reinforce these as necessary.

In Britain, not only are both the autonomous and political pressures even stronger than in America, but the reserve demands which the Government could make effective are much larger. Some of these were listed above – the needs of the under-developed areas, the urgent claims for higher social expenditure, the backlog of social investment, and so on; and even if none of these existed, taxation, which is high by historical standards, could easily be reduced amid general applause. There is no intelligent sense in which one can speak of a likely excess of potential output over potential demand in Britain in the foreseeable future.

The effects of continued full employment on the rate of growth

---

[1] And of course in Britain these may be caused by export fluctuations over which the government has no control. Moreover the government itself may make errors, and provoke a minor recession by carrying anti-inflationary cuts in demand too far.

and economic efficiency are likely, on balance, to be favourable.[1] It is an illusion to suppose that unemployment, because it (allegedly) strengthens incentives to work and the downward pressure on manufacturers' costs, is therefore necessarily beneficial to productivity. No doubt some downward pressure on costs is highly desirable – something is said on this later. But if the pressure is carried to the point where the level of unemployment becomes significant, the balance of advantage rapidly changes, since both labour and management take refuge in protective devices which have an adverse effect on costs.

On the side of labour, the instinctive reaction to unemployment is to resist the introduction of new machinery, and to spread the available work by 'go-slow' methods. The parallel on the side of management is a general flight into the security of cartel and market-sharing arrangements. Even where competition is nominally preserved, it increasingly takes the form of a drive less for the lowest costs or the highest efficiency, than for the greatest possible differentiation of the product from those of other manufacturers, and diversification of output in order to spread risks. The consequence is diminished specialisation and diminished standardisation: in other words, short production runs, and the sacrifice of the potential advantages of large scale. That this is bad for efficiency has been clearly shown by the numerous Anglo-American Productivity Reports which fastened on precisely these characteristics of British industry, which are partly a legacy of pre-war unemployment, as one of the major reasons why British productivity was not higher.

Under full employment, all these pressures are reversed. There is less temptation to restrictive market-sharing arrangements, and less need for defensive sales and output policies. The buoyant level of demand stimulates not only the direct expansion of capacity, but also more audacious risk-taking, more rapid technical innovation, and a greater expenditure on research. Moreover, the shortage of labour acts as a powerful spur to more economical methods of production and the instalment of labour-saving machinery. On the side of labour the enhanced security of em-

---

[1] Even if they were unfavourable, it would not of course constitute a sufficient argument against having full employment. The social benefits of full employment are of far greater importance than the economic ones.

ployment, although it undoubtedly creates some difficulties in the field of labour relations and discipline (e.g. in industries such as building),[1] nevertheless weakens the attraction of restrictive practices, and fosters a greater willingness to accept technical change.

But the most significant change is in the sphere of investment decisions. It is not simply that investment will be currently higher than in an under-employed economy, since the transition from depression to boom will seldom be accomplished without the help of a rise in investment: but the inducement to a still further expansion will also be strong.

This is partly for obvious economic reasons. Decisions about investment, in public as well as in private industry, are based on expectations about future demand, prices, and profits; and these in turn are influenced by the level of current demand and current profits. With the economy producing to full capacity, not only are current profits high; but because full employment leads, for the reasons just mentioned, to a healthy rate of increase in productivity and hence in personal incomes and consumption, they will tend to advance, and with them expectations about the future, with every year that full employment continues. The result is a constant tendency for investment plans to be revised upwards, and for the level of capital formation to increase.

Of course these optimistic expectations depend wholly on the conviction that full employment will be maintained, and will not at a certain stage give way, as it invariably has done in the past, to a cyclical depression. For some time after the war this conviction was far from being universal. Most businessmen imagined that they were caught up in a conventional post-war

---

[1] Though to listen to employers' complaints about 'slackness' and 'insubordination', by which nothing more is often meant than a less docile demeanour on the part of workers, one would think that the post-war British experience in this respect was unique. But of course this change in attitudes always accompanies prosperity. 'Sir,' exclaimed Dr. Johnson, dining at Mr. Scott's, 'subordination is sadly broken down in this age. No man, now, has the same authority which his father had – except a gaoler. No master has it over his servants; it is diminished in our colleges; nay, in our grammar schools.' On being asked why this was, and after attributing it first to the coming in of the Scotch, Dr. Johnson went on: 'Why, Sir, there are many causes, the chief of which is the great increase of money. The shoe-black at the entry of my court does not depend on me. I can deprive him but of a penny a day, which he hopes somebody else will bring him; and that penny I must carry to another shoe-black; so the trade suffers nothing.' (*Life*, 1867 ed., p. 333.) The parallel is exact.

boom, to be followed by a conventional (though unusually long-delayed) post-war depression.

But the persistence of full employment for more than a decade of peace has now largely cured the depression psychosis which dominated industrial attitudes, with such insidious results, in the inter-war period. The business community accepts the fact that prosperity is here to stay, not only because full employment will be maintained, but also because we have entered a period of rapid growth in personal incomes and consumption. This too little noticed revolution in business psychology is the most important economic event of our generation; and its implications for the rate of capital formation are too obvious to need under-lining.[1]

These economic pressures are fortified by more subtle social pressures. The country now accepts, in a way that was impossible in the pre-war era of excess capacity, the need for rapid growth, and for high investment to attain it; and these have become accepted national aspirations. Successive Chancellors, all political parties, City opinion, weekly journals, economists, and even less elevated publicists, all preach to industry that it has a patriotic duty to invest, and praise it when it does so. It is a mistake to assume that a social consensus of opinion of this sort has no influence on economic decisions – it has, and the fact that expansion is now 'the done thing', and applauded on all sides, is a significant inducement to business growth.

This influence communicates itself to the *personal* motives of industrial executives. I have already argued in Chapter I that with the transition from family to joint-stock enterprise, the growth of the firm has partly replaced personal consumption as the basic motive and rationale of business behaviour, and that this stimulates a policy of heavy ploughing-back and re-investment of profits. Now that rapid expansion has become a national and not merely an occupational goal, the prestige of a firm, and so of its executives, rests even more completely on its rate of growth of output and profits. This naturally exerts a strong influence on the investment attitudes of managements. It is often said that the expansion of capitalism in the nineteenth century was fundamentally the product not of any set of economic institutions, but

[1] And we must remember that scarcity in the labour market creates an additional inducement to new investment.

of the 'entrepreneurial' psychology of the capitalist. Whether or not this is true, it seems clear that the modern top management team (in nationalised as well as private industry), though from different motives and acting within a different social and institutional framework, often has an equally expansive group psychology.

It is, of course, always imprudent to dogmatise about economic trends. What the position will be in the long run, no one can say. Even in the short run, it may be that industry and governments[1] will not be willing to invest up to the limits which the supply of savings and risk-capital makes possible; and in that case we shall need measures to stimulate demand. But if one has to hazard a guess for the next decade, it seems more likely that in a democratic, semi-egalitarian, full-employment economy of the post-war British type, investment incentives will remain buoyant, while on the other side the tendency will be towards high consumption and inadequate savings.

III   *The Threat of Inflation*

Sufficient savings are necessary not only for economic growth, but also to preserve stability. This was not the case before the war, when instability had nothing to do with inadequate savings, but was the result of cyclical fluctuations in investment; and when indeed the persistence of secular under-employment even through the boom was basically a symptom of excessive savings.

To-day the secular under-employment has disappeared, for the reasons given in the previous section. But it does not follow that the trade cycle has also disappeared. One might still have deep fluctuations in investment, even though the trend-line round which they occurred, and hence the average level of employment through the cycle, were much higher. Yet I believe that the cycle in its classical form – in the form, that is, of deep and rhythmical fluctuations – is unlikely to reappear in Britain. Not only are governments both more competent and more anxious to suppress it, should it show signs of re-emerging, but investment itself is tending to take on a rather more stable character. Over one-half of total capital expenditure is now incurred by public autho-

[1] The latter being under equally heavy, though quite different, pressures towards high investment, e.g. in the field of social capital or roads.

rities (central and local government, and the Nationalised Boards); and this large component, although sometimes rather unpredictable in its behaviour, is at least not liable to fluctuate directly in response to short-term cyclical changes in profit expectations. Even in the private sector matters are slowly changing. Deep investment cycles presuppose, first, that most capital projects are physically capable of being postponed and resumed, curtailed or augmented, easily and at short notice (as might be the case if investment consisted mainly of purchasing single machines): and, secondly, that decisions about investment are taken in the light of short-term cyclical expectations.

Neither of these is as true as formerly. Physically, investment is increasingly a matter of major expansion schemes, the result of long-range planning for several years ahead, and involving simultaneous and co-ordinated expenditure on plant, machinery, factory building, and research. Such schemes are often too indivisible to be easily curtailed, too large to be lightly foregone, and too lengthy in execution to be cut off at short notice. And decisions about investment also take on a more and more long-range character, not only on account of these physical factors, but also because psychologically businessmen now pay more attention to the long-run sales outlook and less to short-run market changes; and because, in addition, the rate of investment in many industries is almost dictated by the pace of research and technological change. Thus long-run capital budgeting, based on expectations about the fairly distant future, is becoming increasingly common; and although this certainly does not rule out sharp fluctuations, such as occurred, for example, in 1955, it does make the recurrence of a deep, classical trade cycle rather unlikely.

Stability is now almost as much threatened from the opposite direction; that is, by fluctuations in savings leading to periodic crises of inflation. Full employment is necessarily divided by only a narrow margin from inflation; and in a democratic country with free Trade Unions, recurrent appeals to the electorate, and rising standards of consumption, this margin is in constant danger of being crossed as a result not only of changes in investment, but equally of sudden changes in savings and consumption. These may be caused on the one hand by the Government, and take the form of a decline in net public saving due to an excessively popular Budget: and on the other hand by the decisions of consumers. The latter possibility becomes more likely as rising consumption increasingly takes the form of expenditure on durable goods, the purchase of which can always be either accelerated or postponed; and this growing 'lumpy' element in consumption makes fluctuations in personal saving and spending almost inevitable.

Each time a sudden decline in saving occurs, and the margin is crossed, a minor crisis ensues, reflected perhaps in a fall in the exchanges and a drain on the reserves, and certainly in lengthening delivery-dates for goods; and the reaction of most governments is to cut that element in total demand which seems most easily under control, namely capital investment. Thus, by a curious irony, a second (though highly irregular) investment cycle appears in the planned economy, caused by the panic response of governments to sudden increases in demand.

These periodic attempts to cut investment, although only partially successful owing to the long-term nature of many capital projects just discussed, are clearly not good for growth. Not only do they interrupt and delay the immediate process of investment, but they may have psychological effects which slow down the future rate of growth even after the immediate crisis is over. As was pointed out above, rapid growth requires a confidence that the existing rate of growth will be maintained, and a climate of opinion in which investment is assumed to be thoroughly desirable. Both these are threatened by periodic announcements of investment cuts.

It is sometimes argued that an occasional tendency to demand-inflation does little harm, and that the sensible way to deal with it is simply to allow the reserves to take the strain – that, after all, is what reserves are for – instead of attempting to reduce demand by cutting back investment. Matters will then gradually right themselves through a continued rise in productivity; and a certain instability of the exchanges is a small price to pay for the overwhelming advantages of driving the economy at top speed. Even ignoring the severely practical objections that our existing reserves are quite inadequate to fulfil this role, and that a rise in productivity cannot be guaranteed by itself to remove inflation, how true is it that demand-inflation does no damage?

Now to run the economy flat out, as was argued above, is unquestionably not only on balance beneficial to productivity, but an absolute condition of high investment and rapid growth through its repercussions on business confidence. Demand must therefore be kept very high indeed. Nevertheless, there is a point at which flat-out full employment is converted into definite excess demand and inflation. When this occurs the balance of advantage shifts, and the losses begin to outweigh the gains.

This is not, it is true, a point which can be either accurately defined in theory, or exactly identified in practice. It gives a false impression to speak of a 'razor's edge' between full employment and inflation, as though these were both precise concepts, and the productive system had no elasticity of output.[1] Nor, even if the critical point could be defined in theory and recognised in practice, are planning techniques so subtle and refined that demand could be exactly set, as though by a thermostatic control, at just the right point.

Yet one can make broad, impressionistic judgments which are not meaningless. It is not absurd to say that full employment has turned into inflation if demand can be seen to exceed supply at current prices in the majority of important markets – if, that is, markets for goods are characterised by lengthening delivery-dates and waiting lists, with a clear upward pressure on prices, and the market for labour by a rapidly growing excess of vacant jobs over applicants.

When this occurs, certain adverse consequences follow. First, managerial efficiency may deteriorate. Here, as always in this field, there is a golden mean. Deflation and unemployment are clearly bad for efficiency, for the reasons explained in the previous section. But at the other extreme, heavy excess demand tends to breed a general carelessness about costs. With a long waiting-list of customers, profit margins can be all too easily maintained in the face of rising costs by an increase in selling prices; and even if neither costs nor prices are actually rising, there is no competitive pressure to *reduce* costs if demand greatly exceeds supply.

It is often said that the crucial psychological difference between British and American businessmen lies in their respective attitudes towards expansion. I doubt if this is true to-day. I believe it now lies rather in the sphere of cost-consciousness. American managements are engaged, to a far greater extent than their

[1] v. P. D. Henderson, *Bull. Inst. Stat.*, May and June 1954, for a discussion of this point.

British counterparts, in an unceasing search for lower costs –
through labour-saving machinery, the rapid introduction of automation, the study of personnel management, and the almost mass
employment of all manner of specialists from scientists to input-
output experts.[1] No doubt part of the difference is to be explained
by historical factors. But part is surely due to the fact that American business, faced *even in non-recession years* with less inflation of
demand, has been under a forcible pressure to look for sales;
and British industry has not (at least to the same extent). Full
employment need not, but excess demand inevitably must, exclude some competitive pressure to sell, and hence to attend to
costs.

Secondly, excess demand may weaken the incentive to export.[2]
This is a familiar point, of which too much was made in the post-
war years when economic conditions were, for structural reasons,
so wholly exceptional, and the required increase in exports so large
and rapid, that no practicable changes in home demand would
have made much difference. But to-day the picture has altered.
The post-war export targets have been substantially attained, and
even in bad years the foreign balance is only narrowly separated
from a reasonably healthy surplus – it is a 10% rather than a
70% increase in exports which is needed even in a 'crisis' year.
Thus a comparatively small change in the volume of exports
makes all the difference between an adequate surplus and a
dangerous deficit.

Now the volume of exports is certainly not violently susceptible
to changes in home demand. Firms have built up their export
connections and sales organisations to the point where their
entire sales and output policy is now attuned to, and depends on,
a generally high volume of foreign sales. But *at the margin* the level
of home demand is certainly important. If firms are both working
to capacity and faced with long waiting-lists at home, why should
they bother to *increase* their exports? And if exports fall off in
some especially competitive foreign market, why not absorb the

[1] Not to mention psychiatrists to help maintain the mental stability of top executives, and sociologists to help in market research.

[2] Of course its most immediate effect on the balance of payments is on the side
of imports – both generally in raising demand for all types of imports, and specifically
by compelling the importation of marginal supplies of essential goods, the home
output of which cannot be quickly expanded (e.g. coal and steel). But I am assuming
that at least the general 'income' effect on imports can be counteracted by import
controls without the need to cut down home demand.

frustrated exports into home sales rather than make painful and hazardous efforts to maintain the volume of sales abroad?

Even if there is no effect on the incentive to export, the lengthening of delivery-dates itself causes a loss of export orders as dissatisfied foreign customers turn elsewhere. A fully-employed economy can probably never offer *immediate* delivery of all capital-goods – there will always be some excess of demand over supply in the investment-goods sector. But this can be either greater or less; and when it becomes too great, the effect on exports may be exceedingly serious. Indeed changes in the (relative) volume of exports in recent years have commonly been a function less of changes in relative price or quality, or the behaviour of wages, than of the degree of sales effort exerted, and the delivery-dates offered; and both these are necessarily affected by the presence or absence of demand-inflation at home.

Thirdly, however, excess demand in the labour market may also have a damaging effect on prices by inducing a wage and price spiral. It is true that rising wage-rates may be neither so undesirable nor so dangerous as people often assume, and also that there are other possible causes of wage-inflation apart from excess demand. Nevertheless it is obvious that a demand-inflation may easily cause a dangerous degree of wage-inflation.

None of this means that as a matter of past history inflation was the major cause of our post-war difficulties, or that more disinflation would have had any appreciable effect on the exceptional structural problems created by World War II and the Korean War. Nor does it mean that the mere avoidance of inflation is a sufficient condition for economic progress. It simply means that under normal peacetime conditions, progress and efficiency require, amongst other things, the avoidance of periodic crises of serious excess demand (though it may be that a continuing mild inflation is inseparable from full employment).

Thus considerations of stability, as well as of growth, direct attention to the central role of savings, and to the responsibility of the Government for securing a volume of savings sufficiently steady to avoid inflationary crises, and sufficiently high to sustain the desired long-run rate of capital creation.

XVII

―――

THE PROBLEM OF PRIVATE PROFIT

I *Profit as Surplus Value for Accumulation*

THE required level of total saving, whatever may happen in the field of personal or governmental savings, will certainly call for a high level of business savings, and hence for high profits in private as well as in public industry. These are a precondition of rapid growth, not only for their contribution to savings, but also as an inducement to industry to expand, and as a source of new capital. So long as we maintain a substantial private sector, therefore, socialists must logically applaud the accumulation of private profit.

This naturally raises an acute political problem. Not only are high profits unpopular (the more so when they occur under a Labour Government which is thought to have the duty of preventing them), but from the earliest days of the Labour Movement they have been anathematised; and for a Labour Government deliberately to encourage them seems a betrayal of everything that socialism stands for. The problem of profit is thus the central economic dilemma facing contemporary social-democracy; and attempts to resolve it will arouse profoundly traumatic emotions on the Left. The inner contradiction of capitalism, according to Marx, was its tendency to huge accumulations of profit. The inner contradiction of social-democracy may be its refusal, in changed conditions, to recognise the need for such accumulations.

The social objections to private profit – that it must lead to a 'maldistribution' of resources, or that it is immoral as an incentive – have already been discussed in previous chapters.[1] We are here concerned with the economic role of profit in the sense of a surplus for accumulation.

Even this role has often been rejected, implicitly if not overtly, by socialists in the past. This was because the role of profit as a source of accumulation became inextricably confused with the Marxist view of profit as 'exploitation'. In Marxist theory, as is well known, labour is 'forced' to work for longer hours than would be needed merely to produce the goods required for its own remuneration at existing standards of living: that is, labour produces a total value greater than its current wage. This surplus value, which would have accrued to the workers themselves had they owned the means of production, in fact accrues to the capitalists, who have alienated the means of production. It is the appropriation of this surplus value in the form of profit which constitutes exploitation.

But in fact the emergence of surplus value, or profit, is in no way dependent on the conditions of capitalist production. It must occur in any society, whoever owns the means of production, in which one of two conditions are fulfilled.[2] The first is simply that the economy is dynamic, and not static. Economic growth depends on the setting-aside of some part of current output for the expansion or improvement of the instruments of production; that is, it requires the deduction of surplus value, and its use as capital for investment. The creation and appropriation of surplus value are thus an absolute pre-condition of economic growth. This is equally true of a communist as of a capitalist country; it is wholly irrespective of how and to whom the surplus value initially accrues. The only society which could forgo the deduction of surplus value as capital for investment, that is, which consumed its entire output of goods in current enjoyment, would be one which had resigned itself to a static population, a static standard of living, a static scientific knowledge, and no technical innovation.

In fact, even in a wholly static society, some surplus value would be required to finance the political, military, and administrative functions of the state. Those who perform these functions

---

[1] *v.* Chapter III, Section III, and Chapter IV, Section IV.

[2] For an excellent discussion of this subject, *v.* Daya, 'Surplus Value, Profit and Exploitation', *Review of Economic Studies*, No. 58, 1954-5. These pages owe a great deal to Mr. Daya's analysis.

create no 'value' in the Marxist sense; and their remuneration must be provided out of the surplus value created by the workers. Again this is equally true whatever the relations of production, for a communist as well as for a capitalist country. Thus Marxist 'exploitation' can be inferred from, and is a condition of, both the fact of economic development and the existence of a central state.

In the light of this manifest indispensability of surplus value, or profit, it hardly makes sense for socialists to object to it on principle. This of course was quickly grasped by the hard-headed rulers of the Soviet Union, who have probably extracted more surplus value from their subjects than any set of rulers since the pyramid-building Pharaohs. Marx never considered the possibility of exploitation in a socialist society, since he assumed on the one hand that the state would gradually 'wither away', and on the other that the transition to socialism would take place only *after* capital had already fulfilled its 'historic function' of developing the productive system to a saturation-point where further growth would be superfluous.[1]

These two conditions are naturally never likely to be fulfilled. And in Communist Russia, not only is an exceptionally large amount of surplus value required and employed for the upkeep of a vast military and bureaucratic machine, but the accumulation of profit for capital formation has been the central, obsessive aim of economic policy. The Soviet Government has enforced a rate of investment (i.e. extracted a degree of surplus value) which not only – or so Communist apologists maintain – exceeds that attained by any capitalist country even in the heyday of its growth, but also certainly required more ruthless exploitation, and more widespread suffering amongst a reluctant and backward peasantry, than ever occurred during the industrial revolutions of the West. But although one may resent the excessive priority given to it in Soviet Russia at the expense of more humane and liberal values, it remains true that capital creation must be a prime motive of economic activity in any developing economy;

---

[1] 'Marx was in the happy position of assuming that the dirty job of exploiting the peasantry and the proletariat would already have been done by the capitalists. [They] would already have created an industrial apparatus and technology that would have taken production to unknown heights when the socialists would take control and get all the glory by distributing equitably all the goods thus produced.' (loc. cit., p. 101.)

and this presupposes the creation of surplus value, i.e. the accumulation of profit.

Presumably every British socialist would now concede the need for such accumulation. But what bothers him, naturally enough, is the fear lest the surplus should be used (or the belief that it is already being used) not, or at least not solely, for capital investment, but to increase the consumption of the bourgeoisie. This possibility appears to arise from the private ownership of the means of production, which confers on the shareholders (or their representatives) the choice of how to dispose of surplus value, and the power to sequester it for their own consumption.

Now in fact this possibility does not depend on private ownership. It also exists in a state-owned economy, where the state bureaucracy responsible for appropriating and disposing of surplus value may equally well use it to allot themselves a privileged consumption-position. The possibility of the 'misuse' of surplus value arises inevitably from the alienation of the means of production from those who operate them. But under conditions of large-scale production, this alienation has little to do with ownership. The Soviet worker is no more able than the British worker to determine the disposal of his surplus value. Conversely, the Gosplan manager is as easily able as the British shareholder or director to appropriate surplus value not for re-investment, but to allocate himself a differential income. In practice, of course, he is far more easily able, since he has neither free Trade Unions nor political opposition to contend with. In any society in which the disposal of surplus value is determined from above (i.e. in all except small-scale peasant or syndicalist societies), the possibility of its sequestration for privileged consumption must exist. But the likelihood of this occurring depends far less on the pattern of ownership, than on the strength of democratic institutions.

The problem facing British socialists is therefore so to use our democratic institutions as to ensure that profit in the private sector is used primarily for re-investment, and not (either currently or ultimately) for distribution to private shareholders – is used, that is, mainly as a source of collective capital accumulation, and not as a form of personal income. Naturally shareholders are entitled to an income commensurate with the risks entailed in investment. But dividend incomes larger than this are justified neither by the performance of an active entrepreneurial function, nor (to put it mildly) by considerations of the right distribution of total personal income.[1] The rest of the chapter discusses the practical methods of securing this divorce between profit as a surplus income accruing to the rich, and deserving by every socialist canon to be squeezed: and profit as a surplus for accumulation and expansion, deserving by every (sensible) socialist canon to be enlarged.

II *Profits Taxation and Incentives*

There are three possible approaches: through corporate taxation (i.e. to tax the profits themselves in such a way as to discourage high dividend disbursements), through personal taxation (i.e. to allow a free distribution of dividends, but to tax the dividends and, more important, the resultant capital gains, in the hands of the recipient), or through statutory dividend limitation. The post-war Labour Governments relied mainly on the first approach; not only was total corporate taxation kept high, but there was in addition a differential tax on distributed as opposed to undistributed profits.

This policy of heavy and differential corporate taxation was notably effective in reducing the relative share of dividend income. Yet it has been consistently criticised, not only of course by Right-wing and orthodox City opinion, but even by some economists on the Left.

The first criticism is that high profits taxation may weaken the incentive to invest, and so cause private investment to fall below the level permitted by the supply of savings and risk-capital. It is not clear at first sight why it should. The differential element in the profits tax exerts a bias in favour of retaining profits, and the greater availability of internal finance (as compared with a non-differential tax giving the same yield) itself creates an atmosphere favourable to expansion. And profits taxation is, after all, proportional and not progressive; and it has always been conceded that a proportional tax has comparatively little effect on incentives. It is often said: why should a business take the risk of expansion when half the profits will go to the Exchequer? But this is a misleading question, since it ignores the fact that half of

---

[1] *v.* Chapter XV for a fuller discussion of both these points.

any losses are also borne by the Exchequer; the loss on one venture can be set off against the taxable profits on another, while overall losses can be carried forward and offset against future profits. It is thus not correct that profits taxation discriminates against risky investment.[1]

It is sometimes said that the bias against high dividends in some way affects the personal incentives of business leaders. It is not obvious why it should, since most of them own only an infinitesimal proportion, if any, of the stock of the businesses which they manage. It therefore seems unlikely that they wish to maximise profits primarily in order to maximise dividends, or become less interested in expansion if dividends are held down. Such a supposition is contrary both to the reiterated (and no doubt genuine) statements of business leaders that they owe responsibilities not only to shareholders but also to workers and consumers, and that they endeavour to strike a balance between the three: and also to the strong conservatism of many large companies in respect of distribution policy, and the (overt or covert) conflict between management and shareholders' representatives which this often creates.

From what motive, then, does the modern business leader seek to maximise profits? He may do so occasionally in order to maximise his own remuneration, if his salary contains a bonus element; but mainly he does so, as I have argued in a previous chapter, from a mixture of psychological and social motives. He tends to identify himself closely with his firm, which comes to have for him a genuine personality of its own, with interests quite separate from those of the shareholders. And not only his corporate loyalty to the firm, but all his personal motives – professional pride, desire for prestige in the business world, self-realisation, desire for power — find their fulfilment in high output and rapid growth, and hence in high profits, these being both the conventional source of business prestige and the ultimate source of business power.

Now from the point of view of these incentives, the absolute level of net profits is of less significance than the relative level.

[1] Except in so far as there is a serious risk of total bankruptcy, in which case naturally there is nothing to offset losses against. This risk scarcely exists in the case of the large public company, which these paragraphs are mainly discussing. The unabridged edition contains a separate discussion of the special problem of the new or small business.

Business power and prestige are judged by, and depend on, the rate of growth of output and profits from one year to the next, or the relationship between the profits of one firm and those of its rivals. It follows that a flat-rate tax on profits, falling equally on one year with another and on one firm with another, since it has no effect on the relative magnitudes, will have little effect on the managerial incentive to maximise profits. It is therefore hard to see how either dividend restraint, or a high absolute level of company taxation, can do much harm to the personal incentives of business leaders.

Even if the main limit on investment *should* prove to come from the side of business incentives, there is still no need to react by crude and indiscriminate reductions in profits taxation; for governments now wield a powerful weapon for inducing more investment, and one which can, moreover, be employed with no undesirable results on dividend policy or share values.

This is the investment allowance, first introduced in the 1954 Budget.[1] Whereas income and profits taxes are a positive tax on company savings, the investment allowance is a negative tax or subsidy on investment.[2] Thus under a combination of the two a company pays less tax, the more of its profits it re-invests and the less it distributes or puts to reserve; and conversely. By varying the tax and/or the subsidy, governments can exert a strong direct pressure on the investment as well as the savings decisions of industry.

This may be seen by taking, as a *reductio ad absurdum*, the extreme case of 100% rates. A 100% investment allowance would mean that companies paid no tax on that part of their profits which they re-invested, and that a company which re-invested all its profits had a zero tax liability.[3] A 100% profits tax would

---

[1] I ventured to call it, in a speech on the 1954 Finance Bill at 3 o'clock in the morning, 'a completely new fiscal device of great moment . . . one not seen before but which will be criticised or supported for many years ahead'. (*H.C. Deb.*, Vol. 528, col. 2176.)

[2] So in most cases was its predecessor, the initial allowance, contrary to the conventional view (supported even by the first Millard Tucker Committee) that it was only an interest-free loan. (v. my article 'The Initial Allowances Reconsidered', *The Banker*, September 1953.)

[3] And despite the fact that the entire cost of the investment could be written off for tax in the first year, the company would still receive the normal depreciation allowance over the life of the investment. A 100% investment allowance would thus mean that it could ultimately set 200% of the cost of the investment against its tax liability.

mean that all profits not re-invested would go to the Exchequer, and that a company which invested nothing would pay its entire profit away in tax. This combination would give rather a strong inducement to managements to invest, since the only alternative would be to let the Inland Revenue have the lot. (The inducement would be even stronger, given the political bias of most managements, if a Labour Government were in office. The disinclination to surrender everything to what Gibbon once called 'the insolent vexation of the farmers of the revenue' would then be overwhelming; and there would be a positive rush to cheat the farmers by raising capital expenditure.)

This limiting case illustrates the fact that different combinations of negative and positive tax will give different scales of preference between investment and non-investment. Furthermore, different combinations of investment allowance, distributed profits tax, and undistributed profits tax will give different scales of preference between investment, dividend distributions, and the accumulations of reserves. Thus a Labour Government could encourage investment by raising the investment allowance, yet prevent either a fall in the total yield of profits taxation, or an increase in dividends, by simultaneously raising the rates of profits tax. We therefore have in the investment allowance a reserve weapon of no little precision and power, should industry prove to have too little incentive to capital formation.

III *Profits Taxation and the Supply of Risk-capital*

The second alleged danger of heavy business taxation is that it may adversely affect the supply of risk-capital, so that companies cannot invest as much as they would like for lack of the necessary finance.

This has not occurred so far, despite all the talk in the City and industry to the contrary. But of course the situation might change in the future, as companies seek, and physical resources permit, a higher level of investment, with a correspondingly greater strain on industry's financial resources. The fear most commonly expressed is that the low distribution ratio which high taxation enforces may make it too difficult for companies to raise outside finance, since these 'artificially' low dividends will not suffice to attract the necessary volume of risk-capital from shareholders.

How important, then, is the shareholder as a source of new capital?

It must be noticed, first, that British industry has historically been largely self-financing, except for new businesses. Even a generation ago, when personal savings were relatively higher than now, they were channelled mainly into foreign investment, housebuilding, railways, and the utilities, leaving industry to rely largely on its own ploughed-back profits.

This tendency is still evident to-day. To a significant extent public companies are, as they have always been, self-financing, and can carry through their investment programmes without recourse to the market and without the need, therefore, to offer inducements to investors in the shape of very much higher dividends. Some two-thirds of new capital expenditure by private industry is financed out of undistributed profits. To this extent, the relation between dividend payments and industrial expansion is less close than is sometimes imagined.

Even to the extent that public companies do have recourse to the market for new funds, they need not always offer very generous dividend prospects. It is an illusion to suppose that 'risk-capital' consists solely of equity capital. Much industrial borrowing takes the form not of share issues, but of debentures and fixed-interest-bearing loans of various kinds.[1] The popularity of such issues in recent years proves at once that investment in large British companies is not considered particularly risky, and that a large volume of funds is available to take up stock which offers no possibility of a rising income. Moreover much of the supply even of equity capital is in search only of a steady yield slightly above that obtainable on gilt-edged, combined with a high degree of security. This applies – not, it is true, to wealthy private investors – but to a significant extent to institutional investors, and also to many small investors who have neither the time nor the inclination to be constantly on the phone to a stockbroker in a daily search for capital gains.[2]

[1] The proportion of new borrowing which took this form was 36% from 1933 to 1938, and has averaged nearly 40% since 1949 (though the figures show large year-to-year fluctuations due to changes in profits tax or rates of interest, and to the inclusion in particular years of large issues by a few giant firms).

[2] In fact the institutions largely dominate the new issue market, since it is only here that they can buy in large quantities without (so huge are the funds which they wield) forcing prices up against themselves. And since they cannot (at least the life assurance and pension funds), in view of their fixed future obligations, stay out of the market for long, they constitute a supply of new capital which is comparatively inelastic to changes in dividends or the prospect of capital gains.

Thus since a high proportion of new capital is found from internal sources, and since of the remainder a further proportion comes from fixed interest-bearing bonds,[1] and since of the residue obtained from new share issues a further proportion is subscribed by investors in search of security rather than large capital gains, it seems unlikely that the lower level of distributions (which after all still offers the prospect of some annual increase and capital appreciation) will have much influence on the overall supply of new capital.

This conclusion is supported by the experience of other countries whose rate of investment is higher than our own, yet where a conservative and even ungenerous attitude is adopted towards the claims of shareholders. Norway, which can boast the highest post-war ratio of fixed investment to gross national product of any country in Europe, has actually maintained a statutory limitation of dividends. Sweden, investing nearly 20% of its gross national product and enjoying a rapid rate of productivity-increase, has had only a moderate rise in dividends and share values since the end of the war; new share-issues play a minor role in the supply of new capital, which comes mainly from company reserves, bank credits, and bond issues; no one worries too much about the relation between share values and asset values; and the social and political climate is such that it would scarcely occur to industry to behave in any other way.

But the most striking example is that of Germany. Here is the country eulogised by the champions of private enterprise not merely for its unmatched investment record, but also for its alleged attachment to the classical virtues of *laisser-faire* and high rewards for risk. Yet the whole spectacular post-1948 German expansion of output and investment was accomplished with only the bare shadow of a free capital market, and indeed with the whole financing of industry largely a matter of State *dirigisme*. What market existed was dominated by municipal and state borrowing, and to a much lesser extent by industrial fixed-interest-bearing issues. Industrial share issues played a negligible part, and almost the entire expansion of fixed investment,

---

[1] The same is also true in the U.S.A. An analysis of corporate financing in 1953 by the Department of Commerce showed that industry financed its requirements to the extent of $22 billion through retained earnings and depreciation, compared with only $7.6 billion through new borrowing; and of the latter figure $5.2 billion took the form of loan stock, and only $2.4 billion of new share issues (preference as well as ordinary).

which has so rightly alarmed opinion in this country, was carried through by a process of self-financing, bank credits, and government funds. Approaches to the market for new capital were on a negligible scale; and the role of the shareholder, and of dividends, was insignificant.[1] Nor can this be put down solely to exceptional post-war factors, since it is well known that German industry has never relied at all heavily on new public issues of ordinary shares, or been at all generous in its distribution policy. The German experience should at least give people pause before they assume that new issues of equity shares must always be the predominant source of new capital, or that any limitation of dividends must inevitably slow down the rate of growth.

IV   *The Choice Facing Socialists*

I conclude that the alleged ill-effects of high business taxation have been exaggerated in the past, and that ample counter-measures are open if they should materialise in the future.[2] We can thus choose dispassionately, without being stampeded by terrible forewarnings, between this and other methods of preventing shareholders from gaining disproportionately from the high profits inevitably associated with rapid growth.

There are two other possible methods. The first would be to transfer all or part of the taxation of the shareholder from corporate to personal taxation; the second would be the statutory limitation of dividends.

The latter, for the reasons set out in Chapter XV, would be the most complicated of all possible methods, and should be treated as a possibility of last resort. But there is much to be said for a partial transfer as between corporate and personal taxation, by combining a capital gains tax with perhaps some reduction in profits taxation.[3] The former is not necessarily much more (or less) efficient from an economic point of view. But it is certainly more equitable and efficient from a distributive point of view,

---

[1] The most striking example of self-financed growth was provided by Volkswagen, whose entire expansion of output (at very competitive prices) from 1948 was financed out of retained profits – and indeed without making any dividend payments to anyone, since the firm had no shareholders.

[2] The counter-measures are described in detail in the unabridged edition.

[3] *v.* Chapter XIII, Section III, for a discussion of the capital gains tax.

since it both falls on gains as they are actually realised by the individual (in contrast to corporate taxation, which is very haphazard as between individual gains), and taxes gains on other forms of property besides securities. But it can only be a partial substitute. There are powerful incentive reasons why it must be a flat-rate and not a progressive tax; and business taxation could therefore not be wholly revoked without an excessive gain to the rich.

Whatever combination of methods is finally chosen, there is no evidence yet to suggest that we cannot run a mixed economy at a high level of employment and a healthy rate of growth, but without a progressive enrichment of the shareholder at the expense of the rest of the community. Some Left-wing economists, it is true, might not accept this conclusion; and the whole attempt is of course in the nature of an experiment. But the more one considers the experience of other countries, the more one becomes convinced that there is no unique source of supply of new industrial capital, no unique position that the shareholder needs to occupy, and no unique level of property-incomes necessary for the growth of capital. All these can be, and are, conditioned by social, cultural, and historical factors. It is the task of the Labour Party, if we accept, as I personally do, that the mixed economy both has great practical advantages and is in tune with the inclination of the British people, so to condition these attitudes that the experiment succeeds.

XVIII

THE ECONOMICS OF NATIONALISATION

I   *The Pre-war Case for Nationalisation*

IN the 1930s, the central importance of nationalisation was taken for granted in the Labour Party. Occasional rumbles of dissent might be heard from those with traces of anarchism or guild socialism still in their blood, but such people were few and far between, and considered rather crankish; and generally it was assumed that every Labour programme would be built round a number of major acts of public ownership.[1]

Nationalisation was desired partly for reasons specific to particular industries, that is, in order to control the use to which particular capital assets were put; and partly for reasons common to all industries, that is, because it was thought that 'socialism' was ultimately consistent only with the public ownership of all (major) capital assets. The specific reasons, which naturally determined the order in which industries were to be nationalised, were as follows.

First, the Public Utility argument. It is a characteristic of certain industries providing essential services either that the basic size of plant is very large in relation to the market (gas, electricity), or that an elaborate 'octopoid' system of distribution (by piping, cabling, wiring, railway lines, etc.) involves extremely heavy

---

[1] There were a few, but very few, exceptions. The most notable was Mr. Jay, in whose book *The Socialist Case* nationalisation only appears, in his own words, 'at a very late stage in the argument' – to be exact, on p. 321 in a book of 356 pages; and even there it only attracts some 15 pages of argument. But Mr. Jay, writing as a financial expert, devoted far more space than was usual to the problems of redistributive fiscal policy and monetary stability.

capital costs. Any duplication of such productive or distributive equipment would be clearly wasteful, and simply cause under-utilisation of the competing capital assets. It has therefore long been recognised that such public utility industries were unsuitable for competition, and that monopoly (either on a local or national scale) must be permitted. But all Governments have insisted, as a safeguard against possible exploitation, on an elaborate super-vision of such monopolies; and the tradition of public regulation had grown to the point where outright public ownership seemed a simpler and more logical solution.

Secondly, the Monopoly argument. While it was conceded that cartels might perhaps be disrupted by suitable legislation, it was argued that large single-firm monopolies, or trusts, were often justified by technical economies of scale which would be lost, to the disadvantage of the consumer, if competition were to be forcibly restored. Since it appeared, to most economists as well as to socialists, that private monopoly inevitably constituted a threat of exploitation (political and social even if not economic), the natural solution seemed to be to substitute public for private monopoly by means of nationalisation.

Thirdly, the Basic Industry argument. There are certain commodities, used normally by a wide variety of other industries, on which the prosperity of the community depends to an especi-ally marked degree, so that any breakdown or weakness in their production, and indeed generally the level of their output and prices, is a matter of particular public concern – to such an extent as to require the extreme solution of public ownership.

These three arguments all relate to the essential structure of an industry, or its strategic position in the economy – that is, to certain inescapable characteristics which make it a natural can-didate for state monopoly. The Efficiency argument, however, which comes fourth, has a more general application. It was most commonly based on the economies of large-scale organisation. These were thought to apply almost universally, and virtually without limit, and to provide a general argument for unification and co-ordination such as would be possible only under a single ownership. The word competition was always preceded by the epithet 'wasteful', and efficiency was held to be largely a function of monopoly control.

There were some industries in particular where the advantages of unification seemed likely to be overwhelming – industries, for example, where the optimum size of plant was larger than the average existing size (electricity, gas), or where redundancy clearly demanded large-scale re-organisation (coal and steel, as it seemed in the 1930s), or where wide differences in efficiency separated the best and worst plants, pointing to a redistribution of output within the industry (coal and steel again), or where overheads were so high that competition must lead to a wasteful under-utilisation of capital equipment (road versus rail). It was, in theory, admitted that there were industries to which these strictures did not apply, and which might be well served by a purely competitive solution. But this was thought to be an academic point, owing to the inexorable tendency of capitalist industry, always forecast by the Marxists and strongly in evidence in the 1930s, towards large scale and the concentration of control.[1]

Thus the efficiency argument came to be bound up with a justification of monopoly control. Naturally, existing single-firm monopolies were to be taken over – but because they represented a dangerous concentration of power, not because they were inefficient. Indeed, they represented, so far as their organisation was concerned, the ideal to which large-scale industry ought to conform; where it failed to do so under the spur of market forces, it must be compelled to do so under the aegis of state enterprise.

Lastly, the Planning argument. Generally, this was based on the belief that the profit motive and the national interest must always be in conflict. Specifically, it was applied most commonly to the basic heavy-investment industries, in which the level of investment dictated by profit-maximising considerations was both on the average too low to ensure full employment, and also too fluctuating to avoid cyclical instability. These were also the industries in which private and public interest were most liable to clash when it came to questions of the location of new plant or the shut-down of old; and Jarrow and Ebbw Vale became notorious symbols of this divergence.

---

[1] A typical judgment, which could be duplicated from almost any pre-war book on socialism, was that of G. D. H. Cole. 'Monopoly, or at least something approaching it, is the rule, and keen competition the exceptional case. . . . It is not possible, even if it were desirable, to go back to the old system. . . . The choice to-day is no longer between competition and monopoly, but between monopoly-capitalism and socialism.' (*A Plan for Democratic Britain*, pp. 29-30.)

In addition to these economic arguments for nationalising particular industries, there were also the wider (and older) social arguments for the public ownership of all major industries, irrespective of the order in which they were taken over. First, it was thought by some socialists that the profit-motive as such was ethically wrong, and could be eliminated only by nationalisation. Secondly, it was thought that harmonious labour relations and the creation of industrial democracy could be achieved only under public ownership.

Thirdly, it was assumed that equality required the extinction of private incomes from property, which in turn required the expropriation of the capitalist. Originally this was conceived as occurring automatically with the transfer of ownership. But later it came to be realised that complete confiscation of private property by nationalisation was neither just nor politic, and that reasonable compensation must be paid. The argument was then that nationalisation, although it would not destroy, would yet diminish property incomes, since equity holdings, carrying with them the likelihood of a gradual rise in dividends and capital values, would be replaced by fixed-interest compensation stock, carrying with it no such long-run prospect, and even in the short run generating an income that was smaller as the risk was smaller.

When it came to deciding what industries to nationalise, these arguments all pointed in broadly the same direction. The wider social arguments pointed to taking industries over in order of size. And the largest industries were in fact either public utilities (gas, electricity, railways), effective monopolies (coal, steel), basic (coal, transport, steel, electricity), notably inefficient under private enterprise (coal), apparently in need of larger scale or central re-organisation (coal, gas),[1] heavy capital-users (electricity, steel, transport), or subject to exceptionally bad labour relations (coal). Other, less important, industries were added for special post-war reasons (raw cotton purchasing, civil aviation, cable and wireless). But broadly the 1945–50 list seemed obviously dictated by these various criteria. Indeed it was so far accepted by public opinion that the greater part of it is still in public ownership after several years of Tory rule.

---

[1] cf. the Reid Report on coal (Cmd. 6610) and the Heyworth Report on the gas industry (Cmd. 6699).

II　*Post-war Experience of Nationalisation*

But do we now simply go on, and in our next period of office take over the next five largest industries, and so on *ad infinitum*? Not many socialists would now definitely answer yes; and for the first time for a century there is equivocation on the Left about the future of nationalisation.

For this there are several reasons. The first and most obvious is that the reality proved rather different from the blueprints. Some of the anticipated advantages did not materialise; while certain unexpected disadvantages emerged.

The planning argument, for example, looks a good deal less clear-cut than it used to. I am not thinking simply of the considerations (sufficiently discussed elsewhere in this book), first, that the distinction between public production for use and private production for profit has in any case lost much of its force at present levels and distribution of purchasing power, and secondly that one can scarcely argue, after the experience of the last ten years, that full employment requires as an absolute condition a much larger public sector: but of the fact that even where planning was admitted to be desirable, it proved scarcely easier to achieve under public than private ownership.

This was due to changes on both sides. On the side of private ownership, whereas before the war it was assumed – surprisingly, in the light of the total control of the Nazi Government over a privately-owned economy – that power resided in titular ownership, so that a change in ownership was a condition of state control, to-day it is realised that planning can be made effective even in the private sector. The government has access to a wide variety of fiscal, physical, and monetary controls; and although these are not of perfect efficiency, and too much is sometimes expected of them, yet they do enable the government broadly to impose its will on private industry.[1]

While control over the private sector thus exceeded expectations, control over the public sector fell short of them. Chapter I has already drawn attention to the independence of some of the Nationalised Boards, and their lack of public accountability. Indeed it was a common saying that the Government had less

[1] *v.* Chapter I for a full discussion of the loss of economic power by private industry.

power over Lord Citrine than over I.C.I.; and the quip was not without force. The Bank of England, for example, continued to pursue a highly independent policy of its own, especially in the field of the foreign exchanges. In the crucial fuel and power industries, control was almost non-existent. The three industries were allowed to go their own independent way: each competing and advertising against the other, each charging the lowest price it could (and indeed encouraged, and in the case of coal compelled, to do so by the Government itself), each unrestrictedly pushing sales in every direction, oblivious of the fact that coal was desperately scarce and large economies clearly possible if policy were only unified. It was a situation which cried out for government co-ordination, either through prices or physical controls; but none was forthcoming.

Investment policy was similarly unco-ordinated. It was argued before the war that one of the advantages of nationalising heavy-investing industries was that their large investment plans would become a stabilising factor in the trade cycle – to be retarded when private investment was booming, accelerated when private investment was lagging. This never in fact occurred; and fluctuations in private investment simply increased or diminished the degree of inflation, with little effective attempt at countervailing action.

The reasons for this outcome were twofold. First, the planning issues which arose had not been properly anticipated, nor were they always clarified even as time went on. The Ministers themselves, therefore, often had no clear policy which they *wanted* to impose on the Boards; and so they took the line of least resistance, which was to allow the Boards to do more or less as they wished.[1]

Secondly, however, even when Ministers held clear views, they were often reluctant to impose them on account of a rather dogmatic attachment, rooted in the Morrisonian conception of nationalisation, to the theory of the independent public board.[2] In so far as this helped to ward off detailed Parliamentary supervision, or even state department nationalisation, it was thoroughly healthy. But it was often pressed to an undesirable extreme in which the Minister, nervous of intervention though enjoying far

[1] This was true for quite long periods in both the transport and fuel and power industries.

[2] cf. Mr. Morrison's *Socialisation and Transport* (Constable, 1933), and his evidence to the 1953 Select Committee on Nationalised Industries.

greater powers under the post-war than under corresponding pre-war Acts, simply tended to behave, especially in Parliamentary debates, as counsel for the defence, and rarely used his powers of direction.[1]

Of course this is largely a question of politics. The truth is that there is now no insuperable *economic* difficulty about the Government imposing its will, provided it has one, on either public or private industry. Indeed post-1945 experience in the planning field strongly underlines one of the main arguments of Part One, namely, that ownership is not now an important determinant of economic power. The Government has all the economic power it needs – the only question is whether it chooses to use it; and from this point of view the mere change in ownership did not always make a decisive difference.[2]

At any rate, whatever the reasons, the planning argument for more nationalisation has, for the moment, fallen into some disrepute. It can now only be held to apply if three conditions are fulfilled: first, that Ministers have a clear idea of what their planning objectives are; secondly, that these objectives cannot be achieved by fiscal or physical controls; thirdly, that Ministers are in fact prepared to plan for their achievement under nationalisation.

Allied to the planning failure was a pricing policy which prevented the full achievement of another of the objects of nationalisation, the transfer of wealth from private to public hands. This has already been discussed elsewhere.[3] Briefly, the refusal to allow the Boards to build up large surpluses (besides often leading, as in the case of coal, to a serious misallocation of resources) meant that savings in the public sector were zero or negative, and hence that total savings were more heavily concentrated than they need have been in private hands.   A quite different pricing policy would have been required to achieve the objective of greatly increasing public relative to private capital.

These two failures are in principle remediable, in the sense of having been due to freely-chosen government policies (for which, to be fair, there were some strong practical arguments). But other

---

[1] Of course questions of personality also came in. Lord Citrine in particular emerged as an apparently untamable figure, beyond the control of any Minister.

[2] The question of planning is further discussed in Chapter XX.

[3] It is discussed in the unabridged edition.

difficulties emerged which appear to be inseparable from nationalisation as so far envisaged; that is, they are inseparable from monopoly and large (indeed enormous) scale.

We now understand rather better that monopoly, even when it is public, has definite drawbacks. Not only is there a genuine restriction of freedom involved in forbidding the citizen by law to start producing certain goods, and an even more dangerous restriction, notably in those cases (such as the B.B.C.) which call on highly specialised talent, in having only one employer:[1] but competition is seen to bring greater advantages than pre-war socialists realised – in preventing sloth and encouraging initiative, and in increasing the sense of consumer welfare (as we observed from the public reaction to the end of rationing) by allowing a free choice of goods and suppliers. Naturally this does not mean that monopoly has no advantages and competition no faults, but only that the balance of advantage now looks rather different. Nor of course does it mean that competition is always physically possible; on the other hand, pre-war Marxist prophecies of its inexorable decline have not been fulfilled, and we have a wider choice between competition and monopoly than was once supposed.

But perhaps the biggest change of view has occurred on the subject of large scale. Before the war, it was treated as axiomatic that, in the words of a typical and well-known judgment, 'large-scale production, especially when conducted in large-size firms and plants, results in maximum efficiency'.[2] To-day we are not so sure – at least beyond a certain size. It is not that the technical economies of scale are in dispute, but that doubts have arisen as to whether these may not be offset by diseconomies in other spheres, such as labour morale (leading to a higher accident rate, more absenteeism, and a less willing attitude to work),[3] or managerial responsibility and control, with the risk that the process of decision-making may become over-centralised and hence slowed

[1] 'The Fabian Society does not suggest that the State should monopolize industry as against private enterprise or individual initiative. . . . The freedom of individuals to test the social value of new inventions; to initiate improved methods of production; to anticipate and lead public enterprise in catering for new social wants; to practise all arts, crafts, and professions independently; in short, to complete the social organization by adding the resources of private activity and judgment to those of public routine, is . . . as highly valued by the Fabian Society as Freedom of Speech, Freedom of the Press, or any other article in the charter of popular liberties.' (G. B. Shaw, Fabian Tract No. 70, 1896.)

[2] P. Sargant Florence, *The Logic of Industrial Organisation* (Kegan Paul, 1933), p. 11.

[3] *v.*, for example, *Size and Morale* (Acton Society Trust, 1953).

down.[1] So far, none of these points is proven one way or another. But it seems clear that at any rate enormous scale is not an unmixed blessing, and in particular that it must bring with it at least the danger of over-centralisation.

This danger has not in practice always been avoided; and this is one of the reasons (though there are others) for the disappointment of yet another of the hopes of nationalisation, namely that it would rapidly and significantly improve labour relations, offering at the same time the hope of a steady advance towards industrial democracy.[2]

Some of these problems may recede as we gain a clearer idea of how to run these vast organisations. At the moment we have a huge area of disagreement – about the degree of public account-ability and Parliamentary control required (the 1953 Select Committee showed a glaring divergence of view not only amongst politicians, but even amongst members of different Boards): on the issue of centralisation or decentralisation of management control, and how much latitude to allow to the operational man-agement level: about how to make joint consultation effective: on what role (if any) to allot to Consumer Councils: on promotion policy, on which the Unions lean to seniority and the management to merit, with no agreement about the recruitment of University graduates: and so on. But for the present, at least, it can hardly be denied that public-monopoly nationalisation, despite con-siderable achievements in certain exceptionally difficult industries, no longer seems the panacea that it used to.

III   *The Case against a Proliferation of State Monopolies*

Even if these difficulties had not arisen, we should still face the fact that the specific economic, as opposed to the wider social, criteria, do not now point unequivocally to a particular list of industries. There are no more public utilities (except for water), and no more industries (except for steel) which can be described

---

[1] Another source of doubt is the growing realisation that neither the average plant nor the average firm is significantly larger in the U.S.A. than in Britain (*v.* Florence, *The Logic of British and American Industry*, Ch. I).

[2] *v.* Chapter XIV, Section III, for a discussion of nationalisation and labour relations.

as basic in the sense that coal or railways are basic. And if we adopt the policy of simply tackling industries in order of size, we find that the next most obvious candidates – chemicals, motor-cars, aircraft, shipbuilding, radio, electrical equipment, and so on – are not for the most part monopolies, nor in need of centralised planning, nor obviously inefficient, nor indeed suitable for organising on a national scale. They are industries quite different in kind from the 1945–50 list, above all in respect of their suitability for monopoly control and their level of efficiency.[1]

On the first point, they are not (with the exception of certain heavy chemicals) monopolies, but competitive oligopolies. (Plenty of monopolies exist, but mostly either in small industries (e.g. matches), or else of the cartel variety which can and should be dealt with by anti-monopoly legislation). Nor are they 'ripe' for nationalisation in the sense that although not yet monopolies, they would be improved by becoming monopolies. On the contrary, most of them would be damaged if this occurred; the element of competition is essential to their efficiency, the units are not obviously of less than optimum size, and their type of product and market is such that centralised control would be disadvantageous. Old-model nationalisation would mean imposing a state monopoly on unsuitable and competitive industries, with the corollary of a large increase in the area of unitary control.

They are unsuitable for old-model nationalisation for other reasons also. The 1945–50 industries had, for the most part, clearly defined boundaries, a relatively simple and homogeneous output normally consisting of a service or raw material, few marketing problems, and a fairly predictable (in the short run) demand. These industries, on the other hand, have indistinct boundaries, a diversified range of output, and a much less stable final demand. Thus once we move from the basic industries into the sphere of manufacturing, an industry becomes extremely hard to define. As multi-line production has spread, overlapping has become general; and most large firms to-day sprawl over several 'industries' at once. The lack of coincidence in the boundaries between firms and those between industries faces the would-be nationaliser with problems of definition far more intricate than

[1] I am assuming that steel and road transport belong to the 1945–50 list, and are re-nationalised. I also ignore certain of the next largest industries for whose nationalisation no demand appears to exist on the Left, so obviously unsuitable are they (e.g. textiles).

those which caused such difficulty even in the relatively simple case of steel.

The fact of multi-line production, moreover, elevates sales and marketing policy to a position of much greater importance than it occupies in the existing public sector. The demand for manufactures tends in any case to be less predictable than that for basic services. But, in addition, the more variegated the output (and the more products are 'branded'), the more central becomes the role of sales policy. This would be so even in an industry catering solely for the home market. But the metal, engineering, and chemical industries are also producing for the export market, where the competition is fiercer, the risks greater, and the fluctuations much more marked. Here the marketing problem, and the need for continuous rapid adaptation to the vagaries of a buyer's market, assume an even greater importance. There is a wealth of difference between selling cars or electrical goods in a highly competitive export market, and selling coal or electricity in a monopoly home market; and it is not clear that the routine type of management which appears to be characteristic of centralised public boards, suitable though it may be for the basic utilities, would be flexible and dynamic enough for this quite different task.

At any rate it is evident that highly competitive and export-oriented manufacturing industries, often producing branded goods, and faced with demand curves at once volatile and strictly indeterminate, are very different in character, and in the problems they present, from the industries nationalised in 1945–50. The latter might reasonably be expected to fare well under a centralised public corporation; it is not self-evident that the former would.

The economic arguments do not, then, give the same clear answer when applied to the next group of industries as they did when applied to coal and railways.

IV   *The Criteria and Conditions for Successful Nationalisation*

The diminished importance of nationalisation on economic grounds is only one aspect of the diminished importance, analysed in Chapter II, of industrial ownership for social relations as a whole. Socialism, whether viewed in social or ethical or economic terms, will not be brought much nearer by nationalising the aircraft industry. A higher working-class standard of living, more effective joint consultation, better labour relations, a proper use of economic resources, a wider diffusion of power, a greater degree of co-operation, or more social and economic equality – none of these now primarily require a large-scale change in ownership for their fulfilment; still less is such a change a *sufficient* condition of their fulfilment.

The gradual (though still often sub-conscious) realisation of this truth[1] has brought a reaction against making state monopoly the central feature of Labour policy. This reaction is stronger than can be explained simply in terms of lazy satiation after so large a meal, or of an intellectual void now that those industries which were preached and studied and perorated about during half a century of opposition are safely in the public sector. It is obvious enough at the level of public opinion, as every Labour candidate knows; and it is also obvious amongst the workers both in some nationalised industries (notably the railways), and in certain industries (notably chemicals) which appear to be threatened.

But it is evident in the official Labour Movement itself – in the Co-operative Movement,[2] in the T.U.C.,[3] and even in the Labour Party, as shown not only by the regular rejection of sweeping nationalisation proposals at Annual Conference, but also by the ambivalence of its election programmes – one list of candidates in 1950, none at all in 1951, and a different list again in 1955.

Nor are the doubts confined to the 'Right-wing' of the Party. They were most trenchantly expressed in *Keeping Left*, a statement by 12 Members of Parliament normally thought to be rather 'Left-wing'.[4] 'Most early socialists thought that the job

[1] Or rather of most of this truth. The exception is the still widespread belief, which is discussed fully in the next chapter, that nationalisation is essential to the diminution of property-incomes, and hence to equality.

[2] *v. Social Ownership.* 'There is a tendency for people at both the red and blue ends of the political spectrum to think that to advocate more and more nationalisation is to advocate more and more socialism. "Nationalisation" may be only a convenient slogan to avoid the necessity for new thinking.' (p. 22.)

[3] *v. Public Ownership: an Interim Report* (1953).

[4] *New Statesman* pamphlet, 1950. Among the authors were Mr. Crossman, Mr. Mikardo, Mrs. Castle, Sir Richard Acland, Mr. Wigg, Mr. Harold Davies, Mr. Hale, and Mr. Stephen Swingler.

of changing the nature of society was exclusively a matter of changing the proprietors of industry. For them the ownership of the means of production, distribution, and exchange was the sole criterion of whether a community was a capitalist or a socialist one. They therefore identified socialism with public ownership, and believed that all the world's ills could be dispersed through the formula of nationalisation. In the last few years we have learned to distinguish the means of socialism from its ends, and the tools of social revolution from their uses. We are now less concerned about who owns a factory. . . . It was right in the first period of Labour's power to transfer the basic industries and services in one sweep to national ownership. . . . But the next steps are not so obvious or so simple. We are approaching the end . . . of the "natural monopolies"; and we can therefore move beyond the technique of nationalising whole industries one at a time by one Act at a time. . . .We cannot disguise the fact that the public corporations have not, so far, provided everything which socialists expected from nationalised industries.'

All this is perhaps a little harshly stated. But it does reflect the contemporary mood in the Labour Movement, and the diminished role now allotted to nationalisation by most socialists. (*Keeping Left* contained no list of large industries to be taken over, and indeed barely mentioned a single industry by name; out of 114 lines of 'Conclusions', the whole subject of nationalisation was only given 5.)

In this new situation, probably most thoughtful socialists would agree on two points. First, any nationalisation proposals must be capable, given the present climate of public opinion, of being justified to the electorate as likely to lead to an economic improvement. The approach must therefore be precise and selective, concentrating not on the next industries in order of size, or on those which happen to be in the public eye, but on those where a genuine economic case can be made out. Secondly, in the light of the evident disadvantages, outside the public utility field, of state monopoly and enormous scale, the method should be to take over not whole industries, but individual firms, leaving others still in private hands: or to set up new government-owned plants to compete with existing private firms. This is the 'competitive public enterprise' approach. It need not rule out occasionally nationalising whole industries where the arguments for doing so seem overwhelming; but it should have a preference wherever possible.

So far as economic efficiency is concerned, it will already be clear that no general statements about public versus private ownership can ever be justified. Examples can be quoted of efficient private industries; they can equally be quoted of efficient nationalised industries – e.g. the civil air corporations, the trunk fleet of British Road Services, or the electricity industry (except for its pricing policies).

Efficiency has little to do with ownership because in the modern corporation ownership has little to do with control. Thus a change of ownership, by itself, makes little difference. The steel industry in recent years has undergone the most kaleidoscopic changes: first private ownership, then the Iron and Steel Corporation, later an anomalous period of ownership by the Realisation Agency, and now back to a (different) private ownership again. Yet management was hardly affected by all these changes in Whitehall; and output continued to rise (though never fast enough, since public ownership never had time to compel a better view of the long-term optimum capacity). Volkswagen, the most efficient unit in the German motor industry, has no legal owners at all, nor has had since 1945. Short Brothers, the aircraft firm, neither improved nor deteriorated significantly after it was taken over by the Government during the war.[1]

The basic fact is the large corporation, facing fundamentally similar problems and acting in fundamentally the same way whether publicly or privately owned. Its efficiency depends on the quality of its top management, and on whether the firm or industry is structurally well adapted from a technical point of view. There are, of course, exceptions – as when a dynamic and progressive top management (or an all-important research team) has a strongly marked private-enterprise outlook, and is very allergic to Whitehall; or where the whole enterprise revolves round a refractory individual genius like Frank Whittle;

---

[1] Another example, taken from a generally small-scale industry, is building. Public operation by direct labour schemes for new housing in some cases shows lower costs than private builders, in others higher; the average for the country is about the same (v. *The Cost of House-Building: First Report of the Committee of Inquiry*, H.M.S.O., 1948, Paras. 195-8). Everything depends on the relative competence of the particular local government officers and private contractors; and this shows wide variations.

or, in the opposite case, where the workers would refuse to
co-operate with private owners (as they would in coal). But with
these exceptions, ownership as such makes little difference;
and a transfer to public ownership will improve efficiency only
if either (1) the Government puts in a better management, or
compels the existing management to take greater long-term risks,
or (2) it is able to adapt the structure of the industry (e.g. by
amalgamations) in a manner obviously required by productive
efficiency. Conversely, it will make things worse if it does the
opposite.

In certain cases it might easily do the opposite. Thus the
imposition of centralised monopoly control on an efficient competitive industry would certainly lead to a fall in efficiency. This
danger is now well understood. But a further danger is not – that
nationalisation might actually lower the calibre of management.
This will occur if we continue to pay such stingy salaries in the
public sector. We have heard too much objection to the allegedly
high, but in fact relatively low, level of salaries in nationalised
industry; we can begin to worry about these when we have removed many far more glaring (and socially unjustified) sources of
inequality. As it is, we simply place nationalised concerns under
a hopeless handicap in competing with private enterprise.

The second condition is that we give the industry a more
efficient structure than it had before. There are certainly cases
where this is in theory possible – cases, that is, where larger
scale would be a positive advantage: where the average existing
scale is too small for maximum technical efficiency: where there
are too many small, non-specialised firms each producing a wide
range of output, and consequently gaining no advantages of
scale: and where competition is too imperfect to compel a greater
concentration.[1] In such cases, the public acquisition and subsequent amalgamation of a number of separate firms might
greatly improve the structural fitness of the industry.

I have no intention of drawing up a detailed list of industries
where such improvements might occur, having always thought

---

[1] Long-distance road haulage was such an example. Even the *Economist* now speaks
of 'the efficient and profitable trunk network that BRS made out of the patchwork
of haulage businesses it took over. The advantage of one such organisation covering
most of the country was slow to emerge but it has [now] been proven by experience.'
(9 July 1955.) But of course BRS has no monopoly of long-distance traffic – indeed
it is now an example of competitive public enterprise.

this a task for industrial experts rather than for laymen. But one interesting *prima facie* case may be quoted – the machine-tool industry. All the recommendations of the Anglo-American Productivity Report on this industry appear to point to the need for public intervention on the lines suggested – standardisation within and between companies, specialisation between companies, and a considerable reduction in the number of companies by absorption or amalgamation. The Report remarks that 'an efficient monopoly is of far more worth to a country than an inefficient highly competitive industry', and points out that in Russia and Germany a dictator, and in the U.S. the pressure of a few large users, were needed to impose standardisation on the machine-tool industries of those countries. This sounds like a remarkable justification for state intervention in a case where a competitive industry fails to adapt itself to an obviously more efficient structure.

At any rate, whatever industries are chosen, we should now have a definite preference for the 'competitive public enterprise' approach;[1] although there will occasionally be cases where state monopoly still provides the right answer. There are, it is true, some difficulties about the form of competitive public enterprise which is usually envisaged. But I leave a detailed discussion of the appropriate forms until after a consideration of the one remaining popular argument for rapid and large-scale nationalisation.

[1] Which is in any case a good Fabian concept. Shaw wrote in Fabian Tract No. 2, in 1884, that 'since Competition among producers admittedly secures to the public the most satisfactory products, the State should compete with all its might in every department of production'. This is the Tract which also contains his acid phrase about 'the division of society into hostile classes, with large appetites and no dinners at one extreme, and large dinners and no appetites at the other'.

XIX

—◇—

THE FORMS OF PUBLIC OWNERSHIP

1 *Nationalisation and Equality*

THIS last argument is in terms of the distribution of wealth, and is thus a reversion to the oldest (even pre-Marxist) argument for public ownership, namely as a means of appropriating the property income of the capitalist. Given that we pay full compensation, it relies on (*a*) the difference between the yields on gilt-edged and equities, (*b*) the fact that nationalisation precludes rising dividends and share values, and (*c*) occasionally, the lower level of salaries in the public sector.

'We [nationalise]', writes Mr. Strachey, 'in order to extinguish the great *unearned incomes* which are to-day derived, not from anything that those who draw them do, but from what they own. . . . The real purpose of socialization is to secure the proper distribution of the net national product among those who create it.'[1] On this view it is more or less irrelevant in what order industries are taken over. The approach is wholly *a priori*. We can dispense with detailed study of the structure, the performance, or the suitability for nationalisation of different industries, and concern ourselves solely with 'the pursuit of certain social and economic objectives, specific in the sense of being quite sharply definable but general in the sense of being quite external to any industry or service which it is proposed should change hands'.[2]

It would probably be conceded that nationalisation had not so far made much difference to equality. Some £2,100 millions

[1] 'The Objects of Further Socialization', *Political Quarterly*, January-March 1953.

[2] Jenkins, *Pursuit of Progress*, p. 101. I must confess at once that I at one time supported this approach (*Socialist Commentary*, February 1950).

of compensation stock was issued in respect of the industries nationalised from 1945 to 1951; it carried an average rate of interest of just over 3%, compared with a yield on ordinary shares during the critical years of 4½%. The incomes of the erstwhile owners thus dropped from some £95 millions to £63 millions per annum; allowing for taxation, the transfer of net income must have amounted to under £20 millions per annum. Even allowing for new borrowing at a cheaper rate, the whole transfer must have been rather small as a proportion of total personal incomes amounting (in 1951) to well over £12,000 millions per annum – certainly infinitesimal as compared with the effects of high taxation.

Nor was there much of a transfer in respect of new savings or capital gains. Once nationalised, the industries were forbidden to make large profits, and had instead (with one or two exceptions) to cover their capital programmes by borrowing from private investors in the open market. And the previous owners can hardly have forgone large gains. In the case of gas and electricity prices were already subject to regulation (and the owners were largely local authorities), in the case of the railways (which accounted for almost half the total compensation stock issued) the owners probably missed making capital losses rather than gains, and only briefly in steel (as the behaviour of steel shares since denationalisation shows) did they forgo any considerable capital profits.

However, it can quite well be argued that the experience of the 1945-51 industries is no guide to what might occur in future, at least in respect of capital profits – the income aspect would probably never be other than negligible.[1] The next group of industries, if we were to go by size (that is, the chemical, metal, and engineering industries), are distinctly more profitable than those already taken over; and with full employment and rapid growth the annual increase in the value of industrial capital will be larger than in the past. Under these circumstances private capital gains might well, over a period, be very considerable;[2] and the only effective method of preventing them, it is said, is by public ownership.

---

[1] Mr. Strachey's 'great unearned incomes' (that is, dividends on ordinary shares) are, after taxation, only some 3% of total net personal income.

[2] v. Chapter XIII, Section III.

Now the problem is not in question; indeed it has taken up a large part of three previous chapters.[1] But the discussion in those chapters showed that it was perfectly possible, even in a rapidly-growing economy, to limit the net rewards to shareholders by methods other than nationalisation (notably by a capital gains tax, and a system of corporate taxation designed to hold down distributions). And the experience of Norway and Sweden, much more egalitarian countries than our own, also proves that wholesale nationalisation is not a necessary condition of greater equality.

Why then should it be preferred to these other methods? Let us consider the implications of asserting such a preference. If it is meant seriously as a method of redistributing wealth, and not merely as a sop to the Party militants, nationalisation must first be fairly rapid, and secondly concentrate on the most prosperous industries where the largest capital gains are made. The first condition requires a return to the policy of taking over entire industries at a time, since only thus should we make any impression on property distribution within a measurable period. The second requires that the industries taken over shall be the largest and most efficient, showing the highest rates of increase of productivity and the fastest rates of expansion.[2] It follows that we must refurbish the 'list' approach discussed in the previous chapter; and each Labour programme must contain its quota of future state monopolies, chosen by no economic criteria (except that of profitability), but simply in order of size. So much is implicit in the view that the objectives of nationalisation are 'external to the industry which it is proposed should change hands'.

I believe that such a policy is both wrong and impracticable. It is impracticable for the obvious reason that the electorate, already suspicious, as the 1955 election showed, of proposals for nationalising efficient industries where no convincing case could be made out on economic grounds, would be rather intolerant towards it. And it is wrong because there is no guarantee that productive efficiency will not suffer. The obvious candidates

---

[1] *v.* Chapters XIII, XV, and XVII.

[2] Although this would mean that another egalitarian advantage sometimes mentioned, namely the disappearance of nepotism, would not be achieved. It is not in large joint-stock concerns such as these that nepotism flourishes, but in small family businesses (and in the City).

as judged by this approach (chemicals, vehicles, the electrical and engineering industries, etc.) are now performing tolerably well. They are mostly competitive industries, heavily engaged in the export market, enjoying reasonable labour relations, structurally well organised, and expansionist in outlook. They are not obviously suitable for wholesale nationalisation; and in the light of the unsolved problems in the existing public sector, the tendency towards centralisation, and the query still overhanging the level of managerial salaries, it is at least conceivable that their performance would deteriorate if they were to be taken rapidly into public ownership. None of this would matter quite so much if we had no balance of payments problem, and no urgent need for higher output. But in fact we have both; and since these are precisely the industries on which our export performance primarily depends, and which are currently responsible for the greater part of the annual rise in output, it seems rather frivolous to propose that they should be nationalised on the scale, and at the speed, required to make a visible impact on income-distribution.

Competitive public enterprise, on the other hand, which was adopted by the Party precisely in order to avoid these difficulties, would have only a marginal effect on income-distribution. First, if we confine ourselves to single firms, and especially in the light of the practical difficulties of choosing and justifying the choice of firms – these are discussed below – progress would inevitably be slow as judged by the proportion of total industrial capital involved. Secondly, since proposals for competitive public enterprise are supposed to justify themselves on grounds of efficiency, it follows that they would apply mainly to those industries where the smallest, and not the largest, capital gains were being made. The two sets of criteria are thus in conflict; and it is inconsistent (though very common) to stress the egalitarian argument, and say that it 'demands a much more vigorous and far-reaching nationalisation policy',[1] and then to abjure the rapid creation of State monopolies and take refuge in the inevitably much slower policy of selecting individual firms. This would merely lead to general discontent when it was found that a deception had been practised, and that nothing whatever was happening to the division of incomes.

Naturally if we accept, as probably most people in the Party

[1] Jenkins, op. cit., p. 104.

now do,[1] that we cannot go bull-headed at nationalisation without regard to the economic consequences, this does not mean that we must passively endure a prodigious annual increase in private property values. It simply means that we must adopt instead the various alternative proposals discussed in previous chapters.

II *Competitive Public Enterprise*

However, even though these proposals could, if adopted, quite well prevent the maldistribution of wealth from getting rapidly worse as a direct result of economic growth, yet some accretion to the real value of private property is likely as a result of growth; and any such accretion is to be deplored so long as private property remains distributed as it is to-day.

But the problem is then fundamentally one of the distribution of property: of how to redistribute existing property, both for its own sake and in order that future increases in its value may be more equally distributed, and how to ensure that new savings, and the capital which they create, are also better distributed than now. Clearly there are many other ways of doing this besides nationalisation; and in so far as nationalisation is one way, it need not take the form, in order to achieve this object, of the compulsory purchase of an entire unit of production, a firm or an industry. It is now the individual ownership, and not the productive unit, that we are concerned with: the title-deeds, and not the physical assets: simply ownership, and not control. Indeed it becomes, from this point of view, a tiresome and unnecessary nuisance to be saddled with control.

The other methods of redistributing property have already been discussed. It can be directly transferred to the State by death-duties, a tax on gifts, and a capital tax. The ratio of new public

---

[1] 'We advocate nationalization only for those industries where the immediate national need makes the case overwhelming. Increased production . . . must remain our main concern, and the extensions of public ownership which we propose are, therefore, limited to those which are essential to the fulfilment of this prime purpose.' (*Challenge to Britain.*) 'It [the balance of payments] must have priority. . . . We must, willy nilly, concentrate for the present largely on the productivity issue. . . . Projects of nationalisation and ambitious welfare plans should give place to insistence on abolishing large fortunes. . . . There will be no nationalisation for the sake of nationalisation.' (G. D. H. Cole, *New Statesman*, 21 November 1953.)

to private savings can be increased by Budget surpluses, heavy taxation of company profits, and allowing the existing nation-alised industries to accumulate a surplus. The ratio of small to large property holdings can be increased by measures to en-courage working-class savings, by inserting the 'legacy' principle into the death-duties, by effective profit-sharing schemes, and (indirectly) by the growth of pension and other eleemosynary funds. All these are alternatives to nationalisation, which need no longer be seen as the one and only large-scale method of redistri-buting the benefits of economic growth.

Even so far as nationalisation is concerned, any method by which the community (or the working class) acquires a capital stake in economic growth is equally efficacious; since the object is not to acquire control, we need not confine ourselves to the compulsory purchase of whole firms. However, since the previous chapter made out a case for sometimes doing this on economic grounds, I shall first consider how 'competitive public enterprise' might work in practice: and then turn to other methods of increasing the community's ownership of capital assets.

There would be no insuperable problems in running a com-petitive public unit, once it was chosen or set up. The main essential would be to establish at the start the right conditions for efficiency. The first is a competitive level of managerial salaries. The second, since the whole *raison d'être* of these companies is the need for greater entrepreneurial initiative than was previously being shown, is the maximum degree of freedom and independ-ence in their day-to-day affairs. They should certainly not be subject to detailed Parliamentary control; and although they should consult the Minister on matters of importance, as the board of a private company might consult a dominant shareholder, and be subject to his directives on major points of policy, this must not extend to the point where decisions are normally taken in White-hall. Suggestions for a special and active Control Board, or for constant meetings between the different State directors to concert a common policy, are quite inappropriate. State enterprises should be as free to develop as private enterprises. They must be able to use their profits for new investment, to negotiate wages and conditions in the ordinary way, and to decide their price and output policies subject only to any planning controls which apply to the whole of the industry; to these, of course, they will be more than usually susceptible, and indeed a useful instrument for making them effective.

Naturally, since public money is involved, there must be some public accountability. But the degree of supervision (theoretically) exercised by Parliament over the Royal Ordnance Factories would be wholly excessive in this case; while Parliamentary time would not permit an annual debate on each concern such as now takes place on each nationalised industry. It has been suggested that a holding company might be set up, containing Members of Parliament and representatives of both sides of industry; it would hold the shares of all the companies, and employ experts where necessary to supervise or examine their activities, just as a finance house or the I.C.F.C. employs experts to watch over concerns to which they are heavily committed. A better suggestion is for a new Public Corporation, responsible for all the state companies, bearing the same relation to Parliament as the existing public boards, but acting otherwise as a rather passive holding company. At any rate, the bias must always be towards the maximum of independence, and the minimum of central interference.

Where a number of firms in the same industry are taken over, the case is different, and some co-ordinating body will clearly be required. Development Councils have not proved a great success; and a less cumbersome solution would again be a public holding company on the lines of the Iron and Steel Corporation, holding the shares in the public companies, and with strong powers of control over the private ones. But of course separate legislation will be needed whenever a number of firms in the same industry are nationalised together, and the whole balance of ownership changed; each such case can therefore be treated empirically, and if need be differently, as it comes along.

The next condition is that competition between public and private firms should be, and should be seen to be, scrupulously fair. There must be no favouritism in the allocation of contracts, raw materials or labour; comparative performance must be the sole test – if the public companies cannot compete on equal terms, they do not deserve to be set up. This also means that new capital should not be supplied on tap from the Treasury at gilt-edged rates, as it has been to some of the nationalised industries. Private firms must borrow from the market; the State concerns should borrow from a public finance body (to be discussed later) which charges full market rates, and applies normal commercial conditions.

The new companies would thus hold a position rather like that of Short Brothers. Although the Government has a controlling interest in the equity, the Ministry of Supply controls the appointment of directors, and the Under-Secretary of State is *ex officio* a director, yet the firm operates on a wholly commercial basis, enjoying no favouritism and subject to no more controls than the rest of the aircraft industry.

III *The Difficulties; and Alternative Methods*

There seems to be no insoluble difficulty about running State companies in competition with private industry; indeed many such companies already exist, and operate successfully, in other countries (notably Sweden and France).[1] The real difficulty is a different one, namely, how they are to be chosen and set up in the first place, and how the choice of this one rather than that should be justified. This difficulty has hardly arisen so far. In France, where most of the firms were taken over immediately after the war, the choice was usually justified by special wartime factors (e.g. a collaborationist owner). In Sweden (where almost all the companies have in fact been set up by Conservative governments), the choice was invariably dictated by considerations external to the industry – the need to raise government revenue, or social-moral reasons, or local unemployment. In the U.K. the acquisition of Short Brothers was justified by imperative wartime needs, and in the U.S.A. the establishment of T.V.A. on anti-depression grounds.

First, under what legislation are the companies to be set up or

[1] In Sweden the state companies include (besides the monopoly of tobacco manufacture and liquor import and distribution) a bank, a chain of restaurants, a large iron and steel works, saw and pulp mills, shale oil production, peat production, and bus services. In France the state owns many of the largest banks and insurance companies, the Renault Company, the S.N.E.C.M.A. (the largest aircraft firm), the Berliet factory, and numerous printing works; while there are more than 40 mixed enterprises, in which the State's participation ranges from 99% to 3%, in such diverse industries as film production, broadcasting, chemicals, news agency, oil distribution, and the merchant marine. (*v. Problems of Nationalized Industry*, ed. W. A. Robson, Allen and Unwin, 1952, pp. 245 seq.) Even the U.S. has its State company – the T.V.A. – which competes at many points with private enterprise, and most successfully.

acquired? Where most of the firms in an industry are acquired, a separate Bill will no doubt be needed on each occasion. But where it is a case of acquiring (or establishing) a single concern, it would be most extravagant of Parliamentary time, and dampening to the spirit of enterprise, if a new Bill had to be introduced for each concern. Clearly some general enabling legislation is called for. It would probably not be impossible to draft a State Companies Act, containing a broad definition of the public interest (such as that embodied in the Monopolies Act), and giving the Government powers, subject to an affirmative resolution in both Houses of Parliament or the recommendation of a new independent commission, to acquire existing or establish new industrial enterprises.

The real difficulty is not that of framing the legislation, but of choosing the companies to be acquired, and then justifying the choice to public opinion. The problem arises because the acquisition is compulsory and backed by legislation, and because it involves discrimination between individual firms in the same industry. This goes against our legislative tradition, as we saw from the experience of physical controls and raw material allocations, which even a Labour Government with a huge majority was unwilling to operate in a discriminatory manner as between individual firms. To say that we shall compulsorily nationalise one chemical firm rather than another, or this aircraft firm rather than that, will be attacked as unfair, arbitrary, and dictated by political and not economic motives.

The ideal approach, which would avoid both the element of compulsion and the charge of non-commercial motives, would be to establish a State investment-trust, provided with public funds but independent of the Government, with instructions simply to make a profit by buying, establishing, or selling productive concerns. It would act, in effect, like a take-over bidder, seeking out inefficient firms, assets that were wrongly or under-utilised, slothful managements, and opportunities for new production; indeed it would be a public version of a composite picture of Messrs. Drayton, Wolfson, Samuel, and Clore. Its choice of firms to acquire would be justified on clear commercial principles; and no question of compulsory, legislative discrimination would arise.

The same end could be partially achieved, and the difficulties similarly avoided, if a government investment corporation were to be established along the lines proposed in Chapter XVII. (This would also be the obvious body to provide new capital to any separate State companies which were set up.) It would have the object, not of itself engaging in production, nor even of exercising control, but of providing capital where this was not easily forth-coming from private sources; and its operations might well be, indeed almost automatically would be, slanted towards industries whose rate of expansion or level of efficiency appeared inadequate. It would often operate by providing capital to new groups or individuals wishing to venture into such industries; and in this way it would foster at least part-public competitive enterprise where this was most needed.

An alternative method, similarly non-compulsory and justified on commercial grounds, would be to encourage the horizontal expansion of existing non-governmental but socially-owned organisations. The existing nationalised industries, for example, surely offer distinct scope. They already own substantial productive capacity outside, though allied to, their own main lines of production: land, coke-ovens, brick-manufacturing capacity, by-product plant, hotels, locomotive and wagon manufacturing factories, etc.[1] Private firms of far smaller size are constantly seeking to extend their interests and diversify their output. In Sweden the State railways have acquired bus companies, and the State forestry undertaking pulp and saw mills, without the need for fresh legislation. The tendency in Britain has so far been either to 'hive off', or at any rate somewhat to neglect (like the Coal Board with its brick-making), operations that did not seem central; and this was understandable in the early and difficult days of re-organisation. But now that matters are more settled, there is a strong case for allowing the Nationalised Boards (though subject to firm guarantees about decentralisation) to expand horizontally, by purchasing or establishing subsidiary undertakings, in exactly the same way as any private firm can do.[2]

[1] The British Transport Commission, through its ownership of the former Tilling and S.M.T. groups and its part-shareholding in a number of B.E.T. subsidiaries (and of course through London Transport), already owns a significant part of the bus industry. But this is less deliberate policy than an accidental result of nationalisation stopped mid-way by a Conservative Government.

[2] Or, sometimes, vertically. The Milk Marketing Board has recently announced that it proposes to set up its own retail outlets (i.e. milk-bars) – a minor but admirable precedent!

There is no reason in logic why public industries alone should be debarred from the normal commercial right to expand and diversify.[1]

The Co-operative Movement provides another possible vehicle of advance. In Sweden the most spectacular examples of competitive social enterprise have come from the Co-operatives rather than from the Government. The British movement has perhaps been somewhat less venturesome. But it has large resources; and a more audacious attitude to risk-taking might produce a large increase in competitive social enterprise in many different spheres.[2] However, Co-operative commercial policy is now under examination by an independent Commission; and a clarification may have to await its report.

Even the Trade Unions, in certain other countries, indulge in competitive enterprise. In Sweden they own one of the most lavish and up-to-date hotels in Stockholm; and the building Unions are responsible for a significant proportion of new housing. In the U.S. also a number of Unions (notably the Garment Workers) have built new housing estates (mainly, though not solely, for their own members). The British building Unions have, it is true, a rather unhappy memory of experiments in co-operative production; but now that economic conditions are more favourable, and since the building industry is quite unsuitable for wholesale nationalisation, perhaps the time has come for a renewed experiment.

We sometimes forget that the local authorities were considerable commercial undertakings before they lost their gas and electricity enterprises. It seems a pity that they are not more willing to branch out into new spheres,[3] since there are some (services rather than manufacturing) which seem eminently suitable for local enterprise – e.g. district heating, underground garages, the retailing of domestic fuel appliances,[4] cinemas,

---

[1] But this would require a change in price policy, in any case justified on other grounds, to enable the Boards to build up substantial reserves. It would be very undesirable to insist that all such operations should be financed by Treasury loans.

[2] The Co-operative Insurance Society, almost the most efficient in the insurance business, is an excellent example of what can be done.

[3] Though it would need a Local Authorities Enabling Bill, of the sort that the Labour Party used regularly to press for before the war, if they were to do so on any scale.

[4] As proposed by Mr. Little in *The Price of Fuel* (p. 130).

laundries, restaurants, hotels,[1] etc., quite apart from the municip-
alisation of blocks of rented property. Any efficient expansion in
these directions would be welcome, though it seems unlikely to
occur on a lavish scale – the impetus once given by Joseph
Chamberlain and the Webbs appears to have exhausted itself.

We also forget that the area of socially-owned land is gradually
rising, not as a result of direct purchase by the central State, but
through the decentralised activities of other public bodies – the
Forestry Commission, the New Towns, the Crown Land Commissioners, the local authorities, the National Trust, and so on.
This is an excellent example of how social ownership can grow
without the attendant disadvantages of state monopoly.

All these other and more indirect types of social enterprise are
ideally to be preferred to direct action by the State. They involve
less danger of bureaucracy and Whitehall control; they avoid the
accusation of arbitrary discrimination; and they can be justified
on strict commercial grounds. There will often be cases, naturally,
where direct State action is desirable; though even here the establishment of a new venture is always to be preferred to the compulsory acquisition of an existing one. But generally one should
envisage competitive public enterprise at least as much in terms
of these more variegated forms of social ownership, as of ownership by Whitehall.

IV *The Ultimate Objective*

The notion of competitive public enterprise implies a desire to
control the use to which certain physical assets are put. But from
the point of view of the distribution of property and new savings,
the question of control is irrelevant. It is quite sufficient to own
the shares; and it makes no difference how haphazardly these are
scattered amongst different companies.

Public share-ownership can be fostered in a number of ways,
most of them already discussed. A government investment corporation, acting as lender of last resort to the whole economy,
would gradually build up a large portfolio of stock (as well as

[1] It is curious that despite the low standard of much of our hotel accommodation
and its physical inadequacy at the peak of the tourist season, we should have been
so much more timid in this direction even than Franco Spain, where the Paradors
are an excellent example of public enterprise.

loans). The Death-duty Commissioners proposed in Chapter XII would steadily create a highly prosperous investment trust; their objective would be to maximise income and capital gains, and in so doing they would counter any danger that the state might land itself only with the crocks and liabilities. And, lastly, there might be a case where the State itself supplies public funds which help to augment the capital assets of an industry, for demanding a share of the equity in part-payment.

But we want not only a larger stake in industry for the State, but also a wide diffusion of property amongst individuals. We should therefore welcome effective profit-sharing, and the indirect diffusion which goes with the growth of pension funds, workers' share banks, educational foundations, and charitable trusts. The objective is not wholly to destroy private ownership, but to alter its distribution.

The ideal (or at least my ideal) is a society in which ownership is thoroughly mixed-up – a society with a diverse, diffused, pluralist, and heterogeneous pattern of ownership, with the State, the nationalised industries, the Co-operatives, the Unions, Government financial institutions, pensions funds, foundations, and millions of private families all participating. Since this is still a long way off, we need heavy taxation to limit profits and dividends. And it may be an unpopular solution amongst the traditionalists, who still want (or will be made to want by *ad captandum* speeches) the steady creation of State monopolies.[1]

But it is too late to settle these matters now by evocations of the spirit of Keir Hardie. We no doubt want more nationalisation than we now have. But I at least do not want a steadily extending chain of State monopolies, believing this to be bad for liberty, and wholly irrelevant to socialism as defined in this book. State ownership of all industrial capital is not now a condition of creating a socialist society, establishing social equality, increasing social welfare, or eliminating class distinctions. What is unjust in our present arrangements is the distribution of private wealth; and that can as well be cured in a pluralist as in a wholly State-owned economy, with much better results for social contentment and the fragmentation of power.

[1] Though it is interesting that the British Labour Party is almost the only important social-democratic party in the world in which a strong desire for wholesale nationalisation still exists.

XX

THE ROLE OF PLANNING

I *The Diminishing Area of Controversy*

THE immediate post-war, like the immediate pre-war, generation of socialists, though for different reasons, thought of planning as a central feature of socialism, indeed as constituting one of the most direct antitheses between socialism and capitalism. Before the 1930s, on the other hand, the word was scarcely mentioned, and the concept played an altogether minor role in the history of socialist thought.[1] To-day we can compromise – discuss it, certainly, but relegate it to a lower priority than it enjoyed a decade ago.

The reason for this demotion is partly that most people now recognise how little there is to be said on the subject in general terms – or at least in general terms that are not abstract to the point of futility. We have grown rather less assured than we used to be in the face both of our limited knowledge of how the economic system works, and of the number and heterogeneity of the variables to be taken into account. Most of what can usefully be said is *ad hoc* to specific situations rather than deducible from, or assimilable to, a generalised theory.

Secondly, in so far as the matter is still discussed in general terms, the vigour has rather gone out of the debate; for practical experience has gradually obliterated the two extreme positions. Most people have moved towards the centre; and the debate is no longer an *a priori* one, conducted in terms of fundamental first principles, but an empirical one, in terms of rather more or rather less in particular situations.

---

[1] *v.* Chapter III, Section II.

Thus Right-wing views on planning have undergone a pronounced modification. On the academic level, few serious economists now believe that a free price-mechanism leads in practice to a maximisation of economic welfare.[1] Not only are the 'optimum conditions of production and exchange', which would theoretically maximise welfare, quite impossible of fulfilment in any highly industrialised economy, but the result would in any case only be 'optimum' in relation to a given distribution of income; and if people object, as socialists do, to the existing distribution, they could not consider welfare to be maximised even if these conditions were to be fulfilled.[2]

The business world has also lost much of its ideological attachment to *laisser-faire*, and certainly has no desire to go back to the 1930s. Much as it dislikes detailed controls and high taxation, it now concedes that the government has a clear responsibility to intervene to whatever extent is required to maintain full employment (and hence high profits). In many industries an even wider governmental responsibility is accepted. It is not thought curious that the state should concern itself with the capacity of the steel industry, or be asked to aid industries which find themselves in export difficulties – cotton textile employers, for example, think it a scandal that the government declines to accept full responsibility for the level of their output. Generally, as Chapter I has shown, private business now finds it quite natural that Whitehall should intervene in the economy to a degree which would have been thought outrageous a generation ago.

Indeed it constitutes a major victory for the Left, the significance of which is grossly underestimated by those with short memories, that the majority of Conservatives to-day would probably concede the right, indeed the duty, of the State to hold itself responsible for (1) the level of employment, (2) the protection of the foreign balance by methods other than deflation, (3) the level of investment and the rate of growth, (4) the maintenance of a welfare minimum, and (5) the conditions under which monopolies should be allowed to operate. This is a far cry from the obscurantism of the Tory Party twenty years ago.

[1] *v.* I. M. D. Little, *A Critique of Welfare Economics* (O.U.P., 1950), for a detailed statement of the argument.

[2] This point is still consistently ignored by journals such as the *Economist* (not to mention less elevated papers), where the 'efficiency' of Budgetary and other changes is always discussed without any regard to their distributive effects.

Lastly, no one of any standing now believes the once-popular Hayek thesis that any interference with the market mechanism must start us down the slippery slope that leads to totalitarianism.[1] This was an unplausible enough view, in a British context, even when it was first advanced; it has been thoroughly discredited now that we have experienced a decade of varying degrees of government control, with no sign of a weakening of our democratic fibre.

Socialist views on planning have been similarly modified. The pre-war argument, based as it was on the combination of manifest inefficiency and glaring inequality displayed by the capitalism of the 1930s, has in any case lost much of its force in the expansionist full employment economy and the Welfare State of the 1950s. And the extreme post-war argument has also fallen rather out of fashion. This was based on a different set of considerations, relating primarily to the dollar shortage and the balance of payments, and the apparent need to allocate resources by detailed physical controls if social justice and external solvency were to be combined in a siege economy. The change in opinion is due partly to the easing of the world economic situation as the post-war crisis years gave way to more normal conditions, and in particular as the American economy came to bely the worst fears expressed about it just after the war: but mainly to a general disillusionment with the whole notion of trying to control short-term production decisions from Whitehall through a detailed budget of production.[2]

This necessarily involves an intricate complex of licensing, rationing, and allocation controls; and these were increasingly seen to have serious drawbacks. They deny the consumer a free choice of goods and suppliers. They are highly unpopular, as was clearly shown by the public reaction to derationing. They involve an excessive growth of bureaucracy, with its concomitant dangers of petty tyranny, graft, and corruption.

And they are often economically inefficient. Not only do the planners often make mistakes, so that bottlenecks are created because the production budgets are not internally consistent; but there are also in practice more inescapable weaknesses. Thus raw material allocations, being inevitably, for political reasons,

---

[1] v. F. A. Hayek, *The Road to Serfdom* (Routledge, 1944).

[2] For an excellent discussion of this point, v. Jenkins, op. cit., Ch. V.

non-discriminatory and therefore based on past performance, simply perpetuate the *status quo*, discourage new entry, and protect the less efficient firms from the competition of the more efficient. Price and investment controls (even if the former lead to no deterioration in quality), since they tend to be more effective the simpler and more essential the goods, often create a situation in which wages and profits are higher in the less essential than in the more essential sectors of the economy; and resources are attracted in completely the wrong directions – from new housing to miscellaneous repair work, utility to non-utility textiles, and so on. Many controls, moreover, are impossible to operate effectively once supplies become plentiful; they can be too easily circumvented, and a 'grey' market develops (as happened at different times with commodities as various as steel and eggs). And in the end a detailed attempt to plan the output of different industries is bound to fail unless backed by direction of labour; and this no one was willing to countenance as a permanent measure.

There has thus been, on both sides, a declining tendency to take up extreme positions; and the issue of planning (as opposed to the objectives of planning) is not now one of the fundamental differences between Left and Right.[1] Naturally important differences of emphasis remain, productive of much political heat. But generally the issue now is not whether, but how much and for what purpose, to plan.

II   *Political Limitations on Effective Planning*

Most of what I want to say about planning has already been said in previous chapters. Its prime function is to ensure that the right quantities of resources are allocated to each of the main sectors of the economy, and that these quantities add up to a full employment but non-inflationary level of demand. I do not mean to imply that the government can precisely control what proportion of the national product will next year be devoted to exports, investment, consumption, and so on. But it can influence these proportions in broad terms; and in some cases, where it is itself

[1] Not that it ever really was, in the light of the detailed planning practised by the Nazi Government.

the consumer or the source of funds, it can determine them fairly exactly.

The main objectives of planning, as outlined in this book, are then a steadily rising level of investment, and a sufficient volume of savings and risk-capital to match it: a volume of home demand which does not pre-empt goods away from export: a situation in the labour market which does not give rise to a wage-price spiral: and an increase in the proportion of the national income devoted to social expenditure – all these to be achieved against a background of growing social equality. Of course none of these will occur automatically. They will require a variety of planning policies, already discussed under the separate heads: above all, a skilful and determined fiscal policy, as well as other subsidiary controls where necessary; for with a lazy fiscal policy, low taxation and little governmental planning, the tendency is always for personal consumption to absorb too high a proportion of resources relative to these other claims.

What stands in the way of successful planning to attain these objectives (and also those to be discussed in the next section)? People are sometimes very critical of the planning performance of post-war Labour Governments, and suggest that major changes in policy will be needed when we next come back to power. Certainly there were weaknesses in post-war planning; but it is important to decide exactly where they lay.

It is often said that the essential deficiency was the lack of statistical information: or that it lay in the number, or the economic sophistication, or the political outlook, of the government planning staff: or in the administrative machinery of planning (i.e. in the organisation of government departments): or in the actual controls or techniques available. And no doubt there were weaknesses in some or all of these respects; and useful improvements could be made in future.

Yet I doubt if any of these was, or will be in the future, the crucial limiting influence. Experience shows that those Ministers prepared to plan could do so effectively despite all these deficiencies; and those who were not, would still not even if all the deficiencies were cured. The vital lack, in nine cases out of ten, and of course far more typically under a Conservative than a Labour Government, is in will-power and determination – in the face of vested interests, pressure groups, indifference, electoral opinion, and back-bench revolts. That is, the failure was essentially a *political* one, which reflects the difficulty of planning in a democratic society. If socialists want bolder planning, they must choose bolder Ministers and – just as important – themselves accept a greater degree of self-restraint when the results of planning impinge unpleasantly, as they often will, on their constituents or their own pet spheres of interest. What is wanted now is the political vigour and will-power, and a readiness to take unpopular decisions. This is why it is largely a waste of time to write in detail about the problems of economic planning – the time to do that will be when the willingness to plan has outrun the techniques. And this is also why it is sad that those on the Left most vocal in calling for more vigorous planning, are often those least willing to preach unpalatable economic truths to the rank-and-file of the Party.

III   *How Much Planning?*

But if we achieve the prime objective of successful planning, namely, to get the right distribution of resources between the main sectors of the economy within a framework of non-inflationary full employment, I doubt if we want too much detailed planning *within* each sector.[1] For reasons explained above, the post-war attempts at detailed planning of production and investment decisions were not a great success; and in any case, as is made clear elsewhere in this book, the traditional socialist case for such planning, based on an assumed divergence between production for profit and production for use, has much less application at present levels of material welfare.

The price-mechanism is now a reasonably satisfactory method of distributing the great bulk of consumer-goods and industrial capital-goods, given the total amount of resources available for consumption and industrial investment.[2] The consumer is the best judge of how to spend his money; and even if he were not,

[1] The condition of non-inflationary full employment is of course vital. If we have excess demand, all manner of detailed controls may become necessary which otherwise are better avoided.

[2] I am ignoring here the non-controversial arguments for intervention relating to health and hygiene.

the principle of individual liberty would still require that he should be left free to spend it, subject only to the social service considerations discussed in Chapter V.[1] This does not mean that the distribution of goods *between* individuals will be ideal: on the contrary, it will not, for purchasing power is still too unequally distributed. But that inequality must be corrected directly by attacking the distribution of wealth; and at any given distribution, save in periods of exceptional crisis or acute shortage, people should now be left free to spend their incomes as they choose. Production for use and production for profit may be taken as broadly coinciding now that working-class purchasing power is so high. What is profitable is what the consumer finds useful; and the firm and the consumer desire broadly the same allocation of resources. And while paternalists may dislike this allocation, wishing that less were spent on drink and pools and television sets, they must swallow their dislike in the interests of personal freedom.

Nevertheless, there will be cases where the government wishes to intervene to override the market allocation of resources within the total allotted to a particular sector: that is, where it decrees that there shall be less of this consumption-good and more of that, or (more commonly) less investment in this direction and more in that. One cannot list such cases by reference to general *a priori* principles. The only sensible approach is a strictly empirical one, which concedes on the one hand that the price-mechanism does not work in so marvellous a welfare-maximising way that we shall jeopardise some optimum conditions, or risk upsetting a delicate mechanism, by intervening: but that on the other hand it does work in a general way to produce those goods which the consumer or investor wants, so that intervention must be justified by evidence either that what is being produced is obviously against the public interest, or that the producer is not correctly interpreting the future course of demand.

Socialists often rely on the latter argument, maintaining that industrial investment should be planned from Whitehall (i.e. its distribution between industries determined) on the grounds that the government planners have better information, or a wider

---

[1] These might be held, for example, to justify a subsidy on milk, or rent controls, or the deliberate cheapening of certain goods to old-age pensioners or national assistance beneficiaries.

insight, about future demand than a private industry can have.

Now the planners, if not the politicians, may certainly be expected to have a better idea than private industry of the future rate of growth of the economy as a whole. It follows that in the case of commodities for which demand varies directly with incomes and output – commodities, that is, subject to little cross-elasticity of demand or possibility of substitution (e.g. fuel as a whole, or transport, or steel) – the Government will normally be able to take a sounder view.

But where future demand does not vary directly with output, and possibilities exist of substitution, a change in consumers' tastes, or export fluctuations, the matter is not so clear. Moreover, even in relatively simple cases where the possibilities of substitution are restricted (road versus rail, or different kinds of fuel), and where therefore the central planners themselves may have a perfectly sound view of future demand, effective planning may still be frustrated either because Ministers, or other Departments, or nationalised industries, ignore this view: or because the Government fails to act on it for the political reasons mentioned in the previous section.

Such examples are plentiful. For instance, the short-term objectives of fuel and power planning in the post-war period were reasonably clear. Yet the Government failed, largely for political reasons, to enforce these objectives by co-ordinating the plans of the different nationalised industries. The various road plans, if they can be so designated, are an even more disturbing example. Not only are they founded on no long-term planned assessment of future demand and costs, but they are also a hotch-potch of unco-ordinated schemes given different orders of priority each time the government changes – consider the sad history of the Severn Bridge. Even the present rail plan, although it seems internally quite rational, is not based on any planned economic relationship between road and rail. And the government planning staff appear to have had no influence on either the rail or the road plan.

It follows that planning intervention on grounds of 'superior knowledge' will be justified only if two conditions are fulfilled. (1) The Government must have an obviously clearer view of future demand than private industry; there is no reason why this should normally be true of the great bulk of industries producing ultimately for a free consumer and export market. (2) Even where this condition is fulfilled (that is, in the case of basic commodities whose required growth is broadly related to total growth), we need the further condition that Ministers should in fact accept the view of the central planners, and enforce it (on other Government Departments and the nationalised industries as well as in Parliament) in the face of the political obstacles described in Section II.

But this second condition is much more relevant to the question of planning within the public sector, than to the question of extending planning further over the private sector; for the commodities or industries most obviously concerned – coal, gas, electricity, railways, and roads – are already fully under public ownership.

IV   *The Proper Objectives of Planning*

The case for further intervention in the private sector is normally different. It arises first when the government is willing, but private enterprise is not, to shoulder the risks of expansion: and secondly where divergences arise between private and social cost.

On the first point, there are certain industries which require an exceptionally large amount of capital (and managerial skill) per unit of output; and these are normally the basic industries, whose expansion is a prior condition of expansion in the rest of the economy. This high ratio of fixed capital to output means first that they find it difficult to expand production quickly to meet a sudden rise in demand: and secondly that the risks of long-term expansion, owing to the heavy cost of excess capacity, appear particularly heavy. Thus a fully integrated steel plant costs about 600 times as much to build as a medium-sized factory; and overheads cannot be covered unless the plant is continuously operated at very near full capacity. Businessmen will then want an unusually high degree of assurance about future demand before embarking on large new capital schemes; and they may tend, as the British steel masters have done, to be too cautious, and always lag one step behind the rise in demand. It pays them better to make mistakes in this direction; and the result is a constant tendency to insufficient capacity – even though government and industry may privately agree in their respective projections of future demand.

The importance to the economy of such cases is sometimes overwhelming; and it must be a government responsibility to ensure, where necessary by nationalisation, that the industrial base, characteristically composed of industries such as these, expands fast enough to support the expected rise in total output. But intervention need not be confined to the basic industries. The government should stand ready, by the use of subsidies, guarantees, bulk purchases, or any other method, to shoulder part or all of the risk in any case where it is clear that expansion is required, but where private capital will not venture alone to undertake it. Since the end of the war, the production of aircraft, films, sulphur, hydraulic presses, and titanium have all been encouraged in this way; and this reserve, selective power to foster particularly essential expansion is the most useful aspect of detailed economic planning.

The other group of cases where intervention is often desirable is where private and social costs diverge – where, that is, the costs borne by, or gains accruing to, the community from a particular line of action are not fully reflected in the balance-sheet of the private (or nationalised) unit. This is the oldest of the economist's justifications for state intervention.

An obvious example of this divergence is the location of new factories. When a firm leaves one area and migrates to another, it involves the community in all sorts of costs and gains – in the one area, perhaps unemployment, or an unbalanced labour force, or wasted capital capacity (in social capital or public utilities): in the other, perhaps acute labour scarcity, traffic congestion, urban sprawl, and so on. There is a clear case here for vigorous planning – indeed without it in the immediate post-war years we might well have had serious unemployment in the Development Areas; and the lack of it now is helping to ensure that traffic in London and Birmingham gradually grinds to a standstill.[1]

Another case where private cost fails to reflect the national interest is where the anticipated profit from an 'essential' investment is quantitatively insignificant to the individual firm, and

---

[1] This links up with the question of 'social', or town and country, planning, which is discussed in the next chapter.

scarcely worth the bother; yet, taking the whole of industry together, the total result of such investments would be of major importance. This is the case, for example, with coal economy. Fuel costs are usually a very small fraction of total costs, and the reduction in costs and increase in net profits to be expected from installing fuel-saving equipment seem insignificant to the individual business; and the investment is not made. Yet if the whole of industry installed such equipment, the resultant saving of coal would be of considerable significance to the national economy. Government intervention is fully justified in cases such as this.

Balance of payments factors may also cause private and social cost to diverge. The desirability or otherwise of particular categories or amounts of imports, exports or import-saving output may be affected by considerations of bilateral trade, or foreign policy, or colonial policy (as with synthetic rubber), or the prospect of holding a particular exchange-rate, or a scarcity of particular currencies. And, lastly, I say nothing of the traditional cases of 'social costs', such as smog, river pollution, and the like; these are now on the whole non-controversial.

It will be seen how little can be said in general terms. Occasionally the divergence between private and social cost will be so glaring that everyone agrees. Occasionally expansion is obviously called for, which the industry itself is unwilling to undertake. Occasionally the Government can take a clearer or more enlightened view than private industry.

This certainly does not add up to an argument for a detailed, overall government plan embracing every industry, least of all in an export-oriented economy like our own. Remaining severely empirical, the Government must simply stand ready first to intervene negatively to stop industry from acting manifestly against the public interest: secondly, and of far greater importance, to intervene positively to secure expansion – to search out the weak spots, especially in the basic industries, and concentrate on these with all the vigour at its command. If it fulfils this positive role of enlarging the industrial base – indeed if it achieves the central, overriding objective of getting sufficient coal and steel – the remaining 90% of the economy can increasingly be left to look after itself now that we are moving from a subsistence to an abundant society.

But the whole question of the distribution of output *within* the

main components of demand – consumption, industrial investment, government expenditure, and so on – is of infinitely less
significance than the question discussed in Section II: of how to
allocate the right *totals* to each of these components – how to
ensure sufficiently high investment, exports, and social expenditure without inflation. That remains the essential role of planning; and only if we carry out that role successfully shall we
extricate ourselves from the intolerable situation in which the
economy lurches from one inflationary crisis to another, each
met by haphazard and damaging panic measures. But better
planning in this respect will not be much assisted, as was made
clear earlier, by chapters, or even books, on planning. It mainly
requires Ministers endowed with the inflexible will and resolution of a Stafford Cripps, and political parties ready to back
them loyally both in Parliament and the constituencies.

XXI

―――――――――

CONCLUSION

1 *The Issues of the Future*

As our traditional objectives are gradually fulfilled, and
society becomes more social-democratic with the passing of
the old injustices, we shall turn our attention increasingly to
other, and in the long run more important, spheres – of personal
freedom, happiness, and cultural endeavour: the cultivation of
leisure, beauty, grace, gaiety, excitement, and of all the proper
pursuits, whether elevated, vulgar, or eccentric, which contribute
to the varied fabric of a full private and family life.

There are, after all, not one, but two good reasons for being
a reformer, and on the Left. The first is a belief in the benefits of
socialism. But there are many changes in society which an idealistic reformer might wish to make, but which are not to be
subsumed under any defensible definition of socialism. And one
is also on the Left, and a Labour supporter, because as a matter
of experience most of those advocating such changes are to be
found on the Left, and those opposing them on the Right.

It would be amazing if every important issue of public concern
could be embraced in a socialist-capitalist controversy, or within
some definition of socialism. Socialist aspirations were first
formulated over 100 years ago. Some remain urgently relevant,
and have formed the substance of this book. Others have lost
their relevance through being largely fulfilled. But of course new
issues, not then foreseen, and increasingly important as the old

evils are conquered, have arisen since; and they may be highly significant for welfare, freedom, and social justice, even though not assimilable into the old socialist-capitalist categories.

This may be seen by considering the case of either the United States or Soviet Russia. In the former country, a Leftist, who was a socialist in Britain, would be much less concerned to promote more social equality or material welfare, of which plenty exists already, than with reforms lying outside the field of socialist-capitalist controversy, yet still the subject of acute Left-Right dispute: civil liberties, or the Negro problem, or foreign policy, or crime, or the sociological problems of a mass society. Similarly in Russia, a Leftist, who was even the most old-fashioned socialist in Britain, would scarcely assume that no urgent problems remained simply because nationalisation and planning could go no further; on the contrary, he would concern himself with the promotion of values, notably the rights of personal freedom and dissent, which in Britain are not a matter of socialist-capitalist disagreement.

So in Britain, as we approach the socialist goals described above, the reformer will bend his energies more and more to issues which cannot be classified as specifically socialist or non-socialist, but which lie in other fields altogether.[1] There are two such fields in which social action is already called for: the freedom of personal and leisure life, and social responsibility for cultural values.

II   *Liberty and Gaiety in Private Life; the Need for a Reaction against the Fabian Tradition*

Society's decisions impinge heavily on people's private lives as well as on their social or economic welfare; and they now impinge, in my view, in too restrictive and puritanical a manner. I should like to see action taken both to widen opportunities for enjoyment and relaxation, and to diminish existing restrictions on personal freedom.

[1] One example of such an issue, which many people already believe to be urgent, was quoted in Chapter I: the issue of managerial and bureaucratic power. This has little to do either with socialism, which historically has been concerned only with the economic power of private business, or with capitalism. It is a political and sociological problem of large scale, which now presents itself as strongly in the State bureaucracy, the Trade Unions, the nationalised industries, and the political parties, as it does in private industry.

The first of these requires, it is true, a change in cultural attitudes rather than government legislation. If this were to come about, much could be done to make Britain a more colourful and civilised country to live in. We need not only higher exports and old-age pensions, but more open-air cafés, brighter and gayer streets at night, later closing-hours for public houses, more local repertory theatres, better and more hospitable hoteliers and restaurateurs, brighter and cleaner eating-houses, more riverside cafés, more pleasure-gardens on the Battersea model, more murals and pictures in public places, better designs for furniture and pottery and women's clothes, statues in the centre of new housing-estates, better-designed street-lamps and telephone kiosks, and so on *ad infinitum*. The enemy in all this will often be in unexpected guise; it is not only dark Satanic things and people that now bar the road to the new Jerusalem, but also, if not mainly, hygienic, respectable, virtuous things and people, lacking only in grace and gaiety.

This becomes manifest when we turn to the more serious question of socially-imposed restrictions on the individual's private life and liberty. There come to mind at once the divorce laws, licensing laws, prehistoric (and flagrantly unfair) abortion laws, obsolete penalties for sexual abnormality, the illiterate censorship of books and plays, and remaining restrictions on the equal rights of women.[1] Most of these are intolerable, and should be highly offensive to socialists, in whose blood there should always run a trace of the anarchist and the libertarian, and not too much of the prig and the prude. If we really attach importance to the 'dignity of man', we must realise that this is as much affronted by a hypocritical divorce law which, as Matthew Arnold once wrote, neither makes divorce impossible nor makes it decent, as by the refusal to establish a joint production council in a factory.[2] A time will come, as material standards rise, when divorce-law

[1] Though if we remove these last, we should in fairness also remove unequal responsibilities from men. Women cannot claim equal rights, and at the same time continue to bring breach-of-promise or alienation-of-affection cases.

[2] Indeed many of these reforms can be justified by the simple moral judgment that hypocrisy is bad. There is something nauseating about the shocked outcry which greets any proposal to amend the licensing laws or to allow plays to be performed on Sundays, and the sanctimonious assumption of superiority over the immoral and godless Continentals, when we consider that public prostitution is tolerated in Britain on a scale which amazes visitors from more 'godless' countries. Let us at least have a little consistency.

reform will increase the sum of human welfare more than a rise in the food subsidies (though no doubt the party managers will be less enthusiastic for it). Socialists cannot go on indefinitely professing to be concerned with human happiness and the removal of injustice, and then, when the programmes are decided, permitting the National Executive, out of fear of certain vocal pressure-groups, to become more orthodox than the bench of bishops.

Much of this can at least claim the sanction of one powerful stream of socialist thought – that stemming from William Morris; though other, Nonconformist and Fabian, influences wear a bleaker and more forbidding air. For one brought up as a Fabian, in particular, this inevitably means a reaction against the Webb tradition. I do not wish to be misunderstood. All who knew the Webbs have testified to their personal kindliness, gentleness, tolerance, and humour; and no one who reads *Our Partnership* can fail to be intensely moved by the deep unaffected happiness of their mutual love. But many of their public virtues, so indispensable at the time, may not be as appropriate to-day. Reacting as they were against an unpractical, Utopian, sentimental, romantic, almost anarchist tradition on the Left, they were no doubt right to stress the solid virtues of hard work, self-discipline, efficiency, research, and abstinence: to sacrifice private pleasure to public duty, and expect that others should do the same: to put Blue Books before culture, and immunity from physical weakness above all other virtues.

And so they spent their honeymoon investigating Trade Societies in Dublin. And so Beatrice could write that 'owing to our concentration on research, municipal administration and Fabian propaganda, we had neither the time nor the energy, nor yet the means, to listen to music and the drama, to brood over classic literature, to visit picture galleries, or to view with an informed intelligence the wonders of architecture'.[1] And so Sidney withheld approval from the Soviet experiment until workers' control had been suppressed, and Beatrice until the anti-abortion law had been enacted, and she could write with approval of the serious, youthful Comsomols with their passion for self-discipline and self-improvement: and of the emphasis on personal hygiene and self-control – 'there is no spooning in the Parks of Recrea-

[1] *Our Partnership*, p. 14.

tion and Rest'.[1] And historically, without a doubt, this insistence on austerity was a vital service to a young and growing opposition movement.

But now we surely need a different set of values. Permeation has more than done its job. To-day we are all incipient bureaucrats and practical administrators. We have all, so to speak, been trained at the L.S.E., are familiar with Blue Books and White Papers, and know our way around Whitehall. We realise that we must guard against romantic or Utopian notions: that hard work and research are virtues: that we must do nothing foolish or impulsive: and that Fabian pamphlets must be diligently studied. We know these things too well. Posthumously, the Webbs have won their battle, and converted a generation to their standards. Now the time has come for a reaction: for a greater emphasis on private life, on freedom and dissent, on culture, beauty, leisure, and even frivolity. Total abstinence and a good filing-system are not now the right sign-posts to the socialist Utopia: or at least, if they are, some of us will fall by the way-side.

III *Cultural and Amenity Planning; and the Declining Importance of Economic Problems*

In the field of cultural values, what is mainly, indeed desperately, needed is determined government planning – to preserve what beauty we still have left in Britain, and to help create a little more. With personal consumption rising by 2-4% a year and likely to double in 20 years, it will really not much matter a decade from now whether we plan to produce rather more of this and less of that, or exactly what prices are charged for this commodity or that. The level of material welfare will soon be such that marginal changes in the allocation of resources will make little difference to anyone's contentment. If they wish, let the violent economic planners and anti-planners battle the matter out. The rest of us will grow progressively more indifferent.

[1] From a document privately circulated on her return from Russia in 1932 (quoted in *The Webbs and Their Work*, p. 226). And she goes on to relate with approval a warning said to have been given by Stalin to a high-placed Commissar: 'I do not want to enquire into your private affairs, but if there is any more nonsense about women, you go to a place where there are no women.'

But we shall grow progressively less indifferent, or so it is to be hoped, to the question of town and country, and architectural, planning. It is hard to discuss this without a tinge of melancholy. It was always obvious that profit-maximisation and market forces would be inimical to the preservation of beauty – the ribbon-building of the 1930s, the speculative housing estates, the steady destruction of London's Georgian squares, made us sufficiently aware of that. And to jog our memories we have only to see the new and utterly pedestrian commercial buildings now beginning to dwarf the City churches, and soon St. Paul's: or to read of cases such as that recently reported, where the English Electric Company, enjoying annual profits measured in millions of pounds, rejected the highly-commended winning design in a competition for its new head office, in favour of a mediocre but commercially more convenient structure.

The melancholy comes from the gradual fading of the post-war hopes of public planning. The post-war era was to be, in this respect, a brave new world. Brilliant, imaginative town-plans were to re-create our major cities. The new towns were to bring an end to London's urban sprawl, and to provide the greatest social and architectural experiment for centuries past. National Parks, the Land Fund, and in a different sphere the Arts Council, symbolised what was to be a new attention to beauty and culture. Above all the Town and Country Planning Act was to be a sure defence against the vulgarities and atrocities of the past.

And public planning in fact has much to its credit. The new towns have been a brave, and abundantly worthwhile, experiment. Post-war housing estates have, on the average, reached a better architectural standard than their predecessors (though seldom a very high one). The blitzed cities have not grown up wholly messy and haphazard, but with at least an element of design and spaciousness. National Parks are slowly (but so slowly) creeping from theory to reality. Some atrocities have been prevented by the Town and Country Planning Act. One public enterprise, the Forestry Commission, as the Kielder in particular shows, has added something new and imaginative to British life not only in its splendid forests, but in the design of forest villages. Nor has the State been backward, as the Festival of Britain demonstrated, as a direct patron of the arts.

But progress has been terribly slow; and the results terribly patchy. And now the impetus seems to be going out of the whole movement; and a middle-aged, apathetic disillusionment is setting in. A Conservative Minister of Works will not take the trouble to save Coleshill, though all the experts told him that he could. High Paddington is abandoned on grounds of cost. The design and adequacy of council-houses has deteriorated appallingly since 1951. The Government itself all but demolished Colcutt's Imperial Institute campanile. The City of London is almost past saving from second-rate mediocrity; even the limited New Barbican project was turned down time and again by the City Corporation. The new towns are compelled to skimp their amenity building through lack of funds. The Board of Trade, always the enemy of both social and economic enlightenment, by relaxing its licensing controls, is once more permitting industry to expand in London and Birmingham, and making it inevitable that these cities, against all our post-war hopes, will spread inexorably into the countryside again. And this is only part of the problem which overshadows all others in this field: the relentless invasion of the countryside by 'Subtopia', and the gradual obliteration of the distinction between town and country.[1]

This is not a book about architecture, or town and country planning; I am not, in any event, expert enough to go into detail. But detail in fact is hardly necessary, since the enemies to be overcome are attitudes of mind; if they can be conquered, the detailed policies will follow. These enemies are first parsimony, secondly indifference, and thirdly anarchistic selfishness. The parsimony can be overcome by a recognition that the total sums involved are a minute fraction of total consumers', or even total Budgetary, expenditure. It is literally true that an annual increase in 'cultural' spending of £30 millions for the next 10 years, out of an annual increase in output of some £300 millions and a Budget of over £3,000 millions, would revolutionise the situation. It only needs a little, and so little, firmness in the face of the Beaverbrook Press.[2]

[1] v. Ian Nairn, *Outrage* (Architectural Press, 1955).

[2] Personally I should be prepared, to take one concrete example, to pay any subsidy necessary to encourage more high building in cities in the interests of preserving the countryside – whatever the *Sunday Express* said about government waste, or the *Economist* about the 'distortion' of resources.

The indifference can be countered only by a display of savagery on the part of the minority who care for these matters – though it may, in the end, not be a minority at all, once the issues are put and the votes collected; this is a sphere in which determined leadership might yield generous dividends. The selfishness, often dressed up in the plausible language of complaints against bureaucracy or compulsory purchase or inadequate compensation, and fortified by a vulgar philistinism amongst those who articulate it in Parliament and the Press, will never be eradicated by argument or debate. We have here a simple, but deep, dividing line at once of principle and temperament; a clash of values to be resolved, not by verbal compromise, but simply by struggle.

Although this emphasis on culture, and that in the previous section on personal liberty, cannot claim the label socialist, they do provide a justification for supporting the Labour in preference to the Conservative Party. Not that the former's record on cultural or libertarian issues is immaculate – far from it. But it is at least significantly better than the Conservative record. A higher proportion of Labour than Tory Members of Parliament has consistently voted for enlightenment on issues such as the Festival of Britain, town and country planning, divorce-law reform, the censorship of plays and books, the abolition of hanging, and the Arts Council; socialists have even shown more practical interest in the preservation of historic private houses; while post-war Labour Chancellors, under Mr. Dalton's lead, initiated the Land Fund and showed unexampled generosity to the Universities. The mood of the Party is therefore mildly encouraging. But one grows too hopeful. By the time we next come back to power, many opportunities will have been lost irretrievably; as this is written, innumerable pygmies, presented with an opportunity that only Wren has ever before enjoyed, are busy spawning their ugly rectangles all over the City of London.

Nevertheless, I hope and believe that the Labour Party may come to take the lead in this struggle. It would, in the judgment of history, do more for Britain by planning the City of London than by planning the chemical industry, and infinitely more by abolishing hanging than by abolishing the tied cottage. It has a favourable background and tradition for assuming this role – the influence of William Morris, its long-standing belief in social as opposed to private values, and the tender, respectful feeling for culture that characterises the educated working class. And it certainly has the opportunity – not merely because the need is so urgent, but because material standards are rising to the point where we can spare more energy, and more resources, for beauty and culture.

Indeed this is a sphere in which the original co-operative ideal is directly relevant. I discussed this ideal in Chapter IV, and concluded that it was hard to see how it could be realised in practice, and on a national scale, in terms of personal motives or industrial relations. But in the cultural field, such an ideal, which demands that social should be placed above private interests, is practicable as well as relevant; though recent experience has taught us that 'private' in this context has little to do with private profit, and must be defined as 'sectional' – to include city corporations, local councils, nationalised industries, and even government departments, as well as private business. But if we pursue this ideal vigorously, and even savagely, we might make Britain not only a more prosperous, not only a more just and equal and contented, but also a more beautiful and civilised country to live in.

In so doing, and with the aid of rising material standards, we might find that another aspect of this ideal, the weakening of the motive of personal gain, was also being insensibly and imperceptibly realised. 'When the accumulation of wealth', Keynes once wrote, 'is no longer of high social importance, there will be great changes in the code of morals. . . . I see us free to return to some of the most sure and certain principles of religion and traditional virtue – that avarice is a vice, that the exaction of usury is a misdemeanour, and the love of money is detestable, that those walk most truly in the paths of virtue and sane wisdom who take least thought for the morrow. We shall once more value ends above means and prefer the good to the useful.[1]

It is no doubt too early yet to relax into these more humane ways, hemmed in as we still are by squalor and distress, especially in under-privileged lands abroad. But even now, as Keynes went on to say, 'there will be no harm in making mild preparations for our destiny, in encouraging, and experimenting in, the arts of life as well as the activities of purpose'. We do not want to enter the age of abundance, only to find that we have lost the values which might teach us how to enjoy it.

[1] *Essays in Persuasion* (Macmillan, 1931), pp. 371-2.

INDEX